D0871505

A Study in Yellow

A Study in Yellow

The *Yellow Book* and Its Contributors

by

Katherine Lyon Mix

GREENWOOD PRESS, PUBLISHERS
NEW YORK

To
A. J. M.

Preface

In the thirty years since this work was begun, I have had reason to be thankful to many people for their assistance. The late Professor R. D. O'Leary, one-time head of the English department of the University of Kansas, presented me with this subject (the University Library had just acquired a set of the *Yellow Book*) and supervised the writing of the original manuscript for a Master's thesis. To the memory of this fine scholar and stimulating teacher I wish here to pay tribute. Some years later, Professor J. W. Ashton, now Dean of the Graduate School at Indiana University, took an interest in the ever increasing amount of material, and I am indebted to him for several suggestions about the reshaping of the manuscript. Finally Professor C. K. Hyder, Editor of the University of Kansas Press, has given me the greatest help in preparing the book for publication, and I am grateful to him for his acute and perceptive criticism and a devotion to editorial responsibility far beyond the line of duty.

The English writers of the nineties to whom I have made reference in the Notes were exceedingly kind and patient with a young American who was brashly invading their territory, and I regret that no one of them is alive today to receive my thanks. The friends and neighbors of Henry Harland in Norwich, Connecticut, were ready and eager to talk about him, and I have most cause to remember the help of Mrs. Martha Geer, Miss Margaret Fuller, and Miss Louise C. Howe.

In the main, however, the preparation for this book was carried on in libraries, and to the unknown and now dimly recalled members of their staffs who so uncomplainingly responded to my many requests, I wish to acknowledge my debt. The institutions in which I pursued my research include the Reading Room of the British Museum, the Library of Congress, the Hamburg Bibliotek, the New York Public Library, the Boston Public Library, the Utica Free Library, the Wadsworth Athenaeum of Hartford, Connecticut, the Kansas State Historical Society at Topeka and the libraries at the following Universities:

Cambridge, Cornell, Yale, Pennsylvania State, California, and Kansas.

I wish to thank Joan St. George Saunders of the Writer's and Speaker's Research of London, who was zealous in solving certain difficult problems, Mary Ann Caws and Erin G. Marcus, who gave clerical help in checking the manuscript and John S. Lewis, who was responsible for the preparation of the index. I am grateful to Professor Harold Orel for a critical reading of the proof, and to Naomi Burton of Curtis Brown, Ltd., for her enduring faith and interest in this undertaking.

Acknowledgment has been made in the Notes to individuals and publishers who have permitted me to quote from certain books or allowed me to reproduce pictures. I am especially indebted to Eva Le Gallienne for the photographs of her father and mother, to Dr. Richard F. Neibling, who made available to me his thesis on "The Early Career of George Gissing," and to Professor Kenneth Cornell of Yale University for his advice on the French scene.

But it is to my husband, Arthur, who died in 1956, that I must confess my greatest obligation. Only his cheerful support and assistance, his enthusiastic co-operation and interest, and his unfailing encouragement through many years of trials and uncertainty made possible the completion of *A Study in Yellow*.

—K.L.M.

List of Illustrations

Chapter I

No PERIOD OF English literary history has been more discussed than the 1890's. Fondly or with horror the survivors have recalled that troublesome decade, while present-day critics have scrutinized its ambiguities with emotions quite as diverse, each individual influenced by his own experience or by some particular theory of literary criticism.

In the summer of 1945 Sir Max Beerbohm, exiled from Rapallo by the war and living in a Surrey village, said, "Essentially I belong to the Nineteenth Century. My world has died."[1] But Sir Max was only repeating what he had said some fifty years before, in 1896, when in the single volume of his *Works,* he declared, "And I, who crave no knighthood, shall write no more. . . . Already I feel myself to be a trifle outmoded. I belong to the Beardsley period."[2]

The consistency of these statements was irreproachable— their truth of course is another matter—but the fact remains that half a century had not served to change Sir Max's opinion.

Only in this one respect can commentators on the nineties agree. They must all, like Sir Max, look backward. Irrevocably the era lies behind them, belonging to a past which nothing they may say can alter. Their impressions may differ, their judgments may offer conflicting testimony, their interpretation of circumstances may vary, but the record is unchanged. As the ever retreating moment lengthens our perspective and enlarges our field of vision, the affairs of the nineties come into sharper focus. Divergent angles grow closer and once contradictory vistas are seen to overlap. Fifty years hence the pattern will seem lucid and legible; now, past mid-century, the hazes have begun to clear.

Many discrepant ideas about the nineties have been advanced. Writers then "expounded an unscholarly paganism; they made little excursions in flamboyant naughtiness," but "this appearance of depravity was only a pose . . . the real objectives were the sentimentalities and hyprocrisies of a dying age." It was "a period of revolt" and conflict, but "the revolt had al-

1

ready taken place," leaving "an air of great repose." It was the "final flare-up of the great Victorian compromise," "the vanguard of progress," *"fin de siècle,"* and "the seedtime of the new century."

Such adjectives as Romantic, Weary, Glorious, Fighting, Naughty, and Gay have been applied to the nineties. In color, they were described as green, out of deference to Oscar Wilde's "curious love of green which in individuals is always the sign of subtle artistic temperament, and in nations is said to denote a laxity if not a decadence of morals";[3] as mauve, a shade which Whistler identified as "pink trying to be purple";[4] but most frequently as yellow, "the colour of the hour, the symbol of the time-spirit."[5]

Yellow had assumed significance before the dawn of 1890. It gathered importance during the decade, becoming quite meaningless with the arrival of the new century. A favorite color with the Pre-Raphaelites, with Rossetti and Burne-Jones, it was also affected by Whistler, whose yellow breakfasts with orange nasturtiums or darting goldfish in a flat blue bowl inspired Lily Langtry to use the same idea, substituting a yellow water lily in antique blue glass—beautiful Lily Langtry, whom he painted so gorgeously in the yellow robe. Sir Richard Burton also gave yellow breakfasts in his rooms by the book shop of W. T. Spencer in New Oxford Street, and the bookseller, watching the guests depart, observed charitably that these gatherings seemed to have been merry.

Yellow sunflowers, painted on the walls of the Oxford Union by William Morris, became the symbol of aestheticism in the hand of Oscar Wilde, who praised the leonine, gaudy beauty of the flower so fervently that American undergraduates at Harvard and Yale marched to his lectures bearing stalks of the yellow blossoms—probably artificial, since it was winter.

Yellow posters stared from billboards; yellow satin rustled at fashionable parties; Mona Caird had her drawing room done with yellow curtains and carpet; London publishers imitated the bindings of French yellow-backed novels; the word "yellow" popped up in book titles—*The Yellow Aster* by Iota and *Le*

Cahier Jaune by A. C. Benson, poems privately printed, for which Henry James wrote to "thank you for your yellow sheaf."[6]

The editor of *Harper's* wrote on Yellow Literature, declaring, "The Yellow literature is not new. There have always been diseased people seeking notoriety by reason of their maladies,"[7] but Richard Le Gallienne glorified the "Boom in Yellow." "Let us," he invited, "dream of this: a maid with yellow hair, clad in a yellow gown, seated in a yellow room, at the window a yellow sunset, in the grate a yellow fire, at her side a yellow lamplight, on her knee a Yellow Book."[8]

It was undoubtedly the *Yellow Book* that gave to the color its final importance. Published at the Bodley Head by John Lane with Henry Harland and Aubrey Beardsley as editors, bound like a book in strong durable cloth, the periodical began in April, 1894, and ended in April, 1897. Those thirteen fat volumes in their staring black and yellow covers took their place on library shelves as a symbol of the period, documentary evidence for posterity.

Max Beerbohm, in what he called a little "back light," has emphasized the importance of the binding, "not a paper thing, a board thing, a book," something to "last longer than a quarter of a year . . . and we contributors in those days always spoke of the Yellow BOOK."[9]

It has lasted. Within those bright exuberant covers lie the nineties, the best and the worst of what they had to offer in literature and art, a record and a repository open for inspection.

Chapter II

A QUICK RETROSPECTIVE glance at the years immediately preceding the paradoxical nineties is necessary—a period usually described as the Victorian Age. The casual observer has little doubt as to the tenets and mores approved by the English queen. From the moment the round-faced Victoria ascended the throne in 1837 a stiffening of the backbone of respectability was everywhere evident. Behavior turned to decorum, and literature and art propagandized virtue.

"The Victorian age" is a term which, properly speaking, has meaning only when used chronologically. There are rebels in every age, and many of the so-called Victorian writers did not conform to the generally accepted sense of the epithet. George Eliot, for all her concern with ethics, was not conventional in her personal life. (The poet Edward Carpenter denounced her for having preached a respectability she was too advanced to practice.) Browning was considered daring in *Pippa Passes* and "The Statue and the Bust." Tennyson sympathized with Lancelot, and Arnold, Carlyle, and Meredith were critical of contemporary mores. From the middle of the century little fermenting bubbles disturbed the calm surface of Victorian conformity.

One of these disturbances was the Pre-Raphaelite movement under the leadership of Dante Gabriel Rossetti. The quiet pains-taking quest of the Pre-Raphaelites was for beauty in art and poetry, but they sought it in a return to the past, not in the present. To them beauty was youthful, naïve, richly decorated, finding its inspiration in the medieval. To Watts-Dunton the Pre-Raphaelites were part of the Renascence of Wonder, but Robert Buchanan, under the pseudonym of "Thomas Maitland," assigned Rossetti to the Fleshly School of Poetry. The publication of the *Germ* in 1850 gave the movement form and permanence.

Swinburne's *Poems and Ballads* shocked, even stunned, British poetry readers in 1866. Surpassing Rossetti in the beauty and melody of his verse, Swinburne also far outdistanced the Pre-Raphaelites in his disregard for convention. A righteously indignant public, refusing to be soothed by musical phrases and haunting rhythms, so protested this flaunting of esoteric passion that the original publishers withdrew the volume; but a less cautious firm took over its publication and English youth, openly or furtively, bought and read.

For seventeen years after his graduation from Oxford, John Ruskin had been an art critic and apostle, preaching through his *Modern Painters* that beauty in nature was a revelation of the

Divine Good, but in 1860 he forsook the beautiful for the good and became a social reformer, spending his fortune in improving the conditions of London's poor. His disciple Walter Pater, more impressed with the need for beauty and a quickened sense of life in literature than for economic equality, assumed Ruskin's cast-off vestments as high priest of the beautiful. In spite of Pater's diffidence and seclusion the garment was not unbecoming and he wore it boldly. His *Marius the Epicurean* (1885), with its insistence upon vivid sensations and personal appreciation of art, seemed to glorify "not the fruit of experience, but experience itself."[1] This and that other much-quoted passage, from his earlier *Renaissance,* "To burn always with this hard, gemlike flame, to maintain this ecstasy, is success in life,"[2] became part of the philosophy of Oscar Wilde.

Other influences too were broadening the Victorian outlook on religion and life. Matthew Arnold and Arthur Hugh Clough spoke of their doubts and uncertainties in spite of a Church of England upbringing and the reassurance of an Oxford background. Darwin had robbed man of his divine birthright, arguing with cold logic and scientific fact that man was not born in the image of God. Victorian fundamentalists scanned Darwin's life hoping to find some hidden corruption which might be used as a weapon against his defiance of Genesis. An increasing social consciousness led many to survey their own surroundings and those of their neighbors with a view to righting existent wrongs.

William Morris, following in the footsteps of Ruskin, espoused the cause of the working people and by his enterprise in making textiles and furniture tried to provide beauty for all. Wearing the blue shirt of the common man, he presided over socialist meetings in the little building on the Mall adjoining Kelmscott House, Hammersmith. Sidney and Beatrice Webb worked indefatigably for better housing and reform of labor laws. G. Bernard Shaw, Havelock Ellis, and Hubert Bland, husband of E. Nesbit, were pillars of the Fabian Society. Oscar Wilde wrote *The Soul of Man under Socialism.* But socialistic activity was not confined to words alone. On Bloody Sunday in 1887 socialism ran athwart the law in the riots of Trafalgar Square when one worker was killed and many arrested. Among the injured who drew prison terms was R. B. Cunninghame Graham.

By 1890 the ranks of the great in literature had diminished. Browning was dead. Tennyson, the poet laureate, was in mute and unhappy retirement at Aldworth. Matthew Arnold's voice had been two years silent, Dante Gabriel Rossetti had died on Easter night, 1882, at Birchington-on-Sea, attended by Hall Caine ("Whenever a great man dies," said Oscar Wilde, "Hall Caine and William Sharp go in with the undertakers"[3]), and Christina Rossetti was writing poetry and reading her Testament in the seclusion of her Torrington Square home.

Among the survivors was George Meredith, whose "acute but honorable minority of a public," as he termed it, had been augmented by the good services of young Richard Le Gallienne's first critical book, *George Meredith: Some Characteristics*. Meredith was in turn to benefit one of the younger generation by accepting as reader for Chapman and Hall George Gissing's *The Unclassed*. He had rejected Mrs. Wood's *East Lynne* (1861) and was later to refuse Mrs. Grand's *Heavenly Twins,* one of the most profitable books of the decade. (It "deals with sexual questions," the youthful E. A. Robinson explained to his friend Smith. "Something after the manner of Zola, with a more direct moral purpose."[4])

Thomas Hardy was just coming into his own, and his *Tess of the D'Urbervilles* was to be published in 1891. Hardy too was to profit by the appreciation of a young poet, Lionel Johnson, whose *Art of Thomas Hardy* (1894) showed a fine discriminative faculty, though a critic of the period grumbled that Johnson, who prided himself on his sentence construction, "had worked the harmless, necessary comma so hard, and put it in so many false positions, that the humane department of the Philological Society might well speak to him about it."[5]

By 1890 Henry James, the self-exiled American living in London, had turned to his second and more involved style of writing, his "ground-glass style," one cynic called it, through which "by close application you can just discern . . . men and

6

women as trees walking."[6] Edmund Gosse was earning his living at the Board of Trade in Whitehall Gardens and acting, so Walter Raleigh said, "as a kind of Literary Providence"[7] to young writers. Gosse's reputation had survived the scathing attack of Churton Collins on his *From Shakespeare to Pope,* although the young Edward Marsh was naïvely surprised to find that "he had not been hounded out of letters and was still allowed to publish."[8] Austin Dobson, also at the Board of Trade, had nearly finished with poetry and was writing prose. In 1891 he was to be welcomed to membership in the Athenaeum by the poetically witty Canon Ainger. Richard Garnett was Keeper of Printed Books at the British Museum, and Sidney Colvin, in the Print Room, was treasuring every letter from Robert Louis Stevenson in the South Pacific and gloating over each new edition of Stevenson's books. Oscar Wilde, about whom strange things were being said, was living in Tite Street, and his *Picture of Dorian Gray* was to appear in the July number of *Lippincott's.*

Among the younger men whose reputation was to come during the next few years, Kipling was just gaining recognition as a writer of unusual short stories, and his verse was beginning to appear. Barrie at the age of thirty had already published *Auld Licht Idylls* and *A Window in Thrums* and written on Meredith for the *Contemporary Review.* Some of the artists and writers who were to be associated with the *Yellow Book,* like Aubrey Beardsley and Max Beerbohm, were still in their teens. In 1890 Beardsley was a clerk in the Guardian Insurance Office and Max had just matriculated at Merton College, Oxford. Hubert Crackanthorpe was barely twenty; Laurence Binyon, twenty-one; Ernest Dowson and Lionel Johnson, twenty-three. Arthur Symons, Laurence Housman, and W. B. Yeats had achieved the ripe age of twenty-five. John Davidson was considerably older, but it was only the previous year that he had given up his schoolteaching in Scotland and come to London to seek literary fame. Henry Harland was twenty-nine. He too was a newcomer, having put the career of "Sydney Luska" behind him in America to write stories under his own name in London.

The predominant influence on the work of these young men was to come from France. A newly awakened interest in French prose and poetry, as well as in art, was evident in England. Whistler had breezed back and forth between Paris and London, bringing home the swagger of the Latin Quarter. An expurgated edition of Baudelaire's *Les Fleurs du Mal* had been published in England in 1861, but it was not until Vizetelly translated Zola's works into English that the average reader understood Gallic frankness. Vizetelly was given a year in prison to meditate on his rashness in presuming to educate the insular; Arthur Machen, who lived in the garret over old Mr. Vizetelly's printing shop, was visited with the inspiration for *The Great God Pan*, which, published by Lane, "made a storm in a Tiny Tot's teacup."[9]

Gradually, however, the realism of Maupassant, Flaubert's gospel of style, Gautier's pronouncement, *"La forme, quoi qu'on ait dit, est tout,"* had a visible effect upon the content and shape of English prose. In 1888 George Moore's *Confessions of a Young Man* created a sensation not forgotten for a decade. Moore was an Irishman who had lived much in Paris and his work was strongly influenced by French models, especially Huysmans' *À Rebours,* which had come out a few years before. Among English writers he acknowledged only one master, Walter Pater. Combining the meticulous style of Pater with the macabre audacity of Huysmans, Moore achieved his *Confessions,* which he tossed with self-conscious bravado into the midst of Victorian rectitude.

A year later Arthur Symons created a similar impact on English poetry with his *Days and Nights* (1889). He too had lived in France and was a student of the French Symbolists and Impressionists, finding inspiration in the meters of Baudelaire, Mallarmé, and Verlaine. To Symons must go the credit for spreading these forms and concepts in England. "He was," as Thomas Beer pointed out, "a specimen of thermal conductivity in letters, through which the ideas of French artists passed into English perception with little damage."[10]

The new world was not ignored by its older brother. In the eighties Walt Whitman's poetry had been much discussed in England, and in Edinburgh, in 1884, John Mackinnon Robertson had written on *Whitman, Poet and Democrat*. To Grant Allen he was "the good grey Walt Whitman," but to a critic in *Blackwood's* he was "that obscene old American twaddler."[11] Oscar Wilde had visited him in his Mickle Street home in Camden to tell him that only he and Emerson were considered true poets by the English. Swinburne, once enthusiastic, had recanted his early fervor in an article called "Whitmania." Henley and Ford Madox Ford lent a sympathetic ear to Whitman's unrhymed lines, but in general the English poets looked to French forms.

As the last years of the century passed, other foreign currents reached English shores. Edmund Gosse was editing Heinemann's International Library, which included translations of Björnson, Maupassant, Couperus, and Jonas Lie. George Gissing declared, "The writers who help me most are French and Russian," and more enthusiastically, "Tourguenéff is a man I glory in!"[12] Maurice Baring thought Dostoievsky greater than Tolstoi or Turgenev, and George Meredith, though he had little sympathy with Tolstoi's social theories, considered *Anna Karenina* the greatest novel ever written. Italian writers were becoming accessible in English, among them Luigi Capuana and Gabriele d'Annunzio. Mr. and Mrs. Henry Harland translated Matilde Serao's *Fantasia* in 1891.

Most invigorating perhaps was the current from Scandinavia. "George Egerton" dedicated her *Keynotes* to Knut Hamsun, "In memory of a day when the west wind and the rainbow met," and later translated his *Hunger*. Richard Le Gallienne made a sentimental pilgrimage to Norway to see Björnson and Ibsen, whose plays, translated by Edmund Gosse and William Archer, were just reaching the London stage.

The performance of *A Doll's House* with Janet Achurch as Nora precipitated a controversy in which every London critic and playgoer took sides. As Max later put it, "Ibsen began to flutter the London dove-cots, and every one was violently either an Ibsenite or an anti-Ibsenite."[13] One critic characterized the play as "a series of conversations terminated by an accident," and Walter Besant wrote heatedly in the *English Illustrated Maga-*

zine of Nora's behavior in so needlessly depriving a home of its wife and mother. When Shaw read Besant's article, he told a friend that he had decided not to throw himself off a cliff lest his suicide should be considered "the natural end of a reprobate who greatly prefers Ibsenism to Walter Besantism." Besides he thought the act would be more fitting for Besant "after such a performance."[14] Feminists like E. Nesbit and Mona Caird were much impressed with the play (the former perhaps had cause to envy Nora), and on the night of the first performance Olive Schreiner, Edith Lees, who became Mrs. Havelock Ellis, Dollie Radford, the poetess, Mrs. Holman Hunt, Eleanor Marx, daughter of Karl, and Honor Brooke, oldest daughter of Stopford Brooke, gathered outside the theatre afterward, breathless with excitement over the opening of this new world for women.

Honor's Victorian father, however, who had left the Church of England to become a Unitarian minister, did not share her enthusiasm, demanding irately, "Who could touch even with a fishing-rod, ten yards long, the woman in a *Doll's House,* or the Doctor, or the husband?"[15] and when Bernard Shaw espoused the cause of the Norwegian with *The Quintessence of Ibsenism,* Brooke wondered what Shaw could see in him. The Countess Cowper wrote in the *Nineteenth Century,* "In Ibsen's plays, the beloved of the realist, the commonplace and vulgar plot is produced in a vile manner, semi-tragic and semi-comic, and is surrounded by a morbid atmosphere suggestive of unfathomed depths of degradation,"[16] but Henry James encouragingly sent Elizabeth Robins, his friend the actress who was studying Ibsen, a Norse grammar, and Ernest Dowson advised Victor Plarr, "Go to see 'A Doll's House.' I have been twice and go again. It's the finest play that has been seen for some years."[17]

10

Chapter III

THE FLOWER OF aestheticism snatched from the relaxing grasp of Pater by Oscar Wilde and worn jauntily in his buttonhole was a fading blossom in the nineties. Ridiculed by Gilbert and Sullivan's opera *Patience,* travestied in Du Maurier's cartoons in *Punch,* burlesqued by Robert Hichens in *The Green Carnation,* Art for Art's Sake had withered in unfriendly hands. Once the treasure of the few, it had become the plaything of the many. The whole thing was a comedy of errors, as William Gaunt has pointed out in *The Aesthetic Adventure.* "To Whistler . . . a barbarous mockery of severe and exacting artistic principles. To William Morris and his associates it was the opposite of their energetic creed in which the mere appreciation of art had no place." The new art-consciousness had created a "fad and a farce."[1]

But the line of beauty must go on and the responsibility was assumed by the disciples of other cults from across the channel: Symbolism, Impressionism, and that bogy of the nineties, Decadence. Arthur Symons gave all three terms careful and exact definition in an article in *Harper's* for November, 1893.[2] Decadence, he found, was neither classic nor romantic. "After a fashion it is no doubt a decadence; it has all the qualities that mark the end of great periods, the qualities that we find in the Greek, the Latin, decadence: an intense self-consciousness, a restless curiosity in research, an over-subtilizing refinement upon refinement, a spiritual and moral perversity." Impressionism and Symbolism, the two main branches of the decadent movement, "are really working on the same hypothesis, applied in different directions. What both seek is not general truth merely, but *la vérité vraie,* the very essence of truth—the truth of appearances to the senses, of the visible world to the eyes that see it; and the truth of spiritual things to the spiritual vision. The Impressionist . . . would flash upon you in a new, sudden way so exact an image of what you have just seen. . . . The Symbolist, in this new, sudden way, would flash upon you the 'soul' of that which can be apprehended

11

only by the soul—the finer sense of things unseen, the deeper meaning of things evident. . . . This endeavor after a perfect truth to one's impression, to one's intuition . . . has brought with it, in its revolt from ready-made impressions and conclusions, a revolt from the ready-made of language, from the bondage of traditional form, of a form become rigid." Goncourt, he said, was the first to invent this new sensational style in prose. Verlaine had initiated a similar style in verse. Words were not merely color and sound, but alive. "That search after 'l'image peinte,' 'l'epithète rare,' is not . . . a search after harmony of phrase for its own sake; it is a desperate endeavor to give sensation, to flash the impression of the moment, to preserve the very heat and motion of life. . . . To fix the last fine shade, the quintessence of things; to fix it fleetingly; to be a disembodied voice, and yet the voice of a human soul: that is the ideal of Decadence."

This was the gospel of Decadence, according to its evangel, the author of *Days and Nights*. Under this creed some of the finest work of the decade was done—and some of the worst.

Not everyone accepted Symons' exposition, however; some placed a different interpretation upon Decadence. "To notice only the picturesque effect of a beggar's rags, like Gautier," wrote Richard Le Gallienne, himself often linked with the movement in the public's mind, "the colour-scheme of a tippler's nose, like M. Huysmans; to consider one's mother merely prismatically, like Mr. Whistler—these are examples of the decadent attitude. At the bottom, decadence is merely limited thinking, often insane thinking."[3]

"Tommyrotics" was the name bestowed on the work of the decadents, according to a writer in *Blackwood's*[4] who subjected George Egerton, Mrs. Grand, Le Gallienne, Grant Allen, and "their holy, awful, individual freedom" to bitter attack. In Max Nordau's *Degeneration* this critic found that "unsavoury topics are at any rate not handled sympathetically, as by decadent essayists and 'yellow' lady novelists."

Much controversy was roused in England and America over Nordau's philippic against the modern movements in art and literature. To Nordau decadence meant decay: the century was old and dying and civilization was dying with it too. The phrase *fin de siècle,* taken so lightly in France, assumed grave significance in the mind of this Teuton. He called it Degeneration, or debased emotionalism, and he found evidence of its corrupting influence in the work of nearly every important artist, writer, and musician, condemning most contemporary genius as degenerate. Not even gentle, spinsterish Kate Greenaway, who could not read George Moore's *Modern Painting* without a blush, escaped his censure. He found her quaintly garbed children "affected," declaring she had profaned the sacredness of childhood "under absurd disguises."[5]

Others were upbraided with as little cause. Lewis Hind's "Minor Poet" complained, "I who write poetry and make floral designs in the manner of Mr. William Crane: I who am fond of birds, and word-games . . . am a degenerate,"[6] but Professor Saintsbury found "too much of [Nordau's] book a silly . . . exaggeration, not at all ill exemplifying the very weaknesses he discusses."[7] Bernard Shaw observed in his *Sanity of Art* that "this theory of his is, at bottom, nothing but the familiar delusion of the used-up man that the world is going to the dogs."[8] In Maine, the young E. A. Robinson, just home from college, wrote a friend, "I have been a wallowing degenerate ever since I painted the dining-room floor last week. . . . There are seven shades of yellow in it and I have a symbol for every devilish one of them."[9]

Strange stories were circulated about these young writers and artists who took liberties with Art, wrote poems in praise of sin, and considered unpleasant facts unpleasantly. They drank vodka and absinthe, they took hashish in search of new sensations, they reversed the usual order of the day and breakfasted in mid-afternoon, they loved freely and often and wrote about it with relish. Some people laughed at them. *Truth* published a recipe for poetic genius: "Half educate a vain youth at Oxford; let his hair grow; dip him into erotic French literature; add one idea; chop it small; give a grotesque name; then serve up as a rival to Milton, Sheridan and Shakespeare."[10]

Some defended them. A writer in *Tomorrow* on "The Supposititious Wickedness of Minor Poets" (the nineties were the heyday of the minor poet), wondered if they were as "naughty as they would have us believe" and doubted they were any more immoral than "shopwalkers, or divinity students, or artists' models."[11]

Not all the gossip could be taken lightly. Sometimes it was difficult to decide where the smoke became fire, to distinguish the men who found inspiration, in some strange illogical way, in their sin, from those who made abortive dashes into the flames and drew back before the holocaust. Most of the Victorians lived to respectable senility; many men of the nineties died young. Murger's melancholy verdict *(Scènes de la Vie de Bohème)*, "La Bohème, c'est le stage de la vie artistique; c'est la préface de l'Académie, de l'Hôtel-Dieu ou de la Morgue,"[12] applied as well to London artists and writers who seemed hurrying to this last destination. To those who believed that the wages of sin are death, this was incontrovertible proof of guilt.

When Hubert Crackanthorpe killed himself at the age of twenty-six by jumping into the Seine, Jeannette Gilder wrote in the *Critic*, "I am not at all suprised at the tragic death of Mr. Hubert Crackanthorpe. No young man, or old one for that matter, could write such morbid, loathsome stories as he wrote and have a sane mind. He was the most pronounced type of the decadent . . . searching for material after the manner of Mr. Stephen Crane and much the same sort of material. . . . A man must have a diseased mind who finds pleasure in writing of diseased morals."[13]

"I have known twelve men who killed themselves," said Arthur Symons long after, staring into the past with haunted eyes.[14] Though Symons himself lived to be eighty, the Hospital had claimed him. Following some years in an asylum of which he wrote in *Confessions*, his health had been precarious and uncertain. Still, by taking care, he lived. Many of his youthful contemporaries shortened their own lives as surely as Crackanthorpe in the Seine or John Davidson in the Cornish Sea, because they took no care.

Aubrey Beardsley died at the age of twenty-six of tuberculosis. He lay for months at Mentone, clutching at life, before his guttering candle burned itself out. The poet Ernest Dowson died miserably in a cottage in Catford when he was thirty-three. Death came to Charles Conder at a private asylum in England in 1900. When Conder died Symons was a patient in the same institution. Lionel Johnson suffered a fall, possibly when under the influence of liquor, and died from a fractured skull at thirty-five. William Theodore Peters, the young American poet and actor for whom Dowson wrote *The Pierrot of the Minute,* died of starvation in Paris. Francis Adams, who wrote so yearningly of death in *A Child of the Age,* ended his own suffering in 1893. Like Beardsley and Adams, Harland too had tuberculosis but he lived to be forty-three. Francis Thompson was forty-eight when he died of the same disease in 1907.

Not all this generation was lost. Some reached the Academy: Rothenstein who was always well balanced, Beerbohm who was protected by his humor, Binyon who was sanely sensitive, Mac-Coll who was a dour Scot, and Sickert and Rhys and Waugh. Some, like John Gray, took refuge in the priesthood. Yeats found a haven in mysticism as some had found it in the church. In his Autobiography, *The Trembling of the Veil,* Yeats tried to find the reason for the disaster which overtook so many of his generation. He thought it might have been caused by poverty and its hardships, which often meant the abrogation of domestic life; or perhaps by intense emotional writing, which turned the poet's thoughts too much upon himself. In the end, however, he came to the conclusion that Pater's *Marius,* "or the attitude of mind of which it was the noblest expression," was responsible. "It taught us to walk upon a rope, tightly stretched through serene air, and we were left to keep our feet upon a swaying rope in a storm."[15]

"New" was the catchword of the nineties. "Not to be 'new' is, in these days, to be nothing," declared H. D. Traill.[16] There was the new freedom, the *New Review,* edited by Henley after the collapse of the *Observer,* the new woman (Max said that she sprang "full-armed from the brain of Ibsen, who in later years unkindly denied paternity"[17]), the new literature, and the new hedonism. Grant Allen was the prophet of the new hedonism, which held that self-development was greater than self-sacrifice, wanted to restore culture to the place usurped by religion, and emphasized sex as the source of inspiration.[18] Grant Allen was also the press agent of the new woman, in spite of E. Nesbit's complaint that he seemed to despise the fair sex, and his novel *The Woman Who Did* aroused Victoria Cross to write *The Woman Who Did Not,* both of which Jeannette Gilder took very seriously in the American *Critic.*

Havelock Ellis, young and eager, absorbed in his studies of sex, sometimes used himself, his wife, and their friend Amy as laboratory material. His *New Spirit* had been reviewed by Oscar Wilde as "The New Spirit—Not Intoxicating."[19] But a succeeding work, *Man and Woman: A Study of Their Human Secondary Sexual Characteristics,* received no open acknowledgment from the son of Speranza.

The new woman was subjecting her role in the world to deepest scrutiny. Not only Nora, but Tess and Jude, Maggie and Esther Waters, the Heavenly Twins and Mrs. Tanqueray gave her cause to think. If this was the new age of freedom the woman of Victorian upbringing had many shackles to cast off. Such titles as *The Evolution of Woman: An Inquiry into the Dogma of her Inferiority to Man* and *A Study of the Equality of the Sexes* appeared on the book lists for 1894. Constable announced the undertaking of a *Sportswoman's Library,* which, said a critic, "startlingly illustrates the position of the Modern Woman," and the *Nineteenth Century* presented its readers with an article on "A Medical View of Cycling for Women." Clubmen discussed bloomers and bicycles, and Jerome K. Jerome said the final question was almost formula, "Would you like it, if your sister showed her legs? Yes, or no?"[20] *Vanity Fair* defined the New Woman as one who "had ceased to be a lady without becoming a gentleman," and *Punch* lamented laconically, " 'New men, new manners'; 'new women—no manners.' "

16

Some women espoused the cause of socialism and joined the Fabian Society, led by the magnetic, red-haired Mr. Shaw. Others, like Evelyn Sharp, took up suffrage, a question which split as many friendships as the playwright from Norway. H. W. Nevinson and Laurence Housman supported Votes for Women, but A. E. Housman said cautiously, "I think I should like to see some other and less precious country try it first: America for instance...."[21] Ouida from her retirement at Lucca wrote acidly on "New Women" and "Female Suffrage," decrying both votes and bicycles.[22]

Young women flocked to the art schools, and some even went to Paris; many turned to writing as a means of self-expression. Hands which had hovered lightly over piano keys transferred their touch to the typewriter. A club was formed that was called the Pioneers, and what had once been the Literary Ladies changed its name to Women Writers. Its members were displeased when Mrs. Humphrey Ward declined an invitation to speak because of ill health, though she had been well enough to attend an Authors' Tea a few days before. She said she did not want to see "sex emphasized in literature," and put in a plea for the "neutrality of the pen—the sexlessness of intelligence."[23]

Some women attempted to achieve this neutrality by assuming masculine pen names for their writing — Michael Field, George Egerton, John Oliver Hobbes, Martin Ross, Frank Danby, Lucas Malet, George Fleming, and others—but as they let themselves be found out almost at once the ruse did not seem important. The aunt and niece who wrote under the name of Michael Field explained that they "thought it necessary in order to get a hearing."[24] E. Nesbit was mistakenly addressed as "Ernest" by H. G. Wells and felt much flattered when William De Morgan wrote her a letter of appreciation concluding, "Thanking you cordially, believe me, Dear Sir, . . ."[25] On the other hand, one critic thought Ella D'Arcy to be a pseudonym, insisting that Miss D'Arcy wrote like a man—high praise indeed. Such masquerading was not limited to women; men pretended also, as strange names at the end of newspaper columns and Fisher Unwin's Pseudonym Library could testify.

Journalism offered more opportunities to the weaker sex, not in news-reporting, but in writing on cookery, fashions, and books. Mrs. Meynell's "The Wares of Autolycus," written by women for the *Pall Mall Gazette,* was a regular institution. Rosamund Graham Tomson made a verse to immortalize the collaborators, beginning,

> O, there's Mrs. Meynell and Mrs. Pennell,
> There's Violet Hunt and me![26]

Rosamund also did Fashion Notes for the *Observer* and wrote poetry. Katharine Tynan was a contributor to the *Pall Mall,* Ella Hepworth Dixon wrote for the *Westminster Gazette,* and Mona Caird did a series on "Morality of Marriage" for the same paper. Marie Belloc, sister of Hilaire, often argued with her editor, W. T. Stead, about her copy; Ada Leverson parodied Oscar Wilde in *Punch* and interviewed celebrities for the *Sketch.* E. Nesbit reviewed books for the *National Observer* and was one of the first to praise *A Shropshire Lad* when it was brought out by Kegan Paul at the author's expense, seeing in it "the promise of great things, things which will be remembered when our little artists in wired flowers are forgiven and forgotten."[27]

In general, journalistic standards were higher than they had been for a long time. W. E. Henley of the *Scots Observer* and later the *National Observer* was responsible for much of this improvement. Henley was, like Wilde, a disciple of Pater, but his ideals and temperament were far removed from those of the author of *Dorian Gray.* Henley was an "arrant Anglo-Saxon," a gifted poet, and a fine editor, though it was sometimes charged that he edited all the individuality from his staff. His powerful and sincere personality drew keen minds to his side, and Kenneth Grahame, Arthur Morrison, Charles Whibley, H. B. Marriott Watson, and G. W. Steevens were among "his young men," known to Max as "the Henley Regatta" and to Harland as "Mr. Henley's truculent Fifth Form." A strong friend and an invincible enemy, by both comradeship and hostility Henley raised the standards of journalism in London.

Still there were those who decried the *Observer.* Frederick

Wedmore said it was "doing the devil's work,"[28] and in 1892 Coventry Patmore, author of *The Angel in the House,* banned the *Observer* from his home for the protection of his wife and daughters, "decent Englishwomen," because he found at least one article in every issue "at once unwise in the interests of the Paper, and more than dubious in those of good taste and fair morals, to admit," adding that though he admired the "vigour and novelty" of Henley's poems he deplored "their peculiar and . . . uneconomical allusions to sex."[29]

Other weeklies which Patmore might have preferred as less damaging to his Angel were the *Pall Mall,* the *Saturday Review,* and the *Spectator,* to which Stevenson used to refer as "my grandmother." Reviews in these journals increased the prestige of the writers until literary criticism was no longer regarded as hack work. Names, many of them soon to be famous, were signed at the ends of columns. Sometimes they were pseudonyms like "Corno di Bassetto," which Bernard Shaw used for his musical criticisms in the *Star,* but names gave dignity to the profession and added authority.

Opposed to the intelligently edited sheets was Clement Scott's *Daily Telegraph,* written, so Lewis Hind said, for the great middle class, "who in music liked oratorios and 'The Lost Chord,' in art Sir Frederick Leighton and Alma Tadema and in drama, *East Lynne* and *The Silver King.*" Scott was a bitter foe of what he called "the Drama of the Dustbin,"[30] and no more vituperative reception was ever offered a production on the English stage than the *Telegraph* gave to *Ghosts,* which it compared to "an open drain; a loathsome sore unbandaged; a dirty act done publicly; or a lazar-house with all its doors and windows open."[31]

Another incentive to good literature in the nineties came with the passing of the three-volume novel and the subsequent diminution of the power of the lending libraries to mold public opinion. Since the cost of a three-volume novel was high, the general reader did not buy his copy but borrowed it from a book club. Such clubs then were immensely important to publishers. In 1885 George Gissing wrote to his sister, "Mudie, I hear, took sixty copies of *Thyrza* . . . and has sent for another twenty-five.

. . . Over against this was the fact that he has just taken 2,000 of Rider Haggard's new book"[32]—pleasant news for Mr. Haggard but likely to inflict on Gissing another of his "days too miserable to chronicle."

A long story and a happy ending had been the chief requirements of the book clubs, but now publishers and writers united to modify these essentials. Though some of the older authors objected—Walter Besant wrote in the *Dial* of the blow to English literary style, and Sir Henry Lucy grumbled that Mudie's and the other libraries would profit most, since the novels cost them less "whilst the subscription remains the same"[33]—most readers accepted with relief this curtailment of loquacity and consequent reduction in cost. At five shillings it was possible to buy one's own book and not depend on the taste of the libraries. Publishers vied with each other to make their books attractive in form and content to tempt this book-buying clientele. The Kelmscott Press set a new standard with the fineness of its paper and the beauty of its decoration. Ricketts and Shannon at the Vale produced fastidiously bound volumes—collectors' items. Publishers became more receptive to the realistic tale that ignored romance and a cheerful conclusion. Poets too had a chance to see their work in print, though the limited editions did not add much money to their pockets. With the shorter novel came volumes of short stories and the new magazines.

Following in the tradition of the *Germ,* the *Hobby Horse* had been founded by Herbert Horne and Selwyn Image, rector of St. Anne's, Soho. The *Hobby Horse* was a handsome and dignified magazine which ceased publication in 1892. Other short-lived periodicals, conceived in beauty and dedicated to the highest forms of literary art, included the *Pageant,* the *Butterfly,* the *Evergreen* (published in Edinburgh by Professor Patrick Geddes and lasting for only four numbers), the *Yellow Book,* the *Savoy,* and the *Dome,* which included music as well as art and literature.

This outbreak of ephemeral periodicals was not confined to England but ran its course on the Continent and in America as well. Two of the most noteworthy European ventures were *Pan* and *Blätter für die Kunst,* both published in Berlin during the middle nineties, though *Blätter für die Kunst* lasted into the next century. Stefan George founded it as the organ of the decadence *(das Niedergang)* directed *"gegan das stoffliche Bedeutungslos."* In addition to contributions by such writers as Stefan George, Hugo von Hofmannsthal, and Karl Wolfskehl, it included translations from Mallarmé, Swinburne, and d'Annunzio. *Pan* was an exceedingly *de luxe* quarterly, "devoted to creative art and to all interests which spring from art." It was lavishly illustrated under the guidance of Meier Graeffe, who visited the Pennells in London to talk over processes for *Pan* and ask them for prints and drawings.

In the United States, the most noteworthy experiments included *Moods,* "intended to be the *Yellow Book* of Philadelphia," the *Chap-Book,* "going to be published whether it pays or not," and the *Lark,* habitat of Gelett Burgess's "Purple Cow."

Chapter IV

IN THE NINETIES London was the center of a revival of literary life such as it had not known since the days of Dr. Johnson and his tavern convivials. To this misty Camelot on the Thames came young poets from Ireland and Wales, ambitious journalists from the provinces, artists from Scotland, eager young critics from Oxford or Cambridge ("A critic is any undergraduate of Oxford or Cambridge," said Le Gallienne),[1] and returning Pilgrims from America.

Never before had there been such an exchange of literature and ideas, not to mention the persons who promulgated them, between England and the States. A number of American writers took up residence in London. "Mr. James and his attendant Americans" someone called this group of Yankee emigrants.[2] Through his international stories and the active correspondence he carried on with American friends, James did much to unite the two English-speaking currents into one. Lady authors from the States, like Sarah Orne Jewett, Annie Fields, and Edith

21

Wharton, came to call on him at Lamb House, and he meticulously returned their visits when he crossed the Atlantic. Whistler had lived in England so long that he had almost forgotten his American heritage. In the eighties Elizabeth and Joseph Pennell, Quakers from Pennsylvania—A. S. Hartrick called Pennell "the most quarrelsome Quaker that ever was"[3]—came to do an illustrated article on Chelsea for the *Century* and remained to become Whistler's steadfast friends. Other American artists took up abode in London, among them John Singer Sargent and J. J. Shannon, born in Auburn, New York.

Bret Harte had been living in Camberly, Sussex, for some years when in 1894 Rudyard Kipling went to make his home in Brattleboro, Vermont, at the suggestion of his American wife. The editor of the New York *Evening Post* was an Englishman, but Henry Norman, editor of the London *Chronicle*, was a graduate of Harvard. The number of American correspondents in London was mounting steadily. Harold Frederic of the New York *Times* was considered by Ian Maclaren to be the best-read American in London. According to Louise Imogen Guiney, herself a transplanted American, he was also the most untouched by English customs. She said that he dreamt, spelt, and ate American.[4] Frederic's best friend was a writer of romantic tales from Canada, Robert Barr, who, Arnold Bennett declared, had "conquered Yankee prejudices but not the Yankee accent."[5] In the summer of 1897 these two were joined in Surrey by Stephen Crane and his new wife, just returned from reporting the war in Greece for the *Journal* and the *Westminster Gazette*.

Richard Harding Davis, another correspondent, "without whom no war was official," had gone to live the life of an undergraduate at Oxford and write an account of his experiences for *Harper's*. William Dean Howells paid a yearly visit to London. Ernest Rhys was entertained by the Stedmans in New York, made a pilgrimage to see Walt Whitman as he had been urged to do by Dr. Bucke, Whitman's biographer, a Norfolk man ("It is worth your while . . . simply to see Walt Whitman's ear, the most magnificent ear ever modeled and fixed on the head of a man"),[6] and met the Lowells, the Nortons, and the Holmeses in Cambridge. In 1893, Walter Besant found in New York a "blind and stupid hostility to England . . ." though "the individual English-man was received with friendliness. . . ."[7] Bill Nye made a flying trip to England in the fall of 1893 and was a guest of honor at a dinner given by the Authors' Club. Max Beerbohm accompanied his half-brother, the actor-manager Beerbohm Tree, on a the-atrical tour of the States in 1895, going as far west as Chicago, where Max was impressed by a dinner companion who had a quotation from Shakespeare for every topic. Max said that couldn't happen in England: "We think it was enough honor to have bred Shakespeare; we don't need to read him."[8] But about the same time Eugene Field at a party at Mrs. Humphry Ward's was asked, "Tell me, please, something of the habits and customs of Chicago. I have never seen a native Chicagoan before," and answered solemnly, "Well, when they caught me I was living in a tree."[9]

Richard Le Gallienne paid a brief visit to the States at the same time as Max and liked them so well that he later returned to stay. Conan Doyle's literary readings in New York in 1894 re-ceived so much publicity that E. A. Robinson grew "tired of him in any form."[10]

Much English work appeared in the pages of American maga-zines and many American novels were brought out in English editions. Every American periodical with any pretension to be-ing literary published a London Letter with book news from Britain, though few English papers reciprocated. W. B. Yeats, while protesting that he hated journalism, wrote for both Provi-dence and Boston papers. Arthur Waugh contributed a weekly letter to the *Critic,* and Annie Macdonell wrote every month for the American *Bookman.* Meredith and Hardy were regularly serialized in America, Hardy's *Tess of the D'Urbervilles* and *Jude the Oscure* coming out in *Harper's.* Hardy was never so fiercely criticized in the States as he was in England or Scotland. (A Scotch paper chanted, "Swinburne planteth, Hardy watereth and Satan giveth the increase.")[11] But Hardy and his editor J. H. Harper encountered many difficulties before *Tess* and *Jude* were got into serial form, the illegitimate children of both becoming adopted orphans to meet the requirements of a family periodical. *Jude* bore three different titles in *Harper's, The Simpletons* and *Hearts Insurgent* preceding the final choice.[12]

On the other hand, Stephen Crane's *Maggie* was more kindly received in London than America, and the author of *The Red Badge of Courage* was hailed as a "great artist" and a "genius" in England before American critics got around to such superlatives. Douglas Sladen went to America to gather material for an anthology, *Younger American Poets,* since Edmund Gosse had told him, "In America every author writes poetry, and that will make them want to know you."[13]

The brisk exchange of *littérateurs* and artists was also carried on across the Channel. William Rothenstein at the age of seventeen had settled in Paris to study art and see life at first hand. He shuttled back and forth from Dover to Dieppe, and whenever a young writer or artist set out on his first trip to the Left Bank he was provided with a letter to Rothenstein, who would show him the sights. In 1893, abetted by Symons, he arranged for Verlaine's visit to London and Oxford.

This French Symbolist poet, now in one of his occasional periods of reform, was entertained by Arthur Symons in the rooms he shared with Havelock Ellis in Fountain Court, and Verlaine wrote a poem on the view from the window. Gosse took him to lunch and to call on a publisher; Beardsley met him at the Harlands' and thought him "a dear old thing";[14] John Lane bought his dinner before he lectured on "Contemporary French Poetry" at Barnard's Inn, Holborn. A writer in the *London Literary World* complained that there were few people present to hear "this most original and exquisite of living poets," but the ten-shilling admission was partly to blame. As Dowson wrote to Plarr, "I shall try to go . . . though I think, nous autres, rimeurs, should be on the Free List."[15] After the lecture Symons took Verlaine to the Crown, where any young intellectual with the price of a glass of beer could view the great man at close range. Generally Verlaine was considered to have been on his good behavior, but Marie Belloc Lowndes (half-sister of Hilaire Belloc), who wrote of his visit for the London papers, complained that no editor would allow her to describe him as "a great French poet."[16]

Mrs. Lowndes because of her French background and facile style was also asked to write of Zola when he visited London later the same year. He spoke on "Anonymity in Journalism" at a meeting of the Institute of Journalists, advertised with a striking poster by the new artist Aubrey Beardsley. An impressive gathering which attended the dinner honoring this exponent of naturalism included a learned judge who had a short time before sentenced Vizetelly to prison for issuing the English version of Zola's works. Katharine Tynan, who went with Marie Belloc Lowndes to hear Zola speak, admitted, "I am not sure that I was quite satisfied with myself about doing honour to the famous Frenchman. The simplicities of my Irish upbringing still constrained me, and Zola was on my Index. He has never been off it indeed."[17] Still she went.

Though Mrs. Lowndes saw Zola several times she did not learn till later that during his London stay his mistress and two children had been settled in a house near London so that he could visit them whenever possible.

Mallarmé lectured at Cambridge in March, 1894, and Alphonse Daudet visited Henry James the following year. James' preparations were made with all care but had to undergo some alteration when Daudet's wife and three children came too. At least they could be publicly acknowledged; indeed Madame Daudet and the offspring went everywhere. James took them to call on Meredith at Box Hill and privately described the visit as "odious,"[18] though Mrs. Wharton thought his account of the "two great writers, both stricken with the same fatal malady, advancing painfully toward each other,"[19] was moving. James wrote A. C. Benson, who had hoped he might see Daudet at Eton, "I wish he might have done Eton properly—but (though I take them all, woe's the day—7 persons!!!—to Oxford on Saturday) he is unable to do anything properly."[20] James also was mentor to Paul Bourget on two occasions when he risked a Channel crossing.

If lecturers came to London, every spring London poets,

artists, and writers migrated to France, to Paris first for the opening of the Salon, then as the sun grew warmer to Brittany to paint and write and bathe. Whistler had discovered a little Inn there and gradually an English colony took it over. Mrs. Pennell has written of the group that made the journey together for several years—Bob Stevenson, D. S. MacColl, Charles Whibley, Charles Furse, Henry Harland, Robert Ross, and Aubrey Beardsley. Ernest Dowson was happiest in Brittany, but Mrs. Atherton saw him one summer at Pont Avon and described him as "a lost soul,"[21] to the horror of Thomas Bird Mosher.[22] Sickert was often there and Conder, working on his silk paintings. Arthur Symons and Aubrey Beardsley planned the *Savoy* at Dieppe.

These artists found renewed inspiration and a sense of participating in a significant movement when they were in Paris. "London may have been wide awake—for London—in the Nineties," said Mrs. Pennell, "but it was half asleep compared to Paris and would not have been awake at all if it had not gone to Paris for the 'new' it bragged of so loud in art and every excitement it cultivated."[23]

Writers enjoyed the untrammeled atmosphere of the Left Bank and envied their French *confrères* the freedom to live and work without interference. The Englishman discovered that even a brief period away from the critical scrutiny of Mrs. Grundy improved his style. "The British public . . . will forgive anything to a French artist, nothing to his English comrade,"[24] grumbled Aubrey Beardsley, yet Stephen Crane told a woman in New York, "Englishmen aren't shocked as easily as we are. . . . You can have an idea in England without being sent to court for it."[25]

Mrs. Pennell might praise Paris (after all she was an American), Stedman might find New York the best place to compile his Victorian Anthology, Julia Ward Howe's impressive parties might draw the lions of Boston, but London was the pivot of Anglo-Saxon culture. "Paris and London, world flowers twain," sang the poet, but London was his first love.

As earlier poets had looked to Windermere, country churchyards, or ruined abbeys for inspiration, the poets of the nineties looked to London. The *London Voluntaries* of Henley, *London*

Visions of Laurence Binyon, *London Nights* of Arthur Symons paid homage to the city. Le Gallienne hailed

> London, London, our delight,
> Great flower that opens but at night,
> Great city of the midnight sun
> Whose day begins when day is done.

Lionel Johnson wrote "By the Statue of King Charles at Charing Cross," and Ernest Rhys described the beggar at the corner when the lamps were lighted and people were hurrying home:

> He is pious at his trade,
> Thinking of the coin new-laid
> Warm and shining in his palm;
> He is London's evening psalm.

Robert Bridges was inspired by "London Snow," and Oscar Wilde visited Covent Garden in the early morning hours and wrote of it in *Dorian Gray*. A. E. Housman might prefer Shropshire and Norman Gale the orchard and cricket field, but John Davidson was called the "Virgil of Fleet Street" and Arthur Symons the "Herrick of the Music Halls."

The story-writer as well as the poet discovered London—not the snobbery of the West End but the life of the dockside, the narrow passage, or the shabby square. Kipling found romance in India, Conrad in the South Seas, Hudson in the Argentine, Barrie in the Scottish burns. The run-of-the-mill scribe found it in London, as Hubert Crackanthorpe's *Vignettes*, Arthur Morrison's *Tales of Mean Streets*, George Gissing's *New Grub Street*, Richard Whiteing's *No. 5 John Street*, H. W. Nevinson's *Neighbors of Ours*, and Somerset Maugham's *Liza of Lambeth* illustrate.

Many of the young writers knew each other and a spirit of literary *camaraderie* prevailed. Friendships grew over the appreciation of a phrase or the perception of a mood. They read and admired each other's work, often proclaiming their regard to the world. "This flock of youthful bards in London are constantly discovering each other," grumbled a critic, and the Philistine wrote heatedly in the *Westminster Gazette* on "Log-

Rolling," sneering at the superlative praise bestowed on one writer by another. The log-roller under fire was Richard Le Gallienne, who was charged with listing six new major poets in his review of poetry for 1894—Davidson, Symons, Gale, Hayes, Francis Thompson, and Yeats. To the resultant controversy Ricardo Stephens contributed a poem, "Ballade of the Newest Poets," ending each stanza with "Roll thou my log, and I will roll thee thine."[26]

Friends often found lodging in the same part of the city. Some preferred Chelsea, rich in memories but cheap in rent, where the glass-roofed studios welcomed artists. Kenneth Grahame lived in a tiny top flat on the Embankment, where he could watch the misty river as Whistler had done and drink coffee at midnight at the small untidy box of a coffee stall, elbow to elbow with poets, artists, and cabbies. George Moore sometimes stayed with Ellis and Symons in their rooms in Fountain Court. Lewis Hind and Le Gallienne resided for a time in adjoining buildings in Chancery Lane. Lionel Johnson at 20 Fitzroy Street was often host to Ernest Dowson when the latter had lingered so long at the taverns that he could not get back to his home in Limehouse. Yeats had rooms over a cobbler's shop in Woburn Buildings off Euston Road, and here once a week he intoned his poetry to selected guests, sometimes at such length that a departing disciple yawned, "Yeats is a good poet, but he has no sense of time."[27]

Journalists rimmed Fleet Street; students gathered in the plane-tree–shaded squares of Bloomsbury. Embryo critics found the old book shops of Charing Cross Road useful for converting review copies (sometimes with uncut pages) into cash. Cash was so necessary and sometimes so hard to get. A poet once lived for a week on cheese and apples at 2d. a pound. Mussels from a street stall were a treat to an impecunious novelist. When money was plentiful, poets and artists gathered at the various cafés and pubs to which they gave their approval. Some liked to dine at the Monico, "which is not amusing," decreed Arthur Symons, or at the Domino Room of the Café Royal, "which is always amusing."[28] During the early years of the decade Oscar Wilde

28

held court in the Domino Room. The Café Royal with its red velvet seats, marble-topped tables, and gold decorations was the most famous restaurant of the nineties, but it had its drawbacks. Cobden-Sanderson, the bookbinder, recorded in his diary in 1896 that he had dined at the Café Royal because "(Philip Burne-Jones said it was the only clean place in London.) I paid 3s. for a fillet steak! It may suit Phil, but it is really too 'clean' for me."[29]

The Crown, between the stage doors of the Empire and Alhambra, was another favorite rendezvous, not so expensive as the Royal. Beardsley was to be found most often at "Jimmy's," as the St. James's Restaurant in Piccadilly was called by its patrons. Beardsley observed here the women who became types and models for his drawings. "They are the only ones who dress well," he pronounced.[30] Other cafés in Soho where food was good and wine was cheap had their coteries who could call the waiters familiarly "August," "Alphonse," or *le petit Paul.* Ernest Dowson always dined at the Poland on Frith Street, where he could torture himself with his hopeless passion for "Missie," the daughter of the proprietor.

Some of the regulars at various taverns banded together in clubs. Maurice Baring belonged to the Cemented Bricks, an organization of young literary men and journalists who met at Anderton's Hotel in Fleet Street. To them Richard Le Gallienne first read his "Religion of a Literary Man," as he later did with such good effect up and down the provinces. Charles Whibley, Marriott Watson, Harold Frederic, and the artist Charles Furse belonged to the Ghouls. Other clubs included the New Vagabonds, the Odd Volumes, the Omar Khayyám (the last two somewhat beyond the reach of the younger men), and the Rhymers' Club, which met at the Cheshire Cheese.

The best of London's young poets belonged to it—Dowson, Davidson, Lionel Johnson, Le Gallienne, Todhunter, Plarr, Rhys, Ernest Radford, T. W. Rolleston, Symons, and Yeats among them. The club met informally once a month at the old tavern, famous for its lark-and-kidney pie, and, after dining, retired to an upper room where over ale and churchwarden pipes the poems of its members were read and discussed. Occasionally guests who could contribute to the symposium on life and prosody were invited.

"The meetings were always decorous and often dull," Yeats has remembered. "Some one would read out a poem and we would comment, too politely for the criticism to have great value; and yet that we read out our poems, and thought that they could be so tested, was a definition of our aims."[31] It was Yeats who suggested a collected volume of these poems.

The first *Book of the Rhymers' Club* was published in 1892 and received kind reviews in most English papers. The whole project was described at length by an anonymous Pilgrim in the *Mercure de France* for March. Dodd, Mead and Company brought out an American edition. A second volume appeared the next year. Both books were financially successful, but no more were published, for now most of the members were on the way to producing their own volumes and the club dwindled away, leaving these two desirable items for collectors.

Artists sometimes showed their good will by planning the decoration of their friends' rooms. Interior decoration was a serious matter in the nineties, as Mr. Leyland, for whom Whistler did the Peacock Room, had reason to know. Aymer Vallance, disciple of William Morris, arranged the color scheme and furniture for Aubrey Beardsley's studio: black floors, green rugs, black furniture upholstered in blue and white, and walls hung with flaming orange. Frank Richards painted bits of scenery on the walls for Douglas Sladen in Addison Mansions. Roger Fry worked against many difficulties to decorate the house of his friend Hubert Crackanthorpe, and when he had surmounted the problems and the house was finished Bertie "must go and ruin the design—white walls and a black dado— by hanging up photographs."[32] Max Beerbohm, an expert since he had adorned his room at Oxford with Pellegrini prints, advised Mrs. Leverson, "Green curtains for the back room—or how would white silk be *or pale blue silk*. Perhaps a pale blue curtain between the rooms but one must see the colours. Mind the wall green is a dingy green."[33]

Those figures of the literary and artistic world who had their own establishments were hospitable to younger folk. Afternoons at home, evenings in the drawing-room were features of social life in London. Only the shyest and most diffident young artist could avoid inclusion in some such circle. Jerome K. Jerome said that the "At Homes" were so numerous it made his brain reel to remember them and that he usually turned up on the wrong day.[34] Grant Richards thought one of the most important things that could happen to a young man of the nineties was "a meeting with Mrs. Ernest Leverson, Ada Leverson, the Egeria of the whole 'nineties movement."[35] At her evenings in those first happy years one could be almost sure of meeting Oscar Wilde.

Most rarefied and select were the Sunday afternoons at the Meynell house when Alice and Wilfrid Meynell, their children, and sometimes the poet they had befriended, Francis Thompson, or their friend Coventry Patmore received their guests. "One arrived; one drank tea; one heard pleasant stories of what was toward; one spoke nervously to Mrs. Meynell, a sibyl at the fireside, and one had one's nervousness dispelled; one played with the children; and one was asked to stop to supper," Grant Richards reported.[36] But Lewis Hind was there on an afternoon when the fire got low and Mrs. Maynell too withdrawn and far away to notice. At last Coventry Patmore rose and said in his deep emphatic voice, "With your permission, Mrs. Meynell, I will procure my topcoat from the hall, and then return."[37]

The Gosses were at home on Sunday evening, as were the Colvins in the British Museum. A new dramatist said he would be damned if he would be taken up by the Sidney Colvins,[38] but any writer was flattered at being asked to the Edmund Gosses' parties. On Saturday night the young men from the Observer liked to go to Henley's house in Chiswick before the tragedy of his daughter's death. "Show Sundays" at the home of J. J. Shannon drew the young artists, and Mabel Dearmer's "lurid Mondays" in her drawing room on Davenport Street were popular. On Thursday afternoons Mrs. Beardsley poured tea for her artist son and his red-haired sister Mabel, and on

31

Thursday evenings the Pennells were at home in their Buckingham Street flat.

Mrs. Pennell has described those evenings. "Few of the crowd one met on those evenings had not already a name or else were not on the point of making one. We provided no amusements—no music, no cards, no dancing, no recitations. Our refreshments were limited to the Englishman's indispensable whiskey-and-soda, cigars, cigarettes, though, when I was sure wives were to be with us, claret and ˜cake might be added. No particular dress was imperative. . . . The chance to talk was the sole attraction."[39]

During the days of the *Yellow Book* the Harlands' Saturday evenings in "the gay pink drawing room with its Persian carpets, its pictures and old furniture," at their flat in Cromwell Road were thronged with the young men and women associated with the quarterly. "Henry James had a way of dropping in 'just for the space of one moment or so, my dear Harland, for I am mortally unwell tonight.' "[40] If James came he was always the lion, but if the master was not in the chair, the gaiety mounted higher. Evelyn Sharp, recalling those evenings in the *Manchester Guardian,* "wondered if anywhere in the young world to-day there is a literary and artistic circle so full of vitality and promise as the one, absurdly labelled decadent,"[41] that came to the Harlands, and included Netta Syrett, Ella D'Arcy, Kenneth Grahame, Oswald Sickert, Richard Le Gallienne and his brother-in-law Jimmie Welch the actor, Lewis Hind, Hubert Crackanthorpe, and Stanley Makower. Sometimes Aline Harland, who had a sweet soprano voice, sang some lyric of Herrick's that Makower had set to music or *"Gardez-vous d'être sévère,"* considered particularly appropriate to the audience. "If but a few people were present," said Netta Syrett, "one heard Harland and Beardsley discussing drawings, gossiping about John Lane and criticizing recent contributions."[42] The evening often ended by all adjourning to the kitchen to "see a poet and a painter settle a dispute as to the right way to make an omelet—a pleasant change from the customary dispute as to the right way to compose a triolet."[43]

Among the older hostesses, Mrs. Crackanthorpe, mother of Bertie and author of the much-discussed "Revolt of the Daughters" in the *Nineteenth Century,* often entertained such established writers as Meredith and Hardy, Stopford Brooke and Henry James. Hardy recorded attending a "most amusing masked ball" at the home of his friends Mr. and Mrs. Montagu Crackanthorpe, where he and Henry James were the only two men not in dominos and consequently were "recklessly flirted with by the women,"[44] and Henry James noted gratefully in his diary for February, 1894, that at Mrs. Crackanthorpe's the night before, Stopford Brooke had given him two little ideas.

James himself sometimes gave parties, especially luncheons, but he did not entertain on the scale of some bachelors. André Raffalovitch, the Russian poet and man of means, good friend to Aubrey and Mabel Beardsley, was a lavish and frequent host, as was Philip Burne-Jones. John Lane in the days before his marriage gave parties in his rooms in Albany or entertained with teas for authors at the Bodley Head. But expensive hospitality was beyond most of the unmarried men of the literary set, who, as a spinster novelist complained, had "just enough money to make life pleasant and comfortable for themselves and none to spare for a wife and possible children,"[45] and Sydney Pauling of Heinemann's said, "There is one drawback to marrying on a small income: *you cannot entertain.*"[46]

If friendships flourished in the nineties, so too did feuds and animosities. Perhaps Whistler, the butterfly with the sting of a wasp, began the fashion when he sued Ruskin for libel. Whistler was continually engaged in litigations and quarrels with men who offended him. Harry Quilter, his adversary on one occasion, was likewise involved against other men of the day. Two editors, T. W. H. Crosland and Frank Harris, carried perennial chips on their shoulders, and Joseph Pennell's suit against Sickert and the *Saturday Review* cost Harris, the editor, a pretty penny. The feud between Harris and Harland endured for all the days of the *Yellow Book;* Henley did not like Harland, nor did Whistler, though they had once been friends and Whister had painted Aline. Clement Shorter announced in the

Sphere, "Personally I do not like either Mr. Gosse or Sir Sidney Colvin."[47] D. S. MacColl won his spurs early in the Degas controversy; Beerbohm and Le Gallienne gave Kipling uncomplimentary attention. Though Andrew Lang had many admirers, Watts-Dunton is reported to have declared, "I never yet knew a man of genius who did not loathe Lang,"[48] and Oscar Wilde said, "Poor dear Shaw! Nice man, Bernard. He's got no enemies, but his friends don't like him."[49]

Bitterness often followed unkind or uncomplimentary words in print. When Conan Doyle objected to the influence Robertson Nicoll was able to swing for or against a book, he expressed the discomfiture of many authors. Nicoll owned the *British Weekly,* in which he wrote articles under his own name, a long discourse on literature signed "Claudius Clear," and a column of literary gossip by "A Man of Kent." As editor of the *Bookman* and contributing editor of the American *Bookman* his word had power. Since in addition he did a weekly column for the *Sketch* and reviews for the Daily *Chronicle,* his individual opinion had the force of six or seven separate reviews. He had been able to do great service for Meredith, but Conan Doyle was not so favored. When the latter protested this loading of the dice, in the Daily *Chronicle,* many authors and reviewers entered the lists.[50] Such literary tilts are out of fashion today, but the nineties rang with them.

Another preoccupation of the period was the literary gossip columns in which the lives and foibles of writers were examined with the same thoroughness today bestowed upon Hollywood. Though Wilde said the writing of literary gossip was not a fit occupation for a gentlemen,[51] it was a way of making a living and the public eagerly licked up the crumbs of news about those who dined in state. Some authors aided these gossip-gatherers; others, like Austin Dobson and Henry James, withheld their co-operation; and the *Bookman* reported that Dobson "has persistently set his face against the system of interviewing" and refused "in every instance and every circumstance to receive the interviewer."[52] James wrote to Howells, "I have a morbid passion for personal privacy and a standing quarrel with the blundering publicities of the age."[53] Maurice Hewlett deplored even *Who's Who*, declaring, "The public for whom such works are produced is a dirty feeder and ought not to be encouraged."[54]

Richard Le Gallienne was more charitable. "Gossip is the social reward of personality," he wrote. "Whether it be playful or poison-fanged, it is a recognition, a tribute, one of the most gratifying forms of success. . . .Gossip. . .means. . .that you are very interesting. . . .The world will forgive its artists anything but propriety. . . .But to rob a poet of his bad name! that is indeed a dull and doubtful service."[55]

This, then, was the London of the nineties, . . .of the hansom cab and the cabmen's shelters, of Vesta Tilley singing "TaRaRa Boom de ay" and Lottie Collins singing "Daisy," of the tandem bicycle and the double standard, of Mrs. Pat Campbell in *The Second Mrs. Tanqueray* and Beerbohm Tree in *A Pillar of Society*, of the barrel organ in the Strand and the concerts of Isidore de Lara, of the children's plays in Hyde Park and the debacle of Oscar Wilde, of the yellow fogs and the flickering gas lamps, of the Diamond Jubilee and Kipling's "Recessional," of Beardsley's genius and the *Yellow Book*.

Chapter V

THREE MEN CONTROLLED the destinies of the *Yellow Book*—John Lane, publisher, Aubrey Beardsley, art editor, and Henry Harland, literary editor.

John Lane was the senior partner in the firm of Elkin Mathews and John Lane at the sign of the Bodley Head in Vigo Street, London. The partnership had been formed in 1887 when John Lane, then a railway clerk but a bibliophile and book collector by avocation, and Elkin Mathews, proprietor of a secondhand book store in the Cathedral Yard at Exeter, embarked on a new venture in publishing. The symbol of the Bodley Head was agreed upon for their sign because, as John Lane explained, "Bodley, the most pious of founders! . . . Besides, Bodley was one of the most notable worthies of Devon, my native county, and had I needed a contributory motive, this would have been an ample one," and Elkin Mathews, coming from Exeter, Sir Thomas Bodley's birthplace, declared that the very same idea was in his own mind.[1] So the Bodley Head it became, and in 1892 the firm was more fully defined as *"Publishers and Vendors of Choice & Rare Editions in Belles Lettres."*

John Lane, born of a race of Devonshire yeomen from West Putford, was largely self-educated. In 1890 he wore a short pointed beard, sandy, like his hair, and his eyes were blue and clear. A busy, bustling individual, full of talk and energy and always in a hurry, he seemed the antithesis of Elkin Mathews, who was quiet, small, clean-shaven, with a head too large for his body and a deliberate manner. Mathews was shy too, especially with women. But different as the men were in temperament and personality they had one thing in common: they both loved books and were resolved to publish only such fine and beautiful volumes as they themselves would be proud to own.

To that end they engaged artists of recognized standing, such as C. S. Ricketts and C. H. Shannon of the Vale Press, to design covers, borders, and bindings. Details of print, paper, and material were carefully chosen to supplement the artistic craftsmanship.

The first publication of the new firm had been Richard Le Gallienne's *Volumes in Folio,* a limited edition, bound in blue grey boards and printed on handmade paper. Lane liked this charming young poet lately arrived from Liverpool, and made every effort to achieve a book which collectors would prize. Publishers were extremely conscious of "collectors' items," believing that beauty and scarcity made an irresistible combination. Other early Bodley Head items included *Silverpoints* by John Gray, *In the Key of Blue* by J. A. Symonds, and *The Sphinx* by Oscar Wilde, all with bindings by Ricketts, and Francis Thompson's *Poems,* for which Laurence Housman did the frontispiece and title-page on the second attempt, the first having failed to win Lane's approval.

Knowing that it took more than an attractive format to sell a book, Mathews and Lane chose their authors with care too, and from the first surrounded themselves with competent advisers. Frederic Chapman, whom Lane had taken from a circulating library in Leicester, a man of judgment and ability, became their general manager and counselor, remaining with the firm for many years. Grant Richards said that when Lane took fright and wanted to trim his sails it was Chapman who stiffened his back, but Ella D'Arcy thought Chapman sometimes assumed too much responsibility and was actually more timid than Lane. Among the firm's readers were such well-known persons as Le Gallienne, John Davidson, John Buchan, and Grant Richards. A young lad by the name of May who began as a sort of office boy and general handy man, advancing his "literary education by addressing the firm's envelopes,"[2] lived to become the Boswell of the Bodley Head with his *John Lane and the Nineties.*

Within a short time the newcomers were rivaling older and more established firms and snatching authors from Heinemann, Dent, and Fisher Unwin, who put the blame for such desertions partly on that innovation, the literary agent. A. P. Watt was a pioneer as this sort of intermediary between author and publisher, and authors welcomed his introduction of business acumen more heartily than publishers. Anthony Hope described the services of the famous firm by saying, "Watt does the blushing for you."

But the determined policy of the Bodley Head to present a distinguished group of writers and artists was more responsible for these deflections. New writers and artists who found little support from orthodox publishers were encouraged by their reception in Vigo Street. There was "always a little breeze blowing from Vigo Street," said Arthur Waugh, "laden with whispers of Lane's new discovery, which Sidney Colvin (or some other authority of equal weight) had declared to be a thing of amazing virtue."[3] Evelyn Sharp doubted whether any other publisher in London "would have seen anything but immaturity"[4] in her first novel, which Lane accepted, and Gertrude

Atherton was elated when she placed *Patience Sparhawk* with John Lane, "the fashionable publisher of the day."[5] The firm was talked about on both sides of the Atlantic; "those rarely courageous London publishers, Elkin Mathews and John Lane," said a Chicago critic admiringly.[6]

Even the mistakes of the firm were diverted into assets. When a forthcoming book of Edmund Gosse's, *Letters of Thomas Beddoes,* was announced through a typographical error as edited by Edmund Goose, Canon Ainger's little verse,

> Heed not this last *bêtise*
> Of John's;
> We know that all his geese
> Are swans,[7]

made good advertising.

Not all the offerings of the firm, however, met with the approval of the Victorians, and again it was Canon Ainger who expressed the opinion of many when he called for "more of the godly soul / And less of the Bodley Head."[8] Though a number of the firm's books were roundly berated by press and public, John Lane considered even adverse criticism better than none at all. Some of his writers, however, were not pleased when *Punch* cracked, "Uncleanliness is next to Bodliness."[9] Kenneth Grahame in particular urged Lane to take some action, but Lane chose to regard it as all good fun and free publicity.

Elkin Mathews did not always agree with Lane. When two men of such diverse natures are partners, there are bound to be differences of opinion. Lane was never the one who yielded. Mr. May admitted that peace departed from the office when Lane gave up his position in the Railway Company to devote all his time to the Bodley Head. From then on, Mathews had to "play second fiddle, and . . . to a galloping *tempo*. . . . Mathews, who never ought to have left the calm of Cathedral Yard, Exeter, could not go the pace. In the end, he had to fall out. It was something of a tragedy."[10]

It is not clear what precipitated the final break but the event disclosed considerable feeling among the Bodley Head authors, and the little breeze in Vigo Street threatened to become a good-sized gale. In the summer of 1894 notices appeared in the press of the separation of Mathews and Lane, which was to take place in September. "Mathews remains at the premises in Vigo Street and will devote his attention as in the past to second-hand books," said one authority. Lane moved to new offices across the street at No. 8, taking the sign "by mutual agreement." Mathews lingered at the old shop about a year, then moved to larger quarters in Cork Street. For years Bodley Head writers remembered the schism and expressed their sympathy for one man or the other. Stephen Gwynn defended Mathews as the real book lover of the two, but acknowledged that a "natural preference for the loser" might have influenced his judgment.[11] Still Mathews did not do badly, for he took a number of Lane's most cherished writers with him, including Dowson, Johnson, Selwyn Image, Herbert Horne, "Michael Field," and Yeats.

John Lane was left in possession of Vigo Street. Only three numbers of the *Yellow Book* had appeared when the division occurred and the quarterly remained with Lane, so that he has come to be considered its proprietor; but Mathews' withdrawal had an undoubted effect on its history.

John Lane, "little Johnny Lane" in Mr. May's fond remembrance, "that poor fly in the amber of modernity" as Max Beerbohm described him,[12] who was now in complete control of the Bodley Head, continued his pursuit of new talent, of the author who was breaking with tradition and charting fresh paths. But he did not neglect the writer of established popularity whose books had a wide circulation and would sell. Lane's farmer forebears had traded in cattle in the village square with thrifty smartness. Now Lane brought this inherited acumen to the book market. He was a shrewd and canny buyer, wise in the principle of give and take, knowing when to accept a loss and withdraw and when to risk greater involvement. The profit from his popular authors could be used to offset the money he spent on books with only a limited or artistic appeal: Lane had a weakness for poetry.

In a day when A. E. Housman paid Kegan Paul thirty pounds to print *A Shropshire Lad,* the Bodley Head was publishing more verse than any other firm in London, and what was more remarkable, giving the poet a little cash besides—in most cases, however, not as much as he wanted. Then he would press Lane for more—perhaps for an advance on a nebulous idea, still in his brain but about to be born, or for additional payment on work already printed. Under either condition, it was said, Lane was more likely to buy the author a good dinner than to hand over the cash. Lane's business methods were often the subject of inquiry among his writers.

Laurence Housman, after several unsuccessful attempts to collect five pounds which Lane owed him, finally wrote a letter asking him as a friend for a loan of five pounds. Housman assured him that he would repay the sum as soon as his publisher, a most honorable man, should make a payment promised the previous week. Lane was so amused by this ruse that he sent the money by return mail and told the story to all his friends, raising the amount from five pounds to fifty.[13] A difference between Lane and Harold Frederic over a financial reckoning did not have such a happy ending, for the brawny American was said to have put over one or two arguments with such telling effect that Lane took to his bed, and another American, Gertrude Atherton, wrote, "I never liked John Lane. He reminded me of a fat white frog, and I was never too sure that I was receiving all monetary dues on the books of mine he published. It was such an honor to be published by the Bodley Head . . . that Lane always looked pained at any demand for money and yielded it up grudgingly."[14] A fellow-bookman said that Lane's "easy Devonshire frankness" covered "lots of subtlety."[15]

Many publishers thought Lane was making a mistake when he accepted Grant Allen's *The Woman Who Did* after they had all turned it down as too dangerous and iconoclastic. Grant Richards persuaded him to print this novel on the explosive subject of the girl who chose to be an unmarried mother when she might have been an honest woman, and the reverberations were considerable. Nearly every reviewer slated it, and Glad-

40

stone, to whom the author sent a copy, gave him his thanks and best wishes, but added that the wishes "would be very different for him from what he probably wished for himself."[16] Still the book ran to twenty editions the first year, good dividends for a mistake.

Though Lane published much that was considered new and daring, he had a wary ear for the roar of the mob or the sound of cracking ice. E. F. Benson said that John Lane "had no objection . . . to thin ice, provided he felt reasonably sure that it would not let him through,"[17] and Arthur Waugh thought that he was afraid of "offending the proprieties, or indeed of causing any annoyance to any person of importance. 'So-and-so would never forgive you,' he used to say, 'if you did this or that'; and his anxiety in gathering approval of his books in advance was part of the same policy of caution."[18]

Lane was particularly hospitable to women writers when "the prejudices of the time being what the prejudices of the time were," according to W. Pett Ridge, many ladies "elected to be known by the first name of George."[19] George Egerton, Ella D'Arcy, Evelyn Sharp, Ethel Colburn Mayne, Netta Syrett, Gertrude Dix, Victoria Cross, and Mrs. Meynell wrote prose for the Bodley Head, and Edith Nesbit, Rosamund Marriott Watson, Dollie Radford, Olive Custance, Nora Hopper, and Katharine Tynan Hinkson were among its poets. The lyre was strummed so prettily at the Bodley Head that J.M.B. in the *Sketch* referred to it as the Bower of Sappho:

> And now the Maiden Muse has fled
> For shelter to the Bodley Head
> And there with Mr. Lane's *élite*
> Our Sappho sings in Vigo Street . . . .
>
> Nor pipe they for a vulgar set —
> Their price, you know, is always net.
> The hearts of women throb and beat
> For Mr. Lane of Vigo Street.[20]

He often treated his lady authors to luncheon, ordering champagne with a lavish extravagance, but if his guests were not very sophisticated, it was said, he substituted Asti Spumante for Veuve Cliquot, being careful to keep the label turned away.[21]

Though a wag termed him "Petticoat Lane," his poets were not all women. He published Norman Gale, Robert Bridges, A. C. Benson, Ernest Dowson, John Davidson, and Francis Thompson; the similarity in names led to a couplet, versions of which are ascribed to various people, including A. E. Housman:

> There in the Bodley shade they romp,
> The sons of Dow and David, Wat and Thomp,

to which of course might have been added "Ben" and "John."

When Lane chose a pseudonym for a contribution of his own to the *Yellow Book*, he took "Jean de France,"[22] a name which represented his own interests in the country over the channel. He published French poets in translation and English poets who wrote under French influence. When Verlaine made his visit to London, John Lane was one of the sponsors, and tickets could be brought from him or Herbert Horne or Arthur Symons. Lane probably had something to do with that price of ten shillings.

By the middle nineties many changes had taken place in the boy who left the little village in Devon to make his fortune. Perhaps he had not quite made it, but he was well on the way. He was now a cultivated man of affairs, with pleasant quarters in GI, Albany, a member of the best clubs, a collector of rare books, glass, china, prints, and silver, an astute appraiser of wine, women, and cooking, a successful publisher about to open a branch in America, and the *deus ex machina* for a brilliant group of writers and artists. Moreover, he was shortly to bring into being another challenge to the British public and to his own capacity, the *Yellow Book*.

Chapter VI

MANY WRITERS HAVE been concerned with the life and drawings of Aubrey Beardsley. The most comprehensive account has been given by Haldane Macfall (who might be considered a stepson of the nineties; at least that was the relationship he bore to Mrs. Sarah Grand, author of the *Heavenly Twins)*, but Arthur Symons, A. E. Gallatin, Robert Ross, Lewis Hind, and R. A. Walker have made authoritative contributions.

Aubrey Beardsley was born August 21, 1872, at Brighton. His sister Mabel was slightly older than he. Mrs. Beardsley taught music and at an early age Aubrey appeared with his sister on the concert stage as a pianist and was considered a child prodigy. He liked to draw too, imitating Kate Greenaway. "The drawings which I sent you were all copies from different books," he wrote with a frankness he might later have avoided. "...I often do little drawings from my own imagination but in doing figures the limbs are apt to be stiff and out of proportion & I can only get them right by copying. ... I am very fond of drawing."[1] He was never a strong child, and the weakness in his lungs was evident before he was eight years old.

He attended Brighton Grammar School, and one of his schoolmates recalled that when he first appeared he wore short trousers below which his thin calves wobbled uncertainly. This eccentricity of dress was much laughed at, to the new student's unhappiness. When he returned to school next term he was the correct English schoolboy in long trousers and starched Eton collar. For the rest of his life Aubrey made it a point to be sartorially elegant. He suffered on other counts during his school-days, and years later when he mentionetd a house in which he had taken lodgings called "Muriel," he said, "I feel as shy of my address as a boy at school is of his Christian name when it is Ebenezer or Aubrey."[2] He took part in school dramatics, attended the theatre whenever he could get the money, and nourished a secret ambition to go on the stage. A farce which he wrote at fifteen was produced by Charles Cochrane at Brighton. His sister Mabel became a successful actress. One of his masters, A. W. King, encouraged Beardsley to draw and praised his talent.

In July, 1888, at the age of sixteen, when most boys are looking toward the University, Aubrey left the Academy to work in an architect's office in London, where his mother was now living. Drafting was drudgery to a stage-struck boy, but it was valuable experience for an embryo artist. He spent his leisure time in the pleasanter pursuits of music, the theatre, writing, and drawing, but the next year, after he had changed to the Guardian Insurance Company as a clerk, the threat of tuberculosis was so heavy on him that he had no strength for anything beyond daily routine. Two years went by before he was able to resume his drawing.

When he was nineteen Beardsley, having got up "a grand show and drawings for my visit,"[3] went to call upon Burne-Jones, a leading Pre-Raphaelite painter. For some time Beardsley had been selling his drawings to Frederick Evans, proprietor of a book shop in Queen Street, Cheapside, and Evans had urged this visit. Burne-Jones, though he sighed privately that he was always having young chaps on his mind now, looked at his work, gave Beardsley the encouragement he needed, and suggested he study at Frederic Brown's Art School. So Beardsley worked at the office by day and attended art class by night, steeping himself in the conventions of the Pre-Raphaelites.

At the home of Burne-Jones, at the Art School, at Evans' shop, Beardsley now began to meet other young men and women who were on varied rungs of the ladder leading to success. Ernest Rhys sat with him one day in the Kardomah Café, across the street from Evans' shop with its display of Beardsley drawings in the window, while they discussed the relative merits of Balzac and Shakespeare. "Beardsley was an enthusiastic admirer of Balzac, his admiration ran to idolatry," said Rhys. "The trouble was that we were unequally equipped. I did not know Balzac half as well as Beardsley, and he did not know his Shakespeare half as well as I did. But what impressed me in his extravagant claim for Balzac's art was the amazing knowledge he

44

showed of the 'Comédie Humaine.' We drew a comparison between Père Goriot and King Lear. 'How much more subtle,' said he, 'the psychology of Balzac!' "[4]

He stayed at the Art School for about two years. Among those who helped him at this time were his future biographers, Aymer Vallance, interpreter of William Morris, and Robert Ross, apologist for Oscar Wilde. When various claims are examined to ascertain who discovered Beardsley—and there were a number of applicants for the honor—Frederick Evans should receive his due, for he arranged for Beardsley's first big commission, to illustrate the *Morte d'Arthur.*

J. M. Dent, the publisher, was planning an expensive and artistic edition of Malory's famous work, and Evans persuaded him to let Beardsley do the illustrations. It was a tribute to Dent's faith in Evans' judgment that he should have entrusted this important commission to a young man who was relatively unknown. The results of this confidence must have both pleased and surprised Dent, for while none of Beardsley's later abnormalities appeared in the *Morte d'Arthur* drawings, they were not the Pre-Raphaelite imitations he had expected.

Beardsley was now launched upon an artistic career. He gave up his job in the insurance office to devote his whole time to Malory. It was a colossal task, calling for hundreds of illustrations, borders, tailpieces, and initial letters, which taxed his resources and imagination. He worked like a demon and was heartily sick of the whole thing before he had finished (indeed, his mother feared he would throw it over),[5] but as soon as the book came out, Beardsley was on his way to fame. Some critics objected that his style was not suited to this medieval work, but most found much to admire in his intricate and beautiful designs, his black and white masses, so like and yet so unlike the Burne-Jones school. He was soon offered smaller commissions and his work began to appear in periodicals.

While he was at work on the *Morte d'Arthur,* he met the Henry Harlands and was introduced to the Cromwell Road gatherings of artists and writers. They deplored his Burne-Jones discipleship, and Harland sent him to his American friend

Joseph Pennell to help him escape the Kelmscott influence. He was also taken to Mrs. Meynell's Sunday afternoons, and here one day he met Lewis Hind, then editor of a forthcoming magazine, the *Studio*. Sitting next to him, Beardsley hesitantly produced the portfolio he carried everywhere and asked Hind to look at a few drawings. He had now abandoned the decorative manner of the *Morte d'Arthur* and was drawing with a strange original conception queer and fantastical creatures, ugly yet beautiful. Hind, instantly attracted, took several for the *Studio* and asked Pennell for an article on Beardsley to accompany the pictures. Pennell wrote a carefully worded and appreciative analysis of the new artist, though he afterwards acknowledged that he had hedged;[6] but to the casual reader the article did not seem too damning, and Beardsley, certainly not a casual reader, was delighted. Fortune seemed to have turned her warmest gaze upon him.

His youthful elation is revealed in a letter he sent a friend of his insurance office days. Though it is boastful and egotistical, one senses beneath the surface the boy's incredulous surprise at his own achievement; the extravagant phrases are partly to convince his friend and partly to reassure himself.

Behold me, the coming man, the rage of artistic London, the admired of all schools, the besought of publishers, the subject of articles! Last summer I struck for myself an entirely new method of drawing and composition, something suggestive of Japan, but not really japanesque. Words fail me to describe the quality of the workmanship. The subjects were quite mad and a little indecent. Strange, hermaphroditic creatures wandering about in Pierrot costumes or modern dress; quite a new world of my own creation. I took them over to Paris with me and got great encouragement from Puvis de Chavannes, who introduced me as '*un jeune artiste anglais qui fait des choses étonnantes.*' I was not a little pleased, I can tell you, with my success.

On returning to England, I continued working in the same method, only making developments. . . . My next step was to besiege the publishers, all of whom opened their great stupid eyes pretty wide. They were frightened, however, of anything so new and daringly original. One of them (Dent—lucky dog!) saw his chance and put me on to a large *édition de luxe* of Malory's "Morte d'Arthur." . . . The work I have already done for Dent has simply made my name. Subscribers crowd

46

from all parts. William Morris has sworn a terrible oath against me for daring to bring out a book in his manner. The truth is that, while *his* work is mere imitation of old stuff, mine is fresh and original. Anyhow, all the good critics are on my side. . . . Joseph Pennell has just written a grand article on me in the forthcoming number of "The Studio." . . . I should blush to quote the article. . . . My weekly work in the "Pall Mall Budget" has created some astonishment. . . . I have already far outdistanced the old men at that sort of thing. . . . I have fortune at my foot. . . .[7]

Within the next few months Beardsey had even more cause for jubilation when John Lane commissioned him to illustrate the English translation of Oscar Wilde's *Salomé*. Wealth and fame, the handmaidens of fortune, bowed before him, but Beardsley should have stopped to think. He had a strange superstition that Wilde brought him bad luck. He should have heeded it.

Aubrey had met the Wildes at Burne-Jones' in July, 1891, possibly in the same afternoon when he made a little sketch of Burne-Jones with his long hair dripping beneath his hat brim and a background suggestive of dancing nymphs. Beardsley could not resist telling his friend, House Master King, of the exalted circles in which he moved, sending him an immediate post card about the tea with Burne-Jones: "The Oscar Wildes and several others. . . .We came home with the Oscar Wildes— charming people."[8]

The charming Oscar, who could turn a neat descriptive phrase for anyone whose importance justified the effort, confided to Le Gallienne that Beardsley had a "face like a silver hatchet, with grass-green hair."[9] (Beerbohm more accurately noted the color of Aubrey's hair as "tortoiseshell.") Wilde and Beardsley met now and again as people of literary and artistic importance did in London and sometimes enjoyed an exchange of repartee. A post card to King, dated April 20, 1893, bore the announcement, "I'm off to Paris soon with Oscar Wilde,"[10] but though Beardsley went to Paris that spring, it was not with Oscar.

When Wilde's *Salomé* was brought out in the French edition, Beardsley, who had a facile command of French, offered to translate it into English. Lord Alfred Douglas had already attempted a translation which had not satisfied Wilde. Unfortunately he was even less pleased with Beardsley's version, and a modified form of Lord Alfred's translation was given to the Bodley Head. "Anyhow Bozie's name is not to turn up on the Title," Beardsley consoled himself.[11]

Wilde had hoped to produce *Salomé* in London; indeed the divine Sarah had promised to play the lead. He had planned the costumes with Graham Robertson; everyone on the stage was to be in yellow, from clearest lemon to deep orange, with here and there a touch of black, all on a pale ivory terrace against a great empty sky of deepest violet. But the censor refused Wilde a license and the performance was not given.

The *Pall Mall Budget*, however, taking advantage of the discussion that followed, asked Beardsley to do a drawing based on the play or on Wilde, but when the editor saw Beardsley's response, motivated by Salomé's speech, *"J'ai baisé ta bouche, Iokanaan, j'ai baisé ta bouche,"* he threw up his hands in horror. The paper's circulation could not stand that. But Hind used it for the *Studio*, and when John Lane and Elkin Mathews saw the picture they knew Beardsley was the man to illustrate the Bodley Head edition of *Salomé*.

Wilde, who was flattered by Beardsley's admiration of his play and liked to be identified with the moment, was quite willing to be in on the Beardsley craze, though he had not been much pleased with the *Studio* drawing. Secretly, Beardsley had not been at all pleased by Wilde's rejection of his translation, but he realized the opportunity *Salomé* offered for the display of his technique and originality; he put his mightiest efforts into the illustrations, achieving drawings so superb that, as Thomas Beer said, they "convinced people that Oscar Wilde had written a tragedy of the name."[12] In four of the drawings, Beardsley paid Wilde the "doubtful compliment" of caricaturing him.

Soon after the book was out, Beardsley wrote to Rothenstein that he had had "rather severe attacks of blood spitting and abominable bilious attack to finish me off. This is my first day up for some time. The Salome drawings have created a veritable fronde with George Moore at the head of the frondeurs."[13]

Wilde's friends were extremely critical of the illustrations. A biographer declares that they did "not in the least interpret the spirit of the play."[14] Wilde himself praised the drawings in public, overlooking the contempt in the caricatures, but he was not easy about the peculiar grotesqueness of some of the detail. It was one thing to suggest evil subtly and obscurely in a maze of purple phrases; it was another to delineate it openly in stark black and white. "Dear Aubrey's designs are like the naughtly scribbles a precocious schoolboy makes on the margins of his copy books," he said privately.[15]

No open break occurred between them; on the surface everything was pleasant. Beardsley liked to be seen with such a successful playright and familiar of the theatre and Wilde enjoyed leading Beardsley about. "Mr. Aubrey Beardsley," he wrote in a note to his leading lady, Mrs. Pat Campbell, "a very brilliant and wonderful young artist and a great admirer of the wonder and charm of your art, says that he must have the honour of being presented to you, if you will allow it. . . .He has just illustrated my play *Salomé* for me, and has a copy of the *édition de luxe* which he wishes to lay at your feet. His drawings are quite wonderful . . .,"[16] and Mrs. Campbell was delighted to have Oscar bring him around after Act III.

Though Beardsley pretended a cordiality with Wilde, and kept upon his mantel a touchingly autographed picture of him in a coat with a fur collar, the more he knew of Wilde, the less he liked him. He did not enjoy being patronized by this grossly voluptuous man of the world and he ached to puncture his bloated complacency. Perhaps some day he would have the chance.

In 1893 Beardsley was elected to the New English Art Club, an honor which pleased him greatly. He had more orders for work that he could fill and his circle of friends and admirers grew. In the fall of that year he was left a small legacy from an uncle, and he and his sister bought the house at 114 Cambridge Street, Pimlico, one of a row of sandstone houses, darkened by fog and smoke. Here on Thursday afternoons they were at home to guests, with Mrs. Beardsley presiding at the tea table, Mabel, red-haired and charming, making everyone welcome, and Aubrey flitting like an attenuated ghost from one to another, sometimes sinking into the tall wicker chair with its padded wings, his long thin legs stretched out before him and his face suddenly haggard. Sometimes he opened the large leather portfolio of drawings and showed his latest work. And if on Friday morning he was not well, he did not like to have his mother suggest he had tired himself the day before.

At the age of twenty-six, when many young men have not made up their minds what career to undertake, Beardsley was a Success. He played the role with distinction, for he was a born actor. Always impeccably dressed, he allowed himself only the eccentricity of the bang of "tortoiseshell" hair combed low on his forehead. In spite of Whistler's unrestrained outburst to Mrs. Pennell (Whistler did not like Beardsley)—"Why do you get mixed up with such things? Look at him!—he's just like his drawings—he's all hairs and peacock plumes—hairs on his head—hairs on his finger ends—hairs in his ears—hairs on his toes. And what shoes he wears—hairs growing out of them!"[17]—most of his associates considered Beardsley a model of correct grooming.

Though he worked like a fiend he pretended to live a life of little effort and great leisure. Some of his contemporaries said they never saw him at work, but he once invited Rothenstein, temporarily homeless in London, to share his studio, and they got on very well working one on each side of the large table. Beardsley was just beginning the *Salomé* drawings. "He would indicate his preparatory design in pencil," Rothenstein said, "defining his complicated patterns with only the vaguest pencil indication underneath, over which he drew with the pen with astonishing certainty. He would talk and work at the same time; for, like all gifted people, he had exceptional powers of concentration."[18]

The ornamental and intricate detail of his drawings meant long hours of labor in his studio on the second floor of the Pimlico house, the room which Aymer Vallance had decorated in orange and black with its priest's desk, ormulu candlesticks, and piano. Sometimes Aubrey jumped up from his drawing board to sit at the piano; more often he dropped, sweating and exhausted, on the big couch beside the window. Penrhyn Stanlaws, the American illustrator, who watched Beardsley work one chilly autumn afternoon, reported that he used a "slow, certain, steady line free from that nervousness which characterized the man."[19] To Stanlaws, Beardsley said, speaking of Keats, "I shall not live much longer than Keats. . . .The doctors give me five years, but!—oh, have a cigarette."[20]

Though Stanlaws thought that some of the critical onslaughts made on Beardsley "almost broke his heart," Beardsley himself claimed to be immune to public opinion. "I suffer my critics gladly," he said in an interview for the *Sketch*. "Their inconsistencies and futile hyprocrisies fill me with amusement."[21] This callous attitude infuriated the press and public, who failed to recognize it as youthful bravado. But when Whistler, after years of belittling Beardsley's work, apologized, saying, "Aubrey, I have made a very great mistake—you are a very great artist," it was the carefully hidden, sensitive boy who burst into tears.[22]

Much of Beardsley's pose—affectation, his enemies called it, and one of them quipped that even his lungs were affected—was due to his pleasure in playing a part. He had a great sense of drama, and might have gone on the stage, like his sister, if he hadn't been an artist. He loved to masquerade and once in a letter to John Lane in Paris, drew a sketch of himself arrayed in the flamboyant garments of a damosel of Piccadilly, declaring that he was going so clad to Jimmy's (the St. James's restaurant) on the following Thursday and meant to have a "regular spree."[23] On one occasion callers were announced at the Harlands', "Miss Tibbett and Master Tibbett." Harland could recall no acquaintance of that name, but when he went politely to the drawing-room to greet his guests he saw an elaborately dressed young lady, holding the hand of a shy tall boy in an Eton suit and wide starched collar who looked familiar. After

51

a long moment Harland recognized Mabel and Aubrey Beardsley.[24]

Roger Fry, the art critic, called Beardsley the "Fra Angelico of Satanism,"[25] a name which should have pleased the youthful artist, with his reverence for Italian masters. Other writers described him more plainly and less epigrammatically. Mr. Punch's puffed cheeks grew redder as his artists parodied and caricatured Beardsley's eccentricities. E. T. Reed and Lindley Sanbourne became so proficient that they nearly out-Beardsleyed Beardsley, using subjects from Britannia to Stephen Crane, "à la Beardsley." He is "the representation of all that is loathsome in art," said one British artist, and E. Nesbit, who considered herself an "advanced woman," concluded a skit on changing fashions in dress with

> Not even for you will I grow plain
> As Aubrey Beardsley's "lady friends."[26]

The Beardsley girl with her narrow eyes, ambiguous curves, and thick full lips offered a fair field for every humorist and jokester. Most criticized the mouth, always "inexpressive and ugly." Beardsley defended his concept. "I like big mouths. People like the little mouth—the 'Dolly Varden' mouth, if that describes it any better. A big mouth is a sign of character and strength. Look at Ellen Terry with her great, strong mouth. In fact, I haven't any patience with small-mouthed people."[27]

He drew this mouth, he said, with one line, trying to express in it all he felt. The line was all-important to Beardsley. He said, "Of course, I have one aim—the grotesque. If I am not grotesque I am nothing. Apart from the grotesque I suppose I may say that people like my decorative work, and that I may claim to have some command of line. I try to get as much as possible out of a single curve or straight line."[28]

The eccentricities of Beardsley's art and the confusion of motives which prompted them have come under the scrutiny of all his biographers. He was called a satirist, like Hogarth, "inspired by rage against iniquity," but Beardsley himself denied this. "I am trying to show life as it really it," he insisted.

"Yes . . . the everyday life is offensive to me . . . most people are ugly—the sensual face is dominant, and it is this face which I have drawn from life. . . .No, I am not satirizing life. My pictures are life itself."[29]

After his death many of his friends rallied to the defense of his character. Lewis Hind wrote, "I shall always hold that his pen was worse than his life; and I can say that, in all the years of our intercourse, I never knew him, in word or deed, anything but a light-hearted, intelligent youth, full of fun, enjoying every moment of the day, laughing at most things, but always intensely serious about his art."[30] H. C. Marillier, the art critic, noted that "those who imagine from the character of some of his subjects that Beardsley went about preaching or discussing vice are quite beyond the mark. Externally, at any rate, he was a pattern of moral decorum."[31]

His associate on the *Yellow Book*, Henry Harland, wrote in the *Academy*, "And when I hear honest folk deploring, horror struck, the quality in his work which it has been the fashion somewhat cheaply to describe as 'decadent'—when I hear them crying out, 'Ah, yes, monstrous clever, certainly; but so immoral, so depraved!'—I, who knew the boy, can only shake my head and smile. For I know that what they hold up their hands at, as depraved, immoral, was nothing more than the mischievous humor, or, if you like, the devilry of the boy—who, boylike, loved to give Solemnity a shock."[32]

Yet certain obscenities in his work, the drawings for the *Lysistrata*, for instance, and the original version of his novel *Under the Hill*, must be faced. Even in the last year of his life he wrote Smithers, "Do you want any erotic drawings?"[33] Though Beardsley hated evil, he was fascinated by it. A friend declared, "It was always an enigma to me how and where he acquired all the knowledge of the dark side of life which his work seemed to indicate."[34] Beardsley was no such cloistered recluse as that; indeed John Rothenstein, son of William, believed that for one "short period his life was very dissolute,"[35] though some of Beardsley's education in sin was merely academic.

His ailing childhood was at least partly to blame. Exiled from the rough and tumble of the playground, much alone, he curled himself in a chair to read the medical books of his doctor grandfather. Leaving school at an age when most boys are busy with studies and games, Beardsley was condemned by his precarious health to a quiet sedentary existence, and to much reading of every sort. Nothing drew him away from a boy's preoccupation with sex. In the medical books he had made the acquaintance of the human embryo, and his horrible leering adaptation of it was to figure unpleasantly in his drawings. As he wrote concerning the cover for the second number of the *Savoy*, "The little creature handing hats is *not* an infant but an unstrangled abortion."[36] From his reading of Restoration comedies and French novels he absorbed the foibles and caprices of love. He found excitement in the printed word and he infused his drawings with a similar excitement. Some of his associates applauded and encouraged him in this tendency. Beardsley could play any part; chameleon-like, fit himself into any group. With Smithers eroticism was a business; with Beardsley it was a phase of his adolescence. He was caught in the universal struggle of youth between man's two natures, and only at the point of death did he reach maturity.

But art and morals must be judged by different standards, as the men of the nineties were the loudest to declare. When Oscar Wilde was sentenced to Reading Gaol, Dr. Richard Garnett, knowing the public attitude, exclaimed, "That means the death of English poetry for fifty years."[37] Though this did not prove true, Dr. Garnett was aware of the strength of the point of view against which many in his time protested. Whatever the verdict on the materials Beardsley employed or the manner in which he represented them, none can deny the skill of his execution or the beauty of the result. His amazing black masses and his use of decorative detail have never been successfully imitated. As Gleeson White said, "None could raise the flower though all had got the seed."[38]

Beardsley telescoped the accomplishments of a lifetime into six short years. When he undertook the editorship of the

Yellow Book, he still had four years ahead of him—one less than he had counted on in his conversation with Stanlaws. He was approaching his best and most creative period. Buoyed up by his success he entered upon this new assignment, "with a kind of desperate courage and with a degree of force and enthusiasm that is given only to a doomed man," said Max Beerbohm. "Normal genius is in no hurry."[39]

Chapter VII

HENRY HARLAND WAS an American who had come to England in the wake of Whistler and Henry James. A New Englander by birth, he was a cosmopolite by choice, and no single country or city possessed his undivided allegiance.

"Born at St. Petersburg . . . brought up mainly in Rome . . . studied in the University of Paris . . ." were particulars he tossed off to reach no less a destination than the *Dictionary of National Biography.*[1] In conversation with intimate friends he was even more imaginative about his past. With a regretful shrug of his shoulders he would assert that if he had stuck to the Irish College in Rome he might have had a cardinal's hat before he was thirty, or he would refer mysteriously to the bar sinister in his family tree, hinting, with a rueful twinkle for the weaknesses of the great, that he was a natural son of the Emperor Franz Joseph. If pursued by a skeptical questioner he would evade the answer. "Tell him that I was born.—And that, thank God, I'm still alive,"[2] or "I didn't see the place well enough ever to recognize it in later life,"[3] but once he said laughingly when asked about his multiple birthplaces that "a man should never live in the land of his birth; a theory which certainly left [me] few lands to live in."[4]

Perhaps Harland felt that his American nationality put him at a disadvantage among those bred in the older civilization of Europe, and so chose a more colorful background. In the years before he came to England he had already carried through a similar deception, when, as a young man in New York, he had written novels about the Jewish race, stories so accurate in feeling and fact that the author was universally taken to be a Jew. Even his Jewish friends accepted him as one of them and photographs from that time make him look Jewish. So complete was his assumption of the role that he had some difficulty in ridding himself of it when he wanted to turn Gentile again.

After he left the United States he alternated his allegiance between France and England. "Harland was one of those Americans in love with Paris," Richard Le Gallienne explained, "who seem more French than the French themselves,"[5] and Evelyn Sharp observed that "one of his peculiarities was a curious conviction that he was a typical Englishman. . . .He was always surprised and a little hurt that nobody on the Continent ever took him for an Englishman"; however, people who were not Americans sometimes took him for an American.[6]

Though Albert Parry, writing in the final number of the American *Bookman* (1933), was the first to explode publicly the myth of Harland's St. Petersburg birth, his friends of the nineties were well aware of the unreliability of Harland's statements. Said Ella D'Arcy, "Of course he wasn't born in St. Petersburg! How could his dear mother have got to St. Petersburg? A sweet woman she was and he was devoted to her, but she'd always lived in the United States. St. Petersburg, nonsense!"[7] But in America, Mrs. Harland answered a friend's inquiry with that twinkle in her eye so like her son's, "St. Petersburg? I really don't know. I was never there myself."[8]

Harland's claim to an English baronetcy, mentioned in the *Dictionary of National Biography*, was also questioned by his friends, Miss D'Arcy admitting that if the title had not gone to a younger son or run out in 1848, Henry Harland's grandfather might have been a baronet, but even this narrow escape she considered insufficient grounds for Mrs. Harland's assumption of the title after the death of her husband. In the British Museum Catalogue list of Henry Harland's books, *The Light Sovereign*, published posthumously, was edited by "Lady Henry Harland," and in her later years Mrs. Harland's letters to her friends, even her close ones, were signed "Aline, Lady Harland."

The Harlands came of good English stock from an Admiral Harland of Suffolk, whose eldest son, a jeweler and clock-maker, emigrated from London to Boston in 1773 and moved to Norwich, Connecticut, the same year. This was Thomas Harland, great-grandfather of Henry and founder of Sentry Hill, the home of the Harlands which Henry described as Barrack's Hill in his novel *The Royal End.*

Henry was born in the most prosaic of places, New York, to Thomas and Irene Jones Harland in 1861. His father, a Yale graduate and member of the New York bar, was interested in Fourierism (the socialistic system propounded by François Marie Charles Fourier) and for a time was manager of a co-operative house with which Horace Greeley was connected; his mother was a brilliant and artistic woman, a painter of some ability who sympathized with all creative workers. She probably understood her erratic, impulsive son better than his father did, for Thomas had a practical turn of mind which served him well as adviser to the government on internal revenue tax and the patent law. Edmund Clarence Stedman, the poet and critic, who was Henry's godfather, exerted a strong influence upon Henry's literary career, which Harland acknowledged years later by writing with characteristic vehemence, "I owe you everything."[9] The Harlands moved in literary circles that included such figures as Walt Whitman, S. S. McClure, and William Dean Howells, and these contacts stimulated in the youthful Henry a desire to write.

Henry's formal education was extremely varied. He was a student at the College of the City of New York from 1877 to 1880. The following year he studied in Paris (at least he was there), and during 1881-82 he was registered at the Divinity School at Harvard. According to his own account, since he already "held a B.A. from the University of Paris," he enrolled as a sophomore in "the coldest winter which had ever occurred this side of the Arctic circle." By spring he was frozen out. "They gave a Greek play, the 'Oedipus' I believe, and I was one of the gay gamboling Grecians of the chorus. My raiment was fearful and gauzesome and I had to array myself in it in a dressing room which had been carefully chilled to seventy-five degrees below zero. I caught a little applause and much pneumonia and my study of Greek . . . and my Harvard career and very nearly my brave young life all ended together."[10]

After leaving Harvard he went to Rome, but 1883 found him back in New York as a clerk in the Surrogate's Office. He had given up the idea of being a Unitarian minister, though he sometimes spoke of himself as one—indeed his experiences in Italy had inclined him toward Catholicism—but he still wanted to write, and spent his spare hours to that end. Stedman advised and counseled him, suppressing Harland's attempts until he felt the young writer was ready to be launched. Then he sent Harland's novel, *From Generation to Generation,* later called *As It Was Written,* penned in longhand, to O. M. Dunham of the American branch of Cassell and Company. Dunham, though he complained of the difficulty in deciphering the manuscript, accepted it almost overnight, with no idea who the author might be, for Harland had adopted the pseudonym "Sidney Luska." ("Every young Jew I had ever heard of was named Sidney and Luska I thought a good name because it didn't mean anything.")[11]

As It Was Written had such an autobiographical flavor in its account of a young Jewish musician's life that everyone believed a Jew had written it. A reviewer in the New York *Tribune* called it a "triumph of art." Then came *Mrs. Peixada* and *The Yoke of the Thorah* (dedicated to Stedman), both dealing with the life of well-to-do Jewish people in New York, but in *Grandison Mather,* or *An Account of the Fortune of Mr. and Mrs. Thomas Gardner,* Harland assumed his own identity, writing the personal history of himself and his wife Aline, whom he had married in 1884.

Aline Merriam, an American girl of French ancestry, was charming, talented, a musician and a writer, and quite in sympathy with Henry's literary ambitions. It was said that her grandfather was an immortal of the French Academy. In 1897

Stedman wrote of her in a letter, "The paragon of lovely and clever womanhood is here to-day, my old-time pet, Mrs. Henry Harland—on a flying trip to American for the first time in seven years. She is not a day older in looks, nor a bit spoiled by crowded experiences, but with some wondrous added perfection of voice, motion, look, which the years have given her."[12]

Aline encouraged Harland to write; furthermore, she endured uncomplainingly his habit of rising at three or four in the morning to work until it was time to go to the office. In 1886 the couple went to Paris, visiting Aline's family and meeting French authors. Harland wrote Stedman, "Perhaps it may interest you to know that day before yesterday I called upon Madame Blanc (Th. Bentzon)—was introduced to her by one of her intimate lady friends, a relative of Aline's."[13] (Madame Blanc, the French writer, was well known in American literary circles as a friend of Sarah Orne Jewett.)

On his return to America a change was apparent in his attitude toward the Jews. In *The Yoke of the Thorah,* serialized in *McClure's,* he urged intermarriage with the Gentiles and when he was himself revealed as a Gentile, much unpleasantness developed with his Jewish friends. As a result of this situation and other uncertainties, Harland and his wife left America, never to return for any considerable stay. They lived in Paris until 1889, when they went to London.

The Henry Harland who had been "born in St. Petersburg" now emerged from the chrysalis of "Sidney Luska." The style in which he wrote underwent as complete a change as the subject matter. Stedman continued to advise him and arranged for his meeting various literary figures in London, among them Edmund Gosse and Henry James. Harland had long considered Henry James his master and now he was happy to sit humbly at his well-shod feet. But the first years were hard ones, for he met with many discouragements and rebuffs. Still he never considered a return to America and the career of "Sidney Luska," holding steadfastly to the belief that in England he could write as he could not in America, for in England, one "hears the language which he writes, spoken by living people

59

all about him . . . a living language. . . .Any derivation from the mother tongue is not the real language, but a dialect and therefore only an English dialect is spoken in America."[14]

In the spring of 1893 James wrote to Gosse from Paris, "Poor Harland came and spent 2 or 3 hours with me the other afternoon—at a café-front and on chairs in the Champs-Elysées. He looked better than the time previous, but not well; and I am afraid things are not too well *with* him. One would like to help him—and I try to—in talk; but he is not too helpable, for there is a chasm too deep to bridge, I fear, in the pitfall of his literary longings unaccompanied by the *faculty*."[15]

Later James was to amend his opinion of Harland's literary faculties, but he was right about Harland's health. In the winter of 1890 Harland had been told by lung specialists in London and Paris that he could not hope to live more than two years and so long only if he moved to a milder climate. Harland had decided to take his chance in London, had turned his back on the doctors, and had proved them wrong, but the doom was on him, as on Beardsley, and though he outlived the artist by six years, he was always fighting the "dread disease hovering forever in the wall-paper, ready to pounce upon one's lungs."[16]

In 1891 he had finished a three-volume novel, *Mea Culpa*, for Heinemann in London, who also brought out his first book of short stories, *Mademoiselle Miss and Other Stories*. The short story now became to Harland the most important form of literary expression. He looked back on the novels of "Sidney Luska" with extreme distaste. *"Mes péchés de jeunesse,"* he called them, with an apologetic smile.[17] He found his greatest inspiration in France, in the short stories of Maupassant, Daudet, and Mérimée. He was acutely aware of the meaning of style and form, nourishing the vividness of an impression until he could transfer it to well-thought-out phrases.

" 'Art,' with him as with his Parisian prototypes," said Le Gallienne, "was a life-and-death matter. Nothing else existed for him. . . .The polishing of his prose was for him his being's end and aim, and I have often seen him at that sacred task of a forenoon, in his study-bedroom, still in pajamas and dressing gown, with a coffee-pot on the hearth, bending over an exquisite piece of handwriting, like a goldsmith at his bench. . . .Not always a page, by any means—a perfect sentence or two was sometimes a good morning's work, which recalls Wilde's jest about a hard day's work: 'This morning,' he said, 'I took out a comma, and this afternoon—I put it in again.' "[18]

Harland had met Wilde, along with other important writers, in London, but they had little in common. Harland disliked Wilde's sensuality and Wilde did not appreciate Harland's light style. Once Harland tried to impress Wilde with the care he used in his writing, saying that he spent hours over every page until he was "fairly nauseated" by the time he finished it. "I should think you would be," Wilde observed.[19]

Though Harland admired realism in other writers he agreed with his godfather, Stedman, that it was not suited to his own talent, which was "incurably romantic." William Dean Howells recalled that Stedman had given him "quite a scolding" because he had praised in Harland what he thought was a tendency towards realism. "It's all right for you," Stedman had told him, "but I think it is a bad thing for Harland."[20] Harland shrank from the sordid, and coarseness offended him; but he was pained by priggishness and had no use for Victorian inhibitions. He understood his own limitations and tried to comply with them, however recklessly he might wave others on to new experiments. Writing in London at the beginning of a period which saw the passing of the three-volume novel and the emergence of the trim shapely tale, he influenced many writers of the nineties. As a critic in the *Nation* summed it up, "What Mr. Harland has done definitely for the art of the short story is to enlarge its scope, to give it fulness and richness, to link the incident with the rest of life, and to convert what had been feared as embarrassing decoration into essential substance."[21] Younger writers looked to him as he had looked to Henry James. He was eager to help them with criticism or introductions to responsive editors. Although his own position was not entirely assured he was quick to lend a hand to others, a virtue not usual in a young man climbing up.

When Harland's *Mea Culpa* was completed for Heinemann's and the manuscript sent to Lovell's, the firm that handled Heinemann's books in America, Lovell's went into bankruptcy. Arthur Waugh hated to break the news to him, because it meant the closing of Harland's American market and the loss of a good deal of money, but Harland's reply was characteristic: "Of course it is a disappointment, but *à la guerre comme à la guerre*. What grieves my wife and myself much more is the fear that this misfortune will mean the postponement of your own marriage. I must come and see you at once and talk it over."[22]

"The number of those whom he helped, whom he toiled for and encouraged is amazing," said one of his contributors to the *Yellow Book*. She had never known him to shirk a criticism on literary work or "to pass one upon any human being's character or actions . . . where his art was concerned he could be severe . . . he had no patience whatever with sham, with vulgar success, with slovenly and indifferent accomplishment."[23] In *Seven Men*, Max Beerbohm testified that Harland was "the most joyous of men and most generous of critics,"[24] and, in a letter, paid tribute to his excellence as an editor.[25]

Harland's energy and fervor were remarked by all his friends. He "never understood how it was possible for people to be bored," said Mrs. Pennell. He plunged into life headlong to get "everything that is to be got out of it,"[26] and Max Beerbohm discovered he "hated to talk of anything about which he couldn't be enthusiastic."[27] This vivid zest for living seemed a happy quality to his friends, but some English people were horrified by "his exuberance."

Le Gallienne remembered him on the evenings at Cromwell Road, "a slim, gesticulating, goateed, snub-nosed, lovable figure, smoking innumerable cigarettes as he galvanically pranced about the room, excitedly propounding the *dernier mot* on the build of the short story or the art of prose."[28] In "Paris Day by Day: A Familiar Epistle to Mrs. Henry Harland," Le Gallienne wrote of "Aline's smile and Harry's wit," with a poetic tribute to Harland's conversation,

"The prose-man takes his mighty lyre
And talks like music set on fire!"[29]

But Harland did not always preach. Often he was amusing and
whimsical, indulging in absurdities, telling fantastic stories. Yet
even in his most carefree moods he did not abandon his pulpit.
"I learned in sorrow what I teach in jest," he used to say.[30]

On such evenings Lewis Hind watched Harland and Beardsley fraternizing and wondered "which would die first,"[31] so
tenuous was the hold of both on life. Aline, too, worried about
her husband's health and pursued him with glasses of milk which
he drank as he rushed from one guest to another, talking briskly.
Aline was much a part of her husband's life. "You could not
think of the Harlands separately," said a friend. "They were
always together."[32] When Henry was happy, so was Aline. She
also shared his darker moments and then guests at Cromwell
Road suffered too. "I remember enjoying those evenings sometimes and sometimes not at all," said Netta Syrett. "Everything
depended on the moods of the host and hostess, both of whom
were erratic and, when bored, made little effort to disguise
their feelings."[33]

In the spring the Harlands usually went to Paris, "for sheer
love of Paris in the Maytime," Mrs. Pennell said,[34] but actually
because the fogs of late winter in London were bad for his
lungs. Harland loved Paris and delighted in showing it to his
friends. He would dash off an invitation to a young poet or
writer, "Do come and join us in this enchanted town, where
the sun shines, and the coffee-houses prosper, and everybody
has the Artistic Temperament."[35] If the young man yielded to
this temptation, Harland guided him expertly about Bohemian
Paris, took him to the Chat Noir, Bruant's Mirliton, and the
Moulin Rouge. He would arrange sudden excursions to Saint-
Cloud or Saint-Germain, or a boat ride on the Seine. In 1893,
the first summer Beardsley was with them, they spent a hilarious
afternoon playing Living Statues against the broken columns at
Saint-Cloud.

Later that same summer the Harlands and some young

artists including Alfred Thornton, Litellus Goold, Charles Loesser, D. S. MacColl, and Jonathan Sturges, an American novelist, took a cottage at Saint-Marguerite in Brittany. Three young sisters named Robinson were also members of the party and Charles Conder joined them in July. They named the cottage the GROB, a combination of the names Goold and Robinson, and a holiday spirit prevailed, though both the painters and writers were working. A notice on the wall of the little house read "Propriety to Let or Sell," to the amusement of English guests. Mrs. Harland, attractive and obliging, was much in demand as a model for the artists, and her charming figure is to be seen in many pictures of that summer, though the faces resembled that of a beautiful American, Miss Kinsella who lived in Paris. Harland wrote all morning in a Jaeger dressing gown, not appearing until lunch, although at times, as MacColl told his mother, "He lights little bonfires on the garden walks and cooks potatoes by himself."[36] In the late afternoon they all met in the garden of an inn in the pinewood a few steps from the GROB to drink *apéritifs* and discuss their masterpieces. If their mood grew sportive they played the games in which the Harlands delighted, charades, Living Statues, and once a mystery play, "The Garden of Eden," in which Mrs. Harland, playing God, asked an embarrassed Adam (Conder) to show Eve around the Garden while MacColl as the serpent hung head downward from a tree to whisper in her ear and Thornton with a broom enacted Gabriel.

No better idea of the summer could be given than is found in a poem on an illustrated broadside which MacColl presented to the hostess when he departed.

> Reader, this neat and tasteful job
> Delineates the festive GROB.
>
> Upon the one hand you will see
> A piece of sky and poplar tree,
> And on the other one may espy
> An apple-tree and bit of sky.
> Rare are the circumstances found
> To flourish on that foreign ground.

Next you will note how comes in view
The hoary Baptiste named BOUDOUX.
Observe him urge his cattle on,
Rougette, Frisette and *La Brétonne.*

Then does the skilful artist trace
The inmates of this pleasant place.

'ARLAND, a most reclusive gent,
On literary toils intent;
Yet would he, o'er the flowing bowl,
Discourse of Nature and the Soul,
And things less fit for the reporter,
For half of him was Latin Quarter.

ALFY, the next, uncommon quick
At victuals and arithmetic,
And with a taste both free and fine
For hats and ties and turpentine.

LITELLUS, oft in slumber laid,
Or quaffing Eno in the shade;
Yet nimble on his toes was he,
Bit by the dance, or frequent flea.

Our CHARLES the next. You can but love
That most engaging turtle dove,
To hear him croon an amorous air
Through locks of honey-coloured hair.

The PRESENT WRITER of this piece
Was bothered by the Pots of Greece,
And did in the wide ocean drown
The unwritten article on Brown.

The LADY REGENT of the land
Controlled them with a gentle hand,
Her dinners would have graced a lord,
Her singing was the day's reward,
"Who's Sylvia" indeed we say,
Commending her like Sylvia.

And Coco — But the Norman Land
Holds thee, thou animalcule Bland!
How he would cheer our rainy days
With little vacillating ways;

How often has be perched and sung
Quaint ditties in the Coco tongue!

The Grob laments, unreconciled,
Its Toy, its Totem, and its Child.[37]

Litellus Goold was a fellow student of Thornton and Mac-Coll who died young; the "Pots of Greece" referred to a book on *Greek Vase Painting* MacColl was writing (published the next year), and Fred Brown was a professor at the Slade School of Art. Coco, an "absurd mythical insect in a glass of water," with which Henry Harland held nonsensical conversations, was named after Boudoux's horse.

It was MacColl's conviction that during this happy summer the idea of the *Yellow Book* first took form.

Chapter VIII

THE SUMMER OF 1893 passed quickly for the little colony at the GROB, Sainte-Marguerite, and yet it seemed "pluperfect and endless: apples reddened thickly in the orchards, and fields of flax burned blue, like another sky upon the ground."[1] Harland was writing a story for *Black and White* about a ruined château in the neighborhood, and Charles Conder was making sketches for it. Harland was much attracted by this sad eccentric young genius, as yet not recognized by an unperceptive public, and burned with zeal to help him. The illustrations would be one way, and he was certain he could sell some of Conder's paintings. *Black and White* was a relatively new venture, a large-sized magazine using both stories and pictures. The editor, C. M. Williamson, was a friend of Harland's, and Harland had already appeared in it several times.

One day when in the garden, warm from the setting sun, they were discussing this undertaking, MacColl suggested that what was really needed was a periodical composed of literature and art which would be independent of each other, having in common only the desire to break new ground, with the art also to be paid for, "as against the artists' bad habits of letting their work go free for the sake of advertisement."[2] The idea was received with tremendous applause; let MacColl start such a magazine at once! But MacColl, who then preferred the paintbrush to the pen, refused. However, he freely presented the suggestion to anyone who wanted to use it.

Summer waned . . . "the corn ripened and was gathered in great stacks and thrashed by turning horses against the timbers of the steadings." On September 15 the holiday was over, Mac-Coll paid his farewell compliment to Mrs. Harland, and the party returned to London. Harland was busy getting *Mademoiselle Miss* ready for publication, but he often remembered the golden summer sun at Sainte-Marguerite and considered the desirability of a publication which should liberate the writers and nourish the artists.

Beardsley too was casting about for some definitive channel into which he could turn his drawings. He had been formally introduced to art circles by Gleeson White, who had taken over the *Studio. Salomé* was finished and though he was preparing the *Keynotes* covers for Lane and drawings for the *Pall Mall* he wanted a medium which should be particularly his own. He had in mind a *Comedy of Masques* and about this time wrote a friend in America that he had signed a contract for such a book, to consist of his designs only and "without any letter press." A little later he told Rothenstein he had made definite arrangements for such a book; Max Beerbohm was to write the occasional verse. Nothing tangible came from these hopes, but apparently the idea of the new quarterly was gaining momentum, and Laurence Binyon was certain he had heard it discussed in the early autumn. Max Beerbohm in 1930, dramatizing his introduction to the *Yellow Book,* set the time as "an afternoon in the late autumn of '93.

"Scene: Cambridge Street, Pimlico.

"Persons: Aubrey Beardsley and myself.

"A.B. 'How are you? Sit down! Most exciting! John Lane wants to bring out a Quarterly — Writings and Drawings — Henry Harland to be Literary Editor — Me to be Art-Editor. Great fun. . . .'"[3]

But Beerbohm's memory of the moment must have been at fault, for Harland has put the birthday of the *Yellow Book* on record as New Year's Day, 1894, when Beardsley had come to lunch in Cromwell Road.

The *Yellow Book* was first thought of one fearful afternoon in one of the densest and soupiest and yellowest of all London's infernalest yellow fogs. Aubrey Beardsley and I sat together the whole afternoon before a beautiful glowing open coal fire and I assure you we could scarcely see our hands before our faces, with all the candles lighted, for the fog, you know . . . .

So we sat together the whole day and evening and were a gay and cheerful couple I assure you. We declared each to each that we thought it quite a pity and a shame that London publishers should feel themselves longer under obligation to refuse any more of our good manuscripts. Fancy having our brains stowed away for so long in their editorial sideboards that we lost our chance of even having our ideas served up cold.

"'Tis monstrous, Aubrey," said I.

"'Tis a public scandal," said he. And then and there we decided to have a magazine of our own. As the sole editorial staff we would feel free and welcome to publish any and all of ourselves that nobody else could be hired to print.

That was the first day of January . . . and the next day we had an appointment with Mr. John Lane.[4]

Mrs. Harland, writing in 1911, added details, corroborating the foggy New Year's luncheon party, but not limiting the guests to Beardsley. Perhaps others came in later. In the afternoon Harland told his plans for a new English quarterly, "where Letters, where Black and White Art might enter into their own." Aubrey Beardsley responded with gusto and they "plunged into practical consideration of detail incident to the proposed publication. Books were brought from the study . . . were called into consultation; new and rare editions were studied . . . . As a mere piece of book making the Quarterly must be on a par too, with the quality, the artistic virtue of its pages." When they tried to find a name for their creation, "the frolic of the hour inspired Beardsley, who proposed: *The Yellow Book*. This title, its appositeness and humour, struck all the young contingent, and it was decided to cling to it until a better one was found."[5]

One of the young contingent, Netta Syrett, remembered the moment. "I happened to be at the Harlands' when the idea of the *Yellow Book* was first suggested, I think by Henry Harland himself, as we sat round the fire in the drawing-room of the Cromwell Road house, one wet afternoon.

"I remember Harland's excited talk—he was like a boy in his enthusiasms—about starting a magazine that should represent the 'new movement.' "[6]

Then came the meeting with Lane. Perhaps the Bodley Head was Beardsley's suggestion, since he had done work for the Vigo Street firm and Harland's books up to now had been brought out by Heinemann. To continue Harland's account: "At one o'clock precisely the three of us sat down to luncheon. At five minutes after one he had consented to back our publication with Beardsley as art editor and myself as editor. At exactly half past one we had arranged over the telephone with Mr. Henry James for the publication of our first piece of fiction. Thus was the *Yellow Book* conceived in fog and darkness, but brought forth in sweetness, light and joy."[7]

Of the *Yellow Book* said Beardsley to an interviewer, "Henry Harland and I thought of it. We spoke to Lane and he approved."[8]

These statements of the Harlands put the birthday of the *Yellow Book* more than a month earlier than the usually accepted night in February that tradition has fixed as the historic moment. The often reiterated tale of a gathering after an Authors' Club dinner for Bill Nye, the American humorist, at which the idea took form has assumed quite wrongly the aura of authenticity. For one thing, Bill Nye, though he had been in London in the fall of 1893, was then making a tour of the States and could not possibly have been in London, but the legend has persisted through many accounts, with only slight variation in detail. Patrick Chalmers', in his biography of Kenneth Grahame, is as entertaining as any and a shade more spiteful.

On a tipsy (the adjective is not mine) February night Mr. John Lane, of the Bodley Head, gave a dinner-party at the Devonshire Club, to certain of the *literati*. Among the last were Mr. John Davidson, the poet; Mr. Henry Harland, novelist, of U.S.A., lately arrived in London, and that infant magician of black-and-white magic, Mr. Aubrey Beardsley. There, conceived on champagne and enthusiasm, the *Yellow Book* leapt, *cap à pie,* from the callow pate of the latter, an erotic Minerva from the brain of an immature Jove. The great idea was seconded by Mr. Davidson, and the company carried it with acclamation. Even the host (financier, presumed, and paymaster) was so struck with the originality of the proposition that he appointed, on the spot, Mr. Harland as editor (because, so they said, he was more elevated than anyone present) and then, as was only fair and right, he named Mr. Beardsley art editor and ordered another magnum of Pommery.[9]

Additional guests mentioned by other writers include George Moore, Frank Harris, and M. H. Spielmann.

Fortunately there is incontrovertible evidence of the earlier date. On January 3, 1894, Arthur Waugh, a young man of letters from New College, Oxford, winner of the Newdigate prize in 1888, recently author of *Alfred, Lord Tennyson, A Study,* and now London correspondent for the American *Critic,* was lunching at the National Club in Whitehall Gardens and saw Harland and Lane with Gosse, whom they had come to tell of their new project, for nothing could go far without the excellent Gosse. Waugh, who was a friend of Harland and a cousin of Gosse, strolled over to join them and thus became the first historian of the new venture, for he made it the subject of his next Letter to the *Critic,* allowing the American readers to have the news long before the English public.

"There have been rumors flitting about London this week," wrote Waugh on January 4, "with reference to a new literary and artistic quarterly magazine, which, it is whispered, is to make a big sensation in the coming spring. So far these rumors have been entirely confined to literary circles, and I believe I have the good fortune of being the first person to collect them into a sufficiently tangible shape for publication; at any rate, no word of the new enterprise has as yet appeared in any London newspaper." He admitted the plans were tentative, but he

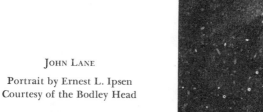

HENRY HARLAND

From the *Bookman* (New York), I (1895)

JOHN LANE

Portrait by Ernest L. Ipsen
Courtesy of the Bodley Head

AUBREY BEARDSLEY

Portrait by Penrhyn Stanlaws

had it on the best authority that Elkin Mathews and John Lane were about to bring out a quarterly "which shall treat, not of the passing moment and its interests, but (in so far as it deals in criticism at all) with the permanent and stable. . . . And, since criticism of so high a calibre could obviously be but a rare bird, it has been thought that such a paper might reasonably be expanded to contain short stories by recognized masters of the craft, poems by 'bards approved,' and illustrations by distinguished artists." An edition of five thousand copies was planned, and the price would be five shillings. "The scheme itself is certainly a bold one," Waugh continued. "It has yet to be proved that the public will buy literature for its own sake: the timely and journalistic contents of our monthly reviews show how keenly editors appreciate the necessity for the interest of the passing hour. And the present moment . . . is the one thing which will *not* be consulted in *The Yellow Book*."[10]

John Lane, writing the Publisher's Note which accompanied the posthumous edition of Beardsley's *Under the Hill*, declared that he and Beardsley and Harland founded the *Yellow Book* one morning "during half an hour's chat over our cigarettes at the Hogarth Club,"[11] but it was not quite so casual as that. Lane always accepted as much responsibility for undertaking the new quarterly as Harland or Beardsley, and he may indeed have had such an idea himself without putting it on record. At any rate the other two would not have got far without him.

Though no announcement was made at this time, gossip was busy and the breeze from Vigo Street freshened perceptibly. On January 11 the charming Mrs. Craigie, who hid her literary accomplishments under the name "John Oliver Hobbes," wrote her new friend and adviser, George Moore: "Do you know anything about a new illustrated Quarterly to be called *The Yellow Book?* Harland and Aubrey Beardsley are the Editors."[12]

So the word slipped quietly around and if, as it appears,, Lane told a number of people one convival evening in February, he was only announcing to them what others already knew. No item seems to have reached the London newspapers, however, until the first of April, when Lane inserted large advertisements of the forthcoming periodical and invited the public to send for a *Prospectus*. On April 11 the editors were interviewed in the *Sketch*. They said that as it stood, the *Yellow Book* was the invention of themselves and Mr. John Lane, but added that "it would hardly be worth while tracing the idea from its first conception, as it grew, shall we say, like a mustard-seed."[13]

Chapter IX

AT WHATEVER TIME during the months of summer, autumn, and winter the nebulous idea of the *Yellow Book* took definite form, the editors and publishers were exceedingly busy during the early months of 1894. Once embarked on the project, they found much to do. It needed more than a smoky-blue half hour at the Hogarth Club to bring to life this splendid creature of their vision. Their greatest concern of course was for its inner soul and spirit, but external appearance was important also, for genius should be suitably garbed. They worried over the details of producing the best possible volume, and busied themselves in choosing type of printing, cloth for the cover of just the desired shade of yellow, and paper suited to the reproduction of the art. The Swann Electric Engraving Company was entrusted with the plates, for its craftsmen understood well the new process which made black and white so successful; the printing went to the Ballantine Press in Covent Garden, which would use a fine grade of handmade paper. And why should this ambitious venture be confined to the British Isles? Let America benefit too; Copeland and Day of Boston would be the right firm for the American edition. They were young and enterprising and had already done very well with *Salomé*. Herbert Copeland was a Harvard man with modern ideas, and Fred Holland Day had plenty of money and was willing to use it.

In all these material items the editors took as much part as the publishers, and John Lane considered the list of contributors as eagerly as Harland and Beardsley, though he said he gave them a free hand. The art and literature were to be quite separate. The art must not in any way illustrate the text. On this point Harland was sure he would have the approval of James, who liked "so little to be illustrated." Indeed he wrote Clement Shorter that he resented it "on behalf of good prose and *real* writing."[1] Both art and literature must be nicely balanced between the traditional and the new; some well-established writers to give backing to the young *arrivistes,* and artists from the Royal Academy to set off the members of the New English Art Club. Editors and publishers agreed on this equitable division; they also agreed on another matter, this time of omission. The bright unsullied pages of the *Yellow Book* should be closed to Oscar Wilde. About this there was no controversy. Neither Harland nor Lane wanted him, but Beardsley was the most determined. He had waited long for the chance to snub the patronizing author of *Salomé.* Here was a heaven-sent opportunity and he intended to use it. Poor Aubrey!

Though Harland, recalling years later the beginning of the *Yellow Book,* said that Henry James was called on the telephone, James himself remembered his invitation differently.

I make the most of this passage of literary history—I like so, as I find, to recall it. . . . It was of a Sunday afternoon early in the spring of that year: a young friend, a Kensington neighbour and an ardent man of letters, called on me to introduce a young friend of his own [Beardsley] and to bespeak my interest for a periodical about to take birth, in his hands, on the most original "lines" and with the happiest omens. What omen could be happier for instance than that this infant *recueil,* joyously christened even before reaching the cradle, should take the name of *The Yellow Book?*—which so certainly would command for it the liveliest attention. What, further, should one rejoice more to hear than that this venture was, for all its constitutional gaiety, to brave the quarterly form, a thing hitherto of austere, of awful tradition, and was indeed in still other ways to sound the note of bright young defiance? The project, modestly and a little vaguely but all communicatively set forth, amused me, charmed me, on the spot—or at least the touchingly convinced and inflamed projector did. . . . I was invited, and all urgently, to contribute to the first number.[2]

And all obligingly James accepted.

Edmund Gosse had already signified his willingness that noon at the National Club. Little happened in the world of letters which escaped the penetrating eye of this poet, essayist, and critic, or in which he was not more than willing to have a part. He was friend and adviser to the *Yellow Book* from its beginning and if he was later tempted to betray its secrets— "Sometime I may tell the real truth," he wrote to Filson Young, "when some sleek withers will wince"[3]—no public record remains of his yielding. On that January day when he first heard the contributors discussed, Gosse was glad to put in a word for his friend the son of the Archbishop, A. C. Benson, a master at Eton and writer of sonnets, and Harland accepted Benson as a foil for Symons and John Davidson.

It was natural to ask Arthur Waugh when he happened by, for he was a good fellow and Harland liked him and wanted to be helpful. (That his assistance was effective Waugh bore witness years later by saying, "The echoes of that first number of *The Yellow Book* followed me for years to come into the offices of editors, and brought me almost as much reviewing as I could do.") Some aspect of literature provocative of discussion was mentioned as desirable, and it was decided that Waugh "should drop a sort of propitiatory garland into the arena, to catch the eye of the prim and prudent," with an essay upholding "Reticence in Literature." Waugh, who felt a deep distrust of "anything like realism," was delighted to undertake this duty.[4]

Richard Le Gallienne, young poet and writer from Liverpool already closely associated with the Bodley Head, must have an opportunity. Indeed it has been suggested that Le Gallienne was the inspiration of the *Yellow Book* as far as Lane was concerned, and his contributions appeared in nine of the thirteen volumes.

Both Lane and Beardsley asked Max Beerbohm for a piece of prose, rather to Harland's surprise, for Harland did not think an undergraduate contribution was wanted, but the deed was done. Beardsley and Harland agreed that Joseph Pennell must be asked for an etching, and that Elizabeth must write something. The editors went frequently to the Pennells for counsel, and Joseph, amused by their perplexities and inexperience, made suggestions and let them have the etching "Le Puy" for a full-page reproduction. To Pennell Le Puy was the most picturesque spot in the world.

The group from the GROB of course must be included, and promises of pictures were obtained from Goold and Thornton. For some reason MacColl was not interested, and a sad misunderstanding had arisen between Conder and Harland, who in his desire to be helpful had taken some of Conder's pictures to sell. In February Conder wrote MacColl, "I had a letter from Harland and he writes in a most abrupt way that he cannot pay me but that he will sell my picture for anything it will fetch over the small sum he advanced on it—as I had not asked him to do so and think the sum I proposed him exceedingly low, I wrote back saying that he would kindly do nothing of the sort. I hope Harland will not give way too much to the habit of buying pictures and not paying for them or his tastes will lead him to prison."[5] But in spite of Conder's unjust suspicions, which he was always having about some one, the rift was healed and his paintings were used in later volumes.

Beardsley worked with furious zeal in his dual capacity as art editor and leading artist. "After Leighton came Aubrey Beardsley, asking me to do a drawing for the *Yellow Book,*" said Laurence Housman.[6] In *Decorative Illustration* Walter Crane, artist and leader of the new book decorators, had mentioned Beardsley as one of the new school of black and white; naturally Beardsley wished to reciprocate. When he hurried to Crane's studio, crowded with Indian idols, carved figures, Japanese prints, Morris designs, Italian engravings, and portraits of Crane's wife and children, to ask a contribution, the kind little Socialist willingly gave him his choice. Beardsley took a photograph of his painting "Renaissance of Venus."[7] He approached E. J. Sullivan and A.S. Hartrick, who shared a studio and did work for the *Pall Mall Budget,* and found them agreeable, Hartrick giving him "The Gardener," originally designed to illustrate the Man with the Muck-Rake in *Pilgrim's Progress,* and done with the flexible steel pen used by lithographers for their finest work.[8] "Mind, it can't stand much reduction," he warned Beardsley.

His worry was not necessary, for Beardsley had uncommon good judgment about reproductions. It was extraordinary that with so little experience he could understand just how the new method of zinc block could be used to get what he wanted. The engravers liked to work for him and he held them up to the highest standards. "The second Mrs. T. has come off splendidly," he wrote jubilantly to Lane. "Annan and Swan will finish it in two or three days. The Furse portrait looks A 1."[9]

Lane examined all of Beardsley's contributions with a wary eye, for he feared that the jokester might get the better of the editor and slip in some hidden impropriety. His alertness was justified when Beardsley nonchalantly handed him "The Fat Woman"; the large dark woman bore an unmistakable likeness to Mrs. Whistler. No one on the *Yellow Book* cared much for Whistler, but Lane had a respect for his sting. In vain Aubrey pleaded, "I shall most assuredly commit suicide if the fat woman does not appear in No. 1 of the *Yellow Book*. I have shown it to all sorts and conditions of men—and women. All agree that it is one of my best efforts and extremely witty. Really I am sure you have nothing to fear. I should not press the matter a second if I thought it would give offence. The block is such a capital one too, and looks so distinguished. The picture shall be called, 'A Study in Major Lines.' "[10] Even this disarming title, however, failed to move the level-headed man from Devon; the picture was banned.

Beardsley also held out a helping hand to Robert Ross, then trying to establish himself in journalism. "We all want to have something charming from you for the first number. Say an essay or a short story. Now *do* send us something soon in your most brilliant style; and make up your mind to be a regular contributor."[11] Ross was interested, and Beardsley wrote again, "5 to 6000 words is about our mark [and] a little longer wouldn't matter. So delighted that we can count on you for No. 1. I have designed a wondrous cover which has received universal admiration."[12] Something went wrong, for nothing by

Ross appeared in the *Yellow Book,* nor was his name included in the list of prospective contributors.

Though most of the contributors were invited by the editors to send in material and a considerable group of writers and artists responded, a few unsolicited manuscripts arrived, among them one from Ella D'Arcy, a short story, "Irremediable," dog-eared from rejections, which Harland recognized at once as the work of a unique and talented writer. He was delighted at discovering Miss D'Arcy, who became one of the *Yellow Book* regulars. Other story writers he chose for the first number were George Egerton and Bertie Crackanthorpe. Lane wanted William Watson, one of his favorite Bodley Head poets. Beardsley wanted Netta Syrett, friend of his sister Mabel. No one wanted Oscar Wilde.

Oscar was not used to being overlooked and he took it badly. If anyone asked him whether he was going to give the new periodical the nod of approval by appearing in it, he turned the conversation deftly to the amount of work he had already on hand, but inwardly he was furious at the slight. He could not believe they would not still call on the smartest wit in London, but when the *Prospectus* was issued with the names of the contributors, he was at last convinced. He blamed the insufferable schoolboy.

The Announcement issued in March was designed to whet the public's appetite for the feast in preparation. Although the editors had arranged for more work than could be used in the first number, names would look well in print, and they hastened to put them there. One of Beardsley's "Lady friends," looking over the books in a bin outside a secondhand shop under the cynical eye of an old Pierrot proprietor done on bright yellow paper, introduced this epicurean bill of fare. Said the editors by way of introduction:

The aim . . . of THE YELLOW BOOK is to depart as far as may be from the bad old traditions of periodical literature, and to provide an Illustrated Magazine which shall be beautiful as a piece of bookmaking, modern and distinguished in its letter-press and its pictures, and withal popular in the better sense of the word. It is felt that such a Magazine, at present, is conspicuous by its absence . . . .

Amongst the artists who will contribute drawings are SIR FREDERICK LEIGHTON, P.R.A., AUBREY BEARDSLEY, R. ANNING BELL, CHARLES W. FURSE, L. B. GOOLD, MAURICE GREIFFENHAGEN, WILLIAM HYDE, LAURENCE HOUSMAN, J. T. NETTLESHIP, J. BERNARD PARTRIDGE, JOSEPH PENNELL, WILL ROTHENSTEIN, WALTER SICKERT, WILSON STEER, ALFRED THORNTON, and others . . . .

The following is an incomplete list of those who will contribute articles, stories, and poems to THE YELLOW BOOK.

E. TRELAWNY BACKHOUSE*	HENRY JAMES
MAX BEERBOHM	LIONEL JOHNSON
A. C. BENSON	RICHARD LE GALLIENNE
HUBERT CRACKANTHORPE	STANLEY V. MAKOWER
ELLA D'ARCY	THEO MARZIALS
JOHN DAVIDSON	GEORGE MOORE
AUSTIN DOBSON	WALTER PATER*
MÉNIE MURIEL DOWIE	ELIZABETH ROBINS PENNELL*
ERNEST DOWSON	RICHARD PRYCE*
GEORGE EGERTON	ERNEST RHYS*
LANOE FALCONER*	GEORGE SAINTSBURY
MICHAEL FIELD*	CHARLES SIBLEY*
JEAN DE FRANCE*	OSWALD SICKERT
NORMAN GALE	F. M. SIMPSON
RICHARD GARNETT	ARTHUR SYMONS
EDMUND GOSSE	NETTA SYRETT
KENNETH GRAHAME	BEERBOHM TREE*
FREDERICK GREENWOOD	WILLIAM WATSON
HENRY HARLAND	ARTHUR WAUGH
FRANK HARRIS*	CHARLES WHIBLEY*
JOHN OLIVER HOBBES	W. B. YEATS
SELWYN IMAGE*	I. ZANGWILL*

. . . In many ways its contributors will employ a freer hand than the limitations of the old-fashioned periodical can permit. It will publish no serials; but its complete stories will sometimes run to a considerable length in themselves. . . . And while THE YELLOW BOOK will seek always to preserve a delicate, decorous, and reticent mien and conduct, it will at the same time have the courage of its modernness, and not tremble at the frown of Mrs. Grundy.

Altogether, it is expected that THE YELLOW BOOK will prove the most interesting, unusual, and important publication of its kind that

---

* Those names marked with an asterisk were never represented in the *Yellow Book*.

has ever been undertaken. It will be charming, it will be daring, it will be distinguished. It will be a *book*—a book to be read, and placed upon one's shelves, and read again; a book in form, a book in substance; a book beautiful to see and convenient to handle; a book with style, a book with finish; a book that every book-lover will love at first sight; a book that will make book-lovers of many who are now indifferent to books.

THE YELLOW BOOK will contain no advertisements other than publishers' lists.[13]

The publication of these promised contributors demonstrated the zeal of the editors to obtain names of importance for the new venture. To be sure, some of the work was not forthcoming, but at least assurance of it must have been given or the careful Lane would not have allowed the names to go on record.

Many an editor of an old-fashioned periodical smiled grimly as he filed this modest statement. At Cambridge one young man did not wait for the advertised product. He began on the Prospectus, and an announcement of *The Yellow Boot,* accompanied by a Beardsleyesque drawing, appeared in the *Granta.*

Yellow as the complexion of the poet and as the gold which inspires him. *Boot,* because Art can dispense with all other clothing, and because our contributors, if they get nothing else, may at least hope to get the Boot—above all because there is nothing like leather. . . . Our complete stories (and they will be as complete as we dare make them) will go to considerable lengths. . . . [*The Boot*] will be coy, it will be saucy, it will be cultured—by Gosse it will! . . . a boot with style, a boot with finish; a boot to be soled and *rissoled;* a pointed boot and in no sense a tight laced boot. . . . The Yellow Boot will not contain any advertisements other than those of its contributors.[14]

However skeptical human nature might be of the inner content of the *Yellow Book,* the exterior would certainly be different. Never before had a magazine masqueraded as a book, taking on airs of permanency and demanding a place on the library shelves. With persistent reiteration the editors emphasized this heritage for posterity, saying in the *Sketch* interview that it ushered in "an absolutely new era in the way of magazine literature." Arthur Waugh, editing this interview for his London

Letter to the *Critic,* interposed gently that "the youthfulness and enthusiasm of these young men must be the excuse for their cock-sure and aggressive attitude."[15] On April 2, 1894, the name of the *Yellow Book* was formally registered at the ancient Stationers' Hall, and as Beardsley added in a letter to Robert Ross, "on the scroll of fame."[16]

Waugh did not stint the American public on news of the forthcoming publication. To a mention of a new book by Ernest Rhys, he added, "Rhys will contribute to the *Yellow Book.*" Early in April he reported that "the first number is now in the printer's hands," and on April 13 he wrote, "On Monday the *Yellow Book* is to come out; and on that evening the editors and contributors, supported by their wives and friends, will dine together, to inaugurate the new career, at a little hotel in Soho. A lively party is promised. . . . . Meanwhile, the new quarterly is on many lips; the editors are being liberally interviewed; and everything looks rosy for the first appearance."[17]

On the morning of April 15, London suddenly turned yellow as the new periodical with its bright daffodil cover and staring black Beardsley design materialized on newsstands and book shops. You could get it at Mudie's or Bumpus' or Quaritch's. Mr. Spencer cautiously insinuated the volumes into his fly-specked window between a book of Baxter plates and *Pickwick* in parts. Charing Cross Road gleamed with yellow. Frederick Evans had the copies in his window on Queen Street open at the Beardsley drawings and pointed them out to customers with happy pride. Even the stands of the respectable and high-minded W. H. Smith and Son were spotted with yellow. This freedom of opportunity surprised John Lane, who had expected that the prototype of Sir Joseph Porter, K.C.B., might ban the sale of the new quarterly, since he had recently refused to handle George Moore's *Esther Waters.* A critic later remarked that far less harm would have been done the public's morals if the counters had been swept clean of the *Yellow Book* and *Esther Waters* put in its place.[18]

The biggest and brightest display was naturally on Vigo Street. Mr. May remembered it well. The lad who spent his days in the back office on a high stool was promoted to service in the front of the shop. Frederic Chapman gave him his first lesson in window dressing, and they filled the little bow window full of copies of the *Yellow Book*, "creating such a mighty glow of yellow at the far end of Vigo Street that one might have been forgiven for imagining for a moment that some awful portent had happened, and that the sun had risen in the West."[19]

That evening the inaugural dinner held in an upper room of the Hotel d'Italia on Old Compton Street presented as festive an occasion as Arthur Waugh had foreseen. Henry Harland was everywhere at once, dashing about the room, in his friendly American way introducing those who had not met before, and stirring everyone to gay good humor. More people than expected had come, and the editors were hard put to find enough places, but at last all were seated. Elizabeth Pennell was honored by the place between Harland and Beardsley in the center of the high table at one end of the room. Her husband had just left for Dalmatia, and in his absence she was "distinguished by this mark of Beardsley's appreciation and Harland's friendliness."[20] Ménie Muriel Dowie sat on Harland's right, with John Lane on her other side. Miss Dowie was a contributor, and since her husband, Henry Norman, was literary editor of the London *Chronicle*, her position was not unmerited.

There were some absences. Henry James was abroad. Could it have been on purpose? Edmund Gosse was ill but had sent some "delightful verses"[21] to represent him. "George Egerton," also ill but not a poet, sent her husband, Mr. Clairmonte. Arthur Waugh noticed that Dr. Garnett was the only one of the older generation who presented himself, and he sat half-hidden in a corner. Hubert Crackanthorpe and Arthur Symons were in Italy; Richard Le Gallienne was delivering a lecture in Liverpool, probably his stand-by on "The Religion of a Literary Man." Netta Syrett was kept away by the death of a "dear relative."[22]

George Moore was conspicuously present, sitting between Olivia Shakespeare and his new collaborator, "John Oliver Hobbes," and receiving congratulations on *Esther Waters* and

81

commiserations over the injustice done it by Smith and Son. Gossip was already linking his name with the handsome Mrs. Craigie's, and his behavior did nothing to scotch the rumor. Mrs. Rhys and Mrs. Harland listened appreciatively to John Davidson in an unusually gay mood telling anecdotes and praising *The Heavenly Twins.* Theo Marzials, translator of folk songs, compared the ballads of yesterday with the lyrics of today for the benefit of W. B. Yeats, who eagerly waited his turn to speak for the poems of tomorrow. Other poets with views to express were Ernest Rhys and Lionel Johnson, "looking years too young for his critical utterances."[23] Although Ernest Dowson had written his friend Victor Plarr, "Are you going to the Yellow Book dinner? I shall, I expect, but I feel that I ought to go to no dinners until this pyramid is pulled down . . ."[24] (referring to a translation of Zola on which he was working), he went and forgot both Zola and "Missie" in the hilarious moment. Among the artists the tawny head of Walter Sickert was plainly visible, and Alfred Thornton sat next to Wilson Steer, as usual mostly silent. Kenneth Grahame looked a little startled at being in such a gathering, and Max Beerbohm betrayed in no way that he was the youngest person present.

The general topic of conversation was the *Yellow Book,* which was reported to have been selling like wildfire all day. Laughter and snatches of talk reached Mrs. Pennell, who sat in a pool of silence at the head table with both her partners so concerned over the speeches ahead that they did nothing to entertain her. One merit all the toasts had in common; they were brief. Beardsley gained instant attention when he began modestly, "I am going to talk about a most interesting subject— myself."[25] Walter Sickert was considered to have made the hit of the evening,[26] however, when he said he "looked forward to the time when authors would be put in their proper places by being compelled to write stories and poems round pictures which should be supplied to them ready-mady by their taskmasters, the artists."[27]

When the speeches were over, the strain at the head table relaxed and Mrs. Pennell's boredom was dissipated by gaiety and banter. Even though the hour was late when the party ended, John Lane conducted a favored few, including the Harlands, Mrs. Pennell, the young Mr. Beerbohm, and Beardsley to the Bodley Head to see the home of the *Yellow Book*, adjourning afterward to the basement of the Monico, where again they drank to its long life.

With such ceremonies was the *Yellow Book* launched on its golden path.

Chapter X

WHILE THE CONTRIBUTORS dined in their own honor, warmed by a glow of pride and—surely on this occasion it would have been Veuve Cliquot — the critics turned the smooth slick pages between the yellow boards marked REVIEW COPY WITH THE COMPLIMENTS OF THE BODLEY HEAD and read eagerly. They had waited long to see what this much-publicized undertaking had to offer. Now the evidence was before them.

The Table of Contents was divided into "Letterpress" and "Pictures," and the editors had bowed Henry James' fifty-page story of literary life, "The Death of the Lion," into the place of honor for literature, while art was introduced with a study of two draped female forms by Sir Frederick Leighton of the Royal Academy; to reach either, one had to pass the title-page on which a Beardsley damsel stood up to play a piano before a background of two trees in a meadow.

After James came Richard Le Gallienne's poem, "Tree-Worship." The Liverpool poet, born Gallienne of Breton descent by way of the Channel Islands, was said to owe his name to Oscar Wilde—at least it was Oscar who had suggested placing the masculine article before the obviously feminine form. "It'll be the making of you, Dick," he had prophesied,[1] and though Henley protested peevishly, "Even his name is ungrammatical," Le Gallienne had done well in London as poet, publisher's reader, and critic. He was already represented on Lane's lists by *The Religion of a Literary Man, George Meredith, Some Characteristics,* and *The Book-Bills of Narcissus.* At twenty-eight, his finely chiseled profile, pale skin, and raven black hair curling over his velvet coat collar set him off from more mundane figures at the Bodley Head. To the young office boy May he was Shelley plainly seen; to Will Rothenstein he looked like Botticelli's "Head of Lorenzo"; William Archer thought "such a name and such a physiognomy . . . hard to live up to,"[2] and Owen Seaman rhymed,

> That London still remains the missus
> Of this Narcissus.[3]

Though tree-worship might seem an innocuous woodland pasttime, the poet had introduced such other fancies into his lines that E. A. Robinson in far-off Maine could not hear or read about the *Yellow Book* without being reminded of "Mr. Le Gallienne's adulterous nightingales."[4]

Max Beerbohm's "Defence of Cosmetics" followed Le Gallienne and shifted the scene from the woods to the dressing table. Max, still an undergraduate at Merton College, Oxford, had already contributed an essay on "The Incomparable Beauty of Modern Dress" to the *Spirit Lamp,* edited by Lord Alfred Douglas, and had on hand a little thing called "A Peep into the Past," which he considered using but discarded for this whimsical essay deriding nature and praising artifice, with some fervent homage for the delicious Miss Cissie Loftus.

New Fiction was represented by Ella D'Arcy's "Irremediable" and Hubert Crackanthorpe's "Modern Melodrama," both unhappily realistic stories of the relations between man and woman. In the first, marriage turned out badly for the husband, and in the second a less formal but more convenient arrangement faced a tragic ending. With the latter especially, the editors were on touchy ground, but George Saintsbury's "A Sentimental Cellar," though exhibiting "within reasonable bounds" the influence of Pater, would offend no one except a teetotaler.

Saintsbury was fifty years old when he wrote for the *Yellow Book* and this was the only appearance of the distinguished critic of literature and wine in the quarterly. The following year he was appointed to the Chair of Rhetoric and English Literature in Edinburgh University, gaining the honor over a field of candidates that included Walter Raleigh, Churton Collins, W. E. Henley, and William Sharp, and went to live in Scotland, to the satisfaction of H. C. Beeching, who recorded his own trip "to Reading to spend some hours in the bookshops, for since Mr. Saintsbury went north to profess in Edinburgh, there is a little more chance of picking up there some unconsidered trifles."[5] When a youth in Merton College, Saintsbury had been stirred by the "wonders" of Swinburne's *Poems and Ballads,* and as a critic for the *Academy* in the seventies he had written in appreciation of the aesthetic principles of such poets as Baudelaire, Whitman, Blake, and Swinburne. The next decade had seen his *Short History of French Literature.* As a proponent of the aesthetic theories of Pater, though with some modification, he was a natural choice for the new quarterly devoted to Art. In 1895 he was to defend the aesthetic doctrine against a moralistic attack by Churton Collins, and in 1898 Collins was to get his revenge by calling Saintsbury's *Short History of English Literature* a "very well of English defiled."[6] Of all this Saintsbury was unaware when he wrote for the *Yellow Book* of the connoisseur Falernius and his museum of magic liquors which recalled to him and his friend the loves of earlier days.

Dr. Richard Garnett, another erudite contributor, revealed "The Love-Story of Luigi Tansillo" with translations of his sonnets, which, though passionate, had been written a long time ago. Dr. Garnett disagreed with some interpretations of Tansillo advanced by John Addington Symonds in the *Cornhill,* but Mr. Symonds had died in 1893 and could hardly object.

A sketch by "George Egerton," the inspiration of Lane's Keynotes Series, and two stories by the literary editor himself completed the fiction. Edmund Gosse had two poems, one dedicated to his friend Benson, who in turn was represented by a poem of disillusionment with an impressive Greek title—after all, he was a schoolmaster. William Watson and John Davidson completed the list of poets. Arthur Waugh's plea for "Reticence in Literature" demonstrated the editors' policy of fair play, though some examples, quoted by Waugh from Swinburne, could not have been termed reticent. But Waugh (who was to become the father of Alec and Evelyn and chairman of Chapman and Hall), though he later said he would not be prepared to defend that standard, "at least without qualifications," at the time believed implicitly that reticence was necessary for immortality, and "so, apparently, did a good many other people."[7]

Though Waugh did not include Arthur Symons' poem *"Stella Maris"* as a specimen of undesirable frankness, no critic could overlook its appositeness. In melodious and outspoken tribute to the Juliet of a night, Symons defended his creed of— could one say, *Carpe noctem?*

> That joy was ours, we passed it by;
> You have forgotten me, and I
> Remember you thus strangely, won
> An instant from oblivion.
> And I, remembering, would declare
> That joy, not shame, is ours to share,
> Joy that we had the will and power,
> In spite of fate, to snatch one hour,
> Out of vague nights, and days at strife,
> So infinitely full of life.[8]

In no other number did Harland include any types of drama, but this first volume contained a play in three scenes by F. M. Simpson, undergraduate of Cambridge, and one act of a three-act play, *The Fool's Hour,* by the two new collaborators, "John Oliver Hobbes" and George Moore.

Among the artists, except for Leighton, J. T. Nettleship, who was just emerging from his shroud of anonymity and was not pleased with the reproduction of his "Head of Minos," and Pennell, the emphasis was on youth, with Walter Sickert's "The Old Oxford Music Hall" and "A Lady Reading," Will Rothenstein's "Portrait of a Gentleman," recognized by many Oxonians as Sir Claude Schuster, and Charles Furse's handsome "Portrait of a Lady," identified sadly by his friends as his late

MAX BEERBOHM

From a photograph by Russell and Sons, the *Critic*, XXXIX (1901)

Mrs. Craigie ("John Oliver Hobbes")

From the *Bookman* (New York), VI (1898)

Hubert Crackanthorpe

From the *Critic*, XXVII (1897)

Ella D'Arcy

From the *Bookman* (New York), II (1895)

fiancée, Eleanor Butcher, whose tragic death had been so heartbreaking to the artist. Laurence Housman's "Reflected Faun" and "A Book Plate" by R. Anning Bell represented the Burne-Jones school.

Beardsley's plump masked woman on the cover smiling encouragingly at the approach of her swain was followed by three plates, "L'Education Sentimentale" of obvious meaning, "Night Piece," with its amazing blackness (dead black, Beardsley thought, used "feelingly and artistically, can be made to express almost anything," even grass. As Boccaccio wrote in the *Decameron*, "The grass was so green that it was nearly black"[9]), and his "Portrait of Mrs. Patrick Campbell," product of that meeting arranged by Wilde.

Such was the fare offered the hungry critics, and to a man they devoured it. Arthur Waugh had euphemistically described the period before the appearance of the *Yellow Book* as one of "rosy expectancy." He should have called it the lull before the storm.

"On Monday," read the review in the *National Observer*, "the great world did Messrs. Mathews and Lane, publishers, the honour to creak on its hinges; for it had been foretold that on that day a new planet—a star of modernity, a yellow asteroid, in fact—should swim into the ken of the nation which hitherto had sat in a most lamentable darkness. Never was the way of a magazine made so plain before it as the *Yellow Book*'s; judicious advertisements planted, and injudicious interviews watered." Never, in the *Observer*'s opinion, had a result been so disappointing. The book itself was termed "bizarre, eccentric, uncomfortably heavy to the hand," with "the audacious vulgarity and the laborious inelegance of the cover" especially offensive, and the contents, "a misarrangement in orpiment," full of "nonsensical and hysterical matter." After praise for Henry James and for Friend Joseph's Etching and kind words for Dr. Garnett and Miss D'Arcy, the remaining contributors were treated in two columns of scathing condemnation. "The publisher has already given the keynote of the criticism he would like to have," concluded the review. "Honesty compels us to strike a discordant strain."[10]

If the *Observer* expected his to be the one dissonant note in the critics' hymn to the *Yellow Book,* he must have been surprised to discover how pleasantly he harmonized with all the others, for most of London's reviewers sang the same tune.

"The *Yellow Book* . . . is . . . we suppose," said the London *Times,* "destined to be the organ of the New Literature and the Art. The cover . . . may be intended to attract by its very repulsiveness and insolence." The note of the journal was taken to be "a combination of English rowdiness with French lubricity. . . . On the whole, the New Art and the New Literature appear to us to compare in this singular volume far from favorably with the old and we doubt if the representatives of the latter will much relish the companionship, to say nothing of the cover, in which they find themselves." However, the *Times'* reviewer was almost alone in his praise of Arthur Symons' *"Stella Maris,"* finding it "graceful and melodious."[11] Most critics used different adjectives for Symons and "his encounter of a night."

A suggestion in J. A. Spender's *Westminster Gazette* has been more widely quoted about the *Yellow Book* than any other in the chorus of disapproval; it called simply for an "Act of Parliament to make this kind of thing illegal." Aubrey Beardsley's designs, "excesses hitherto undreamt of," demonstrated the need for this ban; Max Beerbohm was included as "the only writer who is entirely worthy to be ranked with Mr. Beardsley."[12]

The review in the *Daily Chronicle* was kinder than most, perhaps as a mark of appreciation by Henry Norman for the seat of honor given his wife at the *Yellow Book* dinner. ". . . altogether in its physical aspects, the volume is one which reflects much credit upon its editors and publishers," admitted the reviewer, but "the inside—the yolk of *The Yellow Book*" failed to satisfy him. Moreover, he complained that the portrait of Mrs. Patrick Campbell had been left out of his copy: "the fly-leaf announcing it precedes one of Mr. Aubrey Beardsley's strange *crises de pinceau.* To those who know the trials and tribulations of processing and editing, this is very explicable," but he regretted the "absence of a picture of so charming a lady by so clever an artist."[13]

The "so clever an artist" rose promptly to this bait, and the next day the *Chronicle* published his letter of apology for the omission of the portrait from the reviewer's copy, adding, "for the benefit of your readers," that every other copy contained the picture. An editorial note appended to the letter congratulated the "more fortunate possessors of the portrait. Our own copy, it is true, contained a female figure in the space thus described, but we rated Mrs. Patrick Campbell's appearance and Mr. Beardsley's talent far too high to suppose they were united on this occasion."[14]

This portrait of the slim, willowy Mrs. Campbell (before the war the original was in the Berlin National Galerie) was a favorite point of attack against Beardsley. *Punch* parodied it as "Played Out; or, The 252nd Mrs. Tanqueray—trained down very fine after a long run,"[15] and a Cambridge humorist inquired:

> Pray, Mr. Beardsley, tell us why
> Your elongated fancy made you
> Depict this lady nine feet high?
> What influence conspired to aid you?[16]

Beardsley defended the picture on all occasions. "It is Mrs. Collins" [Mrs. Campbell], he insisted. "It's just like her. I caught the expression of Paula Tanqueray one night when I was standing in the pit of the St. James Theatre. Mrs. Collins had given me lots of sittings but not until that moment did I catch the secret of her face. Then when Mrs. Collins appeared as Dulcie Sarondie in 'The Masqueraders,' everybody . . . said 'How like Beardsley's portrait!' "[17]

The title-page with the young lady playing the piano in the middle of a flowery meadow also came in for criticism. So widespread was the objection to this "unpardonable affectation" that Beardsley justified it in a letter to the editor of the *Pall Mall Budget,* explaining that Christoph Ritter von Glück had been wont to use a piano, adorned on each side with a bottle of champagne, in the middle of a field, and that he had written his two *Iphigenias* and his *Orpheus* under such conditions. "I tremble to think," Beardsley concluded, "of what critics would say had I introduced these bottles of champagne! And yet we do not call Glück a *décadent*." This letter was copied in the American *Critic,* with a comment by the Lounger that only the bottles of champagne would explain the "eccentricity of the lady with a crack down her back."[18]

In spite of the unfavorable tone of the reviews, the *Yellow Book* was selling so fast that the Bodley Head could not keep up with the demand. In five days the entire first edition had vanished and a second appeared. All the lending libraries and book clubs had waiting lists. When the second edition was exhausted, Lane put an advertisement in the *Academy* reassuring a clamorous public that the third would be "ready on Monday, at all Booksellers, Libraries and Railway Bookstalls."[19]

Everyone wanted to see the sensational production; it was the conversational topic of the day. A puzzled clerk asked Arnold Bennett, as if he inquired into a mystery of the universe, "What is this *Yellow Book?*"[20] Undergraduates at Oxford and Cambridge neglected their studies to read it, and the *Oxford Magazine* chided, "We have even seen bold spirits reclining under trees regaling themselves with *The Yellow Book.*"[21]

With wifely pride Mrs. Harland told her friends it was a great success and had really created a furor. The editors had become the lions of the town.

Some of the contributors, however, agreed with the reviewer in the *Times* that they were not happy about the company in which they found themselves, and Sir Frederick Leighton came to the Bodley Head to say that his friends had reprimanded him severely for getting himself into such a predicament and that he had solemnly promised them not to do it again. Moreover, the ungrateful Henry James wrote confidentially to his brother William, "I haven't sent you 'The Yellow Book'—on purpose; and indeed I have been weeks and weeks in receiving a copy of it myself. I say on purpose because although my little tale . . .

appears to have had, for a thing of mine, an unusual success, I hate too much the horrid aspect and company of the whole publication. And yet I am again to be intimately, conspicuously associated with the 2nd number. It is for gold and to oblige the worshipful Harland."[22]

Another man of letters was equally displeased because it was a company in which he did not find himself. Oscar Wilde cautioned Charles Ricketts, "My dear Boy, do not say nice, false things about the 'Yellow Book.' I bought it at the station, but before I had cut all the pages, I threw it out of my carriage window."[23] "Have you seen *The Yellow Book?*" he asked Mrs. Leverson. "It is horrid and not yellow at all,"[24] and to Alfred Douglas he was even franker. "It is dull and loathsome: A great failure—I am so glad."[25]

The literary magazines took up the prosecution where the papers had left off and boosted Lane's profits higher by their horrified comment. The *Spectator* was scandalized by the *Yellow Book,* "a jaundiced-looking indigestible monster, half-book, half-magazine . . . while the sacred fire that was to illuminate and dazzle the world is curtailed to the modest proportion of a guttering candle."[26] The *Sketch* thought it showed the "clever school of writers" who gathered around Elkin Mathews and John Lane "at their very worst and weakest."[27] The *Saturday Review* grumbled that the illustrations certainly did not justify their existence,[28] but the review of the writing was more favorable than Frank Harris gave any succeeding number.

The article in the *Speaker* was prefaced by a discourse on first editions, of which the nineties were so conscious. "Let the lover of first editions take comfort. Foolish he may be—we ask him to admit it for the sake of argument—and vain he may be: but no collector that we have ever heard of is foolish or vain enough to hoard, even if he should be mad enough to purchase, the first or any other edition of 'The Yellow Book.' " The critic then devoted two pages to this "farrago of aspiring affectation and preposterous incompetence," to end "overwhelmed by the feeling that ere three months have come and gone, a second and possibly more terrible *Yellow Book* may be flaunted before our eyes."[29]

Punch found in the new quarterly a never-failing source of inspiration for jokes, parodies, and cartoons. In the issue for April 28 under the heading "Some Colour for the Question" appeared the quip, "The *Yellow Book* is the title of the new eccentric Quarterly published by Elkin Mathews and Company. But will the *Yellow Book* become a generally *Red* Book?"[30] and in the same number a poem "Jaundice," beginning

> Leaves—like Autumn leaves—the tint of custard,
> Cover like a poultice made of mustard,
> General aspect bilious.
> Letter-press (with some exceptions) silly;
> Sentiment like highly-seasoned skilly,
> Posing supercilious,

went on to say,

> Gloomy gulfs of cocky cynicism,
> Give you intellectual rheumatism,

and concluded:

> Waste of time and trouble, ink and paper.
> Sure if "Art" must play such prankish caper,
> Aping the cheap wag's tone,
> There's no need to print it—at a crown.[31]

At Cambridge, the *Granta,* which had already printed the parody of the Prospectus, exclaimed dramatically, "It is out. We have seen it . . . and, thanks to a constitution fortified by the athletic exercises of a University, we live to tell the tale . . . . If a collection of semi-obscene, epicene, sham erotic and generally impotent literary and artistic efforts make up a book, well then, this is a book, and we have nothing further to say,"— a misleading statement, since the writer devoted many burning words to Arthur Symons and "all the rest of the nincompoop brigade."[32]

If this was the opinion at Cambridge one might expect the opposite view from Oxford, but on this occasion the ancient rivals were agreed. "Hearty congratulations to the *Granta* on the brilliance of its criticism of the *Yellow Book*," applauded Mostyn Piggott in the *Isis*. "The observations on 'Stella Maris' and its author, Mr. Arthur Symons, are admirably just . . . . If Mr. Arthur Symons has on one occasion strayed from the path of virtue, why should he take the public into his disgusting confidence? . . . The *Yellow Book* is both dull and foolish . . . an attempt on the part of certain young men, whose merits lie somewhat behind their estimate of them to pitchfork themselves into notoriety."[33]

In the United States, published by the Boston firm of Copeland and Day, the first number appeared a month later than in England, but its reception was no more laudatory, though the outcry was not quite so vociferous. It was after all published in England, though its editor might be an American, and the American public had grown used to being shocked by literary importations from the other side of the Atlantic. As Charles Dudley Warner declared in *Harper's,* "It is hardly safe in these days to give an English novelist free access to the general American public through the pages of a popular magazine without careful scrutiny . . . and if the London life is what it is depicted in many recent romances, it is a pity to risk its diffusion in the middle classes by means of the circulating libraries."[34]

The *Nation* found the "Whistlerian affectations" of Max Beerbohm "particularly intolerable,"[35] and the *Bookbuyer* thought "the spirit of the whole thing . . . simply repellent," and startling even to "hardened readers of police reports."[36] The *Critic* refused to let itself be influenced by the fair promises of Mr. Waugh's London Letter. It dubbed the new periodical a "Yellow Impertinence" and referred to *"Stella Maris"* as a "poem of the gutter." That such respectable writers as Henry James, William Watson, Edmund Gosse, Richard Garnett, and, yes, even Arthur Waugh, should appear among such low associates, only demonstrated, in the opinion of the reviewer, that "amiability makes strange bed-fellows."[37] The *Dial* gave it a better character than most, calling it a realization of the idea of Howells' *A Hazard of New Fortunes,* but saying pointedly, "We doubt if the beginning of the twentieth century will find this volume nearly as readable as we now find it late in the nineteenth."[38]

From Gardiner, Maine, where E. A. Robinson was doing chores and beginning to write, he informed his friend Smith, "Have read the *Yellow Book*—all I care for—and find it pretty thin. Henry James' story and Arthur Waugh's essay are the only things I care for. The *Yellow Book,* in my humble [opinion], is an elegantly got up fake and has no excuse for being that I can see."[39] Yet in two later letters he adjured his friend to be sure to bring him the new *Yellow Book.*

If, as John Lane said, the editors "desired criticism even though adverse to themselves," they were left with few ungratified wants, but they refused to let their belief in the *Yellow Book* be weakened, since the public had bought up three editions and was waiting avidly for John Lane to get the fourth off the press. An analysis of the reviews revealed great differences of opinion. Studying their clippings, the editors noted that what one critic disliked most violently might be warmly praised by another, and they decided to capitalize on these discrepancies. Certain contributors, like Beardsley, Symons, and Crackanthorpe, had received the hardest blows, but even they had won a few kind words.

So the Prospectus prepared for Volume II offered a Resumé of the Opinions of the Press on Volume I, setting one statement against another with good effect. Henry James's story was "very difficult to read" and "chiefly valuable for the sake of the name of its author," but, on the other hand, it was "very near Mr. James's best—there is satire, humour, and epigram enough in its fifty pages for half a dozen ordinary stories." Gosse's poems were "prattling mediocrity" and "among the best in the book." George Egerton's "Lost Masterpiece" was both a "nothingness of words" and "clever." "The Fool's Hour" was described as "a work of the keenest wit," and in this case the editors could find "no difference amongst the critics."[40]

One name was omitted from this symposium and here, too,

the critics were in complete agreement. Nobody had a good word to say about Max Beerbohm. But neither Harland nor Max was daunted by this universal disapprobation. "A Letter to the Editor" by Max Beerbohm was announced as a feature of Volume II.

Chapter XI

IN SPITE OF the advertised acclaim of the critics for the work of "John Oliver Hobbes" and George Moore, nothing by either of these writers was to appear in Volume II. In June just before the appearance of the second *Yellow Book,* their comedy *The Fool's Hour* was performed at a special matinee at Daly's Theatre with enough success to start the collaborators working again on a new play, *Journeys End in Lovers' Meetings,* in which Ellen Terry and Forbes-Robertson later played the leading roles. So the authors were much occupied, but even if she had not been busy, Mrs. Craigie was not to be caught a second time. Indeed, she wrote to George, "He [Harland] wants me to write a poem, a story, an article, anything, for the next number. I fear I cannot oblige him. *The Speaker* on *The Yellow Book* is only too just. I have never seen such a vulgar production." She added virtuously, "Reserve is a great gift: I have always prayed for it."[1]

Some rude persons might have said it was a pity her prayers were so ineffective, for Mrs. Craigie was one of the most talked-about women in London during the nineties; no writer of book gossip was ready for press until he had mentioned her latest novel, love affair, or epigram. She had made up her pseudonym "John Oliver Hobbes" by taking "John" from the name of her father and her son, "Oliver" from Cromwell, one of her heroes, and "Hobbes" from the Malmesbury philosopher, thinking of whom, she said, kept her from being sentimental.[2] An embarrassed editor once addressed her as "Mrs. Joliver Hobbes."[3]

Though Gertrude Atherton described Mrs. Craigie as "a

short dark women who would have been plain but for a pair of remarkably fine eyes,"[4] the New York *Bookman* declared she was "a dark handsome woman with large luminous eyes and a high color, who dresses smartly," and published a drawing by Walter Spindler to confirm its judgment.[5] "Her husband, Mr. Craigie, is one of the young men about London who go everywhere, and are intimate at the most exclusive houses," *Munsey's* told its readers in March, 1894. "He is very handsome and agreeable, with a splendid physique and—a passion for drink! ... Mrs. Craigie lives quietly with her father . . . . She is as beautiful as her husband is handsome . . . very sad . . . interesting . . . artistic, and designs her own gowns, wearing soft crêpes and gold embroideries."[6] Mrs. Craigie had a vivid personality and a quick wit. When she was told that one of her less glamorous contemporaries had said in a moment of exuberance that she'd like to be kissed to death, Mrs. Craigie surveyed the hopeful one through her monocle and drawled, "Ah, I see; she evidently intends to be immortal!"[7]

In April, 1894, the *Bookbuyer* published a little verse:

> John Oliver Hobbes, with your spasms and throbs,
> How does your novel grow?
> With cynical sneers at young Love and his tears
> And epigrams all in a row.[8]

Somewhat earlier Mrs. Craigie was quoted in an interview as saying, "I have been a gentle cynic from babyhood."[9]

If so, Pearl Richards Craigie's cynicism began in Boston in 1867. Her father, John Richards, had made a great deal of money through the manufacture of a patent medicine, reportedly liver pills. When she was three, she was taken to live in London by her family and at the age of seventeen went to study music at the Conservatoire in Paris. At eighteen she wrote letters to a London weekly, signed "Diogenes Pessimis," which brought her offers of an assistant editorship. At nineteen she was married to Reginald Walpole Craigie, and her son, John Churchill Craigie, was born in August, 1890. In the following May she was separated from her husband and subsequently divorced. In the interim she enrolled at London University for a classical degree, but gave up her studies when she began to write. Her first book, *Some Manners and a Moral* (1891), attracted immediate attention. In 1892 she was received into the Catholic Church, though her mother was a pillar of the City Temple, and added the names Mary Teresa to her own. When she wrote Dr. John Parker of the Temple and so signed herself—Pearl Mary Theresa Craigie—he answered politely over the signature Matthew Mark Luke John Parker.[10]

In June, 1893, Thomas Hardy first met "that brilliant woman, Mrs. Craigie" and by September was on such terms of friendship that he spent two hours on a Sunday morning walking on the moors with her while she explained her reasons for becoming a Catholic. Though he owned to being vexed with her and did not consider her logic satisfactory, he could not quarrel with "such an amusing companion."[11]

Having succeeded at fiction, Mrs. Craigie felt the lure of the theatre and wrote to George Moore for advice on the dramatization of one of her short stories. Moore ignored the letter of "that fellow Hobbes" until Arthur Symons identified the writer as a fascinating and wealthy young American, living apart from her husband. That set Moore off in a hurry to offer her every assistance, and once they had met he proceeded to fall ostentatiously in love with her. He was fifteen years her senior and had already indulged in various affairs which he had publicized widely, always, however, dodging matrimony. This time it appeared he was serious; only Mrs. Craigie was married and not yet divorced from her husband. She was not in a position to encourage his passion and would only meet him on the platonic ground of literature. Moore used to call on her in the family mansion in Lancaster Gate, and sitting in the drawing room ornamented with irises painted on the doors, three pairs of lace curtains draped across the window, a life-size statue of Joan of Arc and a motto on the mantel, "What would Jesus Say?", he would discuss with her the intricacies of dramatic construction.

George Moore was an Irishman, born in County Mayo in 1852, but in his late teens he went with his family to London, where he began his art education at the South Kensington Art School. In 1873 after his father's death, he went to Paris, determined to become an artist; but "one day, horrified at the black thing in front of me, I laid down my pencil, saying to myself, 'I will never take up pencil or brush again . . .' " and he turned to writing poetry and prose.[12] In 1878 his *Flowers of Passion* led Edmund Yates of the *World* to declare that the book should be burned by the common hangman and the author horsewhipped at the tail of a cart.[13] Moore wrote poetry under the influence of the French Symbolists, though in prose he called Zola his master and did him the homage of transferring unacknowledged pages into his own books. ("The man I object to," said Moore, "is the man who plagiarises without knowing it; I always know; I took ten pages."[14]) His novel *A Mummer's Wife* (1885) quickly went into three editions, and the same year Vizetelly brought out his pamphlet against the circulation libraries, *Literature at Nurse*. In 1888 his *Confessions of a Young Man* was a sensation in America as well as England. He had now transferred his residence from Paris to London, living first at King's Bench Walk, The Temple, and then moving to a flat in Victoria Street. Though many of his friends disbelieved his self-lauded lustiness in love and made fun of his *Confessions,* they acknowledged his way with prose, and his reading public was too impressive to be disregarded. "I wrote the first serious novels in English," Moore solemnly pronounced. "I invented adultery, which didn't exist in the English novel till I began writing."[15] His *Modern Painting* (1893) had spread the knowledge of Impressionism and added importance to his art reviews in the *Speaker*. He had just reached the height of success with the banned *Esther Waters*. "All experimentation is now over," he wrote a friend, "and henceforth I shall only sow seeds in the garden that is suited to my talent." But Oscar Wilde said, "The next time Moore will get it right. He conducts his education in public."[16]

Now Mrs. Craigie's difficulties with her would-be lover were increasing. He was getting her talked about more than she liked. With a history, self-proclaimed, of many conquests, he was trying to create the impression that here was another and that collaboration might—and did—cover a multitude of sins. She was not sure she wanted this somewhat shopworn suitor, though he laboriously learned to play the piano out of deference for her love of music and read her the letters of Héloïse to Abelard, remarking wistfully that no one had ever written him such letters. Mrs. Craigie's missives were surely models of reticence, though she sometimes consulted him about her new interest in the Honourable George Nathaniel Curzon, a handsome young aristocrat. Her name was now linked with Curzon's in gossip columns until April, 1895, when he married an American girl, Miss Mary Leiter of Washington; after it was revealed that they had been secretly engaged for two years, everyone was sorry for "John Oliver Hobbes."

In June *Journeys End in Lovers' Meetings* was produced, and Thomas Hardy made one of his infrequent trips to London for the opening night. Later Mrs. Craigie went to Hawarden to read the play to Gladstone, who had once sent a complimentary post card to her collaborator. In July she got her divorce and wrote to Ellen Terry, "I can hardly realize the verdict at present. I feel that the trial is still going on—that it is going on for ever and ever! The sensation is hideous. But I have got my child."[17]

Still she was not having George Moore, who took his dismissal badly, talked about it everywhere, and made fun of her and her writing. He had done all the work in the plays; she had only added "little liver pills" in the shape of epigrams and bits of dialogue. In his next book, the "poisonous 'Celibates,' "[18] as an American reviewer called it, he caricatured her cruelly. A few months later she was reported engaged to Walter Spindler, the artist who had painted her picture and to whom she had dedicated her *Bundle of Life*. Though he was somewhat her junior, the match seemed suitable, but again nothing came of it, and soon the gossips whispered that Mr. Arthur Balfour was her next choice, since she wished to shine in the world of "*la haute politique.*"[19]

In the meantime her father had bought the long-established

Academy, "presumably to give his daughter a way of reward-
ing her literary friends and punishing her enemies," and Lewis
Hind as editor was often summoned to confer with Mrs. Craigie,
"all frills, furbelows, scent, epigrams and kindness,"[20] though
he maintained she did not interfere with the Review. In 1897,
apparently forgiving all, she visited Lord and Lady Curzon, and
a few years later again spent a gay time with them at Government House, Calcutta. Her play *The Ambassador* (1898), an
epigrammatic comedy, showed what she could do without benefit
of Moore and ran a season in London. The American Ambassador Choate insisted he was under great obligations to Mrs.
Craigie, for it was from her play "that I acquired most of my
knowledge of the duties of that office,"[21] but Ouida thought it
very poor stuff; "there is no plot at all and the little action
there is, wholly improbable."[22]

As Mrs. Craigie limited her writing to two hours a day, she
had time to enjoy society and did not neglect her literary contacts. In 1902 she wrote a birthday letter to George Meredith,
who replied, "For though I bear in mind our meeting one
welcome day, I did not imagine you to have so lively a memory.
Or was it that a vigorous young sister in the craft was taken
with a kindly feeling for her now mute old brother?"[23] The
following year when she was about to go abroad he begged her
to visit him on her return. "Please, consent," he wrote. "And I
shall look forward."[24]

Again in 1903 she attempted a collaboration with Moore.
He had in the meantime written *Evelyn Innes,* dedicated to
his two friends of the Temple, Arthur Symons and W. B.
Yeats, as the writers with whom he found himself most in sympathy. Yeats was the Pied Piper, as Rothenstein said, who
played Moore into Dublin and the Irish mountains. His association with the Abbey Theatre has been described without
reticence and sometimes without reliability in *Ave, Salve,* and
Vale. His *Untilled Field* was also a result of his Irish experiences. The second collaboration of Moore and Mrs. Craigie, on
The Coming of Gabrielle, again ended in disaster. According
to Moore's acount, which he gave to several friends, they were

walking in Green Park: " 'There is nothing more cruel than lust,' she said. 'There is,' I said. 'What is that?' 'Vanity,' and I let her go a step ahead and gave her a kick behind.' "[25]

Though it was all over, he couldn't stop talking about her. "My dear fellow," he said to Vincent O'Sullivan, "you don't seem to realize that I have collaborated with her. Now when a man has collaborated with a woman it is the same as if he had slept with her. She has no secrets left to reveal."[26]

Mrs. Craigie started a lecture tour in America in 1905 but was obliged to relinquish this strenuous undertaking. She made a "charming impression," always "exquisitely gowned," though sometimes the substance of her speech was not thought as good as its delivery. On her return to England she curtailed her activities, and at a dinner of the New Vagabonds appealed to her dinner partner, G. B. Burgin: "Do ask them to let me off my speech. My heart's queer and I don't want to tumble down dead in the middle of it."[27] She was spared that humiliation, but one morning in the autumn of 1906 she was found dead in bed, a rosary between her fingers.

"Have just read of the death of Mrs. Craigie in the papers," Thomas Hardy wrote in his journal. "Her description of the artistic temperament is clever; as being that which 'thinks more than there is to think, feels more than there is to feel, sees more than there is to see'. . . . It reveals a bitterness of heart that was not shown on the surface by that brilliant woman."[28] In July, 1908, he went with Mrs. Hardy to the unveiling of a memorial to "John Oliver Hobbes" at University College, London, by Lord Curzon.

In summing up her career, the London *Tribune* said that, though she had written many noteworthy novels, plays, and essays, "her style and outlook on life were still unfixt, and the development of her genius seemed to show much greater possibilities."[29] *The Gods, Some Mortals, and Lord Wickenham* (1895) was generally considered her best work. In the epilogue to her last novel, *The Dream and the Business,* a study of religious temperaments, Tessa says, "Women of my type, who are not strong enough physically to bear the strain of mortal suffering very soon, and gladly, flicker out." Perhaps it was so with the woman who wrote it. If she had lived, she might have come closer to "enduring greatness." William Dean Howells said of her, "She cannot be forgotten in any study of her time. Whether her shapely and clever and brilliant books will continue to be read, I should not venture to guess, even. Whose books will continue to be read?"[30]

Though Moore wrote of Mrs. Craigie in *Resurgam* as the only woman he ever loved, he did not seem inconsolable at her death. He later proposed collaboration to Ella Hepworth Dixon and Gertrude Atherton, but they refused his offer of intellectual connubiality. From his residence in Victoria Street he moved his furniture and treasured paintings to the house with the discreet bow-window on the "long lackluster street of Ebury," where he lived till the end of his life—a long one. Here he wrote *The Lake, The Brook Kerith, Aphrodite in Aulis,* and here he turned his talk into *Conversations.* Here his artist friends came to spend the evening, or lady authors known to him from youth to call at tea time. "If you go to tea with him he will probably stir up the teapot with a beautiful Georgian spoon," said Ella Hepworth Dixon,[31] but poor deaf Ada Leverson could never find him at home, because as he told his cook, he had something else to do beside shouting in her ear and what she needed was an ear trumpet. In his age Moore was preoccupied with his youth, writing and rewriting his early books. He died in January, 1933, a lonely, tired old man, and though the Prime Minister and a few artists attended the funeral at Golder's Green, men of letters were conspicuously absent. "It was Moore's own fault that everybody hated him except a few London painters," Yeats had said.[32]

Much has been written of Moore's appearance and personality. He himself objected to Sickert's portrait of him because it gave him a face like a boiled pudding. His similarity to a chestnut worm has been indicated. Mrs. Atherton mentioned his "long colorless face that looked like a codfish crossed by a satyr."[33] Le Gallienne compared his countenance to "a dripping candle,"[34] and Charles Morgan said he had the "face of a fiery sheep."[35] Susan Mitchell wrote of his "egg-shaped face" and "champagne shoulders,"[36] and James Whitall described his "sloping shoulders, drooping moustache and short flipper-like arms terminating in fat white hands."[37]

But Moore saw himself differently. He called his sloping shoulders "agnostic"[38] and said, "Within the oftentimes bombastic and truculent appearance that I present to the world, trembles a heart shy as a wren in the hedgerow or a mouse along the wainscotting."[39] Arnold Bennett found him "naïvely and harmlessly vain, and very agreeable,"[40] but Oscar Wilde, asked if he knew Moore, said, "Know him? I know him so well that I haven't spoken to him in ten years."[41] Edward Martyn told Yeats, "I know Moore a great deal longer than you do. He has no good points."[42] (Moore said, "That man Martyn is the most selfish man alive. He thinks that I am damned and he doesn't care."[43]) Watts-Dunton was only "rather prejudiced" against Moore,[44] but Clement Shorter thought him the "most repellent of all modern authors."[45]

Aside from his role as champion of the need for "speaking out," Moore's stature as a stylist was often considered. Yeats spoke of the "plate-glass window" of his style, but a Dublin critic compared it to "ribbons of toothpaste squeezed out of a tube." Though Somerset Maugham was apprehensive of the critical faculties of a don who had an "inordinate admiration for *Esther Waters*,"[46] Charles Morgan declared in his *Epitaph on George Moore*, "Twice George Moore re-created the English novel—first in 1894 when *Esther Waters* gave us our liberty, and again ten years later when there began that series of tales, extending from *The Lake* through *The Brook Kerith* to *Aphrodite in Aulis*, in which we may discover . . . a new cadence and discipline, a new reconciliation between the written and the spoken word."[47]

Chapter XII

WHEN THE SECOND number of the *Yellow Book* appeared early in July, 1894, an eager public was ready for it, but no one awaited the yellow glow with more anticipation than Mrs. Sickert of Pembroke Gardens, for three of her sons were among the contributors. Though the *Yellow Book* was often called a family affair with husbands and wives, brothers and sisters in the same issue, having three brothers together, Walter Richard, Bernhard, and Oswald Sickert, was unusual. Mrs. Sickert, the English widow of a Munich painter, had lived much abroad but now, back in London in a house filled with her husband's pictures, she encouraged her five sons to follow their father's calling. They all had a gift for drawing, but she had most reason to feel proud of Walter Richard and Bernhard, members of the New English Art Club. Walter, as he called himself then (he became Richard after 1928), had turned to art after an early career as actor in Ellen Terry's company, but he still kept an interest in the theatre as represented by the music halls, which he often visited to make sketches of the stage and audience. He had studied under Legros at the Slade and been a disciple of Whistler, but that friendship was waning and would be broken by the end of the decade. Having turned to Paris and Degas, he had set himself up in Chelsea and was looked on as the leader of the London Impressionists. He had contributed two paintings to Volume I; he had three in the second volume, one a portrait of the art editor himself, the other two drawn from music halls. Indeed, the most frequent theme of his *Yellow Book* contributions was the music halls, which conventional critics did not consider a proper source of inspiration. Sickert's refusal, throughout a long career, to discriminate against unpleasant and ugly subjects was one of his most valuable services to his craft.

In Volume II a portrait of a tall, handsome, impeccably tailored young man by Impressionist P. Wilson Steer, though identified in the Index only as "A Gentleman," was generally recognized to be Mrs. Sickert's famous son. Steer and Sickert were close friends, though dissimilar in character; Steer was silent and retiring, Sickert as wittily talkative as Whistler, and each painted the other "exquisitely," MacColl thought.[1]

Bernhard Sickert, likewise a friend of Whistler (whose biography he wrote in 1908), was somewhat overshadowed by his more assertive brother. He painted in the manner of Camille Pissarro, and George Moore, who saw him and Walter frequently at Dieppe, thought him talented. His study of a head in this volume showed strength and individuality, but this drawing was his only contribution to the *Yellow Book*. Though Bernhard Sickert died in 1932, an exhibition of his pastels was held at the Leicester Galleries, London, in 1953.

Oswald, the third of Mrs. Sickert's charming sons and her favorite, preferred writing, though he had not yet exposed the Sickert name to the public, hiding his identity under the single letter "O." Together with two other young men, Stanley V. Makower, "V.," and Arthur Cosslett Smith, "C.S.," he had published a book of short stories, *The Passing of a Mood,* under the initials "V.O.C.S." in the Pseudonym Library, taken by the critics to be the work of a single writer who, "either he or she," had "a light touch and a sense of proportion." Oswald admired Henry James and wanted to write like him, but his "Purple Patch" in this volume showed an awkward gap between intention and achievement. The following year Oswald amplified his pseudonym to Oswald Valentine, and in Volume XII came out honestly as Oswald Sickert with a story that did credit to the name. Oswald and Bernhard were faithful members of the Harlands' group, as was Makower, a young Jewish musician with money. He and Oswald had been associated at Cambridge in founding the *Cambridge Observer,* which had set out *"épater le bourgeois,* and was defiantly propagandist concerning foreign authors. It contested the claim of contemporary critics, and discovered the best of all art in the New English Art Club."[2] But Oswald in spite of ability and intelligence, or perhaps because of them, deserted journalism for advertising and as agent for the *Times* was to travel over most of the globe, winning friends for himself and his paper. Edward Marsh, a friend of Cambridge days, paid tribute to his gentle charm. "I should like to commemorate him, how slightly soever, for I suppose he has left no dint on the general memory."[3]

Two changes were noticeable in the form of Volume II: the cover was printed in a dark green instead of black, though in the next number it turned black again, and the "Letterpress" and "Pictures" of the Table of Contents had become "Literature" and "Art." As *Punch* explained it,

> No possibility of doubt
> Can stop us now in finding out
>   What "literature" should be;
> No longer dazed by rival claims,
> We read a row of deathless names,
> Not yet renowned, but would-be . . . .
>
> And Beardsley shows us now the nude;
> It would not shock the primmest prude,
>   Or rouse the legislature,
> An unclothed woman ten feet high
> Could not make anyone feel shy,
> She's "Art," she is not nature.[4]

In general, criticism of the second volume was less harsh. The *Times* said it "will not have the same *succès de scandale* that fell to the first, but it will be better liked by people who still think that in literature and art it is well to draw the line somewhere."[5] The *Westminster Gazette* complained that if it was saner, it was also duller.[6] *Punch* was again moved to poetry.[7]

Most critics centered their fire on an essay by Philip G. Hamerton, "*The Yellow Book*, Criticized." The editors had planned to use in each number a criticism of the previous one written on invitation by some well-known man of letters, but after Dr. Hamerton's laboriously honest attempt, the scheme was given up. Hamerton was primarily an art critic and in that capacity he had roused the ire of Whistler by inquiring in the *Saturday Review* why a picture with many colors in it should be called *A Symphony in White*, to which Whistler had shot back one of his famous replies, "And does he then, in his astounding consequence, believe that a Symphony in F contains no other note, but shall be a continued repetition of F F F? . . . Fool!"[8]

But Hamerton was interested in literature too, and his *Intellectual Life* and *Quest of Happiness* had been well received. His own search for happiness had not been very successful, for after a miserable childhood he had struggled to free himself from religious doctrine, becoming a heretic in education as well as theology. But he was a philosopher, too, and when a lady rejected his offer of marriage, said with cold common sense, "I never could understand why men make themselves wretched after a refusal."[9]

Hamerton, considered an authority on good taste, was expected to administer a Victorian rebuke to the new upstart, and when he found much to commend in it, the gentlemen of the press howled derisively. He regretted the publication of "*Stella Maris*," inquiring with a frankness he doubtless considered suitable to his pulpit, "Why should poetic art be employed to celebrate common fornication?"[10] But he rallied to the defense of the much beset Mr. Beerbohm, whose essay he found a *jeu d'esprit*, though its opinions were precisely the opposite of his own. Hamerton offended most gravely, however, when he referred to Beardsley as "a man of genius." No critic could forgive him that extravagance. Indeed no one was much pleased with his "Criticism," not even John Lane, who had asked him to write it. But if Lane had wanted Hamerton's opinion of the second volume he could not have got it, for the critic was dead; indeed this essay was his last published article.

Another target for attack was Max Beerbohm's "Letter to the Editor" in explanation of his previous "Defense of Cosmetics." Though he maintained, rather unconvincingly, that his essay had been merely a travesty, a burlesque on the "precious" school of writers, he devoted most of his letter to a consideration of critics. In spite of a disarming statement of purpose—"After all, I think it is a sound rule that a writer should not kick his critics. I simply wish to make them a friendly philosophical suggestion"—such pronouncements as "Every new school that has come into the world, every new writer who has brought with him a new mode, they have rudely persecuted. . . . It is not until the pack has yelled itself hoarse that the level voice of justice is heard . . ."[11]—won small applause from the pack.

Another voice in this volume raised in justification of the credo of the quarterly was Hubert Crackanthorpe's with "Some Roundabout Remarks," a reply to Arthur Waugh's "Reticence in Literature." The concluding paragraph must have had the strong approval of the editor.

> The truth is, and, despite Mr. Waugh, we are near recognition of it, that nowadays there is but scanty merit in the mere selection of any particular subject, however ingenious or daring it may appear at first sight; that a man is not an artist, simply because he writes about heredity or the *demi-monde,* that to call a spade a spade requires no extraordinary literary gift, and that the essential is contained in the frank, fearless acceptance by every man of his entire artistic temperament, with its qualities and its flaws.[12]

The *Times* reviewer named three items of real interest, Frederick Greenwood's "Gospel of Content," James's "The Coxon Fund," and Alfred Hayes's "My Study."[13] Perhaps he could have included Charlotte Mew's "Passed," for in this short story may be found promise of the poetic and tender understanding later demonstrated in such volumes as *The Farmer's Bride* (1921) and *The Rambling Sailor* (1929). A young woman then in her middle twenties, daughter of a well-known architect, Charlotte Mew had already contributed stories to *Temple Bar* and the *Chap-Book,* and was to continue with fiction until the first decade of the next century before turning to poetry, in which she found her finest expression. Her first book of verse, in 1916, won her the admiration of Thomas Hardy; among his papers after he died was found her poem, *"Fin de Fête,"* which he had copied from the *Sphere.* He and Masefield and De la Mare were responsible for her being awarded a Civil List pension in 1923 (Gosse refused to sign the petition). Siegfried Sassoon, who considered her "one of my spiritual benefactors," thought the 70 pounds "a wretchedly small sum."[14] Though she lived most of her life in Bloomsbury, plagued by poverty and suffering, she loved the country and longed for it.

> Lord, when I look at lovely things which pass,
>   Under old trees the shadow of young leaves
> Dancing to please the wind along the grass,
>   Or the gold stillness of the August sun on the August sheaves;
> Can I believe there is a heavenlier world than this?[15]

Her one *Yellow Book* story, laid in the mean and murky London slums, with its stark portrayal of "this thing called Death," heavy with the sense of unfulfillment and despair, seemed to foreshadow the mood which led her, after the death of her sister Anne, to end her own life in 1923.[16]

Another woman who made her single *Yellow Book* appearance in Volume II was Katharine de Mattos, with a poem "In a Gallery." She was a sister of Bob Stevenson and a cousin of Robert Louis, who had dedicated his *Dr. Jekyll and Mr. Hyde* to her in 1886, with this verse:

> It's ill to loose the bands that God decreed to bind;
> Still will we be the children of the heather and the wind.
> Far away from home, O it's still for you and me
> That the broom is blowing bonnie in the north countrie.[17]

"Here, on a very little book and accompanied with lame verses," he wrote her, "I have put your name. Our kindness is now getting well on in years; it must be nearly of age; and it gets more valuable to me with every time I see you. . . . You know very well that I love you dearly, and that I always will."[18]

But Katharine de Mattos was to cause Stevenson great unhappiness and precipitate the break with his best friend Henley. She was one of Henley's young women, writing verse for his *National Observer*, and, at his encouragement, trying fiction. Stevenson had helped her free herself from an unhappy marriage and promised money for the support of her child. In 1887 he had written his business friend, Charles Baxter, "At Christmas, please send £10 to Katharine. . . . Should Henley be in want of money, £30." Katharine had written a story which she had talked over with the Stevensons, Mrs. Stevenson making a suggestion about a character which the young author had not accepted; but when the story did not sell, Mrs. Stevenson urged that she be allowed to try it her way. Katharine had apparently acceded, but so unwillingly that Stevenson had asked his wife not to do it. However, she had persisted and the story appeared in the March, 1888, *Scribner's* under her name. At once Henley wrote Stevenson—"Private and Confidential"—that he had read the story with considerable amazement—"It's Katharine's; surely it's Katharine's?"—and could not understand why there was not a double signature. Stevenson bitterly resented the implication, referring Henley to Mrs. de Mattos for an account of the circumstances. Her attitude, however, that though Henley had written without her knowledge, "He had a perfect right to be astonished," distressed Stevenson even further. He could not sleep at night, wished to God he had died at Hyères, and wrote pages to Baxter about this "treachery." "She can do what she will with Henley; I have long suspected this, and I fear—perhaps so have others." He tried thus to justify Henley's charging at him like a "poor Knight Errant," but the hurt was too deep. Henley apologized: "I should, I know now, have said nothing. . . . You must not believe, though, that I struck to hurt. . . . Life is short enough and cruel enough, as it is; and you and I, dear Louis, should know better than to waste the good that is in it." But Stevenson could not forgive, and the breach was never healed.[19]

When Stevenson died in December, 1894, five months after Mrs. de Mattos' poem had appeared in the *Yellow Book,* Henley wrote William Archer, "I have hitherto hoped and believed that we had but to meet for the wrong to be made right. And now that's impossible; and there is nothing for us but, as I wrote of and to him langsyne . . . to

> 'Lie in the Peace of the Great Release
> As once in the grass together.' "[20]

Though the *Times* singled out Alfred Hayes's poem "My Study," it did not mention two other writers in the same number who had been formerly associated with him in a volume of poetry. Published at Rugby in 1893, this volume, *A Fellowship of Song,* contained the verse of Norman Gale, Richard Le Gallienne, and Alfred Hayes. Gale and Hayes were both schoolmasters, Gale at Rugby and Hayes at Birmingham. Gale's first book of poems, which had appeared anonymously at Rugby in 1890, was *Cricket Songs and Other Trifling Verse,* and his last book (1937) *Close of Play, Poems on Cricket.* The poems he contributed to the *Yellow Book,* "Betrothed" in this volume and "The Call" in Volume V, departed from the playing field to "the wood on the hill" and "the country where the cowslip nods asleep," and were concerned with an older sport than cricket. Leaving the lure of the city to more sophisticated poets, he wrote of the country and orchard and cricket green; even so the "discreetly fleshly" tone of his verse did not escape criticism, and a poem in *Orchard Songs* (1893), "written on being charged with undue frankness," came to the conclusion,

> Who call me base must think me base;
> But soon afresh for me
> Your speeding footsteps in the grass
> Shall prove my purity![21]

The poet Robinson, reading avidly in preparation for his own song-making, decided, "They are all on the wrong track, excepting Mr. Gale, and he is almost sickening sometimes in artlessness, or whatever he calls it. If I rejoiced in cricket and football as he does I should not write some of the stuff that he has written. I say 'stuff,' but do not quite mean it. Whatever Gale does—at least, what I have seen—he does well; but his country maidens grow a little tiresome."[22]

Ronald Campbell Macfie, an Aberdeen man who alternated books on science with excursions into poesy, had a poem "Dreams" which a reviewer in the *National Observer* said struck "the richest and truest note" in this number.[23] Certainly one line of it, "Hiving hot lips among thy temple hair," excelled in accumulation of metaphor.

One older poet was included in Volume II, Austin Dobson, whose *"Sat est Scripsisse,"* called a "charming epistle" by the

Times, was inscribed "To E. G. with a Volume of Essays," for Gosse was his fellow-poet on the Board of Trade. The last line of it might have been taken for the epitaph of many of his *Yellow Book* friends:

They, too, had once their ardour:—they handed on the fire.

Though he lived until 1921, Dobson already belonged to the older school of poets, having little in common with the new ones who found their inspiration in France, though he himself had looked to that land in an earlier day. Nearly two decades previously he had introduced the villanelle and rondeau to English ears not then attuned to those delicate measures, and Browning was reported to have called his poems "carved cherry stones."[24]

Sir Frederick Leighton was absent from this volume as he had promised to be, but Beardsley had induced John Sargent to represent the Royal Academy with his "Portrait of Henry James." This profile drawing was the artist's second attempt to depict his fellow-American. Sargent had destroyed an earlier full-length drawing, with the wry remark that it was impossible to do justice to a face that was all "covered with beards like a bear." Beardsley was so pleased with this side face sketch of the baldish, bearded author that he asked Sargent for the portrait of another *Yellow Book* contributor, Edmund Gosse. But Sargent, like Leighton, was wary, as his letter to Gosse showed:

My dear Gosse,
I have just replied in the negative to a note from Mr. Aubrey Beardsley asking my permission to reproduce your portrait in the "Yellow Book."

From an artistic point of view I dislike that book too much to be willing to seem an habitual contributor.

My only regret is that it should be *à propos* of your portrait, especially if you ever were willing that it should be reproduced, which I should consider a great compliment.
Yours very truly,
John S. Sargent.[25]

If the general tone of this volume was milder there was no compromise in Beardsley's contributions. "Mr. Aubrey Beardsley is as conspicuous by his vapid and vulgar attempts at French *chic* as before," said the *Nation*.[26] His cover design was judged not so objectionable as the first, but the grotesqueness of his "Comedy-Ballet of Marionettes" gained little admiration. His "Portrait of Madame Réjane" did not arouse the storm of protest accorded to his earlier portrayal of Mrs. Campbell. In fact, one reviewer thought it the best likeness ever made of this "graceful but ugly actress." William Archer was ready with the explanation of Beardsley's success: "Mme. Réjane happens to be the one woman in the world with a Beardsley mouth."[27] But Thomas Beer has related that Réjane wept and screamed when she saw Beardsley's poster of her face "with its Cytherean grin."[28]

In this volume the editors may seem to have violated their principle of allowing no relation between Literature and Art, doing further honor to Madame Réjane with an article from a fellow-countryman, Dauphin Meunier, who saw "the devil in her body, heaven in her eyes."

Meunier was a Parisian friend of the Harlands. In 1894 Harland urged Le Gallienne to join him in Paris. "Therefore— Come. We will spend laborious days and tavern nights. We will dine with Dauphin Meunier, and sup with dear old Verlaine, and breakfast with the Muses."[29] When Verlaine lectured in London in 1893 he had put Meunier in the independent *pléiade* of poets, "all remarkable . . . and of an assured future."[30] Meunier had been part of the Symbolist movement in France from 1885 to 1890 but later associated himself with the *École romane* of Jean Moréas. He was a painter as well as a poet and a linguist. This essay was written in English but poems in later volumes were in French, as, for example, *"Au bord du Lac Léman (Souvenir de Vevey à Madame Paul Vérola),"* "Hyde Park *(Souvenir de Londres à Madame Aline Harland),"* and *"Chapelle Dissidente,* London *(pour* Mr. Aubrey Beardsley)."* Harland liked and admired this talented Frenchman and gave him several opportunities in the *Yellow Book.* Later Meunier reciprocated by translating Harland's *Cardinal's Snuffbox* into French.

Shortly after the appearance of Volume II, announcement was made that Elkin Mathews and John Lane were to part company. The Editor of the American *Chap-Book* regretted the dissolution of a firm that "has done so much," wondered how the "excellent list of books" would be divided, and asked pointedly if there would now be two *Yellow Books*.[31] Lane soon made it known that he would continue the *Yellow Book*. He had indeed taken most of the responsibility for the journal since its beginning, but Mathews had kept a steadying hand on it, and the loss of his influence was soon to be felt.

Chapter XIII

IF IN VOLUME II of the *Yellow Book* the editors felt they had leaned too far to the side of reticence, they righted the balance with a vengeance in Volume III by including work from the most talked-about writers and artists. Indeed the Index read like a roster of all the sad young men of the nineties, with Arthur Symons, Ernest Dowson, Lionel Johnson, Hubert Crackanthorpe, Kenneth Grahame, Theodore Wratislaw, William Watson, S. Cornish Watkins, Arthur Moore, John Davidson, Max Beerbohm, and Henry Harland in literature and Beardsley, Sickert, and Steer in art. Present too were several of Lane's petticoats—Miss D'Arcy, Olive Custance, Leila Macdonald, and Annie Macdonell, London representative of the New York *Bookman*, who was just finishing her book on Hardy.

They made a meaty issue, ushered in by a provocative article, "Women—Wives or Mothers" by "A Woman," a flagrant misrepresentation according to Miss D'Arcy, who fastened the authorship on Frederick Greenwood, founder of the *Pall Mall Gazette*, editor of impressive journals, including the *Anti-Jacobin*, and acknowledged author of "The Gospel of Content" in Volume II. At least once before, when he finished Mrs. Gaskell's *Wives and Daughters* for the *Cornhill*, Greenwood had assumed a feminine point of view. In 1893 he had published *The Lover's Lexicon*, which dealt with such subjects as Abhor-

114

rence, Calf Love, Disenchantment, the Kiss, Old Maids, and Love Letters, and concluded that the "happiest marriages are those wherein the man and wife are chums."[1] Since he had been criticized for "Imagination in Dreams" (purely pre-Freud) in 1894, perhaps it was not unnatural that he should wish to conceal his identity while passing judgment on the Wife-Woman vs. the Mother-Woman and giving a perfunctory verdict for the latter. Greenwood is supposed to have been the original of Meredith's Richard Rockney in *Celt and Saxon.*

Though Greenwood's adjudication in the *Yellow Book* stirred up feminine tempers, by far the greatest sensation of this volume was created by John Davidson's "Ballad of a Nun." This long narrative poem of the nun who left her convent and the "righteous God behind," and went "to worship sinful man," returning at last a broken and repentant sinner to find that during her absence the Virgin had taken her place, had been rejected by several editors (the *Fortnightly* called it "disgustingly licentious")[2] before Harland accepted it, but most critics gave it a respectful consideration. Quiller-Couch, writer in the *Speaker,* said that "all the critics have spoken of 'A Ballad of a Nun' and admitted its surprising strength and beauty. They have left me in the plight . . . of the gentleman who had to be content with saying 'ditto' to Mr. Burke. For once they seem unanimous and for once they are right."[3] W. T. Stead, however, champion of the fallen woman, formed a vociferous minority of at least one, when he abused the poem as "immoral" in the London *Review of Reviews.*[4]

Its publication precipitated a minor crisis at the Bodley Head which the Reverend H. C. Beeching, who succeeded Canon Ainger as Reader at the Temple, described in the *Cornhill.* "On a certain Monday morning late in '94 a *queue* of respectable middle-aged ladies thrust its way along Vigo Street into the 'Bodley Head,' asking for copies of 'The Ballad of a Nun' by a Mr. Davidson. When the pressure was a little eased the publisher ventured to inquire the cause of the sudden demand. . . . The answer was that the Archdeacon of W.—— had charged them on their souls' health to procure it. Dear

Archdeacon! He knew the story from the *Gesta Romanorum* or from Miss Procter's version, and too carelessly assumed that D. meant the same thing."[5]

Beeching had a great fondness for "my poet Davidson," explaining, "I thing it is partly John Davidson's interest in blackbirds that attracts me to him above the other sixty or seventy young gentlemen who make modern poetry,"[6] but he did not like this poem and could not read it a second time.

No other poem appearing in the *Yellow Book* was more widely quoted than this famous ballad. But if the poem was quotable, it was also adapted to parody. The brave lines,

> "I care not for my broken vow,
> Though God should come in thunder soon;
> I am sister to the mountains now,
> And sister to the sun and moon,"

were a tempting target. Owen Seaman (later Sir Owen of *Punch*) wrote "A Ballad of a Bun" about the lady author who

> ". . . trafficked in the mart
> All for a mess of Bodley bun.
>
> "I cannot cut my kin at will,
>   Or jilt the protoplasmic germ;
> I am sister to the microbe still,
>   And second-cousin to the worm!"[7]

Harry Cust of the *Pall Mall Gazette* convulsed a dinner of the Omar Khayyám Club at the Burford Bridge Hotel with a version whose heroine was

> ". . . mother-in-law to the North Pole . . .
> And maiden aunt to the Equator."[8]

John Davidson was thirty-seven when he presented the public with this ballad. A Scotchman with a Scotchman's love of controversy, he looked, said Jepson, "in his short beard, silk hat and morning coat" like a "commercial traveller at loggerheads with the world."[9] For many years he wore a toupee but was quite insensitive about it and would hang it cheerfully on a tree when he went to bat in a cricket game. At the age of six

116

he had read Bunyan, at seven discovered Scott, and at twelve gone on to Shakespeare and Carlyle, all writers he considered to have had an influence on his own work. He thought *Don Quixote* the greatest prose in the world, he admired the poetry of Wordsworth, but in philosophy his man was Nietzsche. Though he later had an additional term at Edinburgh, he left school at thirteen to become a teacher. In 1885 he was married to Annie Smith. From his dominie's stool he looked longingly toward the world of letters, trying to write plays, a critic said, without having "invented a single plot, and scarcely . . . created a character"[10] in the eleven years of dramatic effort. In 1890 he decided to take his chance in London, where he made a slim living from writing reviews and articles, inching his way into the literary world in which he never was to feel quite at home. He had no patience with the affectations of society, but secretly he envied the man with an Oxford or Cambridge degree. He and his family lived in a house so small ("*the* smallest house in London," he said) that he had to rent a room over a greengrocer's shop in which to write. In 1894 he told Robert Sherard that "there was nothing as yet in the shape of an income."[11] But things were about to change. He was yielding to his impulse to write poetry. Though he had belonged to the Rhymers' Club he had not contributed to either of its volumes, but suddenly his poems began to sell. He boasted to Yeats, "I am writing verse. . . . I had been writing prose for a long time, and then one day I thought I might just as well write what I liked, as I must starve in any case. It was the luckiest thought I ever had, for my agent now gets me forty pounds for a ballad, and I made three hundred pounds out of my last book of verse."[12]

Davidson found in London his last and greatest inspiration. The first of his *Yellow Book* poems, "London," reflected the excitement of "The World's central fire-fountain."[13] His third, "Thirty Bob a Week," "a vigorous ugly bit of realism" according to the *Times*, concerned the plight of an underpaid London clerk. Davidson was not especially the poet of the lower classes, but he sympathized with all downtrodden humanity.

Davidson was now riding the crest. In the next number his

five-stanza "Proem to 'The Wonderful Mission of Earl Lavender,' " caught the public's fancy with its satire on the *fin de siècle,* and in Volume V his "Fleet Street Eclogue" rivaled the success of the "Nun." Nearly everyone liked the "Eclogue," though not everyone approved of its setting. Charles Eliot Norton wrote his daughter, "But the best poem . . . is 'A Fleet Street Eclogue,' by John Davidson, which was privately printed by Mr. Lane, the publisher of the 'Yellow Book,' when he was here a month or two ago, and which now appears alas! in the wretched Y.B. itself,—a vile place for a manly, hearty genuine-English poem, with no touch of decadence in it."[14]

Another poet who bore Davidson company in this volume was José Maria de Hérédia, just elected to the French Academy —the victor over Zola, who had been presented unsuccessfully for the twelfth time. Each year the French reviews and English ones, too, seethed with the question of Zola's election: his exclusion was a disgrace; his admittance would be a national insult. This time he had come nearer to success than ever before, but in the judgment of Edmund Gosse the Academy had made no mistake in electing Hérédia, and Watts-Dunton celebrated the event with a poem in the *Athenaeum,* "Apollo in Paris." For more than twenty years Gosse had admired the Cuban poet, born of a Spanish colonial father and a French mother, educated in Paris and founder with Mendès, Prudhomme, Coppée, and others of the *Parnasse Contemporain.* Among his friends Hérédia was a romantic figure. Anatole France called him the "young gentleman of fashion" whose "neckties were as splendid as his sonnets," and was jealous of the sonnets. Gautier is said to have declared, "Hérédia, I love you, because the name you bear is exotic and sonorous, and because you make verses that curl up at the end like heraldic scallops." *Les Trophées,* the book of sonnets in recognition of which he was honored by the Academy, had been circulated in manuscript before publication, achieving such a reputation that the entire edition was sold out on the day it was printed. "And now," said Gosse, "with the slender yellow volume of *Les Trophées* in his hands, he steps lightly up the staircase of the French Academy."[15] No wonder Heredia was welcome at the *Yellow Book* with his sonnet *"Fleurs de Feu."*

For such readers as could not trust their French, a translation by Ellen M. Clerke was provided ("Flowers of Fire"). Miss Clerke was a poet, linguist, and astronomer—a novelist too, for in 1902 she frugally used the title *Flowers of Fire* for a romance in which an eruption of Vesuvius was described.

The contributions of Symons, Dowson, and Johnson to this volume all bear an oddly personal and prophetic touch, only partly appreciated by their contemporary readers. Symons' poem *"Credo,"* eschewing the flamboyance of *"Stella Maris,"* with only a subtle glancing at "the joy of sin" pondered the futile pattern of life and death, "Since life, once lived, returns no more again." The last stanza,

> We are awake so little on the earth,
> And we shall sleep so long, and rise so late,
> If there is any knocking at that gate
> Which is the gate of death, the gate of birth,

foreshadowed Symons' preoccupation with the idea of death during the last years of his life. The feeling was not a moral cowardice, he insisted, but "an intellectual dissatisfaction with an enigma . . . which can be solved only when its solution is of no further use."[16]

Arthur Symons did not solve this enigma until 1945; with Dowson and Johnson the issue was more pressing. Ernest Dowson died in 1900 and since his death, the circumstances of his life and writings have been examined by various authors. In fiction he was the inspiration of Ridmer in May Sinclair's *The Divine Fire,* and of Ernest in Marian Plarr's *Cynara,* his own story. His biographers have included Desmond Flower, Robert Sherard, Victor Plarr, Edgar Jepson, John Gawsworth, and Mark Longaker. "There were certainly two Dowsons," his friend Victor Plarr said, "—one the vexed and torn spirit of the biographers . . . the other a Dowson *intime,* known, I venture to think, to very few, but by those few greatly loved."[17]

He has been longest remembered as the poet of *"Non Sum Qualis Eram Bonae sub Regno Cynarae,"* with these lines,

> I have forgot much, Cynara! gone with the wind,
> Flung roses, roses riotously with the throng,

from which, as is often pointed out, came the title of a best-selling American novel.

There was little to mitigate the tragedy of Dowson's life. From the time he became a man, his career is the story of a descent, physical and perhaps moral, which gained catastrophic tempo at the end. If Dowson had had a Watts-Dunton to limit his drinking and enforce an early bedtime, he might have been spared to round out his allotted three-score and ten. Would his bequest to poetry have been richer? It is a nice question.

Dowson came of more than respectable family. His father, who owned a dry dock at Limehouse on the Thames, had literary ambitions, but his energy was dulled by tuberculosis. From his mother, too, Dowson inherited a frail body and flickering vitality. Taken by his family to the French and Italian Riviera in a shivering search for winter warmth, Dowson perfected his French and Italian until each was like a native tongue. Latin he had already mastered. Later he used this skill in the translations by which he made his living, and less directly, but more significantly, in his approach to poetry.

He had five terms at Queen's College, Oxford, and with his mind set on a literary career went to London to help his father in the uncongenial business of the dry dock. Through his Oxford associations he was soon introduced to the group of young writers and journalists who represented the new literature in London. Dowson thought of himself as a prose writer, concerned like Crackanthorpe with the short story, but in 1890, when he produced for Herbert Horne and Selwyn Image, the directive minds of the *Hobby Horse,* his beautiful *"Amor Umbratilis,"* Dowson the poet was recognized. He became a member of the Rhymers' Club and contributed six poems to the first *Book.* "Dowson was the only poet I ever knew," said Arthur Symons, "who cared more for his prose than his verse; but he was wrong, and it is not by his prose that he will live, exquisite as that prose was at its best."[18]

During the early years of the nineties he collaborated with his friend Arthur Moore on a novel, *A Comedy of Masks,* and worked on translations from Zola and Richard Muther's *History of Modern Painting.* He also fell in love—not reasonably and sensibly with one of the young women journalists who would have made him a good wife, but hopelessly and absurdly with Adelaide Foltinowicz, the daughter of the restaurant keeper in Soho—"Missie" she was called, little more than a child, and quite insensitive to the devotion of this strange young man so far removed from her Polish-Catholic world. She did not even know that he loved her, though he played endless games of checkers with her father that he might be near her, tried to impress her mother with the suitability of the match, joined the Catholic Church to reach her spiritually, and dedicated his verses (1896) to her: "For Adelaide. To you who are my verses, as on some very future day, if you ever care to read them, you will understand." When she was seventeen Missie seemed grown-up, not quite pretty, with dark eyes and hair and no trace of Cockney accent. Then she began to notice the waiter, a plump German with a shiny face. Dowson was alternately encouraged and plunged into despair. When the strain became too great he sought solace from whatever *petite dame* presented herself. His apology for the defeat of his constant soul by his inconstant body has been immortalized in his poem "Cynara" (though neither Professor Longaker nor John Gawsworth believes that Cynara represented Missie).

John Lane had published Dowson's *Dilemmas* and wanted him at once for the *Yellow Book.* His "Apple-Blossom in Brittany" appeared in this volume. Dowson knew Brittany well. He had been on a walking trip there in 1890, and he returned again and again to its peaceful villages. Edgar Jepson thought he was "happiest in the remote Breton villages, whither he now and again withdrew himself, from which he wrote his most delightful letters. . . . The world went well with him there— as well, at any rate, as it ever could go with him."[19] Removed

121

from the daily torture of his visits to Missie he could fill his life with dreams, or more realistically accept the knowledge that his dreams could never come true. The background of this story was given metrical form in his poem "Yvonne of Brittany," and the pictorial representation of it by Conder is now owned by the Tate Gallery.

"Apple-Blossom in Brittany" was an idealized version of his own love story, written by the Dowson who burned candles before the shrine of the Immaculate, not the poet who drank libations to Aphrodite. Here Dowson, in the character of Benedict Campion, an English critic in love with his French ward Marie-Ursula, relinquished her to the convent, though a little pleading would have won her back to him; for he had persuaded himself with a *fin de siècle* submission that "any other ending to his love had been an impossible grossness, and that to lose her in just that fashion was the only way in which he could keep her always. And his acquiescence was without bitterness, and attended only by that indefinable sadness which to a man of his temper was but the last refinement of pleasure."[20]

But Dowson lost Missie to his rival the waiter, whom she married in 1897, and from then on things went badly with the poet. His father and mother had inconsiderately killed themselves, his father by drinking poison and his mother with a noose around her neck. Dowson lived much in France because it was cheaper, but he never had money enough for the drink he craved in ever increasing amounts.

Dowson's collaborator, Arthur Moore, also had a story in this volume. Coming from a distinguished family of artists (his father John G. Moore was a landscape painter and his uncles were famous in painting and sculpture), Arthur ignored heredity by choosing law as a profession and literature as an avocation. At Queen's College he and Dowson were drawn together by a regard for Henry James and planned to write a novel, which, begun in Brittany, was finished after Moore returned to London. They wrote alternate chapters on an outlined plot, and so similar was their style that few readers recognized any difference. However, Moore's story "Second Thoughts," his one appearance in the *Yellow Book,* moved with frank matter-of-factness to a cheerful ending very different from Dowson's. When Missie was married, Moore did his friend another service: he went to the wedding and carried Dowson's gift.

Like Dowson, Lionel Johnson had been at Oxford, had later joined the Rhymers' Club, and contributed to this third volume of the *Yellow Book* a piece which was self-revealing. His essay "Tobacco Clouds" defended the Ivory Tower he had chosen, but it acknowledged the weakness in his philosophy. Johnson had gone to public school at Winchester, a place he loved "intensely,"[21] and where in spite of an absorbing interest in philosophic ideas he served as Senior Prefect, Prefect of Chapel, Editor of the *Wykehamist,* and member of the mission committee. He also played feminine roles for the Shakespeare Society. One of his younger friends at the school with an interest in poetry was Lord Alfred Douglas, whom he introduced to Wilde, an act that he later regretted. Evidence of Johnson's youthful intellectual approach to life was shown in *Some Winchester Letters of Lionel Johnson,* published after his death by Lord Russell, onetime husband of Elizabeth "of the German Garden."

At New College, Oxford, he was president of the Essay Society, advocated Home Rule, considered joining the priesthood, wrote poetry, and acknowledged his four literary passions to be Aeschylus, Lucretius, Victor Hugo, and Newman. George Santayana was one of his friends, the "Son of Holy Avila," who later said Johnson was typical of many of the learned and gifted at Oxford, "saturated with affectations."[22] Douglas Ainslie was another who remembered evening discussions of life and religion with Johnson, lasting so late that the visitor had to depart through the window. "At about midnight Johnson would put down the *Apologia* and say: 'I think, my dear Ainslie, that the labourer is worthy of his hire, especially if he toil through the silent watches of the night. Shall it be champagne or *sal volatile* and water?' "[23] Ainslie invariably chose the former; Johnson sometimes had both. Johnson admitted in a letter to Miss Guiney that his most persistent wrongdoing at Oxford had

123

been "climbing over gates or walls after hours. . . .If I live to be Pope I shall carry the mark of that sin upon me; a scar on my wrist, which was run through by a spike upon the wall."[24]

In 1890 he came up from Oxford to make his living in London by writing. Though he preferred poetry he found criticism more profitable, contributing to the *Anti-Jacobin* and the *Hobby Horse* and writing polished, scholarly reviews for the weeklies. A reverent disciple of Pater (the subject of his last poem), he believed that English should be written with the preciseness of Greek or Latin. Punctuation was a fetish with him and he complained to Miss Guiney, "When I'm dead, the colon won't have a friend in the world but you."[25] Two of Johnson's best lyrics were read aloud to the Rhymers' Club, "Dark Angel" and "By the Statue of King Charles at Charing Cross." A visitor said the reading reminded him of "a mouse's recitative," but Rhys did not think the comparison fair, though in contrast with the "incanting of Yeats or the plain military style of Rolleston, his melic mode was not in tune with church-warden pipes and bowls of punch."[26] Johnson for his part was sometimes pained by Dowson and Symons; he thought "Cynara" called for a libation of cyanide, and lectured Dowson on chastity.

Lane had published Johnson's six essays on *The Art of Thomas Hardy* and now promised an edition of Johnson's poems. Mathews suggested that Rothenstein do a lithograph of the poet for a frontispiece, but Johnson demurred: "Too great an honour! . . . the very portrait itself would blush: which is undesirable for a lithograph."[27]

Johnson was small and slight—"little" was the adjective often applied to him, though he did not like it—and his face was boyish. Miss Guiney said his smile was "pleasant as a bookish fay's."[28] It was rumored that on his first appearance at one of Gosse's Sunday afternoons his host took him for a friend of his young son's and asked him if he'd like to go and play in the garden. Oscar Wilde was reported to have said that "any morning at eleven o'clock you might see him come out very drunk from the Café Royal, and hail the first passing perambulator."[29]

When he wrote for the *Yellow Book* he was living at 20 Fitzroy Street and his rooms, austerely neat and simply arranged, were full of books. He loved books, collected them, treasured them, read them. He liked to show them to his friends, affirming proudly, "In my library I have all the knowledge of the world that I need."[30] A member of the Catholic church (he had joined in 1891) he was well received by the Meynell circle, and admired Mrs. Meynell, though he deprecated "the one mortal sin" of her "damning incapacity" to love dogs.[31] To another Catholic friend, Katharine Tynan Hinkson, he gave his unconditional devotion because of her pug dog, Paudeen. He often spent Sunday at the Hinksons' cottage after going to mass with them at Hanwell.

Religion with its ritual was a necessity for Johnson, though he had turned from the priesthood, perhaps influenced by Newman's pronouncement, "I have always considered the profession of a man of letters a third order of the priesthood." Now Johnson turned to the church for solace of an inner turmoil not then realized by his associates. His quiet reserved exterior gave little sign of his unhappiness and even when he was much under the influence of drink he had the manners of a gentleman. But more and more often his friends called to find his door barred, though the milk sat sour upon the threshold, and feared the shadow of his Dark Angel was upon him.

A foreboding note was struck in his *Yellow Book* essay, "Tobacco Clouds," in which he dwelt with appreciation upon the mode of life he had chosen—"to walk about the old city, with 'a spirit in my feet,' as Shelley and Catullus have it, of joyous aims and energies; and to speed home to my solitary room over the steep High Street; in an arm-chair, to read Milton and Lucretius, with others." He did not see the face of any woman in his Tobacco Clouds; he believed in his "measured way of life; its careful felicities, fashioned out of little things"; he liked to meditate upon the classics and the grace of Rome. One sentence in the concluding paragraph pointed with dreadful prescience to the tragedy ahead: "True, should the terrible issues come upon me, demanding high courage, and finding but good temper, then give me your prayers, for I have my misdoubts."[32]

His friend Santayana said of him, "He was a spiritual rebel, a spiritual waif who couldn't endure the truth, but demanded a lovelier fiction to revel in, invented or accepted it, and called it revelation. In part like Shelley, in part like Rimbaud, he despised the world and adored the unreal."[33]

Only occasionally could Lionel Johnson be found at the Crown, where poets, painters, and dramatists gathered every evening in the saloon bar to talk "learnedly about the ballet and Walter Sickert and the latest art movement in France and Edmund Gosse's last insincerity,"[34] but Theodore Wratislaw, though not a member of the Rhymers', was often there. Aubrey Beardsley thought Wratislaw "really not a bad sort," and when his *Caprices* was published in 1893 considered it "rather a clever volume of verse,"[35] but a reviewer in the London *Bookman* hoped the poet would live to regret it, finding little to commend except the limiting of the edition to one hundred copies.[36] Wratislaw too liked to dine at Jimmy's and in this volume of the *Yellow Book*, he recounted a meeting with a recent portrayer of Salomé,

> . . . in the babbling room agleam
> With scarlet lips and naked arms,

and so on.

The rather depressing effect of Volume III, an effect in which Crackanthorpe, Ella D'Arcy, and C. S. had no small part, was, however, enlivened by Max Beerbohm and his "Note on George the Fourth," which won kinder words from the critics than usual; by Kenneth Grahame's satire on women's rights, "The Headswoman"; and by Charles W. Dalmon's rollicking verse on "Parson Herrick's Muse."

But the most diverting feature of this volume was the hoax perpetrated by the art editor. Beardsley liked practical jokes, and he was slightly tired of being told he could not draw. In addition to his acknowledged group of four drawings, the whimsical "Portrait of Himself" in bed, "Lady Gold's Escort," the wonderful "The Wagnerites," in which a number of celebrities including Mrs. Browning have been recognized, and *"La Dame aux Camélias,"* he inserted two other pictures of quite different character over assumed names, "Mantegna" by "Philip Broughton" and "From a Pastel" by "Albert Foschter." The critics were completely taken in. While treating Beardsley's signed work with their usual disdainful ridicule, several took pains to praise the contributions of Broughton and Foschter. The *St. James's Gazette* commended highly the artistic qualities of Philip Broughton, and the *Saturday Review,* finding Beardsley "as freakish as ever, and in precisely the familiar kind of *capriccio,"* considered Mr. Broughton's "Mantegna" a "drawing of merit" and Foschter's "Pastel" a "clever study."[37] The *National Observer* scorned Beardsley but thought the "Pastel" a "monstrous clever caricature" and had pleasant praise for the "Mantegna.[38] According to the sympathetic Beerbohm, one innocent was even brash enough to advise Beardsley to "study and profit by the sound and scholarly draughtsmanship of which Mr. Philip Broughton furnishes us another example in his familiar manner."[39]

This was sweet revenge for the young man whose spirit had secretly shriveled under adverse criticism. Penrhyn Stanlaws called upon him just after the unmasking of Mr. Broughton and Mr. Foschter. "I never, before or after," Stanlaws reported, "saw him in such a happy frame of mind. His boyish ruse had been successful, and a thorn had been removed."[40]

Chapter XIV

IF IN VOLUME III Harland gave a hearing to the doomed young men, in Volume IV he turned more generously to the hopeful young women. He welcomed such deliciously feminine contributors as Graham Tomson (soon to be Mrs. Marriott Watson), Olive Custance (later wife of Lord Alfred Douglas), Edith Nesbit (Mrs. Hubert Bland), Ménie Muriel Dowie

(Mrs. Henry Norman), Leila Macdonald (Mrs. Hubert Crackanthorpe, Evelyn Sharp (later—much later—Mrs. Henry Nevinson), Marion Hepworth Dixon, and Dolf Wyllarde, to the company of such poets as Le Gallienne, Dr. Garnett, C. W. Dalmon, John Davidson, and Charles Newton-Robinson. The last-named was doubtless of Lane's choosing, for Newton-Robinson's father had been one of the great connoisseurs and collectors of the Victorian period and his son had continued this interest. By profession Newton-Robinson was a barrister, educated at Cambridge, and interested in land development, but the art he loved most was poetry, by which he wished to be remembered.[1] His "Modern Paraphrase" of Horace's *Car.* I. 5 in this volume was included in the Bodley Head edition of his *Viol of Love* (1895).

To the art of this number Sickert contributed a Victorian landscape of the "Hôtel Royal, Dieppe," one of his favorite subjects, and portraits of Le Gallienne and George Moore; Rothenstein, a head of John Davidson (Max congratulated Will on the subtle way he had handled the poet's toupee, but the artist averred he had not noticed it; Max later caricatured a bald Davidson); Wilson Steer, "A Lady in Grey," and a portrait of the currently popular pianist Emil Sauer; and Beardsley, two extremely provocative drawings, "The Mysterious Rose Garden" and the "Repentance of Mrs. ****," a double-page "Frontispiece for Juvenal," and a "Portrait" of the actress Miss Winifred Emery (Mrs. C. Maude).

Dolf Wyllarde, a London journalist, educated at King's College, belonged to the grateful group sponsored by A. P. Watt, the pioneer literary agent. If he had placed her "Rondeaux d'Amour," concerned with passion flowers, golden moments, and blossom-tinted bowers, in Volume IV, he did not establish her as a regular *Yellow Book* contributor, for these rondeaux with their varying refrain, "before the night," "during the night," and oh, dreaded debacle, "after the night," were her one appearance. However, Miss Wyllarde went on to become a successful novelist, with some forty titles to her credit before her death in 1950.

Graham Tomson, "beautiful," Mrs. Pennell called her, "reminiscent of Rossetti in her tall, willowy slimness, with her long neck like a column and her great halo of black hair and her big brown eyes, appealing, confiding, beseeching,"[2] was a poet, and the wife of Arthur Tomson, an artist and member of the New English Art Club, who suffered from the same disease that threatened Beardsley and Harland. She also wrote fashion notes for the *National Observer* and appeared in the *Pall Mall Gazette*. "Vespertilia" was her first poem in the *Yellow Book;* William Archer thought it the best thing she had written. It began,

> In the late autumn's dusky-golden prime,
>   When sickles gleam, and rusts the idle plough,
> The time of apples dropping from the bough,
> And yellow leaves on sycamore and lime,

and such lines as

> When the round moon is low and the night-birds flit,
> When sink the stubble-fires with smouldering flame,
> Over and o'er the sea-wind sighs her name,
>   And the leaves whisper it,

illustrated the Rossetti-like quality of her verse. She had a true ear for rhythm and rhyme and could manipulate sounds pleasantly as in "The Isle of Voices" in Volume V:

> Fair blows the wind to-day, fresh along the valleys,
> Strange with the sounds and the scents of long ago;
> Sinks in the willow-grove; shifts, and sighs, and rallies—
> Whence, Wind? and why, Wind? and whither do you go?

She had poems in seven volumes of the *Yellow Book* and of frequent contributors among the women poets she has most claim to be remembered.

Though she had been a good friend of the Pennells, when the break with her husband occurred the Pennells sympathized with Arthur, and she and Mrs. Pennell ceased to see each other. "As to the Tomson Watson business," Joseph Pennell wrote his wife from Rome, "I only hope *you* wont [sic] be run in as a witness in any scandal . . . it is a nasty business—and I'd keep out of it altogether."[3] The members of the Henley group all took sides when Rosamund left her husband and went to live with the young journalist from New Zealand, H. B. Marriott Watson, of the *Pall Mall Gazette,* in order to obtain her divorce under English law. In the nineties, such an open act of defiance required courage. By the time her second poem appeared in the *Yellow Book* she had legal right to the name Marriott Watson, and dropping the Graham, became simply Rosamund.

Edmund C. Stedman commented to Robert Bridges, "The Armytage-Tomson-Watson sequence is interesting. Well, a woman who can write such ballads has a right to be her own mistress—to touch life, one may say, at as many points as she cares for?"[4]

So the Marriott Watsons went to live in Shere, Surrey, and there Lewis Hind found her one morning, domestically shelling peas in the garden while composing a poem. She was, he said, "a gifted poet, a charming woman, and a remarkable hostess."[5]

Her new husband was also a busy writer. He had worked for Frederick Greenwood on the *St. James's Gazette,* then gone to Henley on the *Observer.* He collaborated with Barrie on a biographical play, *Richard Savage,* which was Barrie's worst failure in the theatre. But Marriott Watson's lifework was fiction; he wrote some forty novels, none of which is remembered today. His style was forced, his dialogue was awkward, and he had little gift for characterization. Though he toiled diligently in the field, he never could raise a winning crop. "Himself the sweetest, gentlest of creatures," said Lewis Hind, who shared a house with him in St. John's Wood before his marriage, "never angry, usually amused, he had no sympathy with any kind of violence. Yet he loved to write about gallant 'Galloping Dick' highwaymen, ladies with dark eyes and noble natures, and bucks."[6]

But he did not contribute stories of this sort to the *Yellow Book.* These tales were painfully and mawkishly realistic, or melodramatic and unconvincing. Only one, "A Resurrection" in Volume VIII, gave evidence of ability. "Marriott Watson," said Grant Richards, "used to sail very close to the wind in his short stories, and I heard that legal notice might be taken of their flourishes, but his manner was of the Restoration and I dare say the rumours were the invention of his enemies. As far as I know he was guilty of only one indictable offence: he warmed his Burgundy."[7]

E. Nesbit's poem "Day and Night" in this volume recorded the duplicity of Earth, who smiled while the sun caressed her but only waited the coming of her lover night. As Mrs. Hubert Bland, E. Nesbit presided over the strangest household with which any contributor could have been connected. Had her *Biography,* published by Doris Langley Moore in 1933, appeared as a work of fiction in the nineties, the righteous Messrs. Smith would have banned it from their counters as an assault on British respectability. But their censorious glances would have been directed at the handsome, insouciant Mr. Bland and not at E. Nesbit.

E. Nesbit, poet, novelist, and "nearly perfect writer of books for children," had married Hubert, ardent young Fabian and journalist, when she was twenty-two. She began writing for *Sylvia's Home Journal,* contributed to the "Wares of Autolycus" column, and collaborated with her husband in work for the Fabian Society, of which he was treasurer and Shaw and Havelock Ellis were leading spirits. Her first book of poems, *Lays and Legends* (1886), was praised by Swinburne in a letter to Philip Bourke Marston, the blind poet who had been engaged to her sister Mary. Children came fast into the Bland establishment, not only her own but those which resulted from Hubert's extramarital adventures, two of whom Edith adopted. Edgar Jepson testified that during the ten years he knew Bland, the *Star* reviewer never had more than two or three mistresses at a time, and "no one can say that that was excessive," said the broadminded Mr. Jepson, "for the days of Edward the Peacemaker."[8]

H. G. Wells, who lived not far from Edith and Hubert at Dymchurch, remarked on the "primitive strand in Bland's make-up. He was under an inner compulsion to be a Seducer—

on the best eighteenth century lines. . . . The astonished visitor came to realize that most of the children of the household were not E. Nesbit's but the result of Bland's conquests, that the friend and companion who ran the household was the mother of one of the young people, that young Miss so and so, who played Badminton with a preoccupied air was the last capture of Hubert's accomplished sex appeal. All this E. Nesbit not only detested and mitigated and tolerated, but presided over and I think found exceedingly interesting."[9]

But it disturbed and depressed her too, and in her unhappiness she turned to Bernard Shaw for comfort. He was near with his flying bicycle, and his rough tweed shoulder offered sturdy assurance. She wrote him passionate love poems and was ready for any recklessness, but Shaw managed to steer her "through her infatuation . . . finally keeping her just off the rocks."[10] In the end she compromised on friendship, a long and enduring one. Her literary career seemed to thrive on adversity, for she needed money to support a growing family, and she tried her hand at many kinds of writing, finding some success at each. Though she herself believed she had a poetic gift (her "Little Brown Brother" is still remembered), she was a better critic of the verse of others. She was one of the first to appreciate *The Shropshire Lad*, sending a copy to Henley, who found the poet "very monotonous" but admitted that the man had "something to say and a very distinguished way of saying it."[11] In 1896 she became one of the poetry critics for the *Athenaeum*. Her pen was so facile that Henley warned her against settling into the "market woman's canter,"[12] but she was at her best as a writer of stories for the young; her *Bastable Children* may prove as immortal as *Little Women*. When it was reprinted in 1928 Christopher Morley wrote the foreword. As a small boy Noel Coward filched a coral necklace to get the money to buy her *Magic City* and when years later he confessed the incident to her, she "was delighted."[13]

During 1958, her centennial, a number of her children's books were re-issued, and Noel Streatfeild published an appreciation of her magic way with the young.

John Lane brought out her *In Homespun* by his Keynotes Series and thought her "the handsomest women when she was young I ever met."[14] Richard Le Gallienne remembered the "boyish, bird-like charm of 'E. Nesbit.' "[15] She was called by her friends a real Bohemian, an advanced woman who smoked cigarettes, cut her hair, and didn't wear corsets—the climax of the unusual for her generation. Laurence Housman, who did the frontispiece for her *Pomander of Verse* (1896), was her devoted friend for years, though they finally parted over the question of suffrage and a "growing uncongeniality" between him and Bland. In 1910 she pained Evelyn Sharp by refusing to sign an authors' memorial to facilitate the passage of a Conciliation Bill for Women's Suffrage. "I am for adult Suffrage," she wrote, "but primarily my political interest is all for Socialism, and I do not wish Socialism to be endangered by an extension of the franchise to a class of women mainly Conservative."[16] Housman thought Hubert was to blame for her attitude.

She had many old friends like Davidson, Le Gallienne, Grant Allen, and Andrew Lang. To her grateful circle of younger friends belonged Arthur Watts of *Punch*, Gerald Gould, H. H. of the *Observer*, E. M. Forster, and Noel Coward. When she died in 1924, C. L. Graves paid her tribute in *Punch*:

> You pass, but only from the ken
>   Of scientists and statisticians,
> To join Hans Christian Andersen,
>   The Prince of all the good Magicians.[17]

Ménie Muriel Dowie, who had been present at the initial *Yellow Book* dinner, and was listed in the Prospectus, was obliged to wait until Volume IV to see her offering between the golden covers. Indeed Miss Dowie's period of waiting had been even longer, for in April, 1893, the *Bookman* reported that "Mrs. Henry Norman (Ménie Muriel Dowie) has just written a new story entitled 'Wladislaw's Advent,' which will be published in one of the illustrated monthlies. Mrs. Norman, we understand, proposes to continue to write under her maiden name," and the date attached to the story in the *Yellow Book* was September, 1891. More than three years is a disheartening wait for any young author. But Miss Dowie had not been idle, for her novel *Gallia,* called "alarmingly modern," came out in 1895, and was gently ribbed in the Chicago *Chap-Book.*[18]

Ménie Muriel, granddaughter of Dr. Robert Chambers of Edinburgh, was considered an advanced woman, too, but adventurous in physical daring rather than in marital experiments. In 1890 her first book, *A Girl in the Karpathians,* recounted her own experiences on a trip through the remote villages of Hungary and though *Munsey's,* often ill-natured about British initiative, hinted that she had never been there at all but had compiled her book in the British Museum,[19] evidence supported the enterprising traveler. In acknowledgment of this achievement she was asked to edit *Women Adventurers,* an account of the exploits of such pioneers as Madame Velazquez, Hannah Snell, and Mary Ann Talbot, for which she wrote so unenthusiastic a preface that one reviewer commented, "The editress is a modern heroine, and feels the superiority of modern ideas, the higher motives of modern adventures."[20]

Henry Norman (Harvard, 1881), whom she married in 1891, was something of an explorer himself—he had at least crossed the Atlantic—and was literary editor of the *Chronicle,* for which she also wrote. They set up housekeeping in a new red brick house on Grosvenor Road, Westminster, where Ménie, tall and slight, with masses of blond hair which she dressed fantastically, according to Marie Belloc Lowndes,[21] gave amusing dinner parties and indulged her passion for collecting lustreware. She had two other stories in the *Yellow Book,* one of these, "My Note-Book in the Weald" in Volume XII being extremely readable. "Wladislaw's Advent" was included in *Some Whims of Fate* (1896). In 1897 her son Nigel was born. In 1905 Henry Norman was knighted, but Ménie did not share the title, since she and Henry were now divorced and she had married another explorer, Major E. A. Fitzgerald, in 1903. After his death she resided in Winchester until the outbreak of World War II; in 1941 she went to live in Tucson, Arizona, remaining in the dry and sunny south land until her death in 1945.[22]

Another contributor who waited long to see his work in the *Yellow Book* although he had been present at its inception at the GROB, was Charles Conder, but his "Design for a Fan," a picture of two eighteenth century ladies before a window, graced this volume. Conder, called a "nonchalant dreamer" by MacColl[23] and "that strange bird" by Sickert—MacColl liked him; Sickert did not, saying, "I can't drink and I am a snob"[24]— had been discovered at Julian's studio in Paris by Will Rothenstein, who was impressed with the unusual charm of his paintings. Will's son, John, later wrote *The Life and Death of Conder.*

Though English, Conder had spent his early youth in Australia, painting his famous "Hot Wind" there when he was only twenty-two. When Rothenstein knew him in Paris he was a heavily built young man with blue eyes and a blond beard and hair which, parted in the middle, fell over his eyes, a soft voice, and a personality attractive to women, who often tried to save him from his vices. Puvis de Chavannes was his lodestar among French painters, but in England it was Whistler, though Whistler disliked this disciple. Aside from his painting, which unfortunately often took last place, Conder loved women and drink. Sometimes wine made him gay and lovable and gracious; at other times his mood turned black and quarrelsome, and he found grievances against his best friends. Besides having a tiff with Harland, he fell out with Rothenstein and challenged Dujardin, friend of George Moore, to a duel. When Conder complained to the French painter Jacques Blanche of the insults he was always receiving, Blanche reminded him, "But . . . did not our dear Master Whistler glory in his battle against the Philistines?" "Yes," Conder retorted, "the Philistines of those days were Ruskin, Holman-Hunt, Dante Gabriel Rossetti; nowadays my enemies are nobodies, simple pamphleteers and such persons as Claude Phillips and Humphry Ward."[25]

Conder painted on silk, and his fans became collectors pieces, Mrs. Jack Gardner having bought the first one he painted. Wilde was much attracted by the fans. "Dear Conder!" he said. "With what exquisite subtlety he goes about persuading someone to give him a hundred francs for a fan, for which he was fully prepared to pay three hundred!"[26] But Joseph Crawhall, the Scotch painter, exclaimed over them, "Umph. Whiskey and Watteau."[27] Indeed Conder's "visions of a voluptuous dreamland, in exquisite vaporous colours"[28] seemed to belong to the eighteenth century rather than the 1890's.

His *Yellow Book* reproductions suffered from lack of color, but he was glad to have them appear there. Beardsley liked Conder and tried to get Lane to let him do a book cover. Later Smithers, publisher of the *Savoy*, gave him *La Fille aux Yeux d'Or* to illustrate.

At the turn of the century Conder was married to an attractive woman with money, and life went more pleasantly. But he could not stay sober for long. Then he began to quarrel with her, his instabilities increased, and in spite of cures and opportunities to work and exhibit, his melancholy was not to be shaken off. After his death, Rothenstein, his earliest and most faithful friend, admitting that "his richly suggestive art is at present underrated," expressed confidence that "its vitality . . . will blossom again in men's eyes."[29]

If the editors were sometimes tardy in getting the work of their contributors into print, sometimes the work was not forthcoming. Though Mrs. Harland said that "no one, old or young, no one with the slightest claim to artistic achievement but chose to make his bow in its pages with the very best he had to offer,"[30] the *Yellow Book* was not always successful in its wooing.

Some, like Henry James, were tempted by its gold, for the quarterly was known to pay well, especially in the first lush year. Le Gallienne once had its generous rates painfully impressed upon him when he read a poem on Stevenson to John Lane, who promptly offered him twenty pounds for it on behalf of the *Yellow Book*. Le Gallienne refused with regret. He had already sold the poem elsewhere for five guineas.

But neither gold nor kind words could lure some of London's leading *littérateurs* to the *Yellow Book*. A definite hostility toward the new journal had sprung up in certain circles, and much of the opposition stemmed from the Catholic household of Alice and Wilfrid Meynell. Alice Meynell, essayist and poet, was the mother of five children and, it was whispered, a more meticulous writer than housekeeper. Desmond McCarthy declared he would not want to read a cookbook by Mrs. Meynell.[31] Wilfrid, her husband, a small brisk man, was editor of *Merrie England,* an organ of the Catholic Church, bearing the hopeful motto, "We shall try to revive in our own hearts and in the hearts of others, the enthusiasm of the Christian faith." The Meynells had discovered and reformed that strange mixture of genius and dissipation, Francis Thompson, the poet. The Meynell establishment was a devout one, and Mrs. Wharton, who once lunched there, was "struck by the solemnity with which this tall thin sweet-voiced woman, with melancholy eyes and rather catafalque-like garb, was treated by her husband and children."[32] She was called "the properest woman in London" by another American, Gertrude Atherton,[33] and Max Beerbohm feared that she would in time "become a sort of substitute for the English Sabbath,"[34] so sacred in the eyes of all London was Mrs. Meynell. Her dislike of the obvious was well known, and she had excluded Gray's "Elegy" from her Anthology of English verse on that ground; George Meredith approved the exclusion of that "funeral march headed by the undertaker."[35]

Mrs. Meynell was a person of great influence in certain Romanist and Victorian coteries. She had a following, a salon, and influential friends in the literary world, among them Coventry Patmore, so fervently devoted to her that he could write, "At rare intervals the world is startled by the phenomenon of a woman whose quality of mind and heart seems to demand a revision of its conception of womanhood . . . one of the very rarest products of nature and grace—a woman of genius."[36] He thought she should be Poet Laureate. Later Patmore's adulation was a little dulled by Mrs. Meynell's "great new friendship with George Meredith," who made her offerings of white violets.

To this "phenomenon" Harland addressed his plea: "I think I have heard that your feeling for that periodical [the *Yellow Book*] is not one of unbounded enthusiasm, *raison de plus* why you should lend a hand to the bettering of it. Won't you do us one of your exquisite essays?"[37] But in spite of this tactful approach, Mrs. Meynell answered nay. (When Patmore's passion had eventually threatened her carefully preserved decorum, Mrs. Meynell had rebuffed him in a poem, printed anonymously in the *Pall Mall Gazette* and beginning:

> Why wilt thou chide
> Who hast obtained to be denied? . . .
> My sacred Nay.[38])

Harland had no better success with Coventry Patmore, to whom he wrote flatteringly, "I wish I could persuade you to let the *Yellow Book* have a poem. It would turn red with pride."[39] But the aged author of *The Angel in the House*, following the example of *Ma Dame*, would have no part in altering the complexion of the *Yellow Book*. Francis Thompson made the same decision, as did George Meredith, for though a hopeful note in the New York *Bookman* hinted, "We hear, on authority that should be good, that a contribution from Mr. George Meredith may shortly be expected within the boards of the *Yellow Book*,"[40] the promise was not fulfilled.

So the cloud of disapproval created by the Meynell circle hovered darkly above the golden orb in John Lane's sky. Since the Bodley Head published the books of Alice Meynell and Francis Thompson, their opinion was important to Lane, how important was soon to be demonstrated.

If some birds were shy and refused to be caught, others fluttered against the bars in an effort to be admitted to the gilded cage. Gertrude Atherton sent Harland "The Striding Place," a story she had written of the West Riding, but Harland declined it on the ground that it was "far too gruesome." As the young American considered it one of her best stories, she experienced an allowable sense of triumph when the *Speaker* accepted it.[41] And Cunninghame Graham objected vehemently, "Fancy the *Yellow Book* refusing a thing of mine on the ground that it was immoral. Cretins, liars . . . ."[42]

Harland always insinuated—more, he said it publicly as the

"Yellow Dwarf"—that some of the bitterest criticism of his quarterly came from the editors who had not been invited to contribute or from their "young men" whose work he had refused. He probably referred, among others, to Henley and Frank Harris. Harris' name appeared on the original list of contributors, but no work by him was included in the *Yellow Book*, and Charles Whibley, Charles Sibley, Richard Pryce, and Israel Zangwill were likewise called but not chosen. In a letter to the *Westminster Gazette*, a certain minor poet, signing himself a "Pariah on Parnassus," said that, though praised by Browning, included by Traill in "his immortal roll," and damned with faint praise by Le Gallienne, he had been rejected by the editor of the *Yellow Book*;[43] and years later Stephen Gwynn thought it necessary to explain, "I never even offered work to the *Yellow Book*."[44]

Four volumes of the quarterly appeared with Aubrey Beardsley as art editor. Though the back cover remained unchanged, he made new designs for each front cover and title-page. Shortly before Volume IV came out he showed the drawing for the cover to a reporter, saying, "I think it the best of the four and my friends think so too. A lot of people will fall in love with that baby," a small tot done with charming simplicity and no touch of the bizarre so usual in his little figures. Asked how long it had taken him to do it, he answered, "About an evening. As I told you, drawing is easy, because it's my life."[45]

On the whole, criticism of Beardsley tended to become less severe as respected and important English artists threw their influence in his favor. But in the mind of the public, uncertain and suspicious since the Marquis of Queensberry, father of Lord Alfred Douglas, had called at the Albemarle Club and left his card with its misspelled but damning inscription for Oscar Wilde, the illustrator of *Salomé* was linked with the author, and the implications of Bearsley's art did not allay this uneasiness. During the libel suit which Oscar brashly brought against the Marquis there was tension and unrest among certain Bodley Head authors, and when the suit failed and Oscar Wilde was

arrested on a charge of homosexual practices, the storm broke
that was to end Beardsley's career as art editor of the *Yellow
Book.*

Chapter XV

IN 1904, WHEN John Lane wrote the introduction to Beardsley's *Under the Hill,* he explained the parting of Beardsley
from the *Yellow Book:* "Beardsley's defect as Art Editor was
Youth. He would not take himself seriously: as an editor and
draughtsman he was almost a practical joker, for one had, so to
speak, to place his drawings under a microscope, and look at
them upside down. This tendency on the eve of the production
of Vol. V., during my first visit to the United States, rendered
it necessary to omit his work from that volume . . . and it must
be frankly confessed that, when he severed his connection with
the magazine, the quarterly suffered an irretrievable loss."[1]

Perhaps in the years which had elapsed since the event he
so euphemistically described, John Lane had convinced himself
that this was the explanation for the removal of the Beardsley
drawings from Volume V. If so, Lane was the only person with
any knowledge of the affairs of the Bodley Head who did not
admit that Beardsley had been fired.

An unfortunate chain of happenings brought about Beardsley's banishment from the quarterly for which he had worked so
zealously. If any one link had been different, the result might
have been less disastrous, both for Beardsley and the *Yellow
Book,* for John Lane spoke truly of its loss.

In April, 1895, Lane, accompanied by Le Gallienne, had
gone to America to investigate the possibilities of opening a
branch of the Bodley Head in the States. A number of other
English visitors happened to be in New York at the same time—
including Max Beerbohm, who had gone over with his half-
brother Beerbohm Tree, Professor Sylvanus Thompson of the
Finsbury Technical College, and Rudyard Kipling, then living
in Vermont. When Lane made his plans for the American trip
Beardsley wanted to go with him, and had written his friend

of Brighton Academy days, G. F. Scotson-Clark in Boston, that he was coming. Joseph Pennell alerted his pretty sister-in-law, Helen Robins of Philadelphia: "Aubrey Beardsley is coming over I believe with John Lane and if you promise to lose your heart to him I'll give him a letter to you."[2] Beardsley confirmed the report in an interview. "Yes, I am going to Boston and New York, probably in early April. I think the sea will do me good. I'm a poor sailor but I can stand it. My object is partly business and partly health. Perhaps I may lecture if anybody cares to hear me."[3] Suggestions of his lecturing appeared in several American papers; "the Rambler" in the *Bookbuyer* noted that he was coming to explain his "own peculiar theories of art," and after some discussion of Beardsley's unorthodox choice of models, concluded that if the eccentric artist wished to lecture in Boston, he doubtless would receive all the appreciation he deserved.[4]

But Beardsley did not go to America. Perhaps he could not face the reception in Boston; more probably his health prevented, for he had been having hemorrhages again; certainly he had work enough in England to keep him busy, but his failure to carry out his intention had unfortunate results.

When Lane sailed for the States the Wilde libel suit against the Marquis of Queensberry had not come up. Lane naturally was interested in the case, for the Bodley Head published Wilde's books and, in the mind of the public, Wilde's writings formed part of the testimony against his character. The subject matter of his prose and his theories of art, as well as his personal code of morals, were regarded with suspicion by many people who *thought* the worst of Oscar Wilde but did not yet *know* they were right. Under this cloud of imputation and disapproval Oscar made no pretense of changing his way of life, apparently unworried by the opinions of middle-class moralists, superior to the accepted standards of good and evil. He could not believe that final judgment would be made against him. But the British public waited and looked for the necessary proof.

Wilde's friends realized the situation better than he. During

141

the rehearsals of Wilde's play *A Woman of No Importance*, Beerbohm Tree had received from an anonymous source a copy of a letter of Wilde's which he had felt it his duty to hand to the playwright.[5] John Lane was only too aware that evidence against Wilde was not lacking, for he had known Edward Shelley, a young clerk at the Bodley Head, and sometimes when he thought of the broken drifting wreck the boy had become, he did not sleep at night. Wilde had met Shelley at the offices in Vigo Street and become interested in the lad, who loved books and hoped vaguely to write. Charmed and flattered by the attention of the great man, Shelley did not know or care where it was leading him; only when Oscar passed on to other friendships did the boy realize his shame. He had lost his place at the Bodley Head, his health was shattered, and his remorse and self-accusation took the form of a torturing melancholia. His life lay about him in ruins and John Lane understood that the ruins were of Wilde's making.

Lane had not alienated his profitable client—that would have been unbusinesslike—but he had heartily concurred in the decision to keep Wilde from the *Yellow Book*. He knew that Wilde's suit against the Marquis was based on sham and that the flimsy foundation was likely to collapse under the buffeting that would be brought against it. If Wilde fell, no one would buy his books and his publisher would suffer. Lane congratulated himself that he had kept his cherished quarterly unsullied by that contaminating touch.

Lane landed in New York on a cold, foggy Sunday morning in April and felt the damp chilliness penetrate his good British tweeds. He was met by his friends and some New York editors, who made the welcome proposal of a hot breakfast and steaming coffee. John Lane felt more cheerful, but first he wanted to know about the Wilde suit. Someone handed him a paper and he read the headline, "Arrest of Oscar Wilde, *Yellow Book* under his arm."[6]

Lane never forgot that shock. "It killed *The Yellow Book*, and it nearly killed me," he said dramatically years later.[7] He was entirely unprepared for this bracketing of Wilde with the *Yellow Book;* it was something he had never foreseen.

Until then he had taken without flinching the many jests about the morals of the Bodley Head. They had been good advertising and he had laughed them off. But this was no laughing matter. He fretted at the meagerness of the accounts in the New York papers. He learned that the boy Shelley had been a witness, and it had been published to the world that Shelley had met Wilde at the sanctum of art and letters on Vigo Street. Over breakfast, for which he now had litttle appetite, Lane discussed his predicament with Tree and Le Gallienne. Perhaps it was not too late to take the step he had sometimes contemplated and rid the Bodley Head of Oscar Wilde. After breakfast he sent a cable to Chapman, in charge during his absence, withdrawing the Wilde books. That done, he breathed a little easier, but not for long.

Early the next morning came a cable from Chapman backed with a message from two of Lane's authors, William Watson and Wilfrid Meynell, urging that Lane part not only from Wilde but from Beardsley as well, and while he was worrying over that, a second cable arrived, this time an ultimatum from Watson, signed by six authors. Either Lane must remove Beardsley or they would take their books elsewhere. In desperation Lane cabled Chapman for further information, and anxiously awaited the answer which did not come. He searched the American press trying to find an explanation for the inclusion of Beardsley in the demand. Kipling, Le Gallienne, and Tree agreed with him that the decree against Beardsley seemed most unjust and they could not understand the reason for it. Lane was forced to believe that Beardsley had been implicated in some way not apparent in the American reports.

The usually level-headed Devonshire man found himself spinning like a top with indecision. Worried as he was about Beardsley he was also concerned with his personal involvement, since Elkin Mathews had got neatly out from under with a letter to the *Times* of April 8: "You mention in your report that the young man Shelley was introduced to Mr. Oscar Wilde by one of the partners of the publishing firm of Mathews and Lane, Vigo Street. Allow me to say that I know nothing of Mr. Oscar Wilde except in a business capacity by publishing his 'Lady Windermere's Fan,' &c., and never introduced Shelley or any person to him in my life, nor knew that he had been introduced. I may mention that for several months I have ceased to be the publisher of any of Mr. Oscar Wilde's books."[8]

Anxious to clear his own coattails as well, Lane hurried to send a cable through the editor of the New York *Times*, a friend of Henry Norman's, denying that he had made the damning introduction. Though the information at hand did not seem to justify acceding to Watson's request, he was beset by dreadful alarm as to what might happen to the business if he held out against these influential writers. Still Chapman sent no word of explanation, and Lane felt he could wait no longer. In a flurry to do something he cabled once more; he protested the ultimatum against Beardsley, but left the decision to Chapman, suggesting he take the advice of Watson and Meynell. Poor Chapman was already taking orders from them.

Miss D'Arcy always blamed Chapman for what happened, but the pressure against him had been overwhelming. On the night that Wilde was arrested and driven to the court in a hansom cab he carried a fat yellow volume under his arm. Angry spectators took it to be the *Yellow Book*. Actually it was a French novel, but none of the outraged crowd stopped to find out. They swarmed into Vigo Street, gathering outside the Bodley Head, home of the *Yellow Book* and of *Dorian Gray,* and manifested their disapproval so thoroughly that the neat bow window was in need of a glazier when they departed. Sticks and stones, shouts and curses left Chapman in no doubt as to the public temper. William Watson, a poet Lane valued highly, had been closely identified with the *Yellow Book* and had a poem in print for the coming number. In Lane's absence he assumed his responsibilities. He was a man of nervous temperament; in fact he had shortly before recovered from a breakdown. Mrs. Humphry

Ward, a pillar of respectability, had told her friends some time previously that William Watson was determined to make a protest over the state of things at the Bodley Head. As a matter of fact, Mrs. Ward was determined that he should make it. She was an important literary figure in the nineties; her current novel often topped the best-seller lists. A Victorian preoccupied with uplift she went about, so Lewis Hind said, "Doing Good with an Air (the Arnold Air),"[9] for she was a niece of Matthew Arnold. Though Matthew Arnold had been surprised to discover she had written a story, Mrs. Ward had made a success of fiction, her reputation being enhanced by one of Gladstone's panegyric post cards.

Watson's first protest had been a letter to Harland. But Harland was in Paris; with the new *Yellow Book* rolling off the presses, he and his wife had taken their usual springtime holiday across the channel, escaping the yellow fog and London's shock at the Wilde downfall. Then Watson, abetted by Wilfrid Meynell, went to work on Chapman. Poor Chapman was an easy prey. When Watson cabled Lane, he had the support of the Meynells and Francis Thompson, as well as Mary Ward. The little group whom Harland had urged to better the *Yellow Book* were now doing it in their own way.

"If Harland had only been at the Bodley Head," Miss D'Arcy mourned, "everything would have been different. He would have made Chapman wait until Lane got back. But Chapman was a little man and he didn't like Beardsley. He took this opportunity to be important."[10]

It was true that Chapman did not try to make a stand against William Watson's feverish excitement. He listened agreeably to Meynell's sober cautioning; he examined the profit sheets on Mrs. Meynell's books with respect; and he cast the die which terminated Beardsley's connection with the *Yellow Book*. But once the deed was done he could not bring himself to tell Lane about it. He ignored Lane's frantic reiterated questions. He had no time, he thought, to spend in justifying his action. The new and reformed *Yellow Book* had to be made and the task was on his shoulders.

145

These seem to be the circumstances of Beardsley's dismissal as nearly as they can be put together so long after the event, with none of the actual characters involved present to testify. It was all in the dark ages. In the years of radio and trans-Atlantic telephone, such misunderstanding would be impossible.

Nothing is more futile than to conjecture what might have happened had some circumstance been different, but the temptation here is great to point out that if Beardsley had been in America with John Lane to settle the publisher's doubts, or if Lane had stayed in London at that particular time; if Elkin Mathews had been at the Bodley Head to carry on in Lane's absence, or if Harland had greeted the spring in Hyde Park instead of the Bois de Boulogne; if the redoubtable Mrs. Ward and the irreproachable Mrs. Meynell had been less zealous for the public good; or, finally, if Oscar Wilde had picked up any other book than a yellow-backed novel when, half-tipsy, he started for the Bow Street Police Station, the ending might have been otherwise.

Afterward John Lane regretted the course he had taken—or failed to take—but he could not bring himself to change it. He knew he had done Beardsley a rank injustice and that Beardsley in no way subscribed to Wilde's philosophy of life. But the public in general did not know this. They took the esoteric quality of Beardsley's art as the outward manifestation of an inner debauchery like Wilde's. They thought the man who wrote *Salomé* and the man who illustrated it were kindred souls and that both represented the *Yellow Book*. Against this false and unfounded belief Lane might have made a stand and saved Beardsley. Instead, groping in the dark fog of uncertainty, he let Chapman take command and watched him toss overboard the first mate, an unwilling Jonah, to the whale of public opinion.

The wheel had come full circle. Beardsley had kept Wilde from the *Yellow Book;* now the tables were turned. Wilde had hated the *Yellow Book* and would have been quite willing to do it harm, and its callow youth of an art editor as well, but

146

when a man is at the mercy of a pursuing vengeance he has little time to think of how he may strike at someone else. His own plight is concern enough. It was with no forethought that Wilde carried the yellow-backed novel. Yet all unwittingly, when he associated himself in the public mind with the *Yellow Book* he set in motion the forces which doomed Aubrey Beardsley and eventually finished the *Yellow Book*.

People had laughed at Aubrey's superstition that Wilde brought him bad luck. There was little laughter that April morning when Chapman ordered the Ballantyne presses stopped and Beardsley's designs removed from the *Yellow Book*. As a journalist of the period Byronically remarked, the *Yellow Book* "turned gray in a single night."[11]

Chapter XVI

THE APRIL NUMBER of the *Yellow Book,* due on the fifteenth, did not appear until the thirtieth, its tardiness a pointed reminder that all was not well at the Bodley Head. When it was finally delivered to the stalls and booksellers, the Beardsley plates had been removed from the volume, except, by a curious oversight, from the rear cover, where his four enigmatic women smiled as blandly as ever over the table of contents. Apparently, in the scramble of providing a front cover, new title-page, and plates for the interior, Chapman had overlooked this last item; here Beardsley clung with a grim finality before disappearing forever from the *Yellow Book*.

One copy of this volume, printed before the Beardsley plates were canceled, has survived, originally the property of Edmund Gosse. On the flyleaf he had written: "Of this dummy copy of the Yellow Book, in its suppressed form, the cover, with Aubrey Beardsley's design, and the four rejected plates by the same artist, were given me by the Editor, Henry Harland. Hardly another copy exists, so rigorously were they destroyed, when W. Watson telegraphed that either Beardsley must withdraw, or he should. The cancelled list of Contents, and his own poem, were given me by Watson." Harland's original inscription was below: "This is, so far as I know, the only copy of this suppressed Yellow Book in existence."[1]

A number of years ago this book was sold at the Anderson Galleries in New York and is supposed to be in the United States. All the Beardsley drawings from this number were later published elsewhere; none of them was in any way different from others which had appeared in the quarterly.

Without Beardsley the general aspect of Volume V was restrained, and several London papers took note of its altered form. The *Times* declared it was "remarkable for the absence of Mr. Aubrey Beardsley's *foudroyante* skill" and "a general tone of striving toward healthiness not hitherto noticeable."[2] The *Westminster Gazette* observed that "among the pictures, Mr. Aubrey Beardsley's are conspicuous by their absence,"[3] while the *Sketch,* remembering Foschter and Broughton, started off on a false scent which must have afforded the deposed art editor a moment of bleak amusement. "Mr. Aubrey Beardsley as we all know, is an absentee—temporarily no doubt—from the *Yellow Book,* and yet I seem to recognize a certain pencil, in a drawing of a child with a hoop, in the current number. . . . Is Mr. Beardsley masquerading again?"[4]

In the States the *Bookman* pointed out, "Certain occurrences in London of recent date, which it is not necessary to mention more specifically, have had a very marked influence upon the tone of the present number of the *Yellow Book.* . . . Mr. Beardsley's name does not appear among those of the artists, and the other regular contributors appear to be more or less depressed in mind."[5]

The contributor most frequently linked with Beardsley was missing too, Max Beerbohm. In Boston with his brother, Max explained airily to a reporter, "I promised to write something for the *Yellow Book* but I have nothing in this number. I am not a worker, you know."[6]

The regenerated *Yellow Book* opened with the triumphant stanzas of William Watson's "Hymn to the Sea." He had raised his standard victoriously at the very portal; only to some it looked like the white flag of surrender. There was, to be sure, a certain slow-moving dignity, sonorous phrasing, and undeniable truth in this long poem, but its total effect was so overweighted and cumbersome that many a poetry lover must have thought John Lane had made a bad bargain in exchanging this for Beardsley's deft and sparkling magic. It has been remarked that Lane was prouder of William Watson than of any other poet of the Bodley Head; certainly his thoughtful, stately verse found a response in Lane's heart. One evening in America at the Stedman home, Lane had given the American poet a folio of Watson's poems to read aloud and as he listened to the sonnet

> Life is still life, not yet the hearth is cold,

Margaret Fuller, Stedman's secretary, saw tears slip down Lane's cheeks.[7]

William Watson's father had been a merchant in Liverpool, and William's early youth was spent on the Mersey, a locality which gave color to his verse. When he was seventeen he paid a visit of homage to Tennyson on the Isle of Wight. His first book of poems, *The Prince's Quest*, was published in 1880, and Helen Thomas remembered how he used to stride up and down her father's study (her father was James Ashcroft Noble, then in Liverpool) reading alternate passages of Milton and *The Prince's Quest* and setting one against the other. In 1887 he had gone to London, where he got encouragement from Hutton and Townsend of the *Spectator*, Walter Besant, and W. D. Howells. In the spring of 1891 Grant Allen, whose attention had been called to Watson by Edward Clodd, praised him in the *Fortnightly Review*.[8]

Watson was proud of his English heritage and had small patience with the Bodley Head poets who courted the Muse from over the channel, a sly wench not to be trusted. "The countrymen of Shakespeare," he wrote, "have no need to borrow either their ethics or their aesthetics from the countrymen of Baudelaire."[9]

149

When Tennyson died in 1892, Watson, along with Kipling, Swinburne, Coventry Patmore, William Morris, Edwin Arnold, Alfred Austin, and yes, Mrs. Meynell, had been mentioned for the laureateship, but even the recommendation of Gladstone was not enough to procure it for him, though he apparently believed he was to receive it. Perhaps his disappointment affected his health; at any rate he became gloomy and melancholic, finally suffering a complete breakdown which was variously reported in the press. A writer in *Munsey's* declared that "one day something gave way in his brain and he lost consciousness of his own acts. He stopped in the park and accosted a royal personage. He was hustled away by the police and his past was looked into. It was found he was insane and . . . a poet."[10] English papers regarded this as a "scurrilous attack" on one of England's leading poets, but whatever the nature of his illness the London *Bookman* reported in April, 1893, "Mr. William Watson has returned from Switzerland, and has joined his mother at Southend. All his admirers will be glad to hear that Mr. Watson has completely recovered, and that so long as he keeps from overwork or undue excitement there is, we are assured, no danger of a return of his malady,"[11] and in November, 1894, his admirers were once more promised that Mr. Watson had "quite recovered his health" and was in town again.[12]

He was a handsome man with an aquiline nose and sweeping mustaches; Edgar Jepson thought he looked like one of Ouida's guardsmen. Miss Hepworth Dixon called him the "most amiable of poets," but thought he had something of "the air of a provincial."[13] Lane was ever on the lookout for a suitable wife for him, and many a Bodley Head authoress was critically considered by the Eros of Vigo Street. Watson was pleasant and friendly with these candidates and continued to live quite happily with his mother until 1909. Then in an impetuous two weeks he met and married an Irish girl, Maureen Pring. Some years later Sydney Cockerell at Cambridge thought she was "wonderfully plucky" with a "wretched little house . . . two children and a poet to keep in trim."[14]

Watson had no wish to be a sequestered poet, a romantic recluse from the affairs of the world. He was impressed with "a sense of the very vastness of man's relation with a world which once looked so simple and intelligible." Of England's foreign policy he wrote,

> Best by remembering God, say some,
> We keep our high imperial lot.
> Fortune, I fear, hath oftenest come
> When we forgot—when we forgot.

He offered knowledge as the solution for the English-Irish feud, and indited epistles to North America on behalf of a better understanding between the two continents. "The Purple East" dealt with the Armenian atrocities. But he sometimes descended to personalities and once epitomized Margot Asquith as "The Woman with the Serpent's Tongue,"

> Who half makes love to you today,
> To-morrow gives her guest away.

For that, Richard Le Gallienne took him to task as "The Poet with a Coward's Tongue."[15] He paid warm poetic tribute to Shelley, Keats, Wordsworth, and Matthew Arnold, in elegies said to have won him a grant of one hundred pounds from the Civil List pensions. Though he admired the poets of the past and was kind to the poets of his youth, he belittled the newcomers of his later years, calling the Georgians, for instance, "long-haired nincompoops"[16] and their verse cheap and slipshod. For their part the Georgians criticized his mechanical rhythms and artificial phrases. In 1928 he was persuaded by his wife to publish his *Selected Poems,* the last of seventeen volumes of poetry. "Nobody reads me any more," he said sadly. "I do not think it will be any good."[17] He was right and Lady Watson (he had been knighted in 1917) bought up most of the edition so that he should not know how dismally it had failed. His friendship with Lane ended in a quarrel, and they were never reconciled. His last years were saddened by poverty as well as failure.

Luckily he could not foresee this unhappiness in the mo-

151

ment of his proud triumph over Beardsley. "William Watson," said Beardsley wryly, "the best poet ever made."[18]

Though Max had done nothing for this number, one of his former classmates at Charterhouse School was present; at the time, however, the two old Carthusians did not know each other. G. S. Street had gone from the Charterhouse to Exeter College and then to London, where he wrote for Henley's *Observer*. His first book, *Miniatures and Moods*, had been well received in 1893, but his *Autobiography of a Boy*, published by Lane just before his appearance in the *Yellow Book*, assured him of a perpetual niche in the corridor of the nineties. These passages selected by the author from the life of Tubby, the boy with a "smile of infinite indulgence," were issued in pale grey-green cloth that shone like watered silk, and the book had already gone to four editions. The prevalent idea that Tubby had some resemblance to Street himself was borne out by his portrait by Francis Howard in Volume XI. As a memorable delineation of the aesthetic type, Tubby ranks with Esmé Amarinth of *The Green Carnation* and Reginald Bunthorne.

Will Rothenstein eventually brought Max and Street together one evening at Solferino's. At first, Will said, "Each aspired to be more coldly aloof than the other; but finally warmth crept into the party, and there and then a close friendship began."[19]

Street became one of Lane's regular readers, and he was a critic as well as a writer of satiric fiction. To this volume he had contributed an essay, "Mr. Meredith in Little," based on an examination of *The Tale of Chloe and Other Stories*. If Harland could not entice the great man himself into the *Yellow Book* he could present him vicariously, and hardly a number passed without some reference to the "now mute old brother." In Volume VI Street wrote on Ouida.

Max himself, writing on Ouida a few years later, said, "At length it occurred to a critic of distinction, Mr. G. S. Street, to write an 'Appreciation of Ouida,' which appeared in the *Yellow Book*. It was a shy, self-conscious essay, written some-

152

what in the tone of a young man defending the moral character of a barmaid who has bewitched him, but, for all its blushing diffidence, it was a very gentlemanly piece of work, and it was full of true and delicate criticism. I myself wrote, later, in praise of Ouida, and I believe that, at about the same time, Mr. Stephen Crane wrote an appreciation of his own in an American magazine . . . three intelligent persons had cracked their whips."[20] (Crane wrote about her in the January, 1897, *Bookbuyer*, having read *Under Two Flags*, which to his surprise he liked.) Max had written in *Tomorrow*, comparing Ouida's champagne with Mrs. Meynell's cowslip wine.

In *Some Notes of a Struggling Genius* (1898) Street said that "American readers do not read my books,"[21] but an American reviewer had read enough of his *Episodes* (1895) to decide that they were "brilliant and audacious enough to satisfy the most eager student of shady human nature."[22] Gradually Street turned his attention to the theatre, succeeding H. G. Wells as dramatic critic on the *Pall Mall* and eventually becoming His Majesty's Examiner of Plays.

In spite of William Watson's suspicion of the countrymen of Baudelaire, his poem had ushered in a volume in which considerable space was given to them, for Anatole France's first story to be published in England, "*L'Evêché de Tourcoing*," an advance chapter of his *Histoire Contemporaine*, was introduced by a critical article on the famous Frenchman by Maurice Baring. The story was presented to the select circle of *Yellow Book* readers in its original tongue and not in translation. Anatole France was at this time little more than a name in England, but this attention in the talked-about quarterly extended his vogue and led to a profitable association with John Lane, who later brought out his works in English. Some years later when France visited the Bodley Head he noticed on the wall a picture by Gertrude Hammond used in Volume VI, of a young woman gazing in some embarrassment at the *Yellow Book* in the hands of a handsome gentleman. "Why is she blushing?" asked the

Frenchman with a twinkle. "He is evidently reading your story to her," Lane answered quickly.[23]

In his *Puppet Show of Memory*, Maurice recalled the circumstances which led to his writing his essay on Anatole France. He was at Edmund Gosse's in the winter of 1895; Harland was there and the conversation turned to the French author. Baring quoted some passages from *Le Livre de Mon Ami,* with which Harland was not familiar, and he suggested that Baring write an article for the *Yellow Book*. It was an appreciative criticism —one of the first on Anatole France in the English press. The young author was still an undergraduate at Cambridge, just entering upon a literary career and when Edmund Gosse praised the article, saying that "there was a unique opportunity for anyone who should make it his aim and business to write gracefully and delicately about beautiful and distinguished things," he decided to continue as he had begun.[24] In carrying out this resolve through the years he produced some fifty books in the fields of poetry, fiction, travel, drama, biography, literary history, criticism, translation, and essay, beginning with *Hildesheim* (1899) and ending with *Russian Lyrics* (1943).

In the middle of the nineteenth century the Duc de Richelieu was supposed to have said, "There are six great powers in the world, England, France, Austria, Prussia, Russia and the Baring Brothers." Maurice was the eighth child of the first Lord Revelstocke, formerly Edward Charles Baring, head of the banking firm of Baring Brothers. Maurice attended Eton, Cambridge, and Oxford, and after failing repeatedly in mathematics, entered the Foreign Office as Secretary in 1896. While he was at Cambridge, he helped found a paper, the *Cambridge A.B.C.,* which lasted for only four numbers but had the distinction of a cover designed by Beardsley. Though the youthful editors had paid ten guineas for the drawing and loudly defended its authenticity, the undergraduate world persisted in considering it a clever takeoff. At Cambridge he was a great friend of Edward Marsh, son of the Cambridge professor. Baring was known for what Archibald Marshall called his "ingenious buffoonery,"[25] and Gosse was the object of one of his practical jokes. Over the signature of his tutor Boughey, he sent Gosse a telegram: "M. Baring passed away peacefully this afternoon." Gosse, quite shaken by the tragic message, hastened to break the news to Baring's brother and directed Arthur Benson at Cambridge to discover the sad circumstances. Only then did he realize that his leg was being pulled. His natural reaction to this gruesome jest may have been the reason for the term in the Baring Language, a secret code belonging to Maurice and his friends, of "An 'Edmund' . . . a display of undue touchiness."[26]

If mathematics was difficult, languages came naturally to Maurice. He won the Prince Consort prize for French at Eton and it was said Russians used to appeal to his authority on points of their grammar. When he lay dying he repeated the Rosary in French, Russian, Spanish, German, and Latin. (Presumably one of these languages would have been understood by the Deity.)

As a young man in Paris he had been a great friend of the divine Sarah, like so many other young Englishmen of the period, but he took his admiration more seriously than some; and she and the stage were his first great love. Russia was his second; he went there in 1901 and continued afterward to study and interpret this enigmatic country. In 1904 he gave up the diplomatic service to become a foreign correspondent. Maurice's third great love was the Catholic Church, into whose membership he was received in 1909. He became one of the great Catholic novelists (in his line have descended Graham Greene and Evelyn Waugh), and a member of that friendly Catholic triumvirate which included Belloc and Chesterton, though the latter's conversion to Catholicism came later than Baring's. "Gilbert could not be hustled," said Baring.[27] Chesterton admired Baring as a man who could celebrate his fiftieth birthday "by dancing a Russian dance with inconceivable contortions and then plunging into the sea in evening dress."[28]

Baring's success as a writer came with the publication of his first novel when he was thirty-seven, for in spite of his prolific versatility he had hitherto failed to achieve a following. He wrote Vernon Lee in 1920, "I have a public of three. You used to be a fourth."[29] Vernon Lee knew and understood him better than most, and paid tribute to his "dry bony style, which looked like no style at all," and his "superb English power of understatement." Coulson Kernahan thought his poetry should be remembered. He had two sonnets in Volume VIII.

Early in the last war his house in London and all his books were destroyed by a bomb, and he went to make his home with his friends the Lovats at Beaufort Castle, Scotland, where he died, after a long invalidism, on December 15, 1943, apologizing to his hosts for the inconvenience of dying so close to Christmas.

Beardsley was responsible for the inclusion of another Frenchman in this volume, the artist Constantin Guys, whose work, though he had died in 1892, had just been exhibited at the Galerie Georges Petit in Paris. Now his black and white of three dandies of a bygone day in tall hats and tail coats demonstrated to the public the editor's awareness of the current topics in art, even though the moment as such was not to be considered in the *Yellow Book*. This painter of Victorian life was not only a countryman but a friend of Baudelaire, who in 1863 had written enthusiastically of his pictures, though in deference to the artist's morbid shyness he did not name him except as "M. G." Living in England in the 1840's, Guys had been an artist for the London *Illustrated News* and a friend of Thackeray, but that friendship ended when Thackeray mentioned his name in print. Even Baudelaire's encomium had not saved Guys during his lifetime from neglect, but the poet's prediction, "We may safely wager that, in but a few years, M. G.'s drawings will become precious archives of civilized life,"[30] has been fulfilled. His drawings have increased steadily in value to become a source of information for many purposes, not least among them the costumes of Roland Petit's ballets.

As though to make up for the noticeable lack in art, Volume V contained more literary items than any previous number, twenty-seven authors appearing in the index, but Ada Leverson's story "Suggestion," with its interest-catching first sentence, "If Lady Winthrop had not spoken of me as 'that intolerable, effeminate boy,' she might have had some chance of marrying my father,"[31] was read with special interest by the literary wiseacres, who knew of Mrs. Leverson's satires of Wilde in *Punch* and her friendship for the playwright. Less than a week after the *Yellow Book* was out, she was to prove her mettle by an act of courage which might have given John Lane cause to blush.

In February, 1895, Wilde had given Mrs. Leverson a box for the opening night of his play *The Importance of Being Earnest,* to which she had invited, among others, Aubrey Beardsley and his sister Mabel. Between the acts the author himself, suave and assured, had joined them, making the box which held the distinguished sportsman, Ernest Leverson, his smart-looking wife, the cadaverously thin young artist, and the pretty girl with the flaming hair, the center of all eyes. Eagerly and a bit suspiciously the pit watched as Oscar received their congratulations on his third successful play. Three months later Oscar Wilde the outcast, released on bail from Holloway Prison, where he was waiting trial, and refused admittance at any London hotel, was finally forced to seek refuge at the house of his mother, to which he came, as his brother Willie explained, "tapping with his beak against the windowpane, and fell down on my threshold like a wounded stag."[32] From this unhappy metaphorical situation he was rescued by Ada and Ernest Leverson, who invited him to stay in their house until his trial. At a moment when Wilde's friends were dropping him with record-breaking haste, the invitation demonstrated courage and a fine disregard of Mrs. Grundy. When after nearly three weeks with them, hidden away on the third floor, he left to go to his trial, he said anxiously to Mrs. Leverson, "If the worst comes to the worst, you'll write to me?" and when it came, she kept her promise.[33] Oscar's replies were published in 1930 as *Letters to the Sphinx.*

157

Mrs. Leverson, who died in 1936, has been introduced to a new generation with the reprinting of her novels in England and a first publication of two in America; Osbert Sitwell paid homage to her memory in *Noble Essences*.

Born Ada Beddington in 1865 of literary and artistic upper-class parents, she had married Ernest Leverson, a wealthy, big-game-hunting sportsman, and become the mother of a son and daughter. By the middle of the nineties, she was not only a writer herself, contributing sketches to *Punch* and *Black and White* and interviewing celebrities for the *Sketch,* but also the friend of many writers; and to her drawing room came such celebrities as Henry James, John Lane, Grant Richards, George Moore, Max Beerbohm, and Aubrey Beardsley. Her conversation was bright and entertaining and her *bons mots* were quoted by people who collected witticisms.

When someone suggested to Mrs. Leverson that a woman whose corn-ripe hair was one of the wonders of London, might possibly dye it, Mrs. Leverson lifted her eyebrows in surprise. "No, I don't think so. But I'm sure she darkens the roots a little."[34] A certain youth had left England under a cloud, she said, but his father had provided the silver lining.[35] Oscar Wilde called her the wittiest woman in the world and indeed her epigrams, sallies, and paradoxes were similar to his own.

When Wilde was released from Reading Gaol, she went with others on a cold dim morning to welcome him back. "Sphinx," he said, "how marvellous of you to know exactly the right hat to wear at seven o'clock in the morning."[36] She treasured the remark, and in *The Limit,* Herry de Freyne said to his cousin who had met him clandestinely at daybreak in the garden, "How did you know exactly what to wear, Val? . . . to choose the *exact* right dress to put on to meet your cousin at dawn in the orchard?"[37] Oscar's note to her next day that said, "When I think that Sphinxes are minions of the moon . . ."[38] also found an echo in Harry de Freyne's "Fancy you, Valentia, a minion of the moon."[39] Brilliant and amusing as she was, she hoarded witticisms and knew that a good idea could bear repeating.

158

The Limit, the third of her novels, was published in 1911; until 1906 she had confined herself to short stories and conversation. In 1911 A. E. Housman wrote to his brother, "The female novel which you gave me when I saw you last was very readable. I forget its name but it contained an indiscreet portrait of Somerset Maugham."[40] Hereford Vaughn in *The Limit,* the playwright whose personal success had not embittered him, was too close a parallel to Maugham not to be noticed. However, her friendship with the original seemed to withstand the indiscretion, and his picture always stood in her drawing room.

Coleridge Kennard was a favored friend and Max Beerbohm was devoted to her, matching his wit against hers, advising her on the decoration of her house, and corresponding with her so briskly that in the 1940's some sixty of his letters to her were offered for sale by an English bookseller. When Theodore Dreiser went to England he wrote Grant Richards, "I am reserving Thursday evening for Mrs. Leverson."[41] George Moore admired her, though he admitted she was a "patterist" of the first rank—as were, in his opinion, Balzac and Shakespeare; and he likened her comprehension of life to Jane Austen's.[42] She continued to write short stories during the 1920's, and when she stopped publishing she turned her attention to helping young writers like Osbert Sitwell and Coleridge Kennard. The Sitwells became her close friends.

Old age was not kind to Ada Leverson. She who had so long been young and charming like her own heroines, hated to admit the years. She grew deaf, a sad predicament for a wit. One by one the circle of her old friends dropped away, some by chance, some by death, some by choice, cruelly, like George Moore. A few days before her death, her daughter, keeping up a cheerful pretense, said to a caller, "Isn't Mother wonderful! She'll soon be the same as everyone else." With an effort Ada Leverson sat up in bed. "That, thank God," she said, "is the one thing I shall never be!"[43]

Both her *Yellow Book* stories (her "Quest of Sorrow" was in Volume VIII) were adroit amusing tales with neat satiric touches very welcome among the heavy realism and purposeful narratives of other writers.

Chapter XVII

IT IS HARD today to realize the impact of the Wilde trial on the London of the nineties. Wilde had been a figure of importance in the literary world, a talented poet, a successful playwright, and, at his best, a charming personality. He was courted for his prestige and sought after for his wit and brilliance. Young writers and artists had been pleased by his friendship, and many of them enjoyed his company and conversation without being touched by his moral idiosyncrasies. When Wilde broke on the witness stand before the inescapable implication of his own testimony, and the public's long-nurtured suspicion turned to certainty, these friends suffered too. The shadow of doubt fell on all with whom he had associated. Many young writers, poets, and painters fled to the Continent. "We were very unpopular," said Arthur Symons with a shrug of his shoulder. "There was a great exodus. We all went; we didn't dare stay."[1]

Those who remained were treated by an aroused society with a hostility which did not distinguish between the guilty and the innocent; as in the case of Beardsley, the suggestion of evil was taken for the fact itself. Similar plumage was noticed on many birds, and much of it was yellow. A number of reasonably upright individuals were unfairly condemned in this wholesale arraignment.

On the other hand, some members of the judicial public were convinced that not all had been done that should have been. Though Oscar Wilde and Alfred Taylor, on trial with him, had drawn prison terms, the British bulldog still sniffed suspiciously at other portals. Robert Bontine Cunninghame Graham, who had commented that Oscar had not shown much pluck at the trial, but that no one expected he would, wrote a friend, "What I want to know is if Oscar is so great a criminal, why are not the people prosecuted whose names the judges know, as they were *written* to them?"[2] And Richard Aldington, a critic of a later generation, said, "Oscar Wilde so bitterly expiated the sin of laughing at the British middle classes. (If every other male homosexual had been proceeded against at the same time with the same ferocity, not to say perjury, there would not have been enough gaols to imprison them.)"[3]

Poor Lionel Johnson suffered more than most, for the Wilde trial brought to a climax his long-festering remorse at having brought the two principals together. Since Johnson had admired *Dorian Gray* and had written its author a set of laudatory Latin verses, *"Benedictus sis, Oscare!"* it was natural that he should take a younger brother poet, Lord Alfred, to call upon the friend of Pater's in Tite Street. That was in 1891. Then year by year he had watched the boy he remembered at Winchester change into a silly corrupt youth, a dissipated disciple of Wilde. His second poem to Wilde, a sonnet, "I hate you with a necessary Hate," asked bitterly:

> Say you my friend sits by me still? Ah, peace!
> Call you this thing my friend? This nameless thing?
> This living body, hiding its dead soul?[4]

For the period following the collapse of Wilde's suit against the Marquis of Queensberry and the trial and sentence of Wilde himself, London's literary and artistic figures who had not vanished to the Continent stepped quietly and carefully. Artists behaved toward their public with anxious deference, essayists leaned heavily upon morality, pointing out the deplorable state of modern literature, and poets were suddenly dazzled by the beauties of nature, the lark and the chaffinch and the hedgerow.

In the *Nation* a writer called attention to this new prudence: "In the latest English poetry, even in that which comes from the Bodley Head and the very headquarters of the *Yellow Book,* we see a reaction towards the standards of the Academy. It is well known that people sooner grow surfeited of the bizarre than even of the tame; and just now the Bodley Head is plainly disposed to forswear sack for a while, and live cleanly. The temporary outcome is, of course, commonplace."[5] Or as *Punch* put it,

When life, each quarter, is made out
    Of still more jaundiced hue,
The needy bard must joint the shout,
    His verse be jaundiced too: . . .

This sere and yellow poesy
    Faint draws its sickly breath,
And—doctors say—Society
    Will soon acclaim its death: . . .[6]

Haldane Macfall has described the circumstances which led to his meeting Beardsley at this time. One of the great English magazines, he said, had attacked the entire field of modern art and literature, using the Oscar Wilde scandal as the basis of its charge. Macfall, who wrote art criticism under the name of Hal Dane, replied to the article by saying that Wilde and Beardsley were not England and had small claim to represent all British genius. He spoke of the art of both men as possessing no manhood and being "effeminate, sexless and unclean." Wilde was in no position to resent the charge, but Beardsley could and did. Momentarily springing to life from the abyss of gloom to which he had sunk since his expulsion from the *Yellow Book,* he penned one of his biting letters and sent it to *St. Paul's,* in which Hal Dane's indictment had appeared.

114 Cambridge Street, S. W.
June 28th

Sir,

    No one more than myself welcomes frank, nay hostile criticism, or enjoys more thoroughly a personal remark. But your art critic surely goes a little too far in last week's issue of *St. Paul's,* & I may be forgiven if I take up the pen of resentment. He says that I am "sexless and unclean."

    As to my uncleanliness I do the best for it in my morning bath, & if he has really any doubts as to my sex, he may come and see me take it.

Yours &c.
Aubrey Beardsley[7]

Beardsley was dissuaded from publishing the letter, however, on being shown Hal Dane's answer, in which he assured the young artist that he was not "overwhelmed with his rollicking devilry in taking his morning bath—a pretty habit that will

soon lose its startling thrill of novelty if he persists in it."
Strangely enough, this exchange of pleasantries led to a friendship between the two men and Macfall became Beardsley's
biographer.

Beardsley had need of friends in those dark months of the
early summer of 1895. Elkin Mathews, Lane's former partner,
had come to his aid almost at once with a commission to draw
the frontispiece for Walt Ruding's *An Evil Motherhood*. Beardsley gave him the "Black Coffee," one of his unused *Yellow
Book* plates, but Mathews did not like it or Lane objected; at
any rate Beardsley later wrote of it, "The dreadful thing was
a blaze up with Lane-cum-Mathews, & a drawing to be produced
at the sword's point."[8]

But in spite of Mathews' good will, sporadic commissions
could not give Beardsley the financial security he had enjoyed
as editor of the *Yellow Book*. His house in Cambridge Street
proved too expensive, and in July he gave it up and the family
moved to St. James's Place. Beardsley's mood was bitter and he
brooded over the injustice he had suffered, drank too much, and
lived in a way dangerous to his health. Yeats in *The Trembling
of the Veil* mentions his unhappiness: "Beardsley has arrived
at Fountain Court [where Yeats was then living] a little after
breakfast with a young woman. . . . He is a little drunk and
his mind has been running upon his dismissal from *The Yellow
Book*, for he puts his hand upon the wall and stares into a mirror. He mutters, 'Yes, yes, I look like a Sodomite,' which he
certainly did not. 'But no, I am not that,' and then begins rail-
ing. . . ."[9] He was hurt and angry, but he was a little frightened
too. He had seen what could happen to one who lived by an
independent code of morals, and his own vaunted impervious-
ness to public opinion was shaken. According to Catholic friends
of a later date, he now felt the first leanings toward the Church
as an authority on which to depend. The priest and poet John
Gray became his "dear mentor." He made attempts at writing,
for he had always wanted to try poetry and stories. But he was
soon so ill that any work was impossible. Without the money

163

advanced him by André Raffalovitch he might have starved. His friends thought he was dying.

In the middle of the summer Arthur Symons went to see him and feared he had come too late, for he wanted to interest Beardsley in a new magazine to be issued by Leonard Smithers as a rival to the *Yellow Book*. Symons was to be editor and he offered the responsibility for the art to Beardsley. As he broached his mission, Beardsley's haggard face brightened amazingly. He was full of ideas and promised eagerly to devote himself to drawings for the new quarterly, to be called, at his suggestion, the *Savoy*,[10] after the famous hotel between the Strand and the Embankment. An assured place again in the world of art was all he needed. His health improved so that he was able to go to Dieppe; Symons was there too, and they planned the new quarterly. In the design which Beardsley made for the Prospectus, a copy of the *Yellow Book* lay carelessly beneath the feet of a small figure in the foreground, but this evidence of pique was deleted before the Prospectus appeared, though the original prints are still in existence.

How much responsibility Harland felt for Beardsley's dismissal is debatable. It has been implied that Harland avoided the issue, taking refuge in Paris and letting the blame rest on Lane. Harland and Beardsley had got on well while editing the magazine, and Harland later spoke of their experience together with warmest appreciation. The families remained on good terms and after the death of both men, Beardsley's mother visited Mrs. Harland in New York. Harland was an unusually sympathetic person and must have been unhappy over his inability to help Beardsley. But Patrick Chalmers, in speaking of Beardsley's retirement, said it happened "to the secret relief of his editor who grudged him his youth and his early fame."[11] When the question was put to Mr. D. S. MacColl as to whether Harland could have saved Beardsley, he replied cautiously that he didn't think you could say that Harland had let him down.[12]

MacColl had an opportunity to demonstrate his loyalty to the deposed artist when Lane asked him to take over the art of the *Yellow Book*. MacColl refused, telling Lane that, other reasons aside, since he was a friend of Beardsley's, he could not supplant him.[13] Other artists, if approached, must have felt the same way, for no new editor was announced. According to J. Lewis May, Lane now acted in that capacity; according to Miss D'Arcy, Harland accepted the responsibility for passing on the illustrations. Probably the two men shared the burden.

Neither was dismayed at the undertaking, for each fancied himself a judge of art. Harland's background was artistic; his mother was a painter of some ability and he was a faithful attendant at exhibitions in Paris and London, always with an eye out for possible *Yellow Book* acquisitions. Lane collected paintings and prints; indeed it was said that he worshiped them even above books and that the walls of the Bodley Head looked like an art gallery. He had great faith in his taste as a connoisseur, but in technical matters he was as ignorant as Harland, and so Lane thought of Patten Wilson.

Wilson was a Shropshire lad, younger brother of the architect Henry Wilson and had been introduced to the Bodley Head by Le Gallienne. He had studied art at the Kidderminster School, but not satisfied with his training had worked to form his own style by copying Dürer, from whom he learned steadiness of hand and economy of line, he said. After temporarily abandoning his career to act as secretary to the director of the Liverpool Gymnasium, he had come to London as designer for a well-known firm of wallpaper manufacturers. At Le Gallienne's suggestion Lane had given him a book of miracle plays to illustrate and asked him to contribute to the *Yellow Book*.[14] His "Rustem Firing the First Shot" had appeared in Volume IV, an elaborate drawing crowded with detail, done with an originality which made his style unique and easily recognized. Wilson's practical experience with the wallpaper firm was just what the theorists needed; so, though he was never dignified by the name of art editor, he became technical adviser and was responsible for the printing and reproductions. A number of his designs were used for the cover and title-pages, examples of his

work were found in all the later volumes, and his back cover
was not changed till the last number.

Chapter XVIII

HARLAND NOW PLUNGED into preparations for Volume VI,
which he wished to make so innocuous as to attract no unfavorable comment, but so interesting as to compensate for the loss
of Beardsley. Again the position of honor at the front of the
book went to Henry James, an author certain of retaining Mrs.
Ward's approval. "I sometimes assist Mary with a little passage,"
he had confided to a friend. But James himself was to suffer
from this exposed position when a writer in *Munsey's* scolded,
"Of late, however, Mr. James has been in bad company. He has
become one of the *Yellow Book* clique."[1]

This was James' first appearance since Volume II, for he
had in the interim been much occupied with the performance
of his play *Guy Domville* at the Haymarket Theatre early in
January, 1895. It had been a tragic venture into the world of
the theatre, a world upon which he had looked enviously, for a
success was so profitable, and actresses, like dear Elizabeth
Robins, were so charming. He had been tempted into it before
on one or two lesser occasions, but nothing like this cataclysmic
failure had ever befallen him. It was a shattering experience
both for James and his friends; indeed Elizabeth Robins
thought his friends suffered more, for he had "at least the stern
comfort of bearing himself in an unprecedented crisis with an
unprecedented candour and dignity."[2] A woman from Boston
was struck with a "sensation of absolute, writhing misery"[3] in
that awful moment when James, led before the curtain by the
manager, Alexander, was met by a fusillade of booing and hoot-
ing from the gallery. Bernard Shaw inquired which patrons of
the drama set its laws—"the cultivated majority who, like myself and all the ablest of my colleagues, applauded Mr. James on
Saturday, or the handful of rowdies who brawled at him?"[4]
Graham Robertson, who sat beside Sargent, thought the Ameri-

can artist was about to leap on the stage to rescue his friend, and afterward Sargent "expressed himself for upwards of half an hour without repeating a phrase or an epithet."[5] But the faithful Harland went to see the play twice and considered it "the prettiest play" he had seen in London.[6] After a few days it was withdrawn, and James wrote Miss Robins that it was "a great relief to feel that one of the most detestable incidents of my life has closed."[7] An American critic found only three objections to Henry James's plays. They were "unactable . . . unreadable . . . unspeakable."[8]

"The Next Time," his story in Volume VI, may reflect obliquely his disappointment over the fate of his play, for in his *Notebook* entry for January 26, 1895, he wrote, "The idea of a poor man, the artist, the man of letters, who all his life is trying—if only to get a living—to do something *vulgar*, to take the measure of the huge, flat foot of the public: isn't there a little story in it, possibly, if one can animate it with action; a little story that might perhaps be a mate to *The Death of the Lion*"[9] (his story in Volume I)? The huge flat foot of the public! Poor James, who had so desired its friendly hand! On June 4, 1895, he took up the idea again and must have carried it through quickly, for the story was ready for the July issue.

The American-born Henry James had gone to England in 1869 and through the kindness of friends had made the acquaintance of such notables as George Eliot, Tennyson, Browning, and Fanny Kemble. In 1875 he permanently deserted America for England and settled happily into the congenial background of the old city on the Thames, feeling that "for one who takes it as I take it, London is on the whole the most possible form of life. I take it as an artist and as a bachelor; as one who has the passion of observation and whose business is the study of human life. It is the biggest aggregation of human life —the most complete compendium of the world . . . if you learn to know your London you learn a great many things,"[10] but Anne Douglas Sedgwick thought he took England "too hard."[11]

On January 9, 1894, a few days after Harland had invited James to be the first contributor to the *Yellow Book*, he confided to his *Notebook* that he seemed "to catch hold of the tail of an idea that may serve as the subject of the little tale I have engaged to write for H. Harland and his *Yellow Book*. It belongs—the *concetto* that occurred to me and of which this is a very rough note—to the general group of themes of which *The Private Life* is a specimen."[12] By February 3 he had the idea well worked out for "The Death of the Lion" (Volume I) in which he considered the problem which has troubled genius from Diogenes to Emily Dickinson: how much of the artist's personal life must he share with his public? Neil Parady, the hero, had been protected by obscurity to do great work; once "discovered," he was lionized to death.

When the first volume appeared James was in Venice. Italy fascinated him, and whenever the winter grime of London grew too oppressive he escaped southward. "Can you resist dipping over into Italy?" he wrote A. C. Benson in Switzerland. "I can't."[13] Joseph Pennell saw him there in the spring and wrote his wife that "he evidently thought he had a suit of duds just like the middle class Italian . . . but to-day that person is a combination of the Frenchman of 1830 and an Englishman of last year—and H. J. dont [*sic*] look like that."[14]

On April 17 at the Casa Biondetti he wrote, "Here I sit, at last, after many interruptions, distractions, and defeats . . . . The last six weeks, with my 2 or 3 of quite baffling indispositions before I left London, have been a period of terrific sacrifice to the ravenous Moloch of one's endless personal, social relations."[15] From James Dykes Campbell's book on Coleridge, he got the idea of "The Coxon Fund" and on April 25 reminded himself, "I have committed myself to the *Yellow Book* for 20,000 words, and I swing back, on 2nd thought, to the idea of *The Coxon Fund*—asking myself if I can't treat it in a way to make it go into that limited space. I want to do something very good for the Y. B., and this subject strikes me as superior."[16]

In "The Coxon Fund" (Volume II) a young man of genius, or apparent genius, was ruined through the security coming from a gift of money by one who might well have used it for herself. James said that its hero, Frank Saltram, "pretends to be of his great suggester [Coleridge] no more than a dim reflexion and above all a free rearrangement."[17] "The Next Time," his story in Volume VI, portrayed the man who tried to produce best-sellers but could write only distinguished failures. On this occasion James took full advantage of Harland's indifference to "the arbitrary limit of length," and it was his longest story. "These pieces," he wrote in the Preface to the New York Edition, "have this in common that they deal all with the literary life, gathering their motive, in each case, from some noted adventure, some felt embarrassment, some extreme predicament, of the artist enamoured of perfection, ridden by his idea or paying for his sincerity."[18]

He originally intended *What Maisie Knew* for the *Yellow Book*, as he indicated on December 22, 1895—"Promising H. Harland a 10,000 (a *real* 10,000) for the April *Yellow Book*, I have put my pen to the little subject of the child, the little girl"[19]—but he apparently could not condense it to the *"real* 10,000" words and gave Harland instead an essay, "She and He," drawn from the recent publication of the letters of George Sand and Alfred de Musset, a revelation which had interested him strongly. That essay was his last contribution to the *Yellow Book*.

Harland's admiration for James was fervent and long-lasting. To Harland, James was *"mon maître,"* and the "supreme prince of the short story writers," but he esteemed as well James' social position, his rooms in London, and his house at Rye, Lamb House, a substantial edifice draped in wisteria, with a mulberry tree in the walled garden. "Here with four or five servants," Harland wrote to an American friend, "Mr. James keeps bachelor's hall, surrounded by fabrics and colours of beauty and marvellous objects of art and interest. In the fine weather he does his writing in a pavilion in the garden, but for the rest he has an inside study. Here he spends his time until the London season calls him, when he goes up to town to dine with his duchesses. You've no idea how popular James is with his duchesses, nor how enormously proud they are of having him to dine with them."[20]

"He dined out every night," reported Mrs. Atherton,[21] but her fellow American, Mrs. Wharton, noted "an anxious frugality" at Lamb House, apparently imposed by the "host's conviction that he was on the brink of ruin. He lived in terror of being thought rich."[22] A. C. Benson maintained that James "spoke with hatred of business and the monetary side of art,"[23] but that he understood well the value and uses of money, though he could at times be generous with it too.

"I hope you read and love Henry James?" Harland asked one of his *Yellow Book* contributors. "To me he seems the only master of considered prose we've got. Ah, but you're not mad about style, as I am. Besides, by the bye, he's one of the two or three 'good' men I know."[24]

James' deliberation, his endless hunting for the exact phrase, his pauses in conversation, though Mrs. Wharton insisted that his slow way of speech was really the victory over a stammer which in his boyhood had been thought incurable, his parentheses, modifications, and quotation marks in writing, sometimes infuriated a waiting listener or reader. "He never lets his characters make clear statements, to say nothing of actions," ranted George Moore. "And their interminable strolling on terraces to smoke cigarettes!"[25] Arnold Bennett found James' "colossal cautiousness . . . very trying. If he would only now and then contrive to write a sentence without a qualifying clause,"[26] and W. Pett Ridge often heard people exclaim, "I can do nothing with Henry James."[27] American humorists found much to laugh at in his mannered prose. Charles Battell Loomis, though considering James a man "who by virtue of his best work must ever loom large in English literature," wrote a translation of one of his stories, and spoke with awe of the "critic who could 'read James in the original.' "[28] Walt Mason, once co-dweller in Emporia, Kansas, with William Allen White, expressed the irritation of the common man when he wrote, "All your people stand and talk, Henry James. Oh, they talk too long, I ween, Henry James; and I can't guess what they mean, Henry James; each one anxiously conceals all emotions that he feels, each one's head is full of wheels, Henry James."[29] Finley

Peter Dunne, creator of Mr. Dooley, sitting next to James at dinner and floundering in the heavy seas of James' hesitations, owned that he had an almost ungovernable impulse to say, "Just 'pit it right up into Popper's hand."[30]

No one appreciated the nuances of James' style more than his friend Max Beerbohm, who said that to read James is "like taking a long walk uphill, panting and perspiring and almost of a mind to turn back, until, when you look back and down, the country is magically expanded beneath your gaze, as you never saw it yet; so that you toil on gladly up the heights, for the larger prospects that will be waiting for you. I admit, you must be in good training."[31] When Max wrote a perfect parody of James in "The Mote in the Middle Distance" he felt a certain nervousness as to its reception, but James told Gosse he had read it with "wonder and delight."[32] Years later Sir Max said that he thought James' published letters revealed a very critical attitude toward some of his friends. In the old days he had been surprised at James' comments about people he had seemed to like. James could be kind but he was not averse to talking about human frailties.[33]

James' stature as a writer and stylist has acquired added dignity with the passage of time. Not always appreciated by the critics of the last century, he has achieved his due in the twentieth. His creative invention and thoughtful approach have been received with understanding and admiration by those who realize how far he looms above most of his contemporaries, but with all the encomiums of present-day discoverers, none has exceeded the homage of Harland: "James . . . the very greatest mind that has ever been devoted to the writing of fiction in any language since the beginning of created literature."[34]

In James's "Death of the Lion" one of his characters used the phrase "the larger latitude." Critics have identified this character, Guy Walsingham, as a reasonable facsimile of a lady author of the nineties who wrote under a masculine pen name and whose *Keynotes* and *Discords* were taken to be experiments in the larger latitude. In both Volume I and VI James had the company of this author, George Egerton. "George Egerton" concealed the very feminine Mary Chavelita Dunne, and since she changed her name by marriage three times during her writing career, from Dunne to Melville to Clairmonte and finally to Bright, considerable confusion must have been avoided by her pseudonym. She was born in Melbourne, Australia, in 1859 and with her father, Captain J. J. Dunne, said to be a Dublin Academician, had traveled on a sailing vessel from Australia to Valparaiso, Wales, and Ireland. She had also worked in America before going to London. Early in the nineties the Bodley Head received a sheaf of stories, unacknowledged by name or address, on which Richard Le Gallienne made such an enthusiastic report that Lane decided to accept them, but no one knew how to notify the author of his or her success. Then one day a young woman, a Mrs. Clairmonte, called to claim her manuscript and be welcomed as the author of *Keynotes*. This volume of short stories, brought out in 1893, gained immediate recognition for its author, both laudatory and abusive. Lane was so pleased that he named after her book a projected series, the Keynotes Series, each book in it having a cover design and keynote monogram of the author by Aubrey Beardsley. To be included in this series was to be of Lane's élite. But Mr. Dooley's originator suggested *Keynotes* was a symptom of "the Beerbohmic plague" of literature.[35]

In June, 1894, readers of the *Bookbuyer* were assured that though Mrs. Clairmonte was thought to be an unusual person, she was indeed an ordinary woman with no views on emancipation, happily married and never so content as when fishing with her husband. Proficient in five or six languages, she was then engaged on some articles for a Scandinavian review dealing with social problems in England, and in her free moments she was writing more short stories, a play, a translation of critical essays from Norwegian, and a vocabulary of fishing terms in four languages.[36] In an interview for the *Bookman*, when asked about her writing, she answered—could she have had Henry James in mind?—"I write just as many [words] as I need, no more, no less—always less if possible."[37]

The busy Mrs. Clairmonte published her second book, *Discords,* as the sixth volume of the Keynotes Series. In the meantime "A Lost Masterpiece: A City Mood, Aug. '93" had appeared in Volume I and "The Captain's Book" in Volume VI of the *Yellow Book.* Ridicule was a handy weapon against the new literature, and the critic of the *Westminster Gazette* used it (not without cause) on George Egerton's "Mood." "She was in an omnibus and 'a precious little pearl of thought,' 'a rare little mind-being' was evolving slowly out of her 'inner chaos' when a fellow passenger with a white-handled umbrella got in, and 'trampled it unto death'. That is all and nothing more. But having lost the idea, it was rather thrifty of George Egerton to persevere with her story."[38] "The Captain's Book," a slender but delicately perceptive tale of a procrastinating author and the disillusionment of his little Jeanet, was a better example of her style.

George Egerton looked to the Northern countries, to the terse realism of the Norwegians. Björnson and Knut Hamsun, both of whom she translated, were her masters. Cornelius Weygandt has said that she "bulked largest of the group to those who took the *Yellow Book* as the gospel of a new faith,"[39] and Malcolm Elwin saw her as the lineal ancestor of A. E. Coppard.[40] She treated love between the sexes with an honesty rare in English fiction, and for this frankness she was condemned by a highly respectable press and suspected by her more subtle and less outspoken contemporaries.

When Henry James satirized her as Guy Walsingham he was perhaps betraying the feeling he expressed to Howells at about this time, that "a new generation that I know not, and mainly prize not, has taken universal possession."[41] It was the fear of the older man who sees himself outmoded by the newcomer. But Henry James need not have worried. Though the trail blazed by *Keynotes* and *Discords* has become a broad highway, today's brave new writers "mainly prize not" George Egerton; indeed it is unlikely they have ever heard of her. They look instead to Henry James, George Egerton having been relegated to a few sentences in books devoted to the history of minor English fiction.

Another young writer, just commencing author, as the phrase was in the nineties, who made a successful first appearance in this volume, was Arnold Bennett—Enoch Arnold Bennett as he called himself then. In 1893 after a brief apprenticeship he had been made assistant editor of *Woman,* for which he wrote breezy paragraphs under the signatures of "Gwendolyn." As he broadened his scope to book notes and articles he used the initials A. E. B. in the *Academy* and the name Jacob Tonson in the *New Age.*

Young Bennett took the business of being an author seriously, totting up the words he wrote each day and struggling to create a style. He studied Continental writers, reproaching himself in his journal, "I have unwisely been reading books by George Meredith and Mrs. Humphrey Ward, and at first my work will certainly reflect their methods . . . both at variance with my natural instincts towards a *synthetic impressionism.* I ought during the past months to have read nothing but Goncourt."[42] And again, "I have been re-reading *Virgin Soil,* and it occurs to me, is indeed forced on me, that I know practically nothing yet of *development* of character."[43]

His *Yellow Book* story, "A Letter Home," in the opinion of its author "the first story of any real decency that I ever wrote,"[44] had been sent first to the editor of a popular weekly, who returned it with praise for its plot but criticism of its style. When Harland took it for the *Yellow Book,* several critics singled it out for special commendation, and Bennett was encouraged in the conviction that he could write.

So he began on a novel, and in the process he said, "I picked out the correct *Yellow Book* from a shelf and read my beautiful story again. That enheartened me a little, restored my faith in the existence of art . . ."[45] and so he wrote the novel which on the recommendation of John Buchan, John Lane promised to publish. Bennett was not entirely pleased with Buchan's report, admitting it was "laudatory and kind, but not (I thought) critically appreciative."[46] Lane put off the publication for two years, preferring to bring out instead the first of Bennett's self-help books, *Journalism for Women: A Practical Guide*, on which Evelyn Sharp had made a "glowing report."[47]

In 1896 he was made editor of *Woman*, a post from which he soon graduated to the staff of the *Academy*, abandoning that in turn for free-lance work. He found a ready market for his reviews, and his reputation for realistic fiction was well established.

Bennett's carefully kept *Journal*, begun in 1896 and published in 1933, was not only a revelation of his own achievements but a chronicle of the years through which he lived and the men and women who made them interesting.

Royalty made its single bow in this volume with a story "Lilla," "*par le Prince Bojidar Karageorgevitch.*" The charming and romantic Prince of the distinguished Serbian family, author of *Notes sur L'Inde* and translator into French of Dostoievsky and Tolstoi, was then living in Paris and perhaps this "*Conte de neige pour mon neveu Rudi*" was one of the results of Harland's visit to the Boulevards when he might so profitably have remained at the Bodley Head.

Several of the controversial names were missing from this number: Crackanthorpe, Sickert, Beerbohm, and of course Beardsley. Kenneth Grahame, Arthur Waugh, and Dick Le Gallienne had survived the winnowing. In art, Conder, Steer, Alfred Thornton, and A. S. Hartrick represented the taste of the former art editor, while Patten Wilson, Gertrude Prideaux-Brune, Wilfred Ball, and William Strang were of Lane's choice.

One water color, "The Screen" by Sir William Eden, Bart., might have had Beardsley's blessing as well, for he would have enjoyed aiming this little barb at Whistler, who had said he could not draw. Sir William had just been the successful plaintiff against Whistler in a suit brought in the Paris courts to recover the money he had paid the artist for a portrait of Lady Eden destroyed by the fiery American in a rage over the insignificance of the fee which he had nevertheless retained. One of the consequences of this Baronet vs. Butterfly case had been Whistler's challenge to George Moore, who had originally introduced sitter to artist, but Moore had neatly sidestepped the encounter, with the excuse that dueling was illegal in England and that it made him seasick to cross the channel. Eden had already had some pictures hung at the New English Art Club and now, in the spotlight of his victory, he exhibited in the *Yellow Book*.

Of this volume, VI, the *Sketch* observed significantly, "It is a good *Yellow Book* on the whole,"[48] and the *Westminster Gazette* rejoiced that the fiction "has lost its distinctly 'Yellow Book' note, which, as some may think, is no great loss."[49] If this was indeed a reformed *Yellow Book,* Harland may have thought he could do no better than bring it to a close with "Two Letters to a Friend," by Theodore Watts. Christened Walter Theodore Watts, he contributed these poems as Theodore Watts, but in 1897 he became Theodore Watts-Dunton by legal act, eliciting the sally from Whistler, "Theodore Watts Dun t'un?"[50]

A friend of George Borrow and a solicitor, novelist, poet, and critic, Watts-Dunton will be best remembered as the man who rescued Swinburne from a sick bed surrounded by empty bottles (not medicine) in Great James Street and eventually transported him to Putney, where he nursed and dominated him for the next thirty years. Mrs. Watts-Dunton in her *Home Life of Swinburne* said that "Walter ruled him by love, guided him by advice, and influenced him by suggestion,"[51] but this was considered a euphemistic acount by Swinburne's earlier friends such as Edmund Gosse. Gosse had reason for his resentment, since Watts-Dunton refused to let him visit at The Pines because of his connection with Swinburne's stormier days. Some thought he was jealous of Gosse's influence. For his part Gosse took the attitude that Swinburne had done no good work since Watts assumed his protectorate. Others, Richard Whiteing among them, shared this opinion. "I have often thought," Whiteing said, "that Watts-Dunton took too much pain with his ministrations of this kind. [He had also served Rossetti.] He

176

seemed to cure his nursling of every bad habit, including the genius."[52]

After Watts-Dunton had reformed Swinburne, limited his drinking, and established a restrained *modus vivendi*, a few acceptable souls were invited to worship at the diminutive feet of the red-haired poet. Rothenstein went just after the conclusion of the Baronet-Butterfly case to make a drawing of Swinburne. Watts, a "little, round, rosy, wrinkled man, with a moustache like a walrus, and a polished dewlap," wanted to hear all the details. "Dear Jimmy . . ." said Watts-Dunton. "What genius! . . . Surely he was in the wrong over Sir William Eden. George Moore I am rather prejudiced against; but of course I don't know him, and I have not read his books. But I trust Jimmy always for being in the wrong, he loves a quarrel."[53]

Luncheon was the usual occasion for these visits, for Algernon did not sleep well after too exciting an evening, and Max Beerbohm has immortalized one such festivity in "No. 2. The Pines." William Archer found the luncheon "great sport. They are the oddest little couple—I really felt my height quite embarrassing when I was standing between them. Both are deaf, Swinburne extremely so. Watts has no chin, and a long moustache, just like a walrus's tusk."[54] "A most *awful* looking little man," Alice Sedgwick said.[55] E. V. Lucas once went to see Swinburne's treasured Lamb manuscripts. "You remember, Swinburne," Watts-Dunton shouted, "that Canon Ainger once paid us a visit for a similar purpose." Swinburne remembered. "And you remember, Swinburne," went on his mentor, "that we thought him a very poor creature." "Yes," the poet echoed, "a very poor creature."[56] Only a strong determination to see the treasures kept Lucas from a cowardly exit.

In spite of the attention he devoted to the Bard, Watts managed a considerable literary output of his own. Besides criticism for the *Athenaeum*, he wrote poetry, being partial to the sonnet and usually mourning the passing of literary figures in fourteen lines; he worked for twenty years on a novel, which he was ever "just about to complete." In 1885 he had been on the point of publishing it, but at the last moment drew back.

In 1887 he wrote E. C. Stedman that the book was not yet published, but would "be out in a few weeks."[57] In 1898 he finally nerved himself, and *Aylwin*, a story of Wales and of gypsies, was presented to the public. "It *must* succeed," said William Robertson Nicoll, and turned the influence of his many reviews to that end. Succeed it did.[58]

In 1905 Watts-Dunton married young and pretty Clara Jane Reich and everyone wondered how Swinburne would receive this feminine presence at The Pines, but the Bard approved heartily. "I am pleased, I am *very* pleased about it," he told Rhys. "You see she will be able to look after me if anything happens to Theodore."[59]

But nothing happened to Theodore until some years after the death of his charge. Swinburne died in 1909 and Watts-Dunton lived until 1914.

Watts-Dunton's sonnets in the *Yellow Book,* "After the Wedding" and "After Death's Mockery," paid tribute to Mildred Le Gallienne, who had died the previous year, and in whose memory her husband Richard was to have a "Prose Fancy" in the next volume.

Chapter XIX

RICHARD LE GALLIENNE's "A Seventh-story Heaven," written "For M. Le G., a Birthday Present, 25 September, 1895" had the place of honor at the opening of Volume VII as a mark of esteem for Mildred Le Gallienne, who had died the year before, and of affection for her husband, the romantic young poet of the Bodley Head. Le Gallienne cultivated a poet's appearance as well as vocation, and E. V. Lucas admired the courage with which he faced the matter-of-fact London world in such a make-up. Dick complained that the street urchins would not let him wear his hair as long as he wanted, and perhaps he described himself in *Young Lives* when he wrote of a "tall young man with a long thin face, curtained on each side with enormous masses of black hair—like a slip of the young moon glimmering through a pine wood,"[1] but a stranger, staring at him in the theatre, asked, "Who's that beautiful woman?"[2] In 1891 he had married his Golden Girl, Mildred Lee, and deeply and romantically in love they had set up housekeeping in a Seventh-story Heaven in Staple Inn. With Richard's sister Cissie, married to James Welch the actor, they enjoyed a Bohemian *camaraderie,* until no one was certain whether it was Jimmy's last shilling or Dick's half crown they had just spent for a bottle of wine and white hyacinths. All this made good material for the young writer who did not shun the personal touch in his compositions. As a fellow-writer said, "We all figure proudly in Richard's latest chants, and so do his sisters and his cousins and his aunts."[3] Later the couple took a cottage at Brentford, and John Davidson inquired:

> What little boat comes o'er the sea
> From islands of Eternity?[4]

But the boat which brought the small daughter Hesper carried away the Golden Girl. Everyone at the Bodley Head sympathized with the poet's grief; Chapman walked the country lanes with him all night after Mildred's death. The poet shared his sorrow too with his readers, and it was none the less real because he dramatized it. His poems "Home" in Volume IV and "A Song" in Volume V mourned his love and in "A Seventh-story Heaven" he told of lost happiness and Beauty, the blue-eyed girl who had gone away. But in Volume VIII a new heroine, the Sphinx, appeared in his story as they dined over white bait. The Sphinx was Julie Norregard, a young Danish journalist, who had been much impressed with Le Gallienne, Lewis Hind had noticed, when he lectured at the Playgoers' Club.

Julie's background was far from prosaic and she was intelligent as well as pretty, if one could judge from her essay on Georg Brandes in this same Volume VIII. She had attended Brandes' lectures at the University of Copenhagen and wrote with personal knowledge and appreciation of the eminent Danish critic. "How well I remember those evenings," she said,

179

"twice a week, when we stood together waiting outside the big door. It was not opened till seven o'clock, but to secure a seat we had to be there long before. All young, all enthusiastic, all dreaming of the possibilities life had in store for us. . . ."[5]

Much was in store for Julie Norregard. A member of a distinguished Danish family, she had been introduced to the social whirl of Copenhagen at an early age, staying up at balls till two o'clock and rising to work in her studio at eight. She wanted to be a painter, but she liked to write. Her father gave her free access to his library and she read *La Cousine Bette* at the age of eleven, and enjoyed it. She was sent to London as the correspondent for two Danish papers and soon was writing as proficiently in English as in her native tongue. She contributed articles to the *Star* on dress and needlework under the pseudonym "Eva" and wrote for the Cassell publications.

While Richard was working on *The Quest of the Golden Girl,* the romanticized tale of his first love, he was paying court to Julie and talking about it in the *Yellow Book*. In April, 1896, the Poet and the Sphinx saw *Romeo and Juliet,* and he made love to her afterward, waiting "the answer of the Rose." In 1897 shortly after the publication of the *Golden Girl*, he and Julie were married. Everyone wished them well, but a reviewer in the *Critic* observed, "It is to be presumed that we shall hear less from the young poet in the future than we have heard in the past of his devotion to the memory of the first Mrs. Le Gallienne."[6]

It was all over by 1903. Le Gallienne had gone to America, where he said he got ten times the price for his writing he could get in England.[7] Julie had taken her small daughter Eva to live in Paris, where she described to Arnold Bennett how diverting it was to live with an artistic temperament. There was one thing she could say: Richard had never bored her; only she had had enough of the artistic temperament. She earned her living by journalism and translations, finally putting her creative ability to work in a hat shop. Netta Syrett and Ella D'Arcy, friends of the *Yellow Book* circle, often came to see her, and Bennett took her and her young daughter for rides in his new auto.

When he left London to make his home in America, Dick was missed by his former associates. Max sent him a post card:

> O witched by American bars!
> Pan whistles you home on his pipes.
> We love you for loving the stars,
> But what *can* you see in the stripes?[8]

Unlike Max, however, Le Gallienne enjoyed New York and got on well with the American people. Sometimes a workman would be surprised when a tall thin man with long hair threw a comradely arm across his shoulder and whispered, "For the Revolution, brother."[9] In 1911 he undertook his third matrimonial venture, marrying Irma Hinton Perry. Later he deserted America for France, but by this time Julie had gone to America with her talented young daughter. She cooked and kept house while Eva hunted jobs in the theatre, but after Eva was established as a star Julie returned to London. Though she and Richard were never reunited, they kept on terms of friendly correspondence. She died in 1943, leaving her daughter a memory of beauty, charm, and courage.

Until the beginning of World War II Richard lived in the attic of an old house on the Left Bank near the Luxembourg Gardens and wrote on Oscar Wilde's table, which he had bought from the Hotel d'Alsace, such books as *From a Paris Attic* and *From a Paris Scrapbook*. He died at Mentone in September, 1947.

In his youth as reader for the Bodley Head and critic for the *Star* he had extended a helping hand to many young authors. Ernest Rhys remembered that he owed the publication of *A London Rose* to Le Gallienne's favorable report. He persuaded Lane to take on Davidson, and he was one of the early critics to appreciate *A Shropshire Lad* He could be harsh in his criticism too, as in his *Rudyard Kipling*, in which he called Kipling one of "the true end-of-the-century decadents," . . . whose aim was "to begin the twentieth century by throwing behind them all that the nineteenth century has won"[10]—democracy, the woman-movement, and the education of the masses. "As a writer Mr. Kipling is a delight; as an influence he is a danger."[11] Le

Gallienne was not without his courage. Though Coventry Patmore hoped that he would one day be led into the bosom of the Church, and at a time when many men of the nineties were turning to incense and images, Le Gallienne wrote *The Beautiful Lie of Rome*, "not as a Protestant" but "as one to whom it seems of paramount importance that the future be kept open for the advancing soul of man."[12]

The Georgians did not give Le Gallienne his due. They saw the poseur intead of the poet and were distracted by the decorations from the reality beneath. His appreciation of poetry outstripped his talent, but his enthusiasm was pleasant. As a critic and historian of his age he should be heeded; he saw most of its foibles and failings, including his own, clearly and with a twinkle in his eye. Never definitely committed to either the sensualists or the Puritans, he was more objective in his judgment of his contemporaries than most. The two volumes of his *Retrospective Reviews* shed light on the era; so too does his *Romantic '90s*, and any student of literary movements will find information and enjoyment in Le Gallienne's contributions to periodicals.

Another interesting young couple appearing in harmonious conjugality in Volume VII were Leila Macdonald and Hubert Crackanthorpe, Leila the poetess with "The Pompeian Cœlia," and Hubert, not with one of his dispiriting studies of realism which Le Gallienne called

> The hideous so-called truth of things,
> Those little documents of Hell,

but with a vivid bit of personal reporting, "Bread and the Circus." One summer at Dieppe, looking for adventure, he had joined an English circus journeying across France to Le Havre, and this account of his experience showed his finest qualities as a writer, which his friend Lionel Johnson enumerated as, first, "skill in dramatic narration—a sense of situation, a lively feeling for the value and interpretation of gesture, posture, circumstance; secondly, analytic skill in the conception and presentment of character; thirdly, descriptive and pictorial power,

RICHARD LE GALLIENNE
Courtesy of Miss Eva Le Gallienne

JULIE NORREGARD LE GALLIENNE
Courtesy of Miss Eva Le Gallienne

JOHN DAVIDSON

Portrait by Will Rothenstein
From the *Yellow Book*, IV (1895)

WILLIAM WATSON

From a photograph by Hollyer, reproduced in the *Bookman* (New York),
IX (1899)

readiness of vision, with a faculty of sifting and selecting its reports."[13]

Though Miss D'Arcy believed that Leila owned her inclusion in the *Yellow Book* to the intercession of her husband and the affability of Harland, her one prose selection, "Jeanne-Marie," in Volume III might have won a place on its own merits, but her poems in Volumes IV, V, and VII seem to bear out Miss D'Arcy's suspicion. After this number neither of the Crackanthorpes appeared in the *Yellow Book*. Indeed before the last volume came out, this exceedingly gifted writer, whom Harland had chosen to bring the desired touch of distinction to *Yellow Book* fiction, was dead. "I hear tragic things of Hubert Crackanthorpe,"[14] Beardsley wrote Smithers when the artist himself was approaching the end, but unlike Beardsley, who wanted to live, Crackanthorpe faced the issue and chose to die.

He was the son of well-bred, well-educated people, his father being a figure in politics and law and his mother a writer and famous hostess. After tutoring by George Gissing, he matriculated at Cambridge, but having come home within a year on the losing side of an argument with the authorities, he began to write, and was soon recognized as a storyteller with a new approach to his material. In 1892-93 he edited the *Albermarle* with distinction, and on Valentine's Day of 1893 he was married to Leila Macdonald, born in Scotland and reputedly a lineal descendant of the famous Flora. Leila too wanted to be a writer and admired her husband's achievements, especially the success of *Wreckage* (1893), which put him at the front of the new realists. They took a workingman's flat in Chelsea, which Roger Fry decorated for them, and all the auspices seemed favorable. For recreation they sometimes went with the Harlands to see the old-fashioned melodramas which fascinated the realist. He dedicated his second book, *Sentimental Studies and a Set of Village Tales* (1895), "To Harry, in Remembrance of Much Encouragement." Though he wrote of life's seamy side and "the pill that's black," Crackanthorpe was content to live a quiet conventional life, finding enjoyment in domesticity. Leila was the nonconformist. "Forty years ago," Rothenstein remembered, "a man felt it more of a disgrace when his wife took the reins into her own hands and drove away with another man on the box seat."[15] Crackanthorpe felt it to the point of heartbreak. On the night of November 5, 1895, after a conference with Leila and his family at the Hotel Voltaire in Paris, in which, to his family's concern, he took Leila's part, he disappeared. At first it was hoped he had run away, but seven weeks later near the Quai Voltaire some river men found a piece of human wreckage, the body of Hubert Crackanthorpe, identified by his brother from the cuff links. Rumors of foul play were persistent and his father and mother requested London papers to make a statement that "according to the medical evidence, there is no doubt that Mr. Hubert Crackanthorpe met with his death on the evening of Nov. 5. He had been with his mother until 11.30 that evening, he went for a walk, and was last seen at 11.50 P.M. on the Quai Voltaire, within 300 yards of which place his body was found. . . . For the last two months of his life he was living in Paris; during that period he had never left it for a single day, and the circumstances of every day of his life there are said to be perfectly well known to his family."[16]

Another young man of letters was caused some embarrassment by Hubert's death, for earlier in the autumn, Crackanthorpe had proposed to Grant Richards, about to set up as a publisher, that he take over the expiring *Savoy*, with Hubert as editor. They were to meet on the night of November 5th to discuss the plan further. But Richards decided not to pass through Paris on his way to Rome and could not keep the appointment. After Crackanthorpe's disappearance a notation of the proposed meeting was discovered, and Grant Richards was held by the police until he could furnish evidence of his presence elsewhere on that night.[17] It has been suggested that Richards' refusal to join Crackanthorpe in the *Savoy* venture may have contributed to the melancholy which led him to end his life.

The work Crackanthorpe had left was gathered together in a volume of *Last Studies*, for which Henry James wrote an appreciation giving much pleasure to Mr. and Mrs. Crackanthorpe but mystifying their friend Stopford Brooke. "I have read Henry James' preface and, to tell you the plain truth," he wrote Mrs. Crackanthorpe, "I do not understand half of it. I *do* understand that he intends to say pleasant and true things, and that he has been at some pains to analyse and describe his impressions of your son's character and work . . . but he has now arrived at so involved and tormented a style that I find the greatest difficulty in discovering what he means."[18] Poor James! and he had undoubtedly so tried to make his praise sincere and memorable.

Crackanthorpe was a realist, a disciple of Maupassant, choosing his subjects from the streets and the people who lived in them. He hated sentimentality and if his starkly effective style was sometimes marred by a clumsy word or phrase, the passing years would have remedied such lapses. He did not live to win the place among English story-writers which should have been his; though his published works were few and the span of his accomplishment short, he cannot be overlooked in a study of the short story.

Lionel Johnson said of the *Last Studies:* "The terrible rapid pages are full of an aching poignancy. The straightforward sentences hide an inner appeal. The telling of the misery becomes a thing of dreadful beauty, and in its intensity goes nearer to the heart of the whole dark matter than many a moving sermon. The artist's abstemiousness in Mr. Crackanthorpe, the refinement of his reticence, never chilled his reader. 'The pity of it! The pity of it!' *That* was always the unspoken yet audible burden of his art."[19]

Crackanthorpe's death was much discussed by his contemporaries. "He was a charming creature," said Miss D'Arcy sadly. "Everyone loved him."[20] Some, like Jeannette Gilder, saw in it the judgment of Providence for worshipping French idols. To others it was as Vincent Starrett construed it, "the perfect conclusion, the consummate touch necessary to round out a brief and tragic existence, leaving its fame a thing of slight and sinister beauty—as complete and perfect in little as a sonnet or a

cameo."[21] He died like a character from one of his stories;
Stopford Brooke said,

> . . . the misery stole
> Into his life till he bade life farewell,[22]

but to his friends the manner of his going echoed the burden
of his art—the pity of it, oh, the pity of it!

Another young poetess in Volume VII, who was beautiful,
talented, and unhappy, was Olive Custance, eldest daughter of
Colonel Frederick Hambledon Custance of Weston Park, Norwich, a wealthy man with rigid views on form and etiquette
but proud of his daughter's poetic achievement. When the
Yellow Book was in preparation Olive was beginning to find
a market for her verse, but lacked sufficient importance to
merit mention in the preliminary announcement. Her first
poem was used in Volume III, and from then on she appeared
frequently, becoming one of Lane's regulars, and an attendant
at his teas, where Richard Le Gallienne stared enthralled at her
"flower-like, girlish loveliness."[23] The Harlands made her welcome at their evenings and she charmed Aubrey Beardsley into
designing a bookplate for her. Bookplates were *recherché* in
the nineties, and one bearing a famous signature was a mark
of importance. After Beardsley left the *Yellow Book* and went to
France she corresponded with him faithfully. "Eleven pages
from Olive this morning, plus 2 pages of verse. Ye Gods! If I
were only Symons!" wailed the ungrateful artist.[24] And again,
"A huge letter this morning from Olive Custance. She must
buy me in large paper if she expects me to read her letters."[25]

But though Olive fluttered enchantingly before many young
men, the one whom she loved seemed curiously obtuse to her
charm. His name was Alfred Douglas. She and Lord Alfred
had met as children and as youthful poets admired each other's
work, writing tenderly romantic poems to each other, which
on her side reflected a personal passion, on his a poetic fancy.
He was her "Prince," and she his "Page." Her first book of
poems, *Opals* (she was fond of those stones and laughed at the

superstition that they brought unhappiness[26]), was published in 1897, and Bosie thought she wrote better poetry than any of her women contemporaries, not excepting Mrs. Meynell. Olive's father disapproved of her infatuation, seeing nothing but disaster in it and was frankly relieved when Lord Alfred went to America and she became engaged to his onetime friend George Montague. But in March, 1902, Lord Alfred returned unhappily from the States, where people still remembered the Wilde affair though Oscar had been dead over a year, and finding his Olive about to marry another, was startled into a declaration of love and a proposal to elope. With the blessing of his mother and a loan of two hundred pounds, he and Olive slipped away to Paris.

At first they lived on the Continent in a glow of happiness, but after a reconciliation with her father, they returned to Weston Park for the birth of their son. Wilfrid Blunt gave a party for Douglas, saying it was time people ceased to cut him, but life in England did not go smoothly for the young couple; too much stood in the way of a successful marriage. She was pitied by her friends and threatened by blackmailers; Lord Alfred's romantic fervor failed to withstand the passing years. He had loved a slim and beautiful girl, his Page; his ardor cooled before a matronly figure and the difficulties of a poetic temperament. In 1913, at the time of the Ransome libel suit, Olive left her Prince, writing his mother, "I have often been very unhappy with him, but I love him above everything, and would never have left him if he had not taken away Raymond [her son]. The Ransome case has done him so much harm; you don't know what people say. . . . Perhaps it would be better for Bosie to divorce me for desertion? I only wish I had courage enough to kill myself!"[27] But she didn't and eventually they achieved a sort of reconciliation, he living in a flat by himself but visiting her every day in a nearby town and preserving the semblance of what he called "a life-long devotion."[28]

Her last book of poems, *The Inn of Dreams,* came out in 1911, though she lived until 1944, dying a year before her husband. Her poetic gift was slight and not always used with discretion, but much of her verse was tender and tuneful and effective in its simplicity:

> I am weary, let me sleep
> In some great embroidered bed.
> Let me dream that I am dead
> Nevermore to wake and weep
> In the future that I dread ...
> For the ways of life are steep ...
> I am weary, let me sleep .... [29]

Though Henry James had no story in Volume VII, his zealous friend and editor could not let him go unregarded, and Lena Milman's "A Few Notes upon Mr. James" kept the candles burning before the altar. The return address which Miss Milman used on the manuscripts she sent to the *Yellow Book* was probably the most unusual ever to reach the Bodley Head—the Tower of London—for her father General Milman was its governor. In December, 1892, James recorded the "intensely picturesque impression of visit yesterday afternoon to the Tower of London—to the 'Queen's House'—by invitation from Miss M., whom I found alone. Very English—quite intensely English." Such London experiences James loved even at fifty. He was impressed with "the whole thing: the homely, historic nook in the corner of a military establishment—the charming girl, daughter of the old Governor of the Tower . . . the memories, the ghosts, Anne Boleyn, Guy Fawkes, the block, the rack and the friendly modern continuity."[30]

In 1894 Lane published Lena Milman's translation of Dostoievsky's *Poor Folk,* with an introduction by George Moore, and she was soon drawn into the *Yellow Book* group, inviting her friends to tea at the Tower in her beautiful room overlooking the river. Evelyn Sharp was glad she did not live there, though she concealed the feeling from her hostess, who spoke with scorn of visitors that stayed in the Tower and saw Lady Jane Grey walking about with her head under her arm. Those who lived in the Tower "never committed the vulgarism of seeing its ghosts."[31]

In a later volume a distinguished and restrained study of

188

a little girl, "Marcel: An Hotel Child," bore testimony to the influence of the master Miss Milman had praised in Volume VII.

Another of Lane's women authors, Susan Christian, made an early bow in this volume with two stories which gave promise of the distinction to be attained by Susan Hicks-Beach. A quiet young lady, living at home in the Victorian manner, she was not at all a part of the literary world when Lane asked her to tea at the Bodley Head to meet Henry Harland. "It was not a very successful party," she recalled, "for Mr. Lane was socially shy . . . and Mr. Harland overexuberant. I thought from both looks and speech he must be a Slav of some sort."[32] Still the occasion was not lost, since it resulted in Miss Christian's "Two Hours: Two Women" in Volume VII of the *Yellow Book*. Though she was a newcomer to the literary scene, the fact was not betrayed in these workmanlike productions.

Her first novel, *A Pot of Honey* (1897), was described in the London *Bookman* as well written and far from commonplace: "Its tone is refined and in some passages distinguished. But the only impression left . . . is that of a murmur by a pleasant voice," and Miss Christian was urged to "speak up."[33] She has done that, indeed too infrequently, but competently, during the subsequent years.

She married a country squire who was a M.F.H. and an M.P. and in 1909 wrote a history of the Hickses and Hicks-Beaches in *A Cotswold Family*. Her most ambitious work was *A Cardinal of the Medici, Being the Memoirs of the Nameless Mother of the Cardinal Ippolito de' Medici*, published in 1937 by the University of Cambridge Press. In *Amabel and Mary Verna* (1944) she wrote a convincing sequel to Charlotte Yonge's *The Heir of Redclyffe*.

Chapter XX

As TIME WENT by, Harland found his editorial duties increasingly burdensome. To plan and manage such a pretentious journal, even with the aid of the publisher, called for tremendous energy. Today such a task would be undertaken only with a staff of editors, readers, and clerical assistants in private offices with names on the doors, but Harland worked alone with inadequate facilities. To be sure, the premises of the Bodley Head formed the editorial sanctum of the *Yellow Book;* but no special provision was made for it, and the Bodley Head hummed with other activities. Harland did much of his work at home; since he wrote letters in long hand, his desk was his office.

Conscientious about trying to help young writers, he often wrote long and careful criticisms of their work. He sent Mabel Kitcat four closely written pages of criticism at a time when he was desperately busy. He kept up his own writing and had at least one story in every number, occasionally slipping in a second under a pseudonym. Small wonder he was always behind in his reading of manuscripts, postponing acceptances or rejections until the big drawer in his desk was crammed so full that it would not shut. Then Ella D'Arcy would take pity on him and lend a hand.

Several people have said that Miss D'Arcy became assistant editor after Beardsley went, but she herself denied any official connection with the quarterly. "I was around a good bit," she conceded, "and I helped as I could. But I never was really an editor."[1]

However, when the overflow in Harland's drawer was too preposterous, she sometimes turned out the whole contents, going systematically through the manuscripts and forcing him to make decisions until everything was cleared away. But it was not long until the accumulation was as bad as ever. "Too many people wanted to write for the *Yellow Book*," she said with a shake of her head.

Evidence of Harland's editorial difficulties was shown in the evolution of the note concerning manuscripts on the fore page of each volume. Originally this read: "The Editor of *The Yellow Book* can in no case hold himself responsible for unsolicited manuscripts; when, however, they are accompanied by stamped addressed envelopes, every effort will be made to secure their prompt return. . . ."

With Volume V this sentence was added in italics: "Manuscripts arriving unaccompanied by stamped addressed envelopes will be neither read nor returned. . . ."

In Volume X all pretense of diplomacy was thrown overboard with the harried statement: "The Editor of *The Yellow Book* advises all persons sending manuscripts to keep copies, as, for the future, unsolicited contributions cannot be returned. To this rule no exception will be made."

Harland found it as onerous to pass judgment on the illustrations as on the literature. He clung to Conder in spite of the artist's ingratitude, and made frequent use of Steer and Thornton, and always Patten Wilson. Rothenstein's loyalties went with Beardsley. Sickert too had gone. In three numbers Harland shifted the responsibility to other shoulders, presenting in Volume VII only work from the Newlyn School in Cornwall, an offshoot of the New English Art Club, in Volume VIII twenty-five pictures and one photograph of a piece of sculpture from the Glasgow School under the leadership of Sir John Lavery, with a cover design by D. Y. Cameron, and in Volume IX decorative designs from the Birmingham School that stemmed from Burne-Jones and William Morris. He found himself calling more and more upon friends—Mabel Dearmer, wife of the Reverend Percy Dearmer, and the original, so Stephen Gwynn said, of many of Harland's heroines;[2] Mabel and Nellie Syrett, sisters of Netta, to whom Beardsley had been helpful; and Bodley Head cover designers. Charming young ladies who did illustrations for children's books suddenly found themselves promoted to sophisticated adult pages.

In literature he depended on the writers of fiction who looked to him for guidance, members of the charmed Saturday night circle, and on poets of Lane's choosing. There were of course others who sent in manuscripts for eventual acceptance.

In Volume VIII appeared one such, "A Slip under the Microscope," by H. G. Wells, then just advancing upon the world of letters. With a degree in Science from the University of London, Wells had done teaching and coaching, written for the *Fortnightly* in 1890, and extended his field to the *Pall Mall Gazette,* until in 1893 by writing and teaching he earned as much as 380 pounds. In August, 1894, he wrote his father, "The *P.M.G.* is still my bread and cheese. I do from six to ten columns a month and get two guineas a column."[3] He was now writing articles for the *Saturday Review* and the *National Observer,* but stories he found harder to sell. Encouraged, however, by reports of the *Yellow Book's* high rate of pay, he wrote what he called "a very carefully done short story,"[4] based on an experience in the biological laboratory, and sent it to Harland. Understanding that pay was by the word, the canny young author, who kept careful accounts, drew out his tale to its fullest length, only to be told by the editor when he returned a favorable verdict that the limit of pay was ten pounds and that words in excess of this amount were the gift of the author. Still Wells must have been satisfied, for in his Introduction to *The Country of the Blind,* he spoke of the "generous opportunities of the *Yellow Book.*"

So began the career of one of the most eminent writers of the new century, an indefatigable worker whose mind boldly ranged over the entire universe. When Wells died in 1946, his friend J. B. Priestley said at the services at Golder's Green, "This was a man whose word was light in a thousand dark places."[5]

Wells's friendship with George Gissing dated back to a dinner of the Omar Khayyám Club in the winter of 1896, when the coming young author told his senior brother how much he had liked *The New Grub Street,* in which the hero reminded him of himself. Gissing's only *Yellow Book* story, "The Foolish Virgin," appeared in the same volume as Wells's.

One of the most significant prose writers of the nineties, Gissing did not share the gay companionship of the pressmen: belonging to no coterie, he was a man apart, an outsider. "I can not get to know the kind of people who would suit me," he wrote his sister, "so I must be content to be alone."[6] His early friendship with Frederic Harrison (who got him a job as tutor to young Bertie Crackanthorpe), and his later friendship with Jane and H. G. Wells were happy exceptions.

"He was to be at outs with society all his life long; he was to suffer terribly from loneliness, bewail his friendless state, and at the same time make himself believe that isolation was best for him after all," said Richard Niebling.[7]

Though in fiction Gissing was a pitiless realist, in behavior he was a hopeless romantic and spent much of his life regretting his quixotic impulses. His misfortunes began at Owens College, Manchester, where he was accused of stealing in order to meet the financial demands of an affair with a young street-walker. An honor student who had taken first prize in Senior Latin, he was rescued by friends, who shipped him to America, where he wrote for the Chicago *Tribune,* but, tiring of his exile, he returned to England and celebrated his homecoming by marrying the girl. He endured a dismal life with Nell until her death a few years later. His second marriage, to a servant girl he picked up one Sunday afternoon in Regent's Park, was no better, though he found some satisfaction in his children. By 1897 he had escaped from a home life which seemed "impossible. Oh quite impossible."[8] In the summer of 1897 Wells and his wife stayed near Gissing in the country, and the next spring the three of them made a trip to Italy, of which Wells wrote in his autobiography. On their return, Gissing, now living apart from his wife at an establishment in Dorking, was visited by a Frenchwoman of the intellectual *bourgeoisie,* who wanted to translate his books. Presently he left England with Gabrielle Fleury for the Continent, where he entered into a supposititious marriage with her. In January, 1902, he wrote Edward Clodd, "You speak of my wife. Oh, yes, she is still with me; and, I devoutly hope, will be until I can no longer benefit by human solace. Our marriage begins to be an old story. . . . I no longer make any mystery of the matter. It has been justified by the event and with quietness and indifference to past troubles. . . ,"[9] but in spite of these brave words he was again unhappy, thin, ailing, and unable to work. During that same month, Henry James wrote to Wells, "I had a saddish letter from Gissing—but rumours of better things for him (I mean reviving powers) have come to me, I don't quite know how, since."[10] But the rumors were unfounded, and Gissing finally escaped to England, throwing himself upon the Wellses' hospitality, until Gabrielle, who had pursued him with letters, got him back again. He was working on a vast historical romance of Gothic Italy, *Veranilda,* when word came to his friends that he was ill. Thérèse telegraphed for Wells, who with unselfish generosity crossed the Channel on Christmas Eve, 1903, to find his friend delirious and dying from pneumonia. He had passed over "into that fantastic pseudo-Roman world of which Wakefield Grammar School had laid the foundation," babbling in Latin or chanting Gregorian music. Wells was with him through the last terrible hours and for the first time in his life saw a man die. "So ended all that flimsy inordinate stir of gray matter that was George Gissing."[11]

Henry James, who had a "persistent taste" for him, called Gissing "an authority . . . *the* authority—in fact on a region vast and unexplored"—saturated with knowledge of the lower middle class.[12] He had achieved this authority by sad experience, but he recognized the value of his knowledge and used it. "Spent day at Crystal Palace," he wrote on Easter, 1888, "and brought back a lot of good notes."[13] Or again, "To-morrow, a Bank Holiday, I must spend in the street; there is always much matter to be picked up on such days."[14]

He looked to the French naturalists and to the Russians for leadership. Turgenev was his hero, at whose request he contributed a literary letter to a Russian magazine for two years, a feat he looked back on "with amused satisfaction." He admitted, "I have not much sympathy with the English points of view. And indeed that is why I scarcely think my own writing can ever be popular. The mob will go to other people who better suit their taste."[15] Though he spoke philosophically he always hoped, like James, to "take the measure of the great flat foot of the

194

public." In the meantime he went on writing for the few, George Meredith among them. "I have found, by the bye," Gissing wrote his brother, "that Chapman's reader, who talked with me so sympathetically about the book, was no other than George Meredith. It is an excellent thing to have got his good word."[16]

His *New Grub Street* (1891) enjoyed a fair success. "The Foolish Virgin," his *Yellow Book* story, was a further development of the theme he had used in *The Odd Women* (1893)—the foolish virgin who idled away a useless precarious existence to find at last a haven in domestic service. Gissing had a genuine understanding of the unattractive incompetent female. He sympathized with her difficulties, was compassionate toward her dreariness, but laid bare her meagre soul with merciless exactness. To his mind the foolish virgin was only one of many "thousands of such women—all meant by nature to scrub and cook," who "live and die miserably because they think themselves too good for it."[17]

As a relief from the sordid problems of city life, Gissing found refuge in the ancient world and the romance of Greece and Rome. His tour of Italy gave him the material for *By the Ionian Sea*. At the time of his death, *Veranilda* was to be the first of a series of historical romances.

In defending realism in fiction in 1895, he said, "Let the novelist take himself as seriously as the man of science; be his work to depict with rigid faithfulness the course of life, to expose the secrets of the mind, to show humanity in its eternal combat with fate. . . . What the artist sees is to him only a part of the actual; its complement is an emotional effect. Thus it comes about that every novelist beholds a world of his own, and the supreme endeavor of his art must be to body forth that world as it exists for him. The novelist works, and must work, subjectively . . . for apart from the personality of the workman no literary art can exist."[18]

Such was his creed and so he wrote. He was "a transitional novelist," said Niebling, "also in that he felt the need of freeing the novel from moral restriction, and yet did little in the final analysis to fight for that freedom."[19] Wells and Bennett were undoubtedly influenced by him, and so, too, was Frank Swinnerton; but these men, by reason of their less limited outlook and unwarped natures, surpassed him.

Wells said, "He spent his big fine brain depreciating life, because he would not and perhaps could not look life squarely in the eyes. . . . But whether it was nature or education that made this tragedy I cannot tell."[20]

Morley Roberts, robust member of the Rhymers' Club, who once pushed a match across the table to Yeats, shouting, "I don't mind lighting a cigarette for the only poet in the whole caboodle,"[21] and a friend of Gissing from grammar school days, turned Gissing's life story into thinly disguised fiction in *The Private Life of Henry Maitland,* in which a number of people of the period are recognizable, Frederic Harrison as Harold Edgeworth, John Morley as John Harley, James Payn as John Glass, H. G. Wells as G. H. Rivers, Clement Shorter as Carew Latter, and Edward Clodd as Edmund Roden. At the time this book appeared, Frank Swinnerton's biography of George Gissing was sent to reviewers, who denounced Roberts for his unkind frankness and commended Swinnerton for his excellent reserve; but Swinnerton admitted that he had only veiled what he did not know, and "whatever credit he deserved for ingenuity in the face of impenetrable silences he had no right to praise for discretion."[22] So well had Gissing's friends kept his secret.

Volume VIII introduced another new name to *Yellow Book* readers, destined to become well known to the English-speaking public, John Buchan, later first Baron Tweedsmuir. Unlike Wells's and Gissing's, his story was not a single item, but was followed by two others in Volumes IX and XIII. Buchan's rise to literary prominence had been meteoric. A note in the *Bookman* for November, 1895, marveled at the appearance of a new writer, "heralded by the announcement of half-a-dozen books."[23] The son of a Glasgow Free Church minister, he had studied philosophy and the classics at Glasgow University on a scholarship, and was now, at the age of twenty-one, at Brasenose, Oxford, and writing for *Macmillan's* and the *Gentleman's Magazine*. He had edited a small edition of Bacon's essays; in 1895 Unwin published his first novel, *Sir Quixote of the Moors*, and Lane announced his *Scholar Gypsies*. The Glasgow artist D. Y. Cameron had brought him to the Bodley Head, and Lane sized him up quickly as a lad he could use. By the middle of June, 1896, as principal reader to the Bodley Head he was considered a literary phenomenon. "Already," sighed Arnold Bennett, "he cannot be more than 23—he is a favorite of publishers." He was, according to the envious Bennett, "a very young, fair man; charmingly shy; 'varsity' in every tone and gesture. He talks quietly in a feminine, exiguous voice, with the accent of Kensington tempered perhaps by a shadow of a shade of Scotch."[24]

He was of course still at Oxford, where in 1897 as a member of the Union he led the attack in a debate on the question of whether or not the Kailyard School of fiction should be condemned. (By the narrow squeak of 58-56 it escaped.) The Kailyard School included such popular writers of romantic Scotch tales as S. R. Crockett, Ian Maclaren, and James Barrie. Buchan gave a "striking exposition of the nature of the real Scotland, the romance and pity of its history, which he placed in strong contrast with the narrow, parochial view of Scottish character spread by these writers."[25] In spite of his eloquence, the merits of Barrie saved the school.

Buchan had spent his summers in the upper Tweedsdale and had learned to know the life of the drovers and shepherds on the border, material he used in two of his *Yellow Book* stories. In "A Captain of Salvation," however, he wrote of Limehouse and the wharves and the seaman who had joined the army of God. All are memorable tales.

All his life Buchan "took situations in hand," and to each he gave his best effort. Like Wells he wrote competently in many fields. Just before he went to Canada as Governor-General, asked about his appearance in the *Yellow Book*, he said he remembered it dimly, except that "I always thought it a very odd medium for work of mine to appear in."[26]

Volume VIII was the fattest of all the *Yellow Books*, containing more than four hundred pages and presenting a fine array of talent. Harland had been especially determined that the buyer should get his money's worth from this volume, for the *Yellow Book* now had a competitor in the field, the *Savoy*, first promised for December but delayed until January. Competition might be the life of trade, but Harland was not sure what it would mean to a literary quarterly.

Chapter XXI

THE FIRST NUMBER of the *Savoy*, produced like the *Yellow Book*, to tempt that discriminating audience, the men and women of modern taste, came out in January, 1896, edited by Arthur Symons, who had contributed poems to Volume I and III of the *Yellow Book*, and Aubrey Beardsley, once its art editor.

The *Savoy* owed its being to the *Yellow Book*, though both sire and offspring would have denied this relationship. If Beardsley had continued as art editor of the popular quarterly, Symons would not have thought of launching a rival venture. Beardsley had contributed more than anyone else to the *Yellow Book*'s shocking but profitable modernity. Until he was sacrificed by the ill-advised Lane, no periodical could have competed with the *Yellow Book*, but now a contest was possible. When Smithers suggested to Symons the idea of the new quarterly, publisher and poet must have agreed that the art could only be entrusted to Beardsley. If Symons could interest the deposed editor in continuing his black and white innovations for a new magazine and if he could lure to its support poets and writers who had sympathized with Beardsley, he would have the essentials necessary for taking over the field once tilled by Lane.

Symons felt no loyalty to the *Yellow Book* nor to the Bodley Head. His poems in the early volumes had received harsh criticism and Lane was not his publisher. In the mind of the public, his flouting of restraint and reserve seemed akin to Beardsley's pictorial unconcern, and though there was no friendship be-

SOME PERSONS OF THE NINETIES
A Caricature by Max Beerbohm

Rear: Richard Le Gallienne, Walter Sickert, George Moore, John Davidson, Oscar Wilde, W. B. Yeats; below: Arthur Symons, Henry Harland, Charles Conder, Will Rothenstein: Max Beerbohm, Aubrey Beardsley

Reproduced by permission of William Heinemann Ltd., owners of the copyright

BEARDSLEY'S PORTRAIT OF MRS. PATRICK CAMPBELL

From the *Yellow Book*, I (1894)

tween the two—indeed they had not met until Symons made the opening move for the *Savoy*—their theories of art and literature were not dissimilar. So with Beardsley and a nucleus of disgruntled turncoats from the *Yellow Book*, Symons began the *Savoy*. Of the thirty-five writers who contributed to the *Savoy*, fourteen had work in the *Yellow Book*.

In the mind of the press and public, the two magazines were closely connected. "If the *Savoy* is half as good as it promises to be," said Arthur Waugh in the *Critic*, "it will knock the reputation out of the *Yellow Book* in one number." The dismissal of Beardsley was usually taken as an indication of a reformed *Yellow Book*, and the *Savoy* was considered to have assumed its aura of iniquity. The older quarterly was said to be stale and humdrum in comparison with the interesting and attractive newness of the *Savoy*. There were, to be sure, other literary projects of the nineties, the *Evergreen*, the *Dome*, and the *Parade*, but none except the *Savoy* was so near an imitator of the *Yellow Book*. Since the aims of the two publications, many of the contributors, and the art editor were the same, some consideration of the *Savoy*, and especially of Beardsley's part in it, seems appropriate.

This rose-tinted venture (its first cover was bound in pink boards not covered with cloth; Le Gallienne had said, "Even pink looks yellow by lamplight") was part of Symons' memorabilia to the nineties and in his brittle and declining years he liked to recall past glory by inditing letters to the press on its left-over stationery.

Arthur Symons' strict upbringing at the hands of his Wesleyan minister father undoubtedly contributed to his later revolt against the conventional in art, literature, and morals. Rebel though he was, he never could quite emerge from the shadow of the manse. As Edgar Jepson said, "To him his harmless enough life among the poets and artists . . . was a patch of the most purple, and he saw their peccadilloes as the sins of Imperial Rome."[1] Haunted by that sense of guilt which festered in the minds of so many of his generation, he brazened his unconcern in order to drown out the small cold voice of conscience. In mid-life, at Bologna, he broke under this conflict, and spent some years in an asylum, later recorded in *Confessions,* but in old age his dull eyes lighted defiantly as he described how Augustus John had painted his picture between two naked women.[2]

Symons' mother had sent him abroad to complete his education and on his return to England he was emotionally and intellectually under French influence. His first poetry had been shaped by his preparation for *A Study of Browning* (1886), but now Verlaine was his model and publication of *Days and Nights* (1889) placed Symons at the front of the Gallic-inspired poets.

He was a handsome youth with a high color, white skin, light brown hair, and blue eyes. He pronounced his name "Simmons" though Oscar Wilde always referred to him as "Simons," insisting it was perfectly clear that Arthur didn't know how to pronounce his own name. Ernest Rhys, Havelock Ellis, and W. B. Yeats were his closest friends, and he shared rooms with the last two in Fountain Court. Though a member of the Rhymers' Club, he did not restrict his interest to poetry, but courted all the Muses and lectured his associates on art, music, and the dance. If, as Archer said, he was a poet of only one mood, he atoned for this narrowness by living vehemently and turning from one stimulus to another with tireless zest. He was a skillful pianist and his knowledge of counterpoint served him well as music critic for the *Star*. Art was important with him too; he could hold his own in discussion with Herbert Horne, George Moore, and Will Rothenstein, and wrote discerningly of exhibitions at the New English or Burlington House. An ardent patron of the dance, he sat in the front row of stalls unless he watched from the wings, worshipping the ladies of the ballet as he had formerly paid reverence to Mlle Eglantine or Yvette Guilbert. When the music halls closed he and his friends sought the settees of the "historic Crown," where over gin and water they talked learnedly of choreography. He liked to travel, and his eager receptivity made his books about foreign cities bright and informative.

Verlaine, Baudelaire, and Villon were Symons' preceptors,

but he found poetic inspiration in his own emotions and sensations. He said his poetry was a "sincere attempt to render a particular mood which has once been mine, and to render it as if, for the moment, there were no other mood for me in the world."[3] Mostly his mood was a sensual melancholy. He took his pleasures seriously, never laughed at himself, experienced love as a "dim pain," and preferred his women beautiful but damned, though he resented the original culprit:

> O my child, who wronged you first, and began
> First the dance of death that you dance so well?
> Soul for soul: and I think the soul of a man
> Shall answer for yours in hell.[4]

Sometimes his verse—"Emmy," for instance—was sillily pretentious, but often it was tuneful and effective. He experimented with rhythms, as in "The Wanderer's Song," whose meter anticipated Masefield's "Sea Fever."

> Give me the long white road, and the grey wide path of the sea,
> And the wind's will and the birds' will, and the heart-ache still in me.[5]

Yeats said, "He is in no accurate sense of the word a 'decadent,' but a writer who has carried further than most . . . that revolt against the manifold, the impersonal, the luxuriant, and the eternal."[6] The editor of the *Chap-Book*, however, thought him "decadent in the unpleasant sense of the word,"[7] and George Moore called him "a man of somewhat yellowish temperament."[8]

During the nineties he published three books of poetry, wrote reviews for the *Athenaeum,* the *Academy,* and the *Saturday,* edited the *Savoy,* and brought out *The Symbolist Movement in Literature,* a helpful chart of literary currents. An astute critic, he could transfer his ideas into clear, readable prose. The *Savoy* illustrated his tastes and judgment.

He and Beardsley planned it partly at Dieppe in August, 1895, under the mentorship of Leonard Smithers, a publisher of strange and exotic books who had undertaken this new quarterly. Like Lane, Smithers had come to London from the provinces, started in a small way with secondhand books, especially unexpurgated editions, and gradually turned to publishing. But unlike Lane he had no interest in uplifting the public's taste, but only a desire to pander to its liking for the doubtful and forbidden. He had found such productions profitable, Burton's *Arabian Nights* in particular, and he could afford to be reasonably generous with Beardsley, but he had a bad influence on the resentful artist, stimulating his erotic tendencies and approving the sensational in his drawings. That he gave Beardsley opportunities to use his limited time with profit is to his credit.

Beardsley enjoyed improved health in the seaside resort, and friends, including Sickert, Conder, and the French artist, Jacques Émile Blanche, commented on his good spirits. He was working hard on drawings for the *Savoy* and gathering contributions from other artists. "Symons has written to Meredith," he told Rothenstein, "to ask if he would sit to you for a portrait. Personally I think Gyp is much more desirable";[9] but Conder wrote Will, "There has been a great deal of excitement about the new quarterly here and discussion. Beardsley is very pompous about it all."[10] Beardsley was indulging his long-cherished desire to write poetry and prose; results of his experimentation appeared in several numbers of the *Savoy*, not entirely to Symons' satisfaction.

Unlike Harland, Symons did not combine the old with the new; all the contributors to the *Savoy* were of the moment and its keynote was modernity. After a Beardsley cover, title-page, and table of contents design, an editorial note referred unmistakably to the *Yellow Book:* "It is hoped that 'THE SAVOY' will be a periodical of an exclusively literary and artistic kind. . . . We hope to appeal to the tastes of the intelligent by not being original for originality's sake, or audacious for the sake of advertisement, or timid for the convenience of the elderly-minded."[11] The opening essay, "On Going to Church" by Bernard Shaw, gave the new venture a start in the right direction. This essay was, as it happened, his sole contribution, but the *Yellow Book* received none. There were stories by Frederick Wedmore, Ernest Dowson, Rudolf Dircks, W. B. Yeats, and Humphrey James and the first three chapters of a romantic novel, *Under the Hill* by Beardsley, poems by Symons, Yeats, Mathilde Blind, Dowson, and Beardsley, and articles by Beerbohm ("A Good Prince"), Havelock Ellis, Joseph Pennell, and Selwyn Image. Beardsley had nine drawings and a large inserted Christmas card; Rothenstein, Sandys, Whistler in illustration of the article by his friend Pennell, Shannon, Conder, Beerbohm, and Jacques Blanche were also present.

Beardsley illustrated his own poem "The Three Musicians," which recounted in unorthodox stanza form the morning's experience of a young soprano, a Polish pianist, and a "slim gracious boy."

> The gracious boy is at her feet,
>   And weighs his courage with his chance;
> His fears soon melt in noonday heat.
>   The tourist gives a furious glance,
> Red as his guide-book grows, moves on,
>   and offers up a prayer for France.[12]

Smithers had vetoed Beardsley's first drawing of the gracious boy at the feet of the "lightly frocked" soprano, and in the accepted substitute, the two were walking arm in arm.

Critics have said much of Beardsley's *Under the Hill,* the expurgated version of *Venus and Tannhäuser,* later published by Smithers, earlier announced by Lane—critics who have deplored its labored and artificial preciosity, or who have seen in it the first stirrings of literary genius to match Beardsley's artistic gift, but who have agreed at least on the magnificence of its illustrations. Of one of these pictures, the artist had written Smithers, "The Toilet is going really grandly but there is such a heap of work in it. It will be finished to-morrow & that will include a night's work."[15] "A heap of work" is a masterly understatement of the effort this drawing must have required, for in fullness of detail and intricate design "The Toilet of Helen" probably exceeded any other drawing. Though he was still worried at staining "many a fair handkerchief red with blood,"[14] he would not spare himself, but worked day and night to make the *Savoy* his finest achievement.

When the number was out he wrote Smithers, "If you have

not already sent a copy of the S'voy to The Sunday Times, do send one round at once by hand. They are so very friendly to me, & have rather important book articles. Pennell &c rave about the Mag. Have got a Whistler for No. 2."[15]

Others than Pennell, &c., have raved about it. The evidence was plain to more than one critic that in comparison with the contemporary *Yellow Book,* the *Savoy* presented more exciting fare. "May the hair of John Lane grow green with Envy," crowed Dowson.[16] The *Sunday Times* described it as a *Yellow Book* "redeemed of its puerilities," the *Athenaeum* declared it was "free from some of the offenses of the older periodicals," and *Punch* observed that it was "bound to have an ennobling and purifying influence."[17]

In May, 1896, Beardsley's health was sufficiently improved for the doctors to permit his return to England. "So glad the Savoy has been well ordered," he wrote Smithers. "Of the Y.B. I know nothing."[18] He found lodgings at Epsom, "a capital place for work,"[19] though he had a slight return of the "hoemorrage"[20] (Beardsley never mastered the spelling of his affliction). He thanked Smithers for the third *Savoy,* in which "Yeats again provides the most interesting item."[21]

Yeats contributed articles to two issues on William Blake, and as a consequence of the reproduction of "Antaeus setting Virgil and Dante upon the Verge of Cocytus," not the work of the dangerous young Beardsley but of William Blake, dead these seventy years, Smith and Company banned the *Savoy* from their stands.

"O, Mr. Symons," the bookseller had said, regarding the naked Antaeus with a frown, "you must remember that we have an audience of young ladies as well as an audience of agnostics," adding as Symons turned away, "If contrary to our expectations the *Savoy* should have a large sale, we should be very glad to see you again."[22]

In this number Symons announced that the magazine would become a monthly. Its policy would remain the same, he assured his readers, and invited them to watch for Mr. George Moore's new serial *Evelyn Innes*—a long vigil, for it never appeared in the *Savoy*. A note at the back brought bad news about Beardsley. "In consequence of Mr. Beardsley's severe and continued illness, we have been compelled to discontinue the publication of 'Under the Hill,' which will be issued by the present publisher in book form, with numerous illustrations by the author, as soon as Mr. Beardsley is well enough to carry on the work to its conclusion."[23]

In demonstration of Beardsley's incapacity, no work of his appeared in the number except the cover and title-page, though he tried to take his failure lightly, writing to Smithers, "I *like* this number of the Savoy vastly, but should have *loved* it had there been an Aubrey or so within its covers."[24]

For the August number he again provided only the cover and title-page, the most significant picture being Conder's frontispiece for Balzac's *La Fille aux Yeux d'Or*. The literary contents included a poem, *"Venite, Descendamus,"* and "The Dying of Francis Donne" by Dowson, three sonnets by Lionel Johnson, *"Stella Maligna"* by Arthur Symons, and "The Song of the Women: a Wealden Trio" by the young Ford Madox Hueffer, a grandson of Ford Madox Brown, who was to write many novels, edit the *English Review*, change his name to Ford, indulge in a tempestuous affair with Violet Hunt, and in his *Transatlantic Review* give opportunities to many new writers of the twentieth century.

Of this fourth number the *Weekly Sun* said, "The Savoyards have taken seriously to literature, Mr. Symons alone keeping steadily to his old manner. Altogether, this is an issue whose promoters need have no fear of criticism. This time, at any rate, it has gone ahead of its rival, the 'Yellow Book.' "[25]

In September, Beardsley's contribution of cover (signed "Giulio Floriani") and title-page was augmented by "The Woman in White," an early drawing lent by Frederick Evans. When this number appeared, Smithers had moved from Arundel Street to the Royal Arcade, Old Bond Street, drawing the query from Beardsley, "Why not call your new premises 'The Sodley Bed?' "[26] Smithers had already broken it to Beardsley that the time on the *Savoy* was about served. Beardsley accepted the news philosophically: "Nothing else could I fear be done with the Savoy. . . . I shall do you some scortching [sic] drawings for No. 8."[27]

The October number saw the reproduction of Beardsley's *Death of Pierrot.* Phil May, the humorous black and white artist, originator of the *Winter Annuals* and on the staff of *Punch,* contributed to this number, as did Havelock Ellis with an article on Hardy. Symons had approached Edward Garnett, friend and literary mentor of the Pole with the unpronounceable name, now known as Joseph Conrad, asking for a contribution to the *Savoy* from the author of *An Outcast of the Islands.* Though Conrad had replied cautiously to Garnett, "Thanks for your hint about the 'Savoy.' I shall wait yet,"[28] his story "The Idiots" now appeared.

Another editorial note in the November issue prepared the public for its coming loss. The *Savoy* would cease publication with the next number, "leaving to those who care for it our year's work . . . presented to you in three volumes, in a cover of Mr. Beardsley's designing."[29] By this device of binding the numbers into book form, Symons hoped to insure for the *Savoy* the permanence of which the *Yellow Book* boasted.

Fiona Macleod's poem in this number gave further impetus to the efforts of those trying to discover the identity of this new Celtic poet who corresponded in a fine ladylike hand with editors and critics but remained elusively invisible. Katharine Tynan Hinkson reviewed Fiona's books in the *Sketch* and the *Speaker,* and Fiona thanked her gratefully, assuring her that there were personal reasons why she must preserve her privacy, but "this much I will confide in you, and gladly! I am *not* an unmarried girl. . . . "[30] George Meredith was pleased when William Sharp after many promises finally brought "Fiona" to call: "a handsome person," he wrote Mrs. Meynell, "who would not give me her eyes for a time. One fears she was not playing at abashment."[31] That was the summer of 1897. In 1905, after several volumes by Fiona Macleod had appeared, William Sharp died and the mystery ended. "Have you looked at the case of William Sharp's claim after death to the works of Fiona Mac-

Leod?" Meredith asked Mrs. Meynell. "He brought her to me, and she accepted my praise. A letter came to me saying that it was to be delivered when his breath was gone . . . but that he was the author. In none of his printed works, verse or prose, was there a sign of imagination or of simple fluency; and the Fiona papers have both. I am puzzled."[32] Meredith had to be convinced, like the rest of the London sceptics, that his fair visitor had been only a cousin of Sharp's, playing a part, and that Fiona was in fact the alter ego of William Sharp. One of the most successful literary hoaxes yet discovered, it could not have been carried on without some help, and one of the few confederates that Sharp admitted to the secret was R. Murray Gilchrist, called the leader of the Symbolist school of fiction. Gilchrist never betrayed his trust, though he must have been sorely tempted by Sharp's patronizing attitude toward his own work. Gilchrist, who lived for some years in the High Peak, was a writer of "great moments and appalling weaknesses."[33] In middle life he was much admired by Hugh Walpole, who visited his dark old house on the moors and thought him a very odd mixture. Walpole dedicated his *Silver Thorn* (1928) to his memory. Gilchrist had one story, a fantastic tale of ancient evil and blood sacrifice, in Volume VI of the *Yellow Book*.

The final *Savoy* was entirely the work of the two editors. Beardsley rushed the magnificent "Rhinegold" drawings into it, as well as the elaborate "A *Répétition* of 'Tristan and Isolde,'" portraits of Mendelssohn and Weber, "Mrs. Pinchwife," and finally *"Et in Arcadia Ego."*

Symons for his part used poetry, a translation of Mallarmé, essays, and "A Literary Causerie" containing this Valedictory Note:

It is a little difficult now to remember the horrified outcry . . . with which we were first greeted. I look at those old press notices sometimes . . . and then at the kindly and temperate notices which the same papers are giving us now; and I find the comparison very amusing. For we have not changed in the least . . . and now that everyone is telling us that we have 'come to stay,' that we are a 'welcome addition,' etc., we are obliged to retire from existence, on account of the too meagre support of our friends.[34]

So *The Savoy* passed from the scene, and the *Critic* consigned it to Nirvana with the acrid epitaph, "No wonder *The Savoy* died. If it had not died a natural death, some one would have killed it."[35] Once again Beardsley had lost a post as art editor.

The contributors to the *Savoy* represented a narrower segment of literary figures than was found in the *Yellow Book*. The proportion of well-known names was perhaps higher: Bernard Shaw, Joseph Conrad, Havelock Ellis, Selwyn Image, John Morley, Ford Madox Hueffer (later Ford), Ernest Rhys, Bliss Carman, and Edward Carpenter never appeared in the *Yellow Book*, though Carpenter was flatteringly mentioned in an essay on "The Poetry of John Barlas" by H. S. Salt.

That essay was one of the few "timely" articles in the *Yellow Book*, and so fulsome in its praise of Barlas (Evelyn Douglas, member of the Rhymers') that it might have been called "logrolling." Salt reinforced his opinion with quotations from Meredith, who had said that, in the sonnet form, Barlas "takes high rank among the poets of his time."[36]

Salt had met Meredith, whom he greatly admired, when he appealed to him for help with a biography of James Thomson. In April, 1894, Meredith thanked Salt for the "little brochure, 'Sex Love' by Edward Carpenter," which he had read "with great satisfaction," adding graciously, "Now and then I see your name. Those least prominent are generally doing the better work."[37] Carpenter and Salt had taken part in the riots of Bloody Sunday, escaping with no harm other than the theft of Salt's watch by a pickpocket. Carpenter advocated the simple life, and in pursuit of it Salt, after twelve years as master at Eton, gave up teaching and took his wife Kate to live in a small cottage in Surrey not far from Shaw. Salt and Shaw were drawn together by the bond of Humanitarianism and Vegetarianism. Shaw enjoyed fireside conversation with Salt at the cottage and piano duets with Kate, who also did volunteer secretarial work for the young playwright. When Shaw married the Irish heiress Miss Payne-Townshend in 1898, Salt stood up with him. After the marriage Mrs. Shaw decided that Kate's gratuitous service was no longer needed. In addition to acting as Secretary of the Humanitarian League and editing its journal, for which Ouida wrote passionately on behalf of abused horses and dogs, though she refused to write an article on Vegetarianism, Salt wrote biographies of Shelley, Richard Jefferies, James Thomson, and Thoreau. Gandhi admitted that he became a "Vegetarian by choice," after reading Salt's *Plea for Vegetarianism*.[38]

A few contributors figured in both the *Savoy* and the *Yellow Book*, among them Yeats, Beerbohm, Dowson, Johnson, Symons, George Moore, Crackanthorpe, Leila Macdonald, Wratislaw, and Edgar Prestage, Professor of Portugese Literature at King's College, London, who made translations for both magazines.

Chapter XXII

HARLAND WOULD NOT have been human if he had not drawn a great breath of relief when Symons announced the coming finale of the *Savoy*. It had been a difficult year for the editor of the *Yellow Book*. Disconcerted at first by the loss of Beardsley, he had tried to accept it philosophically, but the presence of the desirable young artist on a rival publication fretted him. To pick up the current *Savoy* flaunting Beardsley's work and the writings of young authors he had once considered his own and compare it with the latest "milk and waterish" *Yellow Book* was an unhappy experience. In public he disagreed loudly with the critics and reviewers who said the *Yellow Book* was running a bad second to its new rival, but in private he was not so confident. Still it was running, and . . . please God . . . he hoped to keep it so.

He pointed out that the *Yellow Book* offered a broader fare than Symons' quarterly, not only the new and coming but the already accepted men of established reputation, university professors, learned critics, and intellectual journalists such as Walter Raleigh, George Saintsbury, James Ashcroft Noble, H.

D. Traill, Francis Watt, John M. Robertson, Frederick Green-wood, Lewis Hind, and Richard Garnett.

Walter Raleigh, later Sir Walter, then a member of the faculty of the University of Liverpool, wrote on "Poet and Historian" for Volume VIII, enlivening a ponderous dialogue between the proponents with occasional witticisms and epigrams. His *English Novel* (1894) had been so flatteringly received that he hoped he might be appointed to the vacant chair of Rhetoric and English Literature at Edinburgh, but the honor went to another *Yellow Book* contributor, George Saintsbury. After Raleigh's study of Stevenson appeared in 1895 he enjoyed lecturing on the late Tusitala before women's clubs, writing his wife, "I love being a large tom-cat among the pigeons."[1] Later lectures in America did not rouse such enthusiasm, for it was hinted that he merely read the galley proofs of his forthcoming book. He found Americans "quite incredible . . . so bright and snappy—the click without the spark."[2]

In 1904 he was appointed Professor of English Literature at Oxford, a post in which he was very happy. His scholarship and writings were generally respected, though in 1908 Arnold Bennett took him to task for his *Style,* calling it a "too fearfully ingenious mess of words."[3] Raleigh's wife was likewise critical of his writing, finding too many "prig words" in his *Six Essays on Johnson* and complaining, "when you get to the end of a sentence you've mostly forgotten what the beginning was about."[4]

Yet Raleigh applauded brevity, advising a young author, "Mind you don't write any professional English, the garbage of words that conceals lack of thought. . . . Write for Oxford cabmen—in that way you will say more in less space."[5] Still one doubts that "Poet and Historian" was directed toward such an audience.

Like Raleigh, James Ashcroft Noble lived in Liverpool, but he never lectured at a university, had no degree, and had educated himself by reading during a long period of ill health. He first wrote for Dickens' *All the Year Round,* progressing to the *Spectator* and the *Academy.* By 1892 he was living in Wandsworth Common, London, where he lay reading on the sofa in his study over the garden, or sat at his writing desk, "constantly smoking cigarettes and sipping weak whiskey and water,"[6] to write his reviews for the *Daily Chronicle,* the *Westminster Gazette,* and the *New Age.* In 1893 his *The Sonnet in England* won the respect of literary pundits. Young writers came to seek his advice, including the poet Edward Thomas, who later married his daughter Helen. Her father was much interested, she said, in the *Yellow Book* movement, "though never carried away by it." For her part she was "rather repelled by it," detesting Beardsley's drawings.[7] She read *The Woman Who Did,* but being embarked on a similar enterprise herself, as recorded in *As It Was,* was not impressed by Grant Allen's heroine.

In the *Yellow Book* James Ashcroft Noble was represented by an essay on the Glasgow poet and essayist Alexander Smith, whom he called "Mr. Stevenson's Forerunner," in Volume IV, and a well-constructed tale, "The Phantasies of Philarete," in Volume V. Within a year of this last he was dead, having failed to survive an operation on his throat. His death took a fair, capable, and considerate critic from English letters; "his life had been a pilgrimage of pain," said Arthur Waugh.[8]

Henry Duff Traill, critic, poet, and parodist, was educated at the Merchant Taylors' School and at St. John's College, Oxford. After a career as foreign correspondent he returned to London and from 1893 to 1897 edited Cassell's *Social England.* As a parodist he used his satire against many forms of literature from the Rossetti sonnet to the New Humour. When R. B. Cunninghame Graham, the aristocratic Socialist of Gartmore, made the unfortunate statement at the Marxist Congress in Paris that "the English Workmen are degraded by the pipe, the Bible, beer, and admiration for the upper classes," Traill blasted him with a ballad beginning,

> Well! blow me, if that ain't a pretty story,

and expressed admiration for

Upper classes as can manage for to grow you
Such a lovely thing in silly Scottish squires.[9]

In his *New Fiction and Other Essays on Literary Subjects*
(1897) he revealed a strong bias toward the established and traditional, attacking new realism as "unreal with the falsity of
half truth, and as old as the habit of exaggeration . . ."[10] and inquiring of Stephen Crane's *Maggie*, "Is it art? If so, is the making of mud-pies an artistic occupation, and are the neglected
brats who are to be found rolling in the gutters of every great
city unconscious artists?"[11] But in spite of his suspicion of the
new, he contributed a gently derisive study of a psychologist,
"The Papers of Basil Fillimer," to the *Yellow Book* (Volume V).

Francis Watt received his education from the Universities of
Edinburgh and Heidelberg, became a Barrister-at-Law in Gray's
Inn, and went to the Middle Temple in 1898. Though he wrote
many articles on law and *The Law's Lumber Room* (1895) he
had broader interests, contributing critical essays to the *Magazine of Art* and to the *Observer*. He belonged to the Henley-
Stevenson circle, and on the night the news of Stevenson's unexpected death reached London he and Henley were discussing
a memorial to the "Shorter Catechist" when William Archer
arrived. Watt, reported Archer, was a saturnine being who
added greater gloom to the occasion.[12] Later Watt wrote appreciatively of both Stevenson and Henley. His two *Yellow Book*
essays reflected his legal training—"The Sergeant-at-Law" and
"A Pair of Parricides."

John Mackinnon Robertson and C. Lewis Hind were, like
Noble, largely self-educated. Robertson left school at thirteen.
After a journalistic beginning on the Edinburgh *Evening
News* he wrote *Walt Whitman, Poet and Democrat* (1884) and
went to London to the *National Reformer*. In 1893, the year
of his marriage to the American Maude Mosher, he became editor of the *Free Review*. His "Concerning Preciosity" in the *Yellow Book* revealed a mind well stored with the literature of
the past and perceptive of preciosity in Carlyle, Browning,
Swinburne, and Meredith, as well as Pater.

Robertson also succumbed to the lure of the American lecture tour in 1897 and in 1900 joined the exodus of journalists to South Africa. He wrote books on Labor, Free Thought, and Rationalism, good examples today of Edwardian thinking, before turning to studies of Shakespeare in 1917. He was Parliamentary Secretary to the Board of Trade from 1911 to 1915 and a Liberal M. P. from Northumberland for twelve years.

As a young man C. Lewis Hind began a career in the lace business, attended night classes at Birkbeck College, and gradually took up writing, getting his first chance with music criticisms for the *London Illustrated News*. From music he veered to art, and his work for the *Pall Mall Budget,* the *Observer,* and the *Art Journal* won him the editorship of the *Studio* in 1893, and allowed him to open its pages to Aubrey Beardsley. By the time the initial number had appeared, Hind had gone to the *Pall Mall Budget,* just purchased by William Waldorf Astor—the "Golden Astor," Katharine Tynan called him. Hind parted from the *Budget* in 1895, when J. M. Richards, father of Mrs. Craigie, bought the weekly *Academy* and asked him to be editor. He took E. V. Lucas, Wilfred Whitten, and Arnold Bennett to help him, and though many complained that he had abandoned the scholarly tradition of the *Academy,* its circulation jumped upward. One of his innovations was the "crowning" of some notable literary work each year, and the books so elevated included *Pan and the Young Shepherd* by Maurice Hewlett, *Christ in Hades and Other Poems* by Stephen Phillips, and *Youth* by Joseph Conrad.

The first chapter of Hind's novel *The Enchanted Stone* appeared in the *Yellow Book.* When the novel was published Victor Plarr called it a modern romance "in a style beyond reproach," but Hind admitted that "it fell quite flat. . . . Occasionally some nice man or woman would tell me . . . how much they had enjoyed reading it, but when I addressed questions to them I found that they had not perused it carefully."[13]

Hind left the *Academy* in 1903 but continued writing on art. In 1917 he went to America, and his weekly articles in the *Christian Science Monitor* became *Some Authors and I* and *More Authors and I,* recollections far more trustworthy than

Frank Harris' *Contemporary Portraits,* though Arnold Bennett (whose review of *Evelyn Innes* Hind had paid for but refused to print) thought that "nearly all Hind's ideas are sentimental and wrong, and his judgments on literature are quite impossible nearly every time; but he has a charm. Perhaps it is his naïveté —a rare enough quality."[14]

Hind said of his own writing, "I am no British Museum student: nothing has happened unless it has happened to me."[15] Though he felt no need of the resources of the grimy grey edifice crouched along Great Russell Street, a number of other *Yellow Book* contributors could often be found in the domed Reading Room where Dr. Richard Garnett served as Keeper of Printed Books. He had been so appointed in 1890, but had been on the Museum staff since 1857. In all those years, said G. B. Burgin, the museum cat had never lacked a friend.[16] Garnett was nearly sixty when Harland asked his support for the *Yellow Book,* but from his store of learning he gladly contributed prose, poetry, and translations, for he contended that "one needs just as much inspiration or suggestion to make a translation as to write original matter."[17] He was at the time much absorbed by Italian literature and his interest was reflected in his "Sonnets from Petrarch" and story "Alexander the Ratcatcher," to which he said history and Rabelais contributed equally. This tale of Pope Alexander VIII in Rome was later added to his *Twilight of the Gods,* a collection of ironical narratives first published in 1888 but several times reissued. T. E. Lawrence, in his early years associated with Garnett at the Museum, said in his Introduction to the 1924 edition, "Dr. Garnett was a very sure scholar who had done the plain things and the big things and was tired of them. . . . It wants no learning to enjoy *The Twilight of the Gods;* but the more learning you have, the more odd corners and hidden delights you will find in it."

The kind, witty, erudite man died in 1906, but the name of Garnett still shines in English letters, for Edward was his son, Constance his daughter-in-law, and David his grandson.

Two young women poets, Nora Hopper and Alma Strettell, both interested in translations, often consulted Dr. Garnett at the Museum on some problem of syntax or meter. Nora Hopper, of Welsh and Irish parentage, living in Kensington, spent long days in the Museum, poring over the Icelandic sagas and negotiating the misty paths of folklore by academic research under Dr. Garnett's encouragement before she turned to a study of her own Irish heritage. Thus inspired, she soon gained recognition as one of the new poets of the Celtic revival, being hailed by Yeats as "the one absolute dreamer of Irish literature."[18] At this time Miss Hopper was obliged to dream her Irish scene, for she had not yet set foot on the green isle. In 1894 her first book, *Ballads in Prose,* had been published by Lane and she was writing busily for periodicals. Except for one story, a bloody tale of ancient Sligo in Volume III, she contributed to the *Yellow Book* poems that were inspired by Irish or pagan folklore. Archer included her among his Younger Generation poets. Perhaps Miss Hopper's Icelandic approach to Ireland had chilled her blood, for she was wont to dwell on the melancholy and even bloodthirsty aspects of Celtic folklore. In 1901 she married Wilfrid Hugh Chesson, himself a writer who had discovered *Almayer's Folly* for Fisher Unwin, and her last novel, *The Bell and the Arrow,* was published a year before her death in 1906. In 1911 Chesson contributed "Reminiscences of 1898" to the *Bookman.*

Alma Strettell (Harrison) had done translations for Dr. Garnett's *History of Italian Literature,* but her interests extended to German, French, Spanish, Provençal, and Rumanian folk songs. In her *Lullabies of Many Lands* (1894) she was said to have got at the heart of the folk songs as no other had done. As wife of the painter Lawrence Harrison she presided over their beautiful home in Cheyne Walk, the rendezvous for a circle which included Tonks, Steer, MacColl, and George Moore. Rothenstein had known the Harrisons well in Paris, but their closest friend was Sargent, and through him they knew Harland and the *Yellow Book* circle. In the summer of 1886 the Harrisons had been with Sargent in the colony at Broadway, where he and Alma played duets with such assiduity as to be known as the "co-maniacs."[19] Sargent did the illustrations for her *Spanish and Italian Folk Songs,* and Violet Paget ("Vernon Lee") thought the frontispiece "wonderful."

Another *Yellow Book* contributor who earned a living at the Museum while pursuing the uncertain career of letters was the poet Theo Marzials, who had been there more than twenty years when he contributed poems to Volumes III and VII. His first book, *Passionate Dowsabella: A Pastoral,* had been "provisionally printed" in 1872, and a copy inscribed "little Gossie from Theo" had been given to his fellow-worker Edmund Gosse.[20] Later he collaborated with Walter Crane in *Pan-pipes,* for which Crane did the decorations and Marzials the song arrangements. Crane found the poet a charming song composer, "more like a Troubador than a modern person" and "always delightful to meet, apart from his musical gifts."[21] Lane snared his *Gallery of Pigeons* (originally published in 1873) and headed him toward the *Yellow Book.* Marzials' musical setting for Swinburne's "Ask Nothing More of Me, Sweet," has been admired.[22]

In the nineties Edmund Gosse visited the Museum only infrequently, having left his position in the cataloguing department in 1875, convinced that his prospects there were "absolutely nil."[23] But he had begun his literary life in the musty chill of the Reading Room, encouraged by the poetic interests of his fellow-workers whom he thought of as "a nest of singing birds."

In 1867 at the age of eighteen, the son of a noted zoologist and devout Christian, Gosse had escaped from an atmosphere of Victorian piety to the freedom of the B. M. He wanted to write, and not being able to decide between poetry and criticism, tried his hand at both. In 1870 *Madrigals, Songs and Sonnets,* by Gosse and John Arthur Blaikie (also a *Yellow Book* contributor), drew this admonition from P. H. Gosse, "I hope you have already prayed *earnestly* and *importunately,* that if this book should meet with praise and fame, this may not be a snare to your soul. It is a great danger and Satan will subtilely make use of it. . . . 'Forewarned is forearmed,' the adage says.

216

May it be so with you and John. I have personally warned him of the danger and have prayed for you both."[24]

In spite of a parent's qualms the book had little sale, but it served to introduce Gosse to Rossetti and Swinburne, whom he cultivated in the pre-Watts-Dunton days, spending rapt hours listening to the poet's conversation. Arthur Waugh thought that a "not infrequent luxuriance or audacity of expression" in Gosse's work was directly referable to Swinburne's long and animated monologues.[25] In 1875 he was made translator to the Board of Trade and in 1877 contributed to Leslie Stephen's *Cornhill* "A Plea for Certain Exotic Forms of Verse," making clear the rule of the rondeau, villanelle, chant royal, and other French types. His *Studies in the Literature of Northern Europe* (1879) called attention to what was stirring beyond the North Sea. In 1885 after Tennyson, Browning, and Matthew Arnold had recommended him, he received the Clark Lectureship at Trinity College, Cambridge, but the honor was nearly his undoing.

Since Gosse was not a University man, the appointment received much criticism, and when the substance of his lectures was published as *From Shakespeare to Pope,* Churton Collins took issue with Gosse's scholarship in the *Quarterly Review,* pointing out mistakes and inaccuracies with such devastating vigor that Gosse wrote Hardy in October 1886: "The *Quarterly Review* has felled, flayed, eviscerated, pulverized and blown to the winds poor Me in thirty pages of good round abuse. . . . It is rather shocking, and keeps me awake o' nights and affects my liver. But I hope to live it down."[26]

Gosse's friends rallied to his support: Tennyson epitomized Churton Collins as "a Louse on the Locks of Literature";[27] Grant Allen was not at home when Collins came to call ("I can't see him; I won't see him. I can't forget poor Gosse"),[28] and gradually Gosse lived it down. He made the indicated corrections, the book was reissued, and two years later he could smile over a letter from Stevenson at Saranac about a thermometer Mrs. Gosse had given R.L.S. and his wife for their living room. "See what Gosse says," Stevenson wrote, was a frequent word of command. "But the point is this: in the verandah hangs another thermometer, condemned to register minus 40° . . . and to him, we have given the name of the Quarterly Reviewer."[29]

Taking more care, he wrote *A History of Eighteenth Century Literature* (1889). *Father and Son,* an account of his relations with his parent, was first published anonymously, but in 1907 he admitted its authorship. Though he said, "This particular book causes me more nervous anxiety than anything I ever published before,"[30] it was one of his best and was crowned by the French Academy in 1913. Yet the frankness of his revelation surprised his friends. Once at a discussion on Browning when Gosse said he had a warm and almost filial regard for the poet, Mrs. Belloc Lowndes expected someone to shout, "God help poor Browning if the author of *Father and Son* has for him a filial regard!"[13]

Steadily, learning from his mistakes, by the mid-nineties Gosse had climbed to a position of eminence among bookmen from which he could look down and dispense favors or issue decrees. He probably had more influence on the contents of the *Yellow Book* than any man except the editors and publisher. He was always glad to put in a word for a young writer, just starting up the slippery ladder of letters. In the past he had profited by the kindness of such elders as Browning, Tennyson, Swinburne, and Matthew Arnold; now he was willing to pass on the favors, and who knew when the present fledgling might be in a position to return them? When he incribed a gift of *The Naturalist of the Seashore* to "Mr." Siegfried Sassoon on his tenth birthday, he gave much pleasure to a small boy and did himself no harm.[32] Gosse was probably on good terms with more different people in the literary world than any other writer of his day, though Churton Collins, Watts-Dunton, and W. E. Henley were not among them.

Of Gosse's poems in Volume I the *National Observer* had remarked, "Mr. Gosse, too, is always frequent and free with his views on 'The Poet' and his habits: but that does not prove that Mr. Gosse can write poetry any more than his contributions to this miscellany prove it."[33] In Volume V Gosse made use of the father-son theme in "The Ring of Life," which the *National Observer,* had it still been in existence, would have found even less convincing.

Gosse's home at Delamare Terrace was always open to young men from Cambridge or Oxford, coming poets or arrived authors, and trans-Atlantic celebrities. His wife Nellie was a charming hostess and Louise Guiney recalled "divers Devon junkets delectably served at dear Mrs. Gosse's."[34] She sometimes did a little writing herself for the *New Review,* but she was also an artist and when her pictures were exhibited at the Grosvenor Gallery Robert Browning called them "jewel-like."[35] Her daughter Sylvia, student and later patroness of Walter Sickert, inherited this talent.

Aside from his biographies, for which he had a flair, Gosse's most important bequest to literature was a vicarious one, for by his astute criticism and appreciative encouragement he urged on wavering writers. With half the world against him, he called Hardy's *Tess* "simply magnificent," and through his critical studies he turned currents into the English stream.

"Dear, cunning, catlike, crafty old Gosse," Stevenson called him;[36] "the most interesting and consistently amusing talker I ever knew," testified Somerset Maugham;[37] "the lingering, final spark of the Pre-Raphaelite comet," said Osbert Sitwell.[38]

Mrs. Gosse was a sister of Lady Alma-Tadema, wife of the painter and member of the Royal Academy. "Dear Tadema is so much more festive than his pictures," Siegfried Sassoon's mother observed when the artist sent her a flask of red wine from Italy. "He makes the marble the most important part of the pictures."[39]

Alma-Tadema gave marble no small share in the decoration of the elaborate mansion he built in Regent's Park, described by Mrs. Gosse for American readers in the *Century,* with anecdotes of his wife and two small daughters Laurence and Anna. Shortly after the completion of this incredible edifice with its marble stairway and tessellated floors, it barely escaped destruction one night when a barge loaded with hazelnuts blew up in a neighboring canal. During the barrage, Laurence, who, said Mrs. Gosse, had been instructed to call the maid if she wanted anything in the night, sat up in bed and said with great calmness, "Anna, ring the bell!"[40]

Now this same Laurence, grown to young womanhood, was embarked upon a literary course and contributing "A Ballad of the Heart's Bounty" to Volume IX of the *Yellow Book,* perhaps urged on by Uncle Edmund. She had already written a novel, *The Wings of Icarus,* called "unwholesome and unhealthful" by the *Bookbuyer,*[41] and "of very considerable promise" by the *Bookman.*[42] Her *Yellow Book* contribution was later included in her first volume of verse, *Realms of the Unknown Kings,* published by Grant Richards, who said he lost money on it. A reviewer in the *Academy* pointed out its faults and virtues; she was hampered by a narrow range, and did not excel in sheer verbal beauty, but she possessed a passionate sincerity, a true sense of rhythm, and a dramatic faculty, though in "A Ballad of the Heart's Bounty," he thought, she had "rather too patently imitated" songs from *The Bard of the Dimbovitza,*[43] translated from the Rumanian by Alma Strettell, one of her co-poets in this volume.

But Laurence Alma-Tadema was best known to a former generation through her verse about the little girl, long a favorite with elocutionists, beginning

> If no one ever marries me,
> > And I don't see why they should,
> For nurse say I'm not pretty
> > And I'm seldom very good.

Another contributor for whose presence Gosse was responsible was A. C. Benson, the Eton schoolmaster who had poems in three volumes of the *Yellow Book.* In 1893 Benson had published a small work called with questionable optimism *Poems.* Gosse saw promise in it, though he complained privately that it was "too much concerned with God and water-fowl,"[44] and used his influence on Benson's behalf. In 1896 Benson's *Essays,* published by Lane, drew the comment from James Ashcroft Noble that "there is something in his critical work which is a little—or more than a little—irritating," and characterized a passage on William Blake as "merely manner, no doubt, but could any manner be more unfortunate?"[45] Benson's prose style was often discussed unfavorably by critics, and Max Beerbohm's parody "Out of Harm's Way" in *A Christmas Garland* was considered by Bertrand Russell to be "the most devastating of all the satires."[46]

Benson had small use for French poetry and looked to the classics for his inspiration. His sonnet in Volume VII, *"Sic tu recoli merearis!,"* with its wistful adjuration,

> O soul, my soul, before thou com'st to die,
> Set one deep mark upon the face of time,

was thought by the *Times* to be "rather fine."

Of his own struggle to set this mark Benson recorded in his diary in 1898, "I wrote two sonnets in the evening before dinner. I find myself much slower at writing poetry and much less disposed to do it than two years ago. I don't think I have the real spring. . . . I have a certain facility in language, and now and then a gleam of artistic excitement. But this is not enough, and I must, I think, resign all hopes of a poetical future."[47] About this time John Lane sent him a statement. His *Poems* was out of print, of the *Lyrics* (1895) 260 copies were left, of *Lord Vyet*, 230. "I shall publish one more volume and then shut up shop," he decided.[48] It was *Peace, and Other Poems* (1905).

He did not abandon letters as a career. He wrote biographies for the English Men of Letters series, including a life of Rossetti accomplished with the hard-won blessing of Watts-Dunton, who had long considered the Pre-Raphaelite his special property. His *From a College Window*, a volume of essays, seems most likely to leave its mark. He lectured at Oxford and wrote long letters to his friends, Henry James among them. His diary was conscientiously kept and he once sent an excerpt to Gosse "as it had already amused Lady Ponsonby and Henry James." Gosse read it with relish until he came to an account of a visit to his house:

"Breakfast with Gosse. I dislike people who are bright at breakfast.

"Dinner with Gosse—champagne; and yet he complains of poverty."[49]

Hugh Walpole said Benson excelled when he was "thoroughly malicious. He picked out his friends' weaknesses like plums out of a pudding and ate them greedily one by one."[50]

Chapter XXIII

IN NEARLY EVERY number of the *Yellow Book* Harland included the work of one American besides himself and Henry James, but all whom he so honored had one thing in common—they were not then living in the land of their birth. The American author who stayed at home had small chance in the *Yellow Book*. Such old friends as Stedman and Howells were never invited to contribute; indeed many Americans in England were likewise overlooked—Mark Twain, Bret Harte, and the young journalist, Stephen Crane, who stopped in London on his way to report the war in Greece. What a pity Harland did not press him for a story, but Heinemann, not the Bodley Head, published *The Red Badge of Courage*, and *Scribner's*, not the *Yellow Book*, got "The Open Boat."

Crane's best friend in England, however, Harold Frederic of Utica, New York, had appeared in Volume VII with a story "The Truce of the Bishop," written, he said, in contemplation of a cycle of Irish tales of the O'Mahoney coast. Frederic had been in London twelve years as correspondent of the New York *Times*. Primarily a journalist, he worked on novels and short stories in his spare moments, and it had taken him six years to finish *Illumination*, or *The Damnation of Theron Ware*, as it was called in the States, and nearly double that time to complete *In the Valley*.

To his London contemporaries Frederic seemed a typical Horatio Alger hero who had made his way by luck and pluck, principally by pluck, they added. Most of them knew his story, for he liked to talk of his boyhood, of the death of his father and his withdrawal from school at the age of twelve to support a widowed mother. Mrs. Pennell remembered his account of carrying milk to the homes of the well-to-do in the Mohawk Valley and his envy of the owners and their soft Brussels carpets. Now his home in London was all Brussels carpets, she said.

His writing career began when he was seventeen and a proofreader on the Utica *Herald,* with a vacation letter from the Thousand Islands. His first story was published in *Harper's* in 1877. That same year he married Grace Green Williams, granddaughter of the Reverend Beriah Green, famous antislavery agitator. In 1880 Frederic went to the Albany *Evening Journal,* then to New York; in 1884 the *Times* sent him to England.

He had an adventurous spirit and never shirked an assignment or shunned coming to close quarters with danger. In his investigation of the cholera epidemic in France he went where no other reporter dared to go. He studied the landlord-and-tenant problem in Ireland at first hand, he went to Berlin to write *The Young Emperor,* and he visited Russia to observe the persecution of the Jews under the Czar, reported in *The New Exodus* (1892).

He loved London, not the fashionable glitter of the West End, but the old London of Chaucer and Dickens. William Heinemann, his good companion and publisher, has recalled a memorable night when he and Frederic and Brandon Thomas, author of *Charley's Aunt,* "painted London red."[1] Frederic went often to the Shannons', where his repertoire of American college songs astonished the men from Cambridge and Oxford. Stephen Crane and Robert Barr, the Scotch-Canadian novelist, were his best friends and "many a merry night" they spent at Crane's house in Sussex.

"A big, loosely-built man, who talked extremely well, who seemed acquainted with everything and everybody," said Lewis Hind,[2] and Louise Imogen Guiney recalled his boyish smile, firm hand grip, and "face of one who is afraid of nothing."[3] He could write well on any subject, but none of his pains went to the perfecting of a phrase or the placing of a colon. The general effect was what he wanted. He himself preferred his short stories to his novels. Like Howells he wrote realistically of the American town, but he lacked Howells' gentleness and finish. It was sometimes suggested that he wrote Frank Harris' stories as well as his own.

In the Valley was called by the *Athenaeum* "a perfect specimen of an American historical novel," and Brand Whitlock praised the fine realism of *The Damnation of Theron Ware*, advising Octavia Roberts to read it, though he admitted "the whole book is not as distinctly elevating in tone as I like a book to be."[4] Frederic's old associates in Utica recognized characters in it as drawn from life and were not pleased.

But as the nineties waned the American withdrew from his former friends and his presence became an embarrassment in circles where he had once been warmly welcome. He left his home, making the Savage Club his headquarters. Then he was living with Kate Lyon in the country. "He was none the happier, surely," said the charitable Miss Guiney; "the unacknowledged uneasiness of his false position must have helped to break him down so early and so suddenly."[5] But Conrad termed him "a gross man who lived grossly and died abominably."[6]

The circumstances of his death, "unnecessarily by a blunder," the Coroner's verdict, as read, brought the situation into unpleasant publicity. Evidence at the trial showed that he had suffered a stroke but that Miss Lyon, "a member of his household" and a Christian Scientist, had called a healer instead of a doctor.[7] He grew rapidly worse, to the alarm of his friends, and when Cora Crane, Stephen's wife, finally induced him to have medical care it was too late. He died on October 19, 1898. Miss Lyon and the healer received prison sentences which were later remitted. Frederic's new book *The Market-Place* boomed to record sales.

Crane resented Henry James' attitude over the Frederic scandal—"He professed to be er, er, er much attached to H. and now he has shut up like a clam"—but when Cora and Stephen took in the Frederic orphans, James gave fifty pounds to a subscription for them.[8]

After Stephen Crane's death in 1900 Robert Barr wrote to a friend, "Stephen died at three in the morning, the same sinister hour which carried away our friend Frederic nineteen months before. At midnight, in Crane's fourteenth-century house in Sussex, we tried to lure back the ghost of Frederic . . . but he made no sign. I wonder if the less insistent Stephen will suggest some ingenious method by which the two can pass the barrier. I can imagine Harold cursing on the other side, and welcoming the more subtle assistance of his finely fibred friend."[9]

Another New York State writer to whom Harland gave several opportunities on the other side of the Atlantic was Arthur Cosslett Smith from Rochester, the C.S. of the V.,O.,C.S. initials. Besides his share in the V.,O.,C.S. offerings, he had independent appearances in Volumes III, IV, and V. Unlike Frederic, Smith found no inspiration in the Mohawk Valley, its history or customs. He did not look back realistically upon American rural life, but sought intellectual stimulus in foreign capitals.

The son of a Canandaigua judge, he had spent one year at the Naval Academy at Annapolis, was graduated from Hobart College, and later received a law degree from Columbia University. After his marriage in 1870 to Elizabeth Atkinson he practiced law for some years in Rochester, but having independent means, did not let the legal profession interfere with travel and writing. During the nineties he lived much abroad, making use of his reader's card at the British Museum and his permit to the National Library in Paris. In London he found the lively *Yellow Book* group to his liking, and his stories reflect its detached satiric attitude toward life and its concern with art. His *The Monk and the Dancer,* a book of six short stories, appeared in 1900; "the Rambler" called it "one of the best beginnings ever made."[10]

It was followed by *The Turquoise Cup and the Desert* (1903; republished in 1920). He died in 1926. Vincent Starrett wrote of him in *Buried Caesars,* finding his outlook on life "delightfully un-American" and his writing slightly artificial, but deciding that "in his artifice, at any rate, he is a very considerable artist,"[11] and William Rose Benét said in 1946, "When I think of short story writers who should be remembered, I think of him."[12]

Harland's own town of Norwich, Connecticut, was the birthplace of William Morton Fullerton, who contributed a poem in praise of George Meredith to Volume III, a sonnet ending with the unblushing assertion:

> No hand but thine is found to fit the gage
>   The Titan, Shakespeare, to a whole world threw.
> Till thou hadst boldly to his challenge sprung
> No rival had he in our English tongue.

Educated at Phillips Academy and at Harvard, where he helped found the *Harvard Monthly,* Fullerton had been introduced to Meredith's work by Professor Croswell, and the enthusiasm which he developed for the English novelist he put to good use on Meredith's behalf. As Literary Editor of the Boston *Advertiser,* when Roberts Brothers brought out the first uniform one-volume edition of *Richard Feverel,* Fullerton admitted that he "kept the columns as full of allusions to Mr. Meredith, and of editorials upon him, as my editor-in-chief would endure; and as a result had called out a number of responses that kept, as the expression is, the ball rolling"[13]—as "the Philistine" would have said, "the log rolling."

Meredith was not displeased by this complimentary game of bowls and in 1886 wrote Fullerton, "I am sensible of the honour you do me in thinking about my work at all. . . . Good work is the main object. Mine I know to be faulty. I can only say generally that I have done my best to make it worthy." He invited Fullerton to visit him in England where he would find a "small cottage warmly open" to him.[14]

Two years later Fullerton accepted the suggestion and found England so pleasant that he decided to remain there. From 1892 to 1911 he was on the foreign staff of the London *Times.* His writing did not always meet with the success he could have wished. "Do not be disheartened," Meredith advised him, "hug your forces, so as to believe in them, and bide your time. It is sure to come to those who are faithful to themselves."[15]

He became known as an expert on international affairs and from the staff of *Figaro* wrote for American and English journals. In 1910, at the time of the disastrous floods in France, Henry James wrote Mrs. Wharton, "I don't ask you about poor great Paris—I make out as I can by Morton's playing flashlight."[16]

During World War I Fullerton was on the general staff of the A.E.F. He was made a commander of the Legion of Honor in 1926.

Another young American who got his start in the *Yellow Book* was Norman Hapgood, brother of Hutchins. Born in Chicago in 1868, he had finished Harvard with an A.M. degree and an LL.B. in 1893. The law course he had taken under pressure from his family, for his own inclinations were toward writing; Charles Dudley Warner had refused an article on Margaret Fuller, and other manuscripts shared a similar fate. His first encouragement came on a visit to London when Harland accepted an essay on Henri Beyle (Stendhal) for Volume IV of the *Yellow Book*. Reviewers too were kind. The *Sketch* called his essay "the best thing in the new *Yellow Book*,"[71] and the New York *Bookman* considered that the article showed "a true capacity for criticism."[18] Such favorable comment strengthened Hapgood's resolution and soon American editors were taking his work. In 1897 he was made dramatic critic of the *Bookman,* and the veteran William Archer epitomized him as "a young critic, a good fellow and frightfully in earnest."[19] In 1900 he became editor of *Collier's*. His literary career suffered some deflection when he was made American minister to Denmark in 1919. In his autobiography, *The Changing Years* (1930), he referred to the impetus given his ambition by the *Yellow Book,* saying, "The literary debauch I was taking, after my personal grievance against fate is fully admitted, had something that helped to round out the world-outlook of a young American from the middle west."[20]

Beardsley had included the work of three American artists—Sargent, Pennell, and Sydney Adamson, better known as Penrhyn Stanlaws—but after the withdrawal of the art editor no more Americans showed their wares in the *Yellow Book*. In Volume XI, however, Harland admitted the American painter Eugene Benson, but to the side of literature rather than art, with an essay on Gabriele d'Annunzio. Ever since his early stay in Italy, Harland, like most of his London colleagues, had cherished a keen interest in Italian literature. D'Annunzio the poet had already received the consideration of the critics, for the Bodley Head had published *Italian Lyrists of Today*, but this was the first treatment as a novelist accorded him in the English press. Benson based his article primarily on d'Annunzio's new romance, *Le Vergini delle Rocce,* though he discussed his poetry as well. In March, 1897, Ouida's essay on d'Annunzio was to appear in the *Fortnightly* and be hailed as his introduction to the English public, but six months earlier Benson had shown in this volume of the *Yellow Book* an intimate understanding of the Italian writer.

Benson should have known his subject thoroughly, for he had lived for more than twenty years in close contact with Italian art and literature. Beginning as an illustrator for a New York paper under the signature "Proteus," he had gone abroad to study art and become an original and accomplished painter, living in Italy but exhibiting in London and New York. He had a literary side as well, having already published *Gaspara Stampa* (1881) and *From the Asolan Hills* (1891). By his marriage to Mrs. Henrietta Fletcher he had acquired a stepdaughter, Constance, an author in her own right under the name "George Fleming." Constance's first book *Mirage* had been published when she was very young. She had been engaged to an English peer, but such were the mores of the day that he broke the engagement on learning that her mother had been divorced.[21] She emerged from the entanglement, however, with a miniature of the peer's grandfather, Lord Byron, and a tempting bundle of the poet's letters. Today she is most easily recognized as the author of *Kismet*. Constance's best friend in London was Elizabeth Robins; and both belonged to Mrs. Crackanthorpe's circle. Walter Crane knew the Bensons well, visiting them in Venice "in a fine old *palázzo* . . . on the Rio Marin" that was furnished with many treasures collected during their long residence in Italy.[22] Benson died in 1908.

A Canadian poet, Charles C. G. D. Roberts, later Sir Charles, member of a distinguished New Brunswick family and cousin of Bliss Carman, contributed to Volume VI a poem, "Earth's Complines," later included in his *Selected Poems* (Toronto, 1936) under the heading "Poems, Philosophical and Mystical." A dynamic and energetic personality even till his death at the age of eighty-three, he was always in the literary thick of things, had been one of the book judges at the World's Fair in Chicago in 1893, and had written for the *Chap-Book*. Though sometimes called the originator of the modern nature story and the Poet Laureate of the Animal World, he found himself quite at home in the *Yellow Book*.

Charles Miner Thompson (Harvard, 1886), whose grandfather had written a popular book, *The Green Mountain Boys*, was currently writing boys' stories for that sheltered journal of childhood, the *Youth's Companion*, when his contribution, "In an American Newspaper Office," appeared in Volume VI of the *Yellow Book*, a contrast which the Boston *Bookbuyer* did not let go unnoticed. Though a reviewer for *Vanity Fair* declared that for its "originality of idea, vividness of narrative, and literary construction," the story was "quite an important paper even in the company of others such as Henry James,"[23] Thompson was not again tempted by the golden glitter but maintained his allegiance to the *Youth's Companion*, serving as its editor until it ceased publication in 1925. Then he again demonstrated his versatility by going to the Harvard University Press as editor. A collection of stories from the *Youth's Companion* under his editorship was published by his son in 1956.

The romantically Gallic name Renée de Coutans signed to "A Lady Loved a Rose," in Volume X and a short story, "Natalie," in Volume XII concealed the identity of Aline Harland, who, though she played an important part in the life and work of the editor, did not wish to appear openly in his quarterly. Her devotion to his interests probably kept her from becoming a writer herself; her letters show she had ability, but she subordinated her work to her husband's, and her output was small. Up to this time her principal accomplishment had been the translation of Matilde Serao's *Addio, Amore,* "creditably" done according to the *Bookman,* but with some trace of foreign accent.[24] Her contributions to the *Yellow Book* showed a light and delicate touch. Of her lady who "loved a rose," one critic grumbled that she might have loved "something more animate."

The editor himself used a pseudonym on several occasions. As an anonymous "Yellow Dwarf" he wrote letters on books and authors in three numbers, taking the opportunity to pay off a few debts owed authors who had snubbed the *Yellow Book,* Frank Harris, John Oliver Hobbes, and George Moore among them. Harland undoubtedly hoped by this device to lift the periodical out of the placid pool of approbation into which it was gently sinking after the departure of Beardsley and to revive the interest of the critics and public. He was partly successful, and several guesses were offered as to the Dwarf's identity (Frank Harris got it right straight off), but some thought such name-calling vulgar; Arthur Waugh said it showed "lack of breeding."[25] A story "The Elsingfords" by "Robert Shews" in Volume XI was written by Harland, and it may be that a long story of the Peruvian desert, "La Goya," by an unknown "Samuel Mathewson Scott," was from his pen. Miss D'Arcy identified Shews but not Scott.

Harland's acknowledged stories reflected his enchantment with the Continent. "This Europe of the American," James called it, saying, "He is lost in the vision, all whimsical and picturesque, of palace secrets, rulers and pretenders and ministers of bewilderingly light comedy, in undiscoverable Balkan States, Bohemias of the seaboard, where the queens have platonic friendships with professional English, though not American, humourists; in the heavy, many-voiced air of the old Roman streets and of the high Roman saloons where cardinals are part of the furniture; in the hum of prodigious Paris."[26] His *Yellow Book* stories bridged the gap between "Sydney Luska" and popular successes like *The Cardinal's Snuff-box.* Collected in book form in *Grey Roses* (1895) and *Comedies and Errors*

(1898), they represent the best of his writing. A critic in the *Academy* declared that "those few in England who could distinguish a short story from a slice of ham and mustard," ranked these books by the side of Maupassant's and Mérimée's.[27] They were adroitly constructed, with convincing atmosphere and bright entertaining dialogue; the mood lightly humorous, sentimental perhaps, but never entirely mawkish. Under his creation characters assumed unusual and fascinating personalities, for the drab and the dreary had no part in his make-believe. Love often motivated action, not the starkly demanding passion of Crackanthorpe nor the amorous excitement of George Moore, but the gentle impetus of an Eros whose arrows did not slay. As for the plot, it was of lesser concern. The theme and treatment were paramount, though Harland had a gift for dramatizing a situation, his own sensitivity giving it a significance missed by the casual observer. If he sometimes magnified intuitive insight out of proportion to its value, he did not deserve the unkind words of Frank Harris, "I fancy he had made his notes of human nature whilst observing the personages of a melodrama at a provincial theatre."[28] No, he did not deserve that.

Van Wyck Brooks, reading Harland's stories in the middle of the next century, found them brittle and charming and artificial. "Only his charm itself was real,—an effect of meticulous workmanship,—but this was so real that . . . one wondered how such graceful prose could ever have dropped into oblivion so quickly and completely."[29]

Perhaps one other name should be included among these Americans in the *Yellow Book,* an unrecognizable Jennie Eustace, whose "Kit: an American Boy" appeared in the last volume. Miss Eustace must have caught Harland in one of his softer moments, or she was one of those against whom he warned himself in his Birthday Letter, "a friend, or a friend's friend, or a friend's young lady, or a friend's maiden aunt."[30] If she was an American she had been a long time away from home and her ear had become attuned to the English idiom. "Kit could not control his enthusiasm," she wrote, "but . . . gave utterance to the most emphatic expression of approval in his vocabulary: 'By Jove! But that is ripping!' "

Chapter XXIV

MORE AND MORE Harland came to rely on the offerings of his Saturday evening guests, Lane's poets, and the authors and artists linked to the Bodley Head by cold cash. The members of the Cromwell Road coterie have been variously listed by participants and observers, but since the evenings continued for several years many visitors could have been entertained at them. Ella D'Arcy, one of the most frequent, mentioned Kenneth Grahame, Beerbohm, Crackanthorpe, Evelyn Sharp, Netta Syrett, Ethel Colburn Mayne, the Marriott Watsons, Victoria Cross (Vivian Cory), Charlotte Mew, George Moore, Richard Le Gallienne, Arthur Symons, Henry James, and occasionally Edmund Gosse. Evelyn Sharp added Oswald and Bernhard Sickert, James Welch (brother-in-law of Le Gallienne), Stanley Makower, and Mabel Dearmer. Netta Syrett remembered her first meeting there with Stephen Phillips. Lewis Hind, Mrs. Murray Hickson (Mrs. Mabel Kitcat), and Stephen Gwynn have identified themselves as regular attendants. Gwynn said W. J. Locke was often at the gatherings, though he did not write for the *Yellow Book*.

One of the strangest was Baron Corvo. The title was self-bestowed, his real name being William Serafino Austin Lewis Mary Rolfe; Miss D'Arcy said he had confessed that "Corvo" meant "unforgivable sin," but as A. J. A. Symons pointed out, it is Italian for "raven."[1] Rolfe sent Harland the first manuscript of the *Stories Toto Told Me* from Wales and the editor, excited by these lively *contes,* urged this newly discovered genius to come at once to London, later regretting his impetuosity when the Baron left fleas in an upholstered chair on his first visit. In a literary decade which teemed with "queer 'uns" Baron Corvo was pre-eminent, but no trace of his eccentricity was revealed in the stories he wrote for the *Yellow Book*. These Italian folk tales narrated by a sharp Italian peasant boy to his English master were later published as *In His Own Image*. Somerset Maugham, who found the *Yellow Book* bad during a twentieth century rereading,[2] must have missed San Paola and San Pietro, rival patrons of church builders, the good little *cherubini* who could not sit down because they lacked the wherewithal, the young Saints, San Sebastiano and San Pancrazio, kept in order by the *Padre Eterno*, and the mamma of San Pietro who but for her selfishness might have been saved by the onion-top reached down to her from Heaven by her Angel Guardian. In six months misspent as a theological student in Rome Rolfe had assimilated the material for these tales.

He wrote like a genius and quarreled like a madman, but the Harland circle, though urging him into unupholstered chairs, treated the fantastically shabby figure with respect, remembering other derelicts who had risen to fame. Harland believed in him. So did Kenneth Grahame, but the Baron was soon at loggerheads with both. An attempted collaboration with Hugh Benson, priest-son of the Archbishop, led to rupture and recrimination. E. Nesbit and Hubert Bland induced Grant Richards to finance his *Chronicles of the House of Borgia*. His letters to this publisher offer a depressing record of his mental maladjustment. When the book appeared, Harland, forgiving all, declared, "In any land save England, such a book would make its author at once FAMOUS and RICH. It is GREAT."[3] But the Baron gave no ground. He struck out the dedication to Harland from *In His Own Image*, and Harland, Lane, and Richards figured as a trio of villains in an unpublished manuscript discovered by his biographer, A. J. A. Symons.[4] Rolfe died in Venice at the age of fifty-three, insane and a pauper; probably no *Yellow Book* author save Henry James has received more recent attention and republication.

Most of the Cromwell Road habitués, however, were gentle in spirit, though determined in their pursuit of art and letters. Three women—Evelyn Sharp, Netta Syrett, and Ella D'Arcy—who were particularly associated with Harland owed their friendship to the *Yellow Book*. The first two in their autobiographies have recalled the zestful evenings at the Harlands'. Miss D'Arcy left no formal record of her life save in her letters and conversation. She had been unknown to Harland and Lane when she sent in her unsolicited manuscript "Irremediable," but she soon became the trusted intimate of editor and publisher, admitted to their confidence and always welcomed as a contributor. With the exception of Harland no other writer appeared so frequently.

Born in London of Irish parents, Ella D'Arcy had been educated in Germany and France, had lived at Hythe and had known the Channel Islands well. Intending to become an artist she had studied at the Slade, but the failure of her eyesight forced her to give up that ambition. She then turned to the sister art of writing. One of her first stories was accepted by Dickens for *All the Year Round.* She had sold a story to *Blackwood's* and one to *Temple Bar,* but her first real recognition came with the publication of "Irremediable" in Volume I of the *Yellow Book.* Though the story had already been refused by several London publishers (the editor of *Blackwood's* declared that marriage was a sacrament and could not be so summarily treated), Miss D'Arcy's realism won critical acclaim and she was enthusiastically accepted by the Harland circle.

Four of her *Yellow Book* stories were laid in the Channel Islands, a territory in which she preceded Elizabeth Goudge by four decades, though she was prone to walk the shady side of the street while Miss Goudge preferred the sun. The unhappy and unblessed marriage was one of Miss D'Arcy's favorite themes, and she sent her lovers to the altar, said Osbert Burdett, "as if their blood was to be shed."[5] Unlike many men authors of the period, who portrayed gentle femininity trampled by the male's unprincipled brutality, Miss D'Arcy showed the superior and well-intentioned man caught in the snare of a designing or stupid woman. For all that was wrong in these marriages the blame rested on the heroine's drooping shoulders. In considering Miss D'Arcy's place in English fiction, William C. Frierson has said, "Her insistence upon the narrowness and triviality of feminine interests is of sufficient importance in the literary history of the nineties to attract our interest. The intimate and un-romantic detail which characterized her presentations forecast the unsentimental analyses of the late English realists."[6]

In 1895 Lane collected her stories into a volume *Monochromes,* and in 1898 brought out *The Bishop's Dilemma* and *Modern Instances.* Her translation of Maurois' *Ariel* in 1924 completed her published work.

According to Netta Syrett, "But for her incurable idleness she should have made if not a great, at least a very distinguished, writer of elegant and witty prose."[7] Her procrastination was well known, and on one occasion Harland locked her in a room, re-fusing to let her out until she finished her next *Yellow Book* story. She loved to travel, and the Syretts called her "Goblin Ella" because she would suddenly pack and disappear, materi-alizing months later in their household with no explanation for her absence.

Netta's family lived not far from Field's Place, Sussex, where Shelley was born, and Ella, after a pilgrimage to the house, enthusiastically talked of writing the life of Shelley. Perhaps that was why John Lane selected her to translate Maurois's *Ariel,* an achievement for which the French author remembered her with gratitude.

Ella was a friend too of the Williamsons, Alice and C. M., who collaborated on travel books and wrote novels. He had been editor of *Black and White,* and they were on good terms with the Harlands. Netta and Ella once visited the Williamsons' villa at Mentone, where Netta and the Williamsons wrote conscien-tiously every morning. Ella "never did a stroke of work," said Netta.

Beside her aversion to work, two other peculiarities hindered Miss D'Arcy's career. She was always ahead of the age in which she was writing and she was extremely sensitive to editorial re-buffs. Just as the editor of *Blackwood's* was horrified by "Ir-remediable," so in 1930 when she tried to place a life and trans-lation of Rimbaud, whom she considered "the greatest of poets, of any age, or any country," she could not find a "publisher, nor an editor in London who could hear his name without turning purple from hair roots to shirt collar."[8] Yet a few years later books on Rimbaud were well received. When one publisher refused a novel she took his verdict as final and put the manuscript away, though Arnold Bennett begged her to let him see it.

So for one reason and another, this promising and much praised writer of the nineties did not bridge the gap between the two centuries. Most of her later years were spent in Paris on the Left Bank, where on the Rue Jacob she had a small room, a good bed ("What a strange thing it is," she complained, "that the practical Briton has never learned the comfort of a good bed any more than he has ever learned to appreciate great poetry or fine literature"),[9] and the respectful attention of the *concierge* and his wife. She spoke French like a native and was usually accepted as one, though she was to die in England, in September, 1939. In the summer she liked to sit in the sun in front of the *Café des deux Magots*, drinking bock and watching the young Bohemians stroll by. They reminded her of the happy days of her youth.

While Ella D'Arcy wistfully remembered the bygone years, Netta Syrett flung her early experiences into her novels. School days at Myra Lodge figured in *The Victorians,* her teacher-training course at Cambridge in *God of Chance,* her first glimpse of feminine independence in London in *Portrait of a Rebel,* and her acquaintance with *Yellow Book* artists and writers in *Strange Marriage.*

With a freedom unusual for the nineties the five Syrett girls lived in a flat of their own in Ashley Gardens, one keeping house while Kate attended Bedford College, Mabel and Nell studied art (both had pictures in the *Yellow Book),* and Netta taught in the Polytechnic School for Girls. Here she made a friend of Mabel Beardsley—a tall girl with a good figure and ginger red hair who liked teaching no better than she. Netta wanted to write; Mabel yearned to be an actress. One day she invited Netta home to tea and to meet her artist brother Aubrey, whose work was just beginning to catch on. Through Aubrey, Netta was introduced to the Harlands and became a welcome and frequent visitor at the house in Cromwell Road.[10]

236

She was not, however, entirely uninitiated in the ways of authors, for Grant Allen was her uncle and she had already been disconcerted by his frank talk of sex and influenced by his materialism. But she was, as Arthur Waugh wrote of her in the *Critic* in 1896, "practically a product of the *Yellow Book*. . . . . She is by no means of the ordinary depressing type of blue-stocking, but has a merry laugh, a contempt for Ibsen, and a busy bicycle. . . . She can talk of an infinity of subjects, and gathers the materials for her fiction largely from the observation which accompanies her own conversation."[11]

Lane bought her first novel, *Nobody's Fault,* for the Keynotes Series, and Harland took three stories for the *Yellow Book.* Although she remembered herself as "young and shy and very easily overawed" in those days, she made a host of friends, including William Locke, Stephen Phillips, Kenneth Grahame, Hilaire Belloc, and Max Beerbohm among the men and Evelyn Sharp, Ella D'Arcy, Mollie Clugston, May Sinclair, Cissie Le Gallienne Welch, and Julie Norregard among the women.

In 1898 her play *The Finding of Nancy* had one performance at the Playgoers' Club with Lillian Braithwaite, C. Aubrey Smith, and Mabel Beardsley in the leading roles, for Mabel too had realized her ambition. Max praised it in the *Saturday Review* over Pinero's *Letty,* saying, "Miss Syrett, knowing little about her specific art, went straight to life, and threw us a bit of life, for what it was worth, with no clever superfluities."[12] In one of her later plays for children, the youthful Noel Coward made a conspicuous success.

An ardent first-nighter, in 1904, rather by chance, she gave Laurence Housman's *Prunella* its one favorable review. When the drama critic of the *St. James's Gazette,* with whom she had gone to the play, pronounced the performance "rot" she asked to write the review for him.[13] Later most critics came to agree with her.

She too liked to travel, and lived for a time in Paris, where she gained the friendship of Gerald Kelly and Somerset Maugham, whose later characterization of the *Yellow Book* as "jejune" she resented.[14] She once made a pilgrimage to the grave of Aubrey Beardsley at Mentone, sending flowers and leaves from it to his mother and sister. After her final visit abroad she returned to live in a flat in Ebury Street within sight of George Moore's front door, but she never saw him go in or out during the five years of her residency. She met him once, however, at the Gerald Kellys' and talked of Clara Christian, who had gone to Ireland with Moore, finally leaving him to marry a friend of his. Clara was a wonderful mimic, she told Moore, who after a long pause inquired, "Did she ever mimic *me?*"[15]

Miss Syrett wrote busily and successfully from the moment of her *Yellow Book* initiation to the appearance of her last book, *Gemini,* in 1940, three years before her death. Harold Williams thought *The Child of Promise* (1907) the strongest of her novels, "a tale distinguished by intellectual power, fine feeling, and vigorous humour,"[16] but a critic in the *Academy* thought she understood women, but "not men."[17]

Evelyn Sharp went the independence of the Syrett girls one better, for in 1894, at the age of twenty-four, she took a flat alone in London and tried to answer bravely when Whistler chided, "Not understood at home, I suppose? No scope for the development of your personality?"[18] But a budding authoress in a large family of older brothers needed quiet in which to write and a secret niche wherein to pile up rejected manuscripts.

Richard Whiteing was the first literary friend of her emancipation, but she soon became a part of the *Yellow Book* coterie and was often at the Harlands'. Once when Henry James was present Harland took her aside to say in an impressive whisper, "He says he has *heard* of your fairy tales!" for she had begun as a writer for children.[19]

Of her first novel, *At the Relton Arms,* accepted on Le Gallienne's and Davidson's recommendations for Lane's Keynotes Series, a reviewer in *Vanity Fair* had two things to say: it was "brought out by the Bodley Head, and the author is not a fool."[20] On the other side of the Atlantic the *Bookbuyer* considered the morals of the book "hardly to be classed among those which our grandmothers called 'nice.' "[21] Six stories in the *Yellow Book* (Volumes IV, V, VI, VIII, XII, and XIII) led H. D. Traill, remembering Canon Ainger's verse, to greet her as "Lane's latest swan." She found Lane a generous publisher, but she was amused by his attempts to make a match between her and his favorite, William Watson. As the poet was known to be susceptible to feminine charms, she was not excited when Lane confided to her that he had never seen William so attracted by any girl.

Stephen Gwynn remembered the Evelyn Sharp of those days as "an absurdly boyish figure, but with brown eyes bigger than grow in any boy's head."[22] Kenneth Grahame was another good friend. So too was William Locke, but she lost his regard over the suffrage question. Henry W. Nevinson, who with Laurence Housman was an ardent worker for Votes for Women, had welcomed her to the cause, "fresh from the staff of the *Yellow Book*, most unmistakable of writers, always equally ready with her penetrating simplicity, her sympathetic wit, and indignant pathos."[23]

Nevinson, journalist and war correspondent, had himself contributed to the *Yellow Book* a poem, "Fire of Life," which justified Le Gallienne's acumen in always addressing him as "Brother Poet,"[24] though he was better known for his prose. His first book of short stories, *Neighbors of Ours* (1895), had been delayed by his publisher for nearly a year until Arthur Morrison's *Tales of Mean Streets* in similar vein had appeared, with the consequence, Nevinson said, that "mine was praised, and his was bought."[25] The following year his *In the Valley of Tophet* presented an appalling picture of the miners in the Black Country, and his "shamed sympathy with working people became an irresistible torment," so that he could hardly endure to live in the ordinary comfort of his surroundings.

Earlier he had been on the *Chronicle,* disputing violently with Shaw over the rates the red-haired music critic was to be paid, but Shaw got the best of him as he usually did in money matters. Nevinson had married young; his wife, Margaret Wynne Jones, was a writer and student of public affairs, and their son Christopher Richard, born in 1889, became a distinguished painter.

With Nevinson's devotion to liberty and his hatred of oppression he was bound to champion unpopular causes, such as Votes for Women. Miss Sharp's adoption of the suffrage campaign was complete, unhesitating, and effective. The very life of the movement from 1914 to 1918, Nevinson has testified, stemmed from her "brilliant mind and dogged resolution." She spoke eloquently and was twice arrested. Her work was continually hampered by the persecution of a government that declared her bankrupt for tax resistance (she thought taxation and representation should go together), stripped her rooms of furniture, cut off her telephone, and seized her royalties. Of the many who helped and suffered, said Nevinson, she "will always be counted among the highest."[26]

To Nevinson, too, Miss Sharp owed her introduction to the Manchester *Guardian,* with which he was then connected and for which she wrote for many years. She was never long without a cause, and Stephen Gwynn saw her in a "land suit" at the end of World War I, "plucking gooseberries and currants against time in a market garden."[27] After the achievement of suffrage she turned to other causes, child welfare and relief work for the Friends in Germany and Russia.

In 1932 Margaret Nevinson died, and the following year Miss Sharp married her long-time friend. In 1936 she wrote the libretto for R. Vaughan Williams' opera *The Poisoned Kiss.* She and her husband faced the first two years of World War II together. His last poem, "Live Dangerously," in the September, 1940, *Life and Letters,* pictured an old man dozing in his club until an air raid alarm roused him to activity.

> The deathwatch beetle dies within my brain
> And I wake up to living life again.

Not even old age kept Nevinson from championing the oppressed, and at the age of eighty-four he wrote a plea for better treatment of the internees who had come to England for refuge. He died in November, 1941, and a year later Evelyn Sharp edited his last book, *Visions and Memories.* She lived until June, 1955.

John Masefield said of Nevinson's autobiography, *Fire of Life,* that few men had such a noble record to set down. Nor, it might be added of Evelyn Sharp, had many women.

In the *Yellow Book* days Evelyn Sharp and Kenneth Grahame enjoyed each other's companionship and were often at Dieppe together with the colony of writers and artists, Beerbohm, Robert Ross, Oswald Sickert, Reggie Turner, and Conder. They bathed in the morning, watched the children dance at the Casino in the afternoon, and in the evenings listened to a concert or put money on the Little Horses at the gaming tables. Miss Sharp said Grahame was an honest critic and a perfect travelling companion, adding that he was usually taken for an Englishman because he was so Scottish.[28]

Kenneth Grahame was a cousin of Anthony Hope (Hawkins), whose mother was a Grahame, but the two young men sought different paths to literary success, Anthony Hope with his light ironic fiction like *The Dolly Dialogues,* or adventurous romances like *The Prisoner of Zenda,* and Kenneth Grahame with his delightful tales of children ("the only really living people") like *The Golden Age,* or fantasies like *The Wind in the Willows.* Anthony Hope did not write for the *Yellow Book,* and years afterward reported that he found in it "a great deal of pretty writing, though not much great writing, and an airified intellectual arrogance which is amusing."[29] But Cousin Kenneth may be read in eight of those intellectually arrogant volumes.

Kenneth Grahame reached the *Yellow Book* by way of the *National Observer.* In April, 1894, he belonged to Henley; in July, 1894, he appeared in the *Yellow Book,* and the *National Observer* was generous enough to praise his "Roman Road" as a "very subtle study of the thought of a boy, phrased in prose of an exceedingly delicate texture."[30] The Bodley Head had already brought out his *Pagan Papers* (1893), however, with a frontispiece by Beardsley (a nice collectors' item). In the process of negotiating terms for this publication Grahame had asked 10 per cent on the first two hundred copies and 20 per cent on

241

the rest, adding, "I don't call this a grasping proposal—especially from a Scotchman."[31]

He knew the value of money, for he worked with it every day at his post in the Bank of England, of which he became secretary before he was forty. His writing was done outside of office hours, and on Sundays he liked to lie above the Henley backwater on the Thames and plan the next adventure of Harold and his brother. He occupied a top floor flat on the Chelsea embankment and entertained at tea ladies who admired his Chippendale bureau which had belonged to Wellington and his collection of hollow glass rolling pins. He was a blond, temperate, kindly man, whom Netta Syrett thought more attractive than some of the effeminate individuals she saw in literary circles.

In Volume III came "The Headswoman," said to "toe the nose of women's rights," later issued by Lane as Bodley Booklet Number 5. In subsequent volumes appeared "A Falling Out," "The Inner Ear," "Long Odds," "The Iniquity of Oblivion," "*Dies Irae,*" and a poem "To Rollo." Some of these were included in *The Golden Age* (1895), reviewed enthusiastically by Swinburne in the *Daily Chronicle*. Two more were incorporated in *Dream Days* (1899). The kind words from The Pines were useful to the young author, but no amount of unfavorable criticism could have kept the public from taking to its heart these attractive tales. In America as well as England he was loved.

Some of his papers were printed in the "little *Chap-Book* in Big Chicago," and E. A. Robinson wrote, "At last that disappointing little affair has printed something worth reading. I refer now to a little sketch by Kenneth Grahame, called 'The Secret Drawer.' I do not know when I have seen a little sketch that has interested me so much as that, or satisfied me half so much. It took an artist to even think of writing it."[32]

In 1899 Kenneth Grahame married Elspeth Thomsen, and for the child of that marriage, Alastair, his immortal *Wind in the Willows* was written under circumstances later described by Elspeth Grahame in the Introduction to *First Whisper of "The*

Wind in the Willows" (1944). When she made this record Kenneth had been dead twelve years and Alastair more than twenty, having committed suicide in his first year at Oxford.

On such few volumes rests the literary fame of Kenneth Grahame, yet no contemporary's is more likely to endure. A new biography by Peter Green (1959), which reveals many hitherto unrealized complexities and sorrows in Grahame's life, seems to confirm this judgment.

Stephen Phillips was one of Lane's new poets whom the publisher, much taken with this big, heavy-set young man, introduced to the Harland group, but on his first appearance at Cromwell Road Aline was in one of her "moods" and left him unnoticed in a corner until Netta Syrett took pity on him. After that the two young people "became more than a little interested in one another,"[33] but the Harlands never warmed toward Stephen Phillips, Harland calling him the "Hall Caine of poetry." Still he printed two of Phillips' poems in the last two volumes of the *Yellow Book*.

Phillips' literary sun rose quickly over the London horizon and set with the same suddenness. Five years after he came to the city, penniless and unknown, with few influential friends, two of his poetic dramas had been accepted for production at West End theatres and ten thousand copies of his new poems subscribed for before publication. Reviewers could not write of his work without comparing him to Dumas, Milton, or even Shakespeare. Within another ten years he was hawking his verses up and down the street, selling them for whatever a pitying editor would pay for the privilege of suppressing them. Phillips' success, which seemed so easy, was dearly bought. Its price was failure.

Born near Oxford in 1864, he had studied for civil service, had been an army tutor and then an actor, touring the provinces with Sir Frank Benson's Shakespearean company, before he published his first poetry in the *Spectator*. In 1890 with his cousin Laurence Binyon he contributed several poems to a pamphlet *Primavera*, published at Oxford. Though his first book, *Eremus: A Poem* (Kegan Paul, 1894), did not receive much notice, Stopford Brooke and Lionel Johnson spoke well of it, and Lane was impressed. When Elkin Mathews printed *Christ in Hades* in his *Shilling Garland* Lane arranged to take on Phillips as a Bodley Head prize, and brought out his *Poems* (including the two *Yellow Book* specimens and *Christ in Hades*) in 1897. Now Phillips was the center of flattering attention. His friend Hutton of the *Spectator* called *Christ in Hades* "a wonderful dream, a dream which stirs the heart in every line,"[34] and Lewis Hind in the *Academy* praised the "individuality of outlook" and "the perfect fusion of matter into form which is that indefinable, inimitable, undeniable thing, style."[35] His *Poems* won the 1897 *Academy* Award of a hundred pounds, Henley coming off second best with half that sum. Everyone wondered how the irascible editor would endure this eclipse, but he wrote generously to Phillips that he was "proud to be in the same boat as the author of *Christ in Hades*."[36]

Sidney Colvin, convinced of Phillips' genius, befriended him as he had Robert Louis Stevenson a few years before, and the Colvins entertained for him frequently, on such occasions inviting influential people. In August, 1899, William Archer wrote a friend, "On Friday I dine with Colvin at the B.M. to hear Stephen Phillips read Francesca—rather an ordeal!"[37] Stephen Gwynn, invited to the Museum on a similar occasion, was "never so moved" in his life,[38] but G. K. Chesterton heard Phillips read his *Ulysses* under the same auspicious circumstances and remained quite calm.[39]

Though Phillips submitted to these affairs and basked in the applause, he was impatient of formal society and was at his best in a small group of friends. Then he enjoyed reading his poetry aloud, and Coulson Kernahan has testified to the excellence of his performance: "Some godlike spirit, outside himself, seemed, in these supreme and consecrated hours, suddenly to possess him, and, when the hour and the consecration were past, as suddenly to leave him. But, while that hour lasted, there was only one word for Stephen Phillips, poet, and that word was Genius."[40]

His drama *Paolo and Francesca* (1899) was a literary success—even Churton Collins approved of it—and a theatrical money-maker when George Alexander produced it some years later. *Herod* (1900), under the direction of Beerbohm Tree, ran for eighty performances to big houses. Lena Ashwell, whom he had asked to play Francesca, said his plays had most splendid production.[41]

Phillips made a profit from the theatre, and the returns from his published poems were far in excess of those received by most poets; still he always needed money. Stephen Gwynn, who seconded Colvin in his efforts to establish Phillips as Shakespeare's successor, said that "Phillips liked things full-bodied, especially humour; he liked eating and drinking (especially drinking); he liked the traditional English games . . . he liked low company, odd types," and he and his wife, who had been an actress, could not "stay indoors of an evening."[42] Year by year his restlessness and his drinking increased until he plunged into long periods of debauchery, with shorter intervals for working. Constance Benson said he broke engagements and wouldn't come to rehearsals.[43] He tried to add to his income by writing prose, but he couldn't sell it. His poetry grew careless and verbose, a travesty of his earlier style. In his clearer moments he realized and admitted his degradation:

> And men not measure from what heights I fall,

he pleaded in "The Poet's Prayer."

His presence at literary or social gatherings became an embarrassment. "Unluckily, my next neighbor at the table was Stephen Phillips, the poet," said Ernest Rhys of a supper at the Cheshire Cheese.[44] Death charitably removed this embarrassment in 1915.

Though several circumstances contributed to the poet's early and tragic ruin, the underlying cause was in the man himself. Immoderate and overzealous praise not only antagonized his contemporaries but did great harm to his own integrity. The man craved spectacular triumphs; the poet could not survive them. Phillips was betrayed by his own temperament.

After his fall the balance shifted to the other extreme; no critic had a kind word to say for Stephen Phillips. The memory of his good work was lost in the bad. Truly his orotund measures, forced rhetoric, and pedestrian meters should be forgotten, but his simpler, sweeter verse does not deserve that fate.

> Beautiful lie the dead;
> > Clear comes each feature;
> Satisfied not to be,
> > Strangely contented.
>
> Like ships, the anchor dropped,
> > Furled every sail is;
> Mirrored with all their masts
> > In a deep water.[45]

"A Fire" in Volume XII of the *Yellow Book* and "The Question" in the next gave no evidence of genius, though phrases in "A Fire" catch the imagination, and "A Question," echoing the theme of Ibsen's *Ghosts,* is economically handled.

When his *Herod* was produced, Phillips bitterly resented the criticism of one of his old companions in the Harlands' drawing room, Max Beerbohm, then dramatic critic of the *Saturday Review.* Though to most unbiased minds Max seemed quite just, the playwright took offense and made known his resentment through the medium of William Archer's *Real Conversations.* His work should not be condemned, he said, "by men who do not begin to understand what I am trying to do, and are consequently incapable of judging whether, and how far, I have succeeded in doing it."[46] Max answered firmly in the *Saturday* and Phillips took refuge in a horrid limerick. But this was in 1900.

In the mid-nineties Max, the "unsnubbable schoolboy," had not yet turned to criticism, being still absorbed in creating fanciful prose and caricatures for the *Yellow Book,* the *Pageant,* the *Parade,* the *Savoy,* and the *Chap-Book.* In 1896 Lane collected these pieces in a chaste red volume, *The Works of Max Beerbohm,* first advertised in the April *Yellow Book.* This record of accomplishment, with a bibliographical list of sixty-five items, appeared when the author was twenty-three.

At the Harlands' the young man from Merton found himself extremely popular with the lady authors. Netta Syrett felt more at home with him than other male visitors. Ella Hepworth Dixon, a daughter of Hepworth Dixon, editor of the *Athenaeum,* and, like her sister Nora, a contributor to the *Yellow Book,* was entranced with Max's "beautiful manners, long, curling eyelashes, the most marvellous clothes, and a habit of offering subtle compliments to women."[47]

Of course Max was a dandy. "English society is always ruled by a dandy," he had written in the *Works,* ". . . for dandyism, the perfect flower of outward elegance, is the ideal it is always striving to realize in its own rather incoherent way."[48] Max's incoherence often dazzled his admirers. Evelyn Sharp was impressed with his claret-colored dress shirt; Netta Syrett remarked on his tasseled cane with its ivory handle; Ella Hepworth Dixon said he came to call in an exquisitely cut waistcoat of bright green baize.

He had many men friends as well. He knew the young artists who gathered at the Crown, the poets who met at the Cheshire Cheese, the journalists of Fleet Street, and the actors at his brother's theatre. He listened attentively to the advice of Edmund Gosse, deferred to Henry James, and lunched with Swinburne at The Pines. Graham Robertson found him the "perfect companion, because I always part from him with the impression that I, myself, have been brilliantly amusing. He is the most generous of wits."[49]

Five essays and one story "The Happy Hypocrite," as well as two caricatures, formed Max's bequest to the *Yellow Book.* In 1896 Smithers published his *Caricatures of Twenty-five Gentlemen,* with its masterly delineation of such colleagues as Harland, Le Gallienne, Beardsley, and George Moore. In 1898 Frank Harris, flamboyant editor of the *Saturday Review,* asked Max to take over Bernard Shaw's post as dramatic critic. "The younger generation is knocking at the door," Shaw wrote. "And as I open it there steps spritely in the incomparable Max."[50] Seldom has an adjective tossed so nonchalantly into print created so permanent a halo. "I don't quite know what to do with the torch that G. B. S. has handed to me," Max demurred modestly,[51] but his uncertainty was not evident.

He was already well established in his play-going habits. "Out of my very cradle," he said, "I stepped upon the fringe of the theatrical world."[52] Now for nearly twelve years, in tails and top hat, he was a regular attendant at first nights, sustaining London theatre-goers through the poetical plays of Stephen Phillips, the Ibsen period, the social comedies of Pinero and Henry Arthur Jones, and the provocative dramas of Shaw:

>   . . . (that spring-heeled marcher
> In *any* new deparcher).[53]

Though he wrote principally for the *Saturday,* his *More* was published in 1899, a busy year for Max as he was turning his *Happy Hypocrite* into a play for Mrs. Pat Campbell. When a reporter asked him that summer where he'd like to spend his holiday, Max answered feelingly, "A four-post bed in a field of poppies."[54]

He had bachelor's quarters on the third floor of his mother's house at Hyde Park Gardens. (His father, the corn merchant, had died in the mid-nineties.) Perhaps this economical arrangement allowed him to live, as Lewis Hind told Bennett he did, on the £5 a week he received from the *Saturday Review.* "Strange, if true," commented Bennett.[55]

Max was careful to preserve the amenities of his social life. "And when you paid an 'afternoon call' (a habit not then extinct)," he explained later, "you would rather have died than not appear before your hostess hat in hand—and gloves there too. These things you presently placed upon the floor beside your chair, where she could still see them, symbols of good breeding and reassuring proclamations of the fact that you were only a visitor and hadn't come to abide with her forever."[56] But gossip had it that more than one young lady would have welcomed that eventuality. When Mrs. Neville, Max's sister Aggie, declared that Max was cosy to live with, many a gentle heart beat yearningly.

One of Max's romances has been placed in the annals by Constance Collier, distinguished English actress and once leading lady for Beerbohm Tree. She and Max were engaged, she said, and she was the inspiration for *Zuleika Dobson*. "We hadn't much money, but we hoped to be married in the following year."[57] Then she decided her career was more important. Later she married Julian L'Estrange, the actor. Asked a long time afterward by Bennett Cerf about her first engagement she said it was broken because Max had "carpet slippers in his soul,"[58] a notion every Maximilian will recognize as absurd.

Max often deplored his satiric temperament. "I am, personally, capable of the strongest reverence and of the strongest contempt," he said in the nineties, "and, when I am talking I can give a quite straightforward expression to these feelings. But, when I sit down to write, lo! my honesty does desert me, leaving me a prey to irony and poses,"[59] and again, "When I am laughing at any one I am generally rather amusing, but when I am praising any one, I am always deadly dull. . ."[60] and above all he would not be that.

But he meant all he said when he wrote early in 1908 of "A Memorable Performance": "It is difficult to write about Miss Florence Kahn's impersonation of Rebecca; for it is never easy to analyse the merits of great acting. . . . In its appeal to the emotions, Miss Kahn's acting is not more remarkable than in its appeal to the sense of beauty."[61]

Florence Kahn, auburn-haired actress from Memphis, Tennessee, had won recognition when she appeared with the New York Independent Theatre. Norman Hapgood called her part as Chorus in *Henry V* with Richard Mansfield, "the most beautiful thing in the whole performance."[62] From New York, Miss Kahn had progressed to further triumphs in London, and then to matrimony, for in May, 1910, she was married to Max, who had resigned from the *Saturday Review* the week before.

In his farewell to the public he had said, "To seem to write with ease and delight is one of the duties which a writer owes to his readers, to his art. And to contrive that effect involves very great skill and care."[63] So he was escaping from the Thursdays which had come to be the unpleasantest day of the week. Two volumes of his reviews were published in 1924, *Around Theatres*, republished in a single volume in 1953. One year later, when the one-volume American edition was published, Sir Max, speaking of the labor entailed in these criticisms, admitted that since they were done for a weekly, and the dailies had already revealed the plot of the play, he was often forced to resort to other material to fill his column, but perhaps it was these added commentaries, these divagations, which gave the reviews more lasting interest.[64]

In *Contemporary Portraits,* Frank Harris quoted from Mrs. Neville an account of Max's shy behavior at his wedding,[65] but when the book appeared in 1923, Max denied vigorously that the anecdote was true or that Harris had been told it by his sister. The subject, he said, had caused him "deep annoyance."[66] Two years before his wedding Max had been in Italy and written an account of his travels for the *Daily Mail.* He had found much that delighted him in the Italian cities, but in a land where no one spoke English he had felt a foreigner's isolation. "I was as a portmanteau that my friends had left behind them, a locked portmanteau with a human heart inside it."[67] Now he went back to this southern land with another heart to keep him company. He and his bride found the Villino Chiaro on the coast road above the Gulf of Genoa at Rapallo so enchanting that they never wanted to leave it. Only two World Wars forced their return to England. In a roof-top study at the Villa he wrote and drew for many years, with the blue Mediterranean outside his doorway and the scent of his orange and lemon trees filling the air.

In 1939, despite his earlier expressed indifference ("And I, who crave no knighthood, shall write no more"),[68] he became Sir Max, for as he had said when Hall Caine was knighted, "Though all sneer at it, there are few whose hands would not gladly grasp the dingy patent. After all, a title is still a title."[69]

With the death of Florence Kahn in 1951, a gracious presence and a serene strength departed from the Villino, but comrades were loyal, and Miss Elizabeth Jungmann, long-time friend of Lady Beerbohm, came to act as secretary to Sir Max and custodian of the garden. Journalists now spoke respectfully of "beloved old Sir Max Beerbohm" and he dubbed himself "old Gaffer Beerbohm," but to his admirers he was still the youthful Max.

Osbert Sitwell, in writing of Ada Leverson in the thirties, said that through her he met "so public a figure as Max Beerbohm, so private a one as Reginald Turner."[70] Reggie Turner and Max had been friends at Oxford, and in Max's last appearance in the *Yellow Book*, Reggie had kept him company with a story, *"A Chef d'œuvre,"* which could face the challenge of "The Happy Hypocrite" without embarrassment. Herbert Horne, a friend of both these wits, was probably the inspiration for Turner's acount of a man's long quest for literary perfection. Horne had spent years gathering material for a life of Botticelli, investigating every aspect of his hero with such care that Reggie had exclaimed, "Dear Herbert Horne! poring over Botticelli's washing bills—and always a shirt missing!"[71]

In 1896, Reggie Turner, about whose paternal background strange rumors persisted, was a barrister and journalist in London, writing for the *Daily Telegraph,* and trying his hand at fiction. In time he published eleven novels, which nobody seemed to read, said Richard Aldington. It was not a fate one would have foreseen from his *Yellow Book* story. Like Max, Reggie yielded to the spell of Italy, and following the death of Oscar Wilde, whose last wretched days he had brightened with his friendship, he went to live in Florence. D. H. Lawrence is said to have done his portrait in *Aaron's Rod*. Aldington, in *Life for Life's Sake,* described him as "a wrinkled ugly little man, with a habit of batting his eyelids like an owl." He collected every book of reminiscences which mentioned him. Aldington added that his book would not join the collection, for "poor Reggie" was dead. He died at Florence on December 8, 1938. "His is the only funeral to which I have ever sent a wreath," said Aldington. "I did that for his sake and because of what he did for Oscar."[72]

When Max's *Happy Hypocrite* was performed by Mrs. Pat Campbell and George Arliss as a one-act play in 1900 (in 1936 it became a three-act play, with music, for Ivor Novello and Vivien Leigh), Max could not bring himself to attend. On the opening night he nervously paced the Embankment, "á la G. R. Sims," he said, while Stanley Makower and Beerbohm's mother "indulgently" witnessed the play.[73] Makower's story, "Chopin *Op. 47*," had appeared in the same *Yellow Book* as Turner's and Max's.

Makower had been part of the V.,O.,C.S. pseudonym, and in 1894 Harland had written, "That is a stunning tale of yours, 'Touched by the Hand of God,' in 'The Passing of a Mood,' "[74] and invited him into the golden circle. The young Cambridge man, musician, barrister, and writer became one of the best-liked Saturday evening guests, and contributed to four volumes of the *Yellow Book*. Though he looked Irish, his father was Jewish, and he was "something of a cosmopolitan" and "a man of gentle manners." He lived with his family in a house in Chiswick, so big that a small Catholic convent was housed in the rear, and gave evening parties in the garden lighted by Japanese lanterns while the nuns watched secretly from darkened windows. He played the piano, composed music, and wrote a novel, *The Mirror of Music* (1895), dedicated to Yvette Guilbert. From short stories Makower turned to factual prose, proving his ability in this field with biographies—*Richard Savage, Perdita* (Mary Robinson)—and a history of *The Times*, before his death in 1911.

In addition to Makower, a number of women visitors at the Harlands' evenings wrote for the *Yellow Book* under pseudonyms, sometimes maintained, sometimes, like Makower's, replaced by their own names. Ethel Colburn Mayne began as Francis Huntley, contributing three adroit stories whose parenthood she had no reason to disclaim (when Lane brought them out in book form she acknowledged her authorship). In her preface to *Browning's Heroines* (1913) she wrote, "Seventeen years ago, when the *Yellow Book* and the *National Observer* were contending for *les jeunes,* Browning was, in the more 'precious' *côterie,* king of modern poets. I can remember the editor of that golden Quarterly reading, declaiming, quoting, almost breathing, Browning! It was from Henry Harland that this reader learnt to read *The Ring and the Book.* . . . A hun-

252

dred Browning verses sing themselves around my memories of the flat in Cromwell Road. . . . The phrases (how alert we were for the 'phrase' in those days) would fall grave and vibrant from the voice with its subtle foreign colouring: you could always infuriate 'H. H.' by telling him he had a foreign accent."[75]

After the *Yellow Book* debut of Francis Huntley, Miss Mayne wrote busily for many years, reviewing, creating, translating. Though best known for her biography of Byron (1912) and her *Life and Letters of Lady Byron* (1929), she was a story writer of distinction. The young Hugh Walpole benefited from her criticism, and she befriended the sorely beset Violet Hunt during the turbulent years of her affair with Ford Madox Ford and would have been her literary executor, but Miss Mayne died before her friend, in 1941, two years after the publication of her last book, *A Regency Chapter.*

"K. Douglas King," though not a pseudonym, was considered to be one for a time. The *Academy* suggested in July, 1897, that Katherine Douglas King had taken part of her name from history and the first line of one of Rossetti's ballads ("I CATHERINE am a Douglas born").[76] With a publisher for a father (founder of Henry King and Company) and a poetess for a mother (Mrs. Hamilton King), she came honestly by the name of King and by the literary skill she displayed in "Lucretia," in Volume X of the *Yellow Book.* By 1900 she had published five novels and married Godfrey Burr.

Vivian Cory, another member of the Harland circle, wrote under the name of "Victoria Cross," termed an "unfortunate choice" by one critic, but defended by Miss Cory because the initials were the same as her own and because she had an ancestor who had won the decoration. Her novel *A Woman Who Did Not* was considered a telling defense of feminine virtue when it was published in answer to Grant Allen's *The Woman Who Did.* Allen's heroine was advanced, emancipated, unhappy; Miss Cory's heroine was smugly satisfied with the path of womanly duty. Yet in her *Yellow Book* story, "Theodora, a Fragment" (Volume IV), Miss Cory, writing in the person of her hero, did

253

not underestimate the pleasure of love. She continued as a successful novelist into the 1930's.

The name "Mrs. Murray Hickson" made a dignified screen for the rather frivolous-sounding Mrs. Mabel Kitcat, later Mrs. Sidney Austin Paul, who collaborated with Keighley Snowden in *The Whip Hand*. Another feminine disciple of the editor who told her, "I want your whole experience of the *Yellow Book* to be a happy one,"[77] she was rewarded with three appearances between the yellow boards.

Chapter XXV

BY NO MEANS all the women writers whom Harland welcomed to his golden quarterly were to be met at the Saturday evenings. Most of the guest list was drawn from London, and those who lived outside Dick Whittington's city were of necessity barred from the festive fellowship—such women as Mrs. J. E. H. Gordon of Box Hill, Vernon Lee, who lived in Italy, and Eva Gore-Booth, friend of Yeats in County Sligo, Ireland.

Mrs. Gordon may not have missed this intellectual stimulus, for her next-door neighbor was George Meredith, to whom she looked for literary counsel. He had read and corrected her first novel, *Eunice Anscombe* (1892), suppressing passages of which he disapproved. She is supposed to have been the original of Cecilia Halkett in his *Beauchamp's Career*. Her *Yellow Book* essay on "Mary Astell," a pleasantly readable account of this seventeenth century advocate of women's rights, was signed with the matronly name Mrs. J. E. H. Gordon, but *Memories of George Meredith* (1919), written after her husband's death and her second marriage, was by Lady Butcher. (Hers was the last generation of women writers to admit the reassurance of matrimony—Mrs. Grand, Mrs. Linton, Mrs. Humphry Ward. Soon after the new century began, the title "Mrs." vanished from authors' lists.)

Violet Paget, with no husband on whom to rely, had assumed the masculine *nom de plume* "Vernon Lee." Half-sister of Eugene Lee-Hamilton (author of *Sonnets of the Wingless Hours*), she was born in 1865, and enjoyed a life span which permitted her to be mentioned by Browning in *Asolando* as a sister poet, snubbed by Ouida, caricatured in *Le Lys Rouge* by Anatole France, and considered critically as a contemporary by Van Wyck Brooks. When her story "Prince Alberic and the Snake Lady" came out in the *Yellow Book* she was thirty years old, with an impressive career in letters behind her.

Daughter of a distinguished diplomat, she had been brought up in Italy. She liked to read—Cooper and Chateaubriand excited her equally—and to paint. One winter she lent her paint box to an American boy with a passion for color, and so began a long friendship and the artistic career of John Singer Sargent. Sargent had been destined for the Navy, but at the end of that winter his talent was recognized by his family, and Dr. Sargent was "face to face with the startling possibility that God (since Dr. Sargent saw God's work everywhere)," said Vernon Lee, "had given him a son who was a painter." She described herself at sixteen as a "half-baked polygot scribbler,"[1] but it was not long till she was publishing her scribblings. Her *Studies of the Eighteenth Century in Italy,* written when she was just past twenty, won the praise of Browning and Pater, who invited her to visit him and his sister at Oxford. Arriving too late for dinner the self-sufficient young woman decided to forage for herself and descending to the kitchen late at night was met by her host, who took the floating white form for a ghost, to their mutual discomfort.[2]

In 1883 she dedicated to an embarrassed Henry James her first novel, *Miss Brown*, which Van Wyck Brooks considered the "most colossal piece of amateurishness that can still rightly be claimed for literature."[3] In 1893 she defended the moral teachings of Zola in the *Contemporary Review,* and in 1896 she further risked her reputation by telling for *Yellow Book* readers the tale of an Italian noble, a Gobelin tapestry, and a serpent.

Although she lived in Florence in a little villa called Palerino on the Fiesole side of the town, where American and English littérateurs, such as Mrs. Wharton and Maurice Baring, visited her and her invalid brother, she came frequently to London. A. C. Benson met her at Lady Ponsonby's and recorded that her talk, "though fitful and delivered in rather a recherché manner, was full of bright little points of light and well-touched phrases."[4] Mrs. Belloc Lowndes knew her "fairly well," but did not like her, "partly because she was extremely erudite, which frightened me, and also extremely snobbish, which made me feel ill at ease in her company."[5] Mrs. Pennell thought her as "masculine in her looks as in her books."[6] Henry and William James were severe with her because her short story "Lady Tal" contained a character much like Henry. The psychologist had further cause to be displeased when she reviewed his *Will to Believe* in the *Fortnightly*. Anne Douglas Sedgwick wrote in 1899, "The article is written from an Agnostic point of view and I delighted in its cleverness, and *grace,* as it were, of attitude and mental temper . . . she charmingly avows that with her the 'need' is *not* to believe."[7]

For nearly fifty years Vernon Lee ranged indefatigably over a wide field of interests, including history, aesthetics, music, philosophy, psychology, fiction, and poetry. An eminent psychologist called her "the most original proponent of empathy writing in English," and another spoke of her "inexhaustible mind." All her work was received with deference, but she never became popular. Lane admitted that he took great satisfaction in publishing her books though they didn't sell. Grant Richards conceded he made "a trifle" out of *Limbo* (1897). She accepted this lack of recognition philosophically, dedicating one of her books "To the Many Writers I have Read and the Few Readers Who Have Read Me." Perhaps because fame came to her so easily in the beginning she ceased to care for it. As Desmond MacCarthy pointed out, "Fame to-day requires careful tending if it is to flourish, and Vernon Lee has been careless of hers."[8] Van Wyck Brooks thought her reputation as an occasional writer most likely to endure. "Almost every pleasant thing in the lives of cultivated men and women she has touched with a happy phrase. Her gift has been so gracious that she seems not to have asked for austere consideration."[9]

One of her friends of the eighties, Amy Levy, the young Jewish poetess who died by her own hand in 1889,[10] wrote of Vernon Lee:

> On Bellosguardo, when the year was young,
> We wandered, seeking for the daffodil . . . .
> I found for you a scarlet blossom rare.
> Thereby ran on of Art and Life our speech;
> And of the gifts the gods had given to each—
> Hope unto you, and unto me Despair.[11]

Vernon Lee died in 1935.

Eva Gore-Booth and her sister Constance, Countess Markiewicz, have been commemorated by Yeats in his dedication of *The Winding Stair*. His friendship with them was of long duration, the girls, daughters of Sir Henry Gore-Booth of Lissadell, having been companions of his boyhood. Eva was younger, quieter, and not so strong as Constance, with a "sensitive look of distinction about her." Yeats, returning to Lissadell as a young man, confided to Eva the story of his unhappy love affair with the beautiful Maud Gonne and found sympathy and understanding. In return he filled her with enthusiasm for the Celtic revival, set her to study the Irish legends, and appreciated her poetry. From her girlhood she had written poems for the *Irish Homestead* and the *New Ireland Review*. Now, perhaps with Yeats' encouragement, she sent seven of her sonnets across the Irish Sea to find harbor in the *Yellow Book*. She called them "Finger Posts," and they pointed the way of Heaven, Nature, Joy, Sorrow, Life when Joy has fled, Love, and Hope. Written in the Italian form, the sonnets, austere and grave, betrayed little Irish influence, and the paths marked by the posts did not lead through fairy forests. The beauty of the lines was touched with sadness, but not sadness without hope—though the mystic Yeats might have disagreed with

> Men talk of all the strength of love and faith—
> Vain words! and false it is as idle boast
> To dream you hold communion with a ghost,

And bring to earth again a vanished wraith.
No shadow answers to a shadow's call—
This is the way of all things spiritual.[12]

Eva was not only a poet; she was a patriot too, though not so tragically involved as Constance, who was sentenced to life imprisonment following a British court-martial for a treasonable plot with Germany. Yeats felt a responsibility for the part of both sisters in the Irish Rebellion; Eva also served a prison term. She had other causes too, such as the woman's movement and trade unions, and with Evelyn Sharp and H. W. Nevinson she worked for suffrage in Manchester. "For her, pity came early and stayed with her patiently to the end," said Séan O'Faoláin. "She spent her life in the service of the poor."[13] Her first book of poems was published in 1898, and in 1903 A. E. included several of them in *New Songs*. Her best-known poem, "The little waves of Breffny go stumbling through my soul," belongs to the Celtic revival as closely as Yeats' "The Lake Isle of Innisfree" or O'Sullivan's "The Twilight People."

Eva and Constance were to Yeats among the dear memories of his youth, two beautiful figures under the great trees of Lissadell, and after Eva's death in 1926, he pictured them in youth and age:

> Great windows open to the south,
> Two girls in silk kimonos, both
> Beautiful, one a gazelle . . . .
> I know not what the younger dreams—
> Some vague Utopia—and she seems,
> When withered old and skeleton-gaunt,
> An image of such politics.[14]

His poem "On a Political Prisoner" was written to Constance when she was in Holloway Gaol, "to avoid writing one on Maud. All of them are in prison."[15]

Yeats' unrequited devotion to the beautiful Maud Gonne, Irish revolutionist, so lovely, Henry Nevinson said, that "at the first sight of her I held my breath in adoration,"[16] provided inspiration for much of Yeats' poetry of this period.

His *Yellow Book* poem, however, promised in the Prospectus, but not materializing until the final number, "The Blessed," dealt with the mission of King Cumhal to Dathi, the Blessed, but lines in it might have seemed apposite to some of his friends in the golden circle.

> "But I have found where the wind goes
> And follow the way of the wind;
>
> "And blessedness goes where the wind goes
> And when it is gone we die;
> And [I] have seen the blessedest soul in the world,
> By a spilled wine-cup lie."[17]

Years later in "The Grey Rock," Yeats, though he said he had Dowson and Johnson most in mind. did honor to

> Poets with whom I learned my trade,
> Companions of the Cheshire Cheese . . . .[18]

Yeats avoided the Fabians and all politics save Irish, though he wrote Katharine Tynan in 1888, "I was at a sort of Socialistic tea-meeting at Kelmscott House of late and talked a long time to Mrs. Cunninghame Graham, a little bright American."[19]

He should perhaps have said "South American," for though Gabriele Cunninghame Graham now lived on the River Clyde, she had been born in Chile of a French father and a Spanish mother. No *Yellow Book* contributor could boast a more romantic history than she, but more than distance kept her from the Harlands' parties, for her husband had called the editors cretins and liars.

Gabriele had been sent to school in Spain where Robert Bontine Cunninghame Graham ("Don Roberto"), riding an unruly horse, nearly knocked her down on the street. After dismounting to apologize, he fell in love with the beautiful dark-haired girl. His excuses merged into impetuous courtship and after a few secret meetings, Gabriele, unhappy in her convent school, eloped with him to England, where they were married at the London Registry Office on October 24, 1878.

The next five years of their life teemed with adventure, in Texas, in Mexico, and in New Orleans. By 1883 they had enough money to return to England and take over the estate left by the death of Robert's father at Gartmore.

"Don Roberto" was a socialist, but as Arthur Compton-Rickett said, "the most aristocratic Radical that ever mingled Old-World feeling with New-World thinking."[20] In the riots of Bloody Sunday in Trafalgar Square over the right to hold meetings, he and John Burns were so beaten by the police that Gabriele, watching from a neighboring hotel, thought her husband had been killed. During his time in prison waiting trial W. T. Stead and Mrs. Besant (to whom Stead had introduced Theosophy through Mme. Blavatsky) worked hard in his behalf. Mrs. Besant visited the worried Gabriele and cheered her by good reports of her husband's condition. "She was so glad to see me, poor little thing," said Mrs. Besant.[21] In spite of threatening letters, Gabriele stood by her husband and when he was brought up for trial, spiritedly sent cards to her friends:

Mrs. Cunninghame Graham
at Home
Bow Street Police Court.[22]

Eventually the procedure against Graham and Burns was dropped, and Gabriele welcomed her hero home. Shaw seemed to have played a cautious part in the fighting, though he had been vocal enough in advance, and upon a later occasion, Graham, asked to identify Shaw, answered, "He was the first man to run away from Trafalgar Square on Bloody Sunday."[23] Edward Carpenter, who had received harsh treatment from the constabulary, relieved his mind by writing of "that crawling thing, a policeman."

While her husband sat in Parliament, Gabriele took over the management of the estate, but she lived her own life too. In 1891 she went to Madrid and spoke in favor of the eight-hour working day. She began to publish stories and sketches in English periodicals. A great reader, fond of poetry and painting, Gabriele with her soft attractive accent and endless cigarette smoking was much discussed by her husband's friends. Violet Hunt admired her appearance, and E. H. New, the black-and-

260

white artist, described her in his diary of 1895 as "very beautiful."[24]

Soon after the turn of the century her health began to fail. Friends attributed her strained nerves to excessive smoking—sometimes two hundred cigarettes a day. In 1906, on her way home from Spain, where she had been doing historical research, she was taken ill and died in southern France, Don Roberto reaching her just before she died. According to her wishes, she was buried in the ruined Priory on the Island of Inchmahone in Lake Menteith, to which her husband, like an ancient Viking, rowed her coffin across the lake. On her stone was carved in Spanish, "The dead open the eyes of those who live."[25]

Her monumental work on Santa Teresa, for which she had gathered material by reliving the Saint's experiences in Spain, appeared on the bookstands the same week as the first *Yellow Book*. Her "The Christ of Toro," a story of a miracle-working picture in an old Castilian monastery, was printed in the last *Yellow Book*. In 1908 her husband published a book of her stories using "The Christ of Toro" as the title-piece. In *Rhymes of a World Unknown* he collected forty-seven of her poems.

Cunninghame Graham survived his wife by twenty years. To the end he was a picturesque figure, often seen on horseback in the Park and epitomized by Arnold Bennett as "a sporting sort of cuss."[26] A good writer himself, he was the friend of writers, among them Conrad, Edward Garnett, and W. H. Hudson, all members of the little circle revolving about H. H. the Ranee of Sarawak. The Ranee, Margaret Brooke, living apart from the Rajah, was a much discussed and admired figure of the decade. Oscar Wilde called her the "Lady of Wimbledon," and she was responsible for his being allowed pen and paper in jail. A remarkable musician, she was "magnificent to the eye, and agreeable to the ear," said Rhoda Broughton.[27] She had known suffering, her small children having died tragically of the plague. In Paris she had been a friend of Pierre Loti, Bourget, and Maupassant (Kipling disapproved of that friendship),[28] and in London she was on good terms with such diverse notables as Swinburne, Stopford Brooke, Henry James, Will Rothenstein, and Lady Paget. The *Yellow Book* story of Lady Paget's daughter, Vernon Lee, was dedicated to the Ranee. Her friendship with Hudson followed a letter sent him after reading a review by Mrs. Cunninghame Graham in the *Saturday Review* of his *Green Mansions*. She entertained lavishly, and at one of her dinner parties Mrs. Belloc Lowndes met Frank Swettenham, whom she considered by far the most interesting guest. He was reported, and she believed truly, "to be irresistible when he falls in love, which he is said to do frequently."[29] Gertrude Atherton, however, on a later occasion enjoyed his wit but not his appearance, for he "was almost black from nearly forty years of tropic suns, and so dried up that he looked not unlike an animated mummy."[30] The Ranee thought him "one of the really great men of the British Empire."[31]

Swettenham (later Sir Frank and subject of a Beerbohm caricature), traveler, colonial official, and author of *Malay Sketches* (1895), returned to London from Perak before taking up his duties as Resident-General of Malay in 1896, and contributed two stories to the *Yellow Book*, "Death's Devotion," laid in Africa, and "The Unka," in Penang—settings far removed from the domestic scene. He had known Conrad in the East and liked to talk of him as a seafaring man. In World War I Swettenham was joint director-general of the Press Bureau and blue-penciled the galley proofs of Wells's *War and the Future,* but in vain, for the zealous planner of world affairs decided the alterations were intended to "save rather the prestige of the military authorities than the country" and ignored them.[32]

Chapter XXVI

TELL ME WHERE is Fancy bred?
Certes, near the Bodley Head.

So rhymed a commentator on the literary geography of London in the days of the *Yellow Book*. On both sides of the Atlantic John Lane was known as the friend of poets. The editor of the American *Chap-Book* maintained that Lane "could pick poets from a crowd, if only by the way their hair grows behind their ears," but he pointed out the weakness in Lane's judgment of poetry by explaining, "He has believed in the author's work because he believed in the author himself."[1] The poetry of the *Yellow Book* often suffered from Lane's mistaken tonsorial discoveries.

Among the unknown or practically unknown poets to whom he yielded one or two appearances in his quarterly were A. Myron, Ernest Wentworth, Elsie Higginbotham, Ellis J. Wynne, Lily Thicknesse, Rose Haig Thomas, S. Cornish Watkins, Frances Nicholson, Charles Sydney, and Constance Finch. More generally acknowledged bards included Charles Catty, C. W. Dalmon, W. A. Mackenzie, Annie Macdonell, Francis Prevost, Marie Clothilde Balfour, Ronald Macfie, F. B. Money-Coutts, Ada and Dollie Radford, A. Bernard Miall, and Douglas Ainslie.

None of these poets grew wealthy from such undertakings in meter and rhyme. (No one attempted free verse.) Few even made a living, and most supplemented their poetic returns with down-to-earth prose, translations, or literary hack work.

Smithers, not Lane, published A. Bernard Miall's *Nocturnes and Pastorals* (1896), which Le Gallienne in the *Star* declared vibrated "with poetry which has been genuinely felt and spontaneously uttered,"[2] but in which a *Bookman* critic found "quite inoffensive and pretty" sentiments, but "not a word to stir the heart."[3] Miall is far better known for his translations of Rolland, Fabre, Charlemagne, Maeterlinck, and Brieux (with Mrs. Bernard Shaw) than for his poetry. His "The Burden of Pity," in Volume XII, expressed a common *fin de siècle* query:

> O wherefore are you not complete,
> Or, being ruined, wherefore sweet?

Douglas Ainslie had been introduced to the *Yellow Book* by Henry James, and with such a sponsor Harland could but make him welcome. From the poems Ainslie offered he selected two, "The Death of Verlaine" and a love poem, "Her Colours." "Henry Harland . . . was not himself a poet . . . and his selection

263

. . . was not very felicitous," said Ainslie later, "though I think the Verlaine has something."[4]

Ainslie's family name of Grant Duff (Ainslie was a nephew of Sir Mountstuart Grant Duff of diary fame, undersecretary in Gladstone's first government) was changed by the terms of an uncle's will to Ainslie. Under this name he was to achieve an enviable reputation as poet, translator, and student of aesthetics.

Born in Paris in 1865, son of a British diplomat, he was educated at Eton and at Oxford, where he found that reading for a Pass hardly interfered with his usual amusements.[5] He began to write poetry at the University. After three years at Balliol he went to Paris to study French and prepare himself for a career in the foreign service, but he found Sarah Bernhardt more fascinating. He held posts at The Hague and in Paris, remaining Sarah's devoted friend and paying her tribute as "Sarah Lucifer, the queen of light," in his first book, *Escarlamonde and Other Poems* (1893).

At Oxford he had known Edgar Jepson and Victor Plarr; like Max, he had lunched at The Pines, had written reviews for the *Pall Mall Gazette,* and now in spite of a promising political career, decided his greatest interest was in literature. A few months after his *Yellow Book* appearance he met in Dieppe Beardsley's "dear sister Mabel whom all artistic London loved" and saw Beardsley's drawing of Mademoiselle de Maupin, over which Aubrey whispered, "The nearest I have ever been able to get to a beautiful woman."[6]

Ainslie was elected to the Athenaeum, where he and Henry James conversed of literature and life. James was a great talker, he said. Only Turner Palgrave could silence him. "Dear James! Peace to his ashes. I shall always miss him and his gentle art of hesitation, of which he made great literature."[7]

Ainslie was widely known for his translation and interpretation of Benedetto Croce, but his most enduring concern was with Oriental philosophy. Of his *John of Damascus* it was said that no more authentic expression of Oriental spirit had appeared in English poetry since FitzGerald translated Omar.

In his eightieth year, at a Hollywood address, he was considering a third book of reminiscences and corresponding with Hindu philosophers in preparation for a return to India to consult with the prophet, Ramana Maharshi—only "Here there are so many alarums and excursions that I find it difficult to get started."[8] He died in 1948.

Francis Burdett Money-Coutts, later Lord Latymer (once known as the "millionaire poet") and a lifelong friend of John Lane, stood nearly as high in his regard as William Watson and Stephen Phillips. Watson, Lane, and Money-Coutts were cycling enthusiasts, and on one expedition to Glastonbury met Thomas Hardy, who was likewise exploring the town. Together the four spent "a romantic day or two there among the ruins."[9] When Lane married an American widow, Mrs. A. E. King, a surprising event to many of his circle, Money-Coutts gave away the bride.

Kegan Paul's list for 1886 advertised *The Training of the Instinct of Love* by F. B. Money-Coutts, but in the following year the separation by judicial decree of Mr. and Mrs. Money-Coutts cast doubt on the writer's authority. Lane soon superseded Kegan Paul as the poet's publisher, and he never went to anyone else. During the mid-nineties he brought out four volumes of verse, much of it in a philosophical vein. Archer called him "a serious and strenuous craftsman who places a fine and individual faculty at the service of a lofty ideal,"[10] and Lewis Hind said he was "a dear man who loved poetry better than anything."[11]

He had two poems in the *Yellow Book*, "A Ballad of Cornwall," with a quaint rhyme scheme, in Volume XI and "Sir Dagonet's Quest," a gay bit of verse in the last volume.

Asked about his father's relation with Lane, the late Lord Latymer said:

I do not know how he became such an intimate friend, as he was, of John Lane's. I remember very well a lunch he gave at the Mitre Hotel, Oxford, in '98 or '99, when I was an undergraduate, at which John Lane and John Buchan (who was also an undergraduate at that time) were present, but I really don't know what first brought them together . . . in the 90's he led a very unsettled and nomadic existence, seldom staying long in any one place. He played a good deal of cricket in the summer, and more than once came down to Radley, where I was at

265

school . . . to play against the school for the M.C.C. But I only saw him at rather long intervals.[12]

A competent poet but hardly remembered today, he had published eleven volumes of verse before his death in 1923 in his seventieth year.

The Radfords—Dollie, her husband Ernest, and his sister Ada—were often guests at Lane's teas in Albany, but only the women found a place in the *Yellow Book,* Ada with two stories and Dollie with three poems. Ernest Radford, member of the Rhymers' Club, a Fabian, wit, vegetarian, and doughty oarsman,[13] had dedicated his *Translations from Heine and Other Verse* (1882) to his sister Ada: "First let my book be inscribed with your name; then launched upon the world. Like the boats we sailed in childhood, its voyage can not be long. The stream is very broad; its waters are very deep; and ours, dear sister, is still but a paper boat, and a 'perishable' freight is song." In his last book, *Songs in the Whirlwind* (1918), she was his collaborator. The foreword in another of Radford's books was less romantic: "Many of these pieces have appeared in magazines to whose editors, with the rarest exceptions, I am under no obligation."[14]

Radford married Dollie Maitland, herself a poet with five books of lyrics published during the nineties, and the couple started other hopeful craft. In 1891 Yeats wrote Katharine Tynan, "Have you seen a pretty little book called *A Light Load* by 'Dollie Radford'? It seems to me pleasant and is the work of the wife of one of our 'Rhymers.' "[15] H. B. Marriott Watson found her *Songs and Other Verses* (1895) gentle, tender, and sweet; "In this pacific house of dolls we may look for no rude violence."[16] Radford did work for the *Pall Mall Gazette,* and he and his wife became leading spirits in the New Reform Club, which Douglas Goldring called the "rather grim home of plain living and high thinking."[17]

The Radfords moved easily from one literary circle to another during their productive period, making little money but many friends. They went boating at Oxford with Ernest Rhys and his wife, at Spade House with the Wellses they played the

266

strenuous parlor games H. G. delighted to invent, and to their charming house at Hampstead the young David Garnett was taken for tea by his parents, Constance and Edward. Ezra Pound valued Ernest's opinion of his poetry. The drawing room at tea time overflowed with poets, artists, and musicians. But work became increasingly impossible for Ernest as his mind grew cloudy and confused. In his good periods he admitted this misfortune, sometimes shocking afternoon visitors by recalling an experience "when I was in the lunatic asylum."[18] In later years D. H. Lawrence was a good friend, though he belonged to the generation of their son Maitland and daughter Margaret. He once rented their cottage at Hermitage in Berkshire, and so too did Richard Aldington. In this quiet and secluded abode the Radfords lived simply, the last days saddened by Ernest's increasing mental decay.

Ernest Rhys thought Radford's lyric beginning,

> Oh what know they of harbours
> Who toss not on the Sea!

enough to keep his memory alive,[19] but "a 'perishable' freight is song."

Charles Stratford Catty had poems in Volumes IX and XI of the *Yellow Book*. His first published volume, *Poems in the Modern Spirit* (1888), was addressed to the "Rising Generation." He sent a copy with the author's compliments to John Addington Symonds and the inscription, "The chief poem of this series is more especially addressed to those who have cast off the dead weight of tradition, and are now eagerly embracing the truth of science." His last book, *Poems of the Past and Present,* appeared in 1937. With him poetry must have been an avocation, for his obituary in the *Times* in 1938 identified him as a "retired bank official."[20]

Sussex-born Charles Dalmon had come to London to begin a literary career and nearly starved to death before he got a job in the library of the post office. He sent a sheaf of his unprinted poetry to Tennyson, who encouraged him by striking out Dalmon's despairing words about his own poems, "The end is failure."[21] Three years later he was on the fringe of the *Yellow Book* group with poems in Volumes III and IV and *Song Favours* published by Lane. A frail constitution, perhaps caused by his early hardships, hampered his work, and in the last years he was happy to find refuge in the Charterhouse, where he died in 1938.

William Andrew Mackenzie's first poems were published while he was still a student at Aberdeen. During the nineties he wrote for the *Yellow Book* (one poem in Volume V), the *Pall Mall Gazette, Black and White,* and the *Sketch,* enjoying to the full, he said, the life of an irresponsible journalist; but in 1914, having become a Catholic, he dedicated his life to the service of others and as Secretary of the International Federation of Save the Children Fund lived more than twenty years in Geneva, the Muse seemingly forgotten.[22]

Another product of Aberdeen University, Ronald Campbell Macfie (author of "Dreams" in Volume II), supplemented his poetry with books on health and science and with newspaper work. In 1910 the question was raised in the *Academy* as to whether Macfie was a poet,[23] and even the affidavit of Lady Margaret Sackville, with whom he had collaborated on a book of fairy tales, failed to convince some doubters. It was said that Davidson considered him a poet, and Saintsbury had praised his *Granite Dust* in 1892. The embarrassment of metaphor in his *Yellow Book* "Dreams" has been mentioned. He also tried poetic drama after the manner of Stephen Phillips but without his monetary rewards. In 1930 he wrote passionately in the *Observer* on behalf of Sir William Watson, "A Neglected Poet": "How much the world has lost by discouraging his genius it is impossible to say; but the writer—a lesser poet with like ideals— knows too well how enthusiasm can be damped and inspiration checked by indifference, and by ignorant, or indolent, or cowardly criticism."[24] So might have spoken many a poet.

"Francis Prevost" (Henry Francis Prevost Battersby) , having given his first book of poems to Kegan Paul in 1886, managed to publish nearly a volume a year throughout the nineties, though Oscar Wilde charged him with imitating the Brownings and hoped that "some day Mr. Prevost will be able to study the great masters without stealing from them."[25] His "Hand and Heart" (Volume IX) overcame some metrical difficulties to arrive at an effective final line. He made his living, however, not by his poetry but by journalism, and went to South Africa as a reporter during the Boer War. Coming home he had as companion on the boat H. W. Nevinson, who said of Battersby, "About his writing, as about his nature, there has always been something of high distinction—something fine, perhaps almost superfine— and to be with him was a perpetual delight."[26] Battersby died in June, 1949.

Annie Macdonell ("Reiselust," Volume III), sister of James Macdonell, like Arthur Waugh supplemented her income by writing for an American audience, and as London representative of the American *Bookman* discussed many contemporary English authors. Her *Thomas Hardy* (1894) pleased its subject and was enthusiastically reviewed by Lionel Johnson, himself an expert on the Wessex novelist. "She has shown," he said, "that the works of an eminent living writer can be discussed in set form, without idle eulogy, or impatient prophecy, or offensive censure, or unscholarly and ludicrous disproportion of any sort,"[27] but a later biographer thought she denied Hardy "any special gift as poet or thinker."[28]

Marie Clothilde Balfour, a member of the Balfour family from which Stevenson was descended, edited the letters of Stevenson's mother in 1897. Previously she had written one novel, *White Sand,* had contributed to the *Evergreen,* and to Volumes X and XII of the *Yellow Book,* and had collected the folklore of Northumberland. Two later novels, *Maris Stella* (1896) and *The Fall of the Sparrow* (1897), were well received by the London *Bookman.*

A number of minor prose writers as well as poets made ephemeral bows in the *Yellow Book,* among them B. Paul Neuman, whose *Interpreter's House* Frederic Whyte considered "remarkable"; Dora McChesney, whose successful historical novels were often illustrated by Greiffenhagen; T. Baron Russell, whose "A Guardian of the Poor" (1898) first appeared in the *Yellow Book;* Charles K. Burrow, a busy writer with ten books to his credit before 1919; Constance Cotterell, who made a promising beginning with "The Love Germ" in Volume XI; H. Gilbert, whose *Of Necessity* Lane published in 1898; Mary Howarth, art student at the Slade and friend of Norway; R. V. Risley, also interested in Vikings; Cecil de Thierry, disciple of Henley; Hermione Ramsden, interested in feminism and Scandinavia; Sidney Benson Thorp *(The Primer of English History,* 1896); and Charles Willeby, musician and musical critic, whose article on Bizet graced Volume II. J. S. Pyke Nott and T. Mackenzie contributed prose, but are otherwise unknown.

Though each volume was well studded with verse, not all the poets of the period were represented—for example, not Hardy, Meredith, Henley, Kipling, Binyon, Bridges, or Lang. Even some authors published by Lane, such as Lord De Tabley, Mrs. Hinkson, Francis Adams, Francis Thompson, and Mrs. Meynell, were omitted.

The mysterious Aleister Crowley, who aspired to become the wickedest man in the world and was generally thought to have reached his aim, had no poem in the *Yellow Book,* though he had been writing poetry since the age of ten and had achieved six privately printed volumes before 1899. "The Beast" was a fellow-member with Yeats in the magical Order of the Golden Dawn, and the strife between them finally disrupted the society, the gentle Yeats abhorring his demon brother. But Aleister was a frequent guest at the Lanes.

Nor were A. E. Housman and his brother Laurence included among the *Yellow Book* bards, though Lane brought out Laurence's *Green Arras* in 1896, of which A. E. made the "envenomed remark": "I had far far rather have my poems mistaken as yours, than your poems mistaken as mine."[29] Laurence Housman the artist, however, displayed two drawings, "The Reflected Faun" in Volume I and "Barren Life" in Volume X, the latter nearly failing to gain Lane's nod. Housman had intended the drawing as a frontispiece for Francis Thompson's *Poems,* but Lane took fright at its involved symbolism, and

270

Housman's key with its deft avoidance of "one or two smaller touches, such as the leafless and barren thorns girdling the loins," failed to satisfy him.[30] He refused the design for the *Poems* but later admitted it to the *Yellow Book*. Through the nineties Laurence Housman worked only as poet and artist. *An Englishwoman's Love-Letters,* that anonymous excitement of 1900, first demonstrated his hand at fiction, and drama was still ahead.

Poets present and absent proved the great number of versifiers at work in the nineties. At a well-attended meeting of the Rhymers' Club Yeats had said, "None of us can say who will succeed, or even who has or has not talent. The only thing certain about us is that we are too many."[31]

Chapter XXVII

WHEN YOUNG WILL ROTHENSTEIN went to call on Swinburne, Watts-Dunton, catechizing him about the trends of contemporary literature, inquired whether the *Yellow Book* would last.[1] Many interested folk had asked the same question and many critics had guessed at an answer.

On the appearance of the first volume, the American *Bookbuyer* had observed, "But the experiment as outlined . . . is most hazardous. The instant the fever of the novelty and audacity is allowed to flag—*explicit The Yellow Book.*"[2] Another crystal-gazing American had prophesied in *Munsey's,* "Its life is limited to three years. It is to be hoped its owners have money enough to keep it going for that length of time."[3]

But not everyone was so pessimistic. Its writers and artists piously hoped it would prove immortal. Elizabeth Pennell declared that the last thing she "foresaw for the *Yellow Book* was a speedy end or . . . any end at all."[4] In January, 1895, Beardsley had indignantly told an interviewer, "The general idea that the *Yellow Book* is dying is untrue."[5]

When Volume XII appeared in January, 1897, a *Times* reviewer observed, "The principle upon which the *Yellow Book* is edited would seem to be that at intervals of every three months a section of the reading public is seized with a craving for fresh work by Mr. Henry Harland, Miss Ella D'Arcy, and others of the little school of writers whom the Bodley Head has brought into notice. The contributions, therefore, tend to run largely in the same groove, but still, as this is the twelfth issue, one must admit, mindful of the fate of the *Savoy,* that the principle serves its purpose well enough."[6]

The *Times,* however, did not know then that the principle was just about served. Volume XIII was late and did not reach the bookstands until May, drawing a jibe from the *Times,* "The *Yellow Book* though it has outlived its youthful 'wildness,' keeps up a reputation for eccentricity by producing its April number . . . in May."[7]

One change in format was noticeable, the repetition of the front-cover design (Mabel Syrett's "Fighting Cocks") on the back, where the Table of Contents usually appeared. It was a generous number. Though not as bulky as Volume VIII (406 pages), twenty-five literary items and eighteen illustrations had been crammed into its 317 pages. Harland had packed it as full as possible; still a residue was inevitable and Norman Hapgood mourned his essay on Laclos, which Harland had bought but not printed.

This was the last *Yellow Book,* though no one said so publicly. No Editorial Note bade the readers goodbye; no Valedictory Letter from the Yellow Dwarf summed up the accomplishment. The end was unannounced. When Volume XIV failed to appear on the stands in July would-be buyers drew their own conclusions, but the press took no notice. Critics must have observed that the heavy yellow volume no longer burdened their desks; artists passed the word glumly from table to table in the Café Royal; short-story writers and poets set out to find new markets. Perhaps Arthur Waugh had the *Yellow Book* in mind when he wrote to the *Critic* early in July, "The sixpenny illustrated magazines are 'cutting into' the old-fashioned weekly reviews and literary papers in a cruel fashion, and no one will be surprised to hear that one of the best-known of these is likely, either to change hands, or to cease altogether during the course of the next few weeks,"[8] but he named no names.

If John Lane talked over the demise with his friends at the Hogarth Club, extolling the virtues of the late-lamented as he had once praised the newly born, he did not take the press into his confidence. Explaining to Arnold Bennett the delay in publishing his *Man from the North,* he admitted that the "past season had been incredibly bad" and that "everything was in arrears."[9]

Critics so tactfully refrained from pointing out the empty space that many readers failed to notice it, and in September, 1897, Conrad wrote Edward Garnett of his newly finished 23,000-word story, *The Return,* "It won't stand dividing—absolutely not. . . . What Mag: would you advise? *Yellow Book* or *Chapman*—perhaps."[10]

But the *Yellow Book* was dead, quite dead, and Jeannette Gilder felt no sadder over its fate than she had about the *Savoy.* The *Yellow Book* was so dead that in New York the Howard Ainslie Company announced in August, 1897, that hereafter their bi-monthly magazine the *Yellow Kid* would become the *Yellow Book,* in view of the improved character of the periodical, which was to be "a phenomenal compilation of taste, humor and fiction," and "simply unprecedented" at the price of five cents. Contributors included Penrhyn Stanlaws, Ellis Parker Butler, John Fleming, Harrison Fisher, Hall Caine, George Horace Lorimer, and Harold MacGrath.

When the period of mourning was past and the *Yellow Book* had become history, critics began to examine the evidence to discover what had killed it. Some suspected murder; others looked for natural causes.

"Wilde, then, brought down the *Yellow Book,*" declared Ford Madox Ford,[11] and John Lane had said the same thing as he remembered the newspaper headline which linked Wilde and the *Yellow Book.* "It killed the *Yellow Book.*"

In expelling Beardsley the *Yellow Book* was doomed, pronounced Haldane Macfall. "The *Yellow Book* went on without him, to die a lingering death and be buried in the commonplace."[12]

The Boer War and the Diamond Jubilee were blamed for

the deed by two other judges, but in the frank opinion of Mr. A. J. A. Symons, "Lack of principle killed it."[13]

"The *Yellow Book* . . . died of acute preciosity," diagnosed an *Academy* critic in 1902.[14]

"We were all a little tired of it," Miss D'Arcy acknowledged.[15]

That it came to an end in view of the failing health of the editor was Mrs. Harland's explanation.[16]

"Having served its turn," added the editor himself.[17]

But a director of the Bodley Head offered the irrefutable solution, "It had ceased to pay dividends."[18]

That was the last word, the summing up of all answers, set down in pounds and shillings. As the business-like John Lane admitted to James Milne of the *Chronicle,* the public lost interest in poetry after Wilde's fall. "The Bodley Head, until then," he stated, "had made a commercial success of every book of verse it published. Onward from then, it could do no more than get its money back, unless the verse was by quite eminent writers."[19]

In the beginning the *Yellow Book,* like the Bodley Head verse, had been a financial success. The furor created by Beardsley's art and the sensational attacks of the critics on its literature had carried it sweepingly forward. Then the wave slackened. Much impetus was lost with the loss of Beardsley. "Few purchasers of fad periodicals ever get beyond the cover," explained a writer in the *Critic.* "The publishers know this, and they put their best foot on the outside."[20] When Lane's best foot ceased to adorn the *Yellow Book,* many people ceased to buy it.

Beardsley was an asset, but he was also a liability. The feeling against him cannot be shrugged off. Gentle middle-aged Kate Greenaway wrote to Lady Ponsonby, "Tell Mr. Ponsonby I HATE Beardsley more than ever."[21] When W. T. Stead and Grant Richards were planning a cover for their *Monthly Index of Periodicals,* Stead insisted, "Whoever does it let us have none of these modern abominations of the Yellow School."[22]

This uncompromising attitude toward Beardsley extended to those who appeared with him. When Mrs. Lynn Linton wrote in the *New Review* in praise of "that sweet and subtle quality of maidenly modesty, . . . that delicate innocence and ignorance of evil," and against "these loud-voiced, Wild Women with their slang and petty oaths, their bold eyes, swinging gait and doubtful conversation," she was warning Albion's daughters against the *Yellow Book* set.[23] Even the parting with Beardsley, though it fulfilled the demands of a few, did not placate the majority.

The limited public to which the *Yellow Book* appealed, a group, according to George Moore, not recognized by the libraries as readers of books, had little money, and the *Yellow Book* cost five shillings. The *Savoy* started at half that price and still it could not last. (Symons later admitted he made a mistake in "giving so much for so little."[24]) As Arnold Bennett said, "Artists, like washerwomen, cannot live on one another."[25]

The subscription list was small, most sales were made over the counter, and few copies reached the provinces. When Mrs. Crackanthorpe asked Stopford Brooke, then in Bournemouth, his opinion of her son's essay in the *Yellow Book*, he had to admit, "I have not got the Yellow Book. This is not the place for its sale,"[26] just as Beardsley wrote Smithers from Twyford, Sussex, for two numbers of "that chaste publication *The Savoy*. . . . I cannot order them here."[27] In America the circulation was smaller than in England, though as one writer explained, since the *Yellow Book* came from London, many Americans bought it "out of curiosity."[28]

It carried no advertising of Pears' Soap or Bovril, only lists of new books from the Bodley Head and from rival firms, but this boot-strap arrangement netted little in cold cash. (These pages of book lists now distinguish the original editions of the *Yellow Book* from the Sotheran reprints.) Lane kept the quarterly free from commercialism, but such purity was expensive.

Changing times affected its popularity. In the mid-nineties the uncompromising policy of ignoring the passing moment and taking no stand on public affairs lured readers who at the end of the decade looked elsewhere. In times of peace such an aloof attitude is permissible, but when a tidal flood of world affairs breaks against the foot of the Ivory Tower, the occupant must sometimes descend to look to the basement windows. The questions of South Africa, India, Ireland, and the Spanish-American war challenged the attention of even the most intellectual coteries. Imperialism, sympathy for the Boers, criticism of America (in the Meynell circle only Mrs. Meynell defended Uncle Sam), concern for Ireland—all these controversies infringed on the struggle for literary integrity.

So, like the youthful Max, the *Yellow Book* was "outmoded," and its thirteen volumes consigned to lower library shelves to gather dust and await the verdict of posterity. At first the judgments pronounced gave small comfort to those who had graced its yellow pages: "the *Yellow Book*—cleverness, whimsies, novelties, finesse, legerdemain—but O my! all amateur. . . ," the majority of its contributions "thoroughly bad," its "effusions," its "sophisticated whisperings," its "sweet poison." But unanimously damning as these indictments sounded, now and then a dissenting voice was lifted by someone who had actually studied the greying volumes. Examined in the light of our mid-century accomplishment, they took on stature and importance, and a wavering tendency to assign them a place on the credit side of the ledger gathered supporters.

The enthusiastic literary historian is tempted to attribute the virtues of a whole period to the effect upon it of his own particular subject. So Henley and his *National Observer,* Frank Harris and the *Saturday Review,* Arthur Symons and the *Savoy,* Heinemann and the *New Review* have received their glossy laurels. Perhaps a summary of Harland's accomplishments as editor will show that at least a modest share should be apportioned to him and the *Yellow Book.*

Max Beerbohm has testified that "Henry Harland was a very enlightened and fine editor."[29] He offered freedom to his *Yellow Book* contributors, the chance to be individuals, to write as they wanted to write. He let them experiment with form. Stories might be long, like his own and Henry James'; they might be short. The brief sketch finding its impetus in *mood* (the nineties hummed with that magic word), character, or situation rather than plot, was a feature of *Yellow Book* fiction. Today such pieces are termed "casuals." They were then more aesthetically described as "pastels," and a writer in the *Chap-Book* punned:

> It is a little piece of prose
> In form and style excelling;
> But what it means no man knows,
> It is, indeed, pastelling.[30]

To Harland style was a fetish; he was, he said, "mad about" it, and he looked for it in his writers. Though he admired brilliance and hated dullness, he did not demand the same sheen on every piece of work. He approved the subjective approach, the portrayal of "a corner of Nature, seen through the temperament of a single man."[31] Let each writer develop his own particular qualities with care, avoiding shoddy writing as he would the plague. This cultivation of style, the search for the suitable word, *le mot juste* (Max called it "that Holy Grail of the period"),[32] sometimes led to overelaboration and artifice; sometimes to what Crackanthorpe termed "the power of individual expression."

Harland allowed his authors a wide scope of subjects, encouraging the psychological story not then much used in English fiction, which posed a mental rather than a physical problem, or analyzed a personal dilemma. He did not insist on the happy ending; in fact it was conscientiously avoided by many writers in favor of a cynical disillusionment. This disillusion had been felt, but not so openly acknowledged, by the Victorians. The men and women of the nineties paraded their pessimism. If the writer doubted the prevalence of justice, believing that occasionally the mills of the gods ground up the wrong victim, he felt obliged to say so. Frustration, poverty, and death were accepted as inevitable by many whose lives were haunted by those grim spectres. Such stories were termed "sordid and degraded" or "sternly realistic," according to the outlook of the reviewer.

In the treatment of love and marriage Harland permitted a freedom which was considered license. To many Victorian readers of popular fiction, love was a romantic and mysterious beauty and marriage a sacrament. Sex was improper and the advocate of sex education was cut by his friends in the street. In 1894 Hardy, taking part in a *New Review* symposium on the physical aspects of marriage, urged that "a plain handbook on natural processes" be placed in a daughter's hands, and "later on, similar information on morbid contingencies," raising the question "whether civilization can escape the humiliating indictment that, while it has been able to cover itself with glory in the arts, in literatures, in religions, and in the sciences, it has never succeeded in creating that homely thing, a satisfactory scheme for the conjunction of the sexes." But Mrs. Lynn Linton deprecated the public discussion of the whole subject as "indecent and unnecessary."[33]

To many *Yellow Book* writers love was not a sweet and simple passion, leading straight to the altar; it was complex, involved, unsatisfactory and often without benefit of clergy. Marriage was not a sacrament but a disagreeable predicament in which two people were caught. (This iconoclastic attitude angered those who believed marriages were made in Heaven.) Violation of the seventh commandment was admitted if not condoned.

Much of this experimentation undertaken by *Yellow Book* writers was awkward and unconvincing, but it opened up new ground. These tentative approaches in the nineties led to the free discussion of sex taken for granted by every writer today.

St. John Adcock once said that only two kinds of poetry pay, the best and the worst. Harland spent John Lane's money for both kinds, but perhaps the latter got rather more of it. Harland was no poet, as Douglas Ainslie pointed out, nor did he care greatly for poetry. Netta Syrett remembered how he first read aloud Davidson's "Ballad of a Nun," "making mock and scoff of it."[34] Lane cherished a fine enthusiasm for poetry and poets, but his judgment of the former was sometimes misled by his regard for the latter.

Poets of the day as well as the older school were welcomed at

278

the *Yellow Book*. Among them they contributed a respectable core of good poetry, an amount of amiable and melodic verse, and a painful plethora of misconceived stanzas. Still nearly every *Yellow Book* poet published at least one volume of verse. Some *Yellow Book* poems have been selected for anthologies. A. J. A. Symons, apologist for the poetry of the eighteen nineties, said that it "lies shivering at the mercy of every critical wind that blows."[35] Perhaps it is just as well that much of it remains in snug oblivion under the yellow covers.

Harland's opinion, seconded by Lane, that the finely wrought essay had small opportunity in English periodicals as compared with the hospitality shown it in France, led to emphasis on that form of writing in the *Yellow Book,* and it is that which has best survived the years. Pater had set up a high concept of the duty and function of the critic, holding that criticism must be subjective as well as objective and the critic a creative writer. *Yellow Book* criticism for the most part accorded with this theory and seems less "dated" than the fiction and poetry. Harland was discriminating in his choice of subjects, and the level of achievement in most non-fictional prose was high.

The *Yellow Book* was important as a force and influence upon editors and readers, but its stimulus to writers was even more significant. One hundred and thirty-eight men and women contributed to its literature; 106 artists exhibited their art. Of the writers all but seven can be linked to other work; of the artists only three are otherwise unidentified. The periodical attracted a tremendous group of writers and painters of all ages and of all schools, but young men and newcomers were in the majority. Without its encouragement many a novice, "commencing author" in the nineties, might have turned aside to some other profession in which a helping hand was not so necessary. Even the friendships it fostered were valuable, for the way is often tedious to the solitary pilgrim, while companionship helps to strengthen the backbone. As Crackanthorpe put it, "A sound, organized opinion of men of letters is being acquired; and in the little bouts with the *bourgeois* . . . no one has to fight single-handed. . . . Young men of to-day have enormous chances:

279

we are working under exceedingly favorable conditions. Possibly we stand on the threshold of a very great period."[36] Heartened by the *Yellow Book,* and believing, like Crackanthorpe, in their destiny, many young men and women went on to a successful career in the next century.

As the editor of the *Yellow Book* summed up its history: "It continued as a successful quarterly for three years and three months and suspended publication with a memorable thirteenth issue. During this time we made most of the London critics gasp a bit and we forced the recognition of any number of principles and ideas for which we had been striving. It let down the bars of prejudice and tradition in the London publishing offices and so it served its turn."[37]

Two selections of the art and literature of the *Yellow Book* have been published, one edited by Cedric Ellsworth Smith (Hartford, 1928), and one by Norman Denny (The Bodley Head, London, Viking Press, New York, 1950). In 1928 Sotheran brought out a reprint of the thirteen volumes.

Just before the first World War, Wyndham Lewis initiated a new magazine, *Blast,* whose purpose was to express the art and literature of the day. "No periodical since the famous *Yellow Book* has so comprehended the artistic movement of its decade," proclaimed its sponsor. When in 1935 John Lehman launched his *New Writing* at the Bodley Head, he called it the "*Yellow Book* of the thirties." Such identifications are not made without cause.

Chapter XXVIII

In June, 1894, Andrew Lang wrote in *Longman's Magazine* on "Ghosts": "Eccentricities they avoid and their conduct should be an example to the younger artists and authors in the *Yellow Book.* 'Nothing is so commonplace,' says a French philosopher, 'as conscientious eccentricity.' From this error in taste, ghosts are free."

Now more than sixty years after, the eccentricities of these artists and authors, once the life and soul of the quarterly, are hidden in the grave, but one doubts not, should they manage a return to our modern world, their trailing robes would still display a conscientious tinge of yellow.

After Hubert Crackanthorpe's death in 1897, Aubrey Beardsley was the next to go, outliving the *Yellow Book* by little less than a year. He died at Mentone, France, on the 16th of March, 1898, after hovering for months on the brink of death, slowly but unescapably slipping toward the edge. Though he found consolation in the Church, he was to the last unreconciled to death, fighting, hoping, making the most of every arrested moment until a few days before the end, when in his passionate recantation, he acknowledged his "death agony." With fingers almost too feeble to hold the pen he wrote the unheeded command to Smithers to destroy his "obscene drawings."[1]

His mother and sister Mabel stayed with him to the end. He was buried in the graveyard at Mentone, above the hill from the Cathedral where Mass had been said for his soul. Later a requiem was sung for him at the Farm Street Church in London. Gertrude Atherton found it "very impressive," but thought the assemblage "curious. . . . All the women were fashionable, all the men looked epicene."[2] American Catholics prayed for him at the Jesuit Church in Boston.

Symons wrote three poems in memory of Beardsley, included in *Love's Cruelty* (1923), emphasizing a characteristic upon which all his friends were agreed, Beardsley's great zest for living.

> Or this poor inch of pavement,
> Where you and I walk without knowing
> What life meant, and so what the grave meant,
> To him in his coming and going:
> It was only life that he wanted!

An unusually close bond existed between Beardsley and his sister, Mabel Beardsley Wright. After his death she resumed her career as an actress, but within a few years fell ill with cancer. She faced her suffering with bravery, a "sweet Catholic saint," said Violet Hunt, "whom everyone . . . worshipped."[3] Her friends and Aubrey's friends came to sit at her bedside, cheering

281

and amusing her. Max Beerbohm played cards with her and Yeats came every Sunday afternoon in the winter of 1913. "I cannot over-state her strange charm," he wrote Lady Gregory, "the pathetic gaiety." She talked much of her brother and his "passion for reality." She had the same faculty for facing unpleasantness and accepted the approach of death with courage. She knew she would go to Heaven. "Papists do," she told Yeats. She sometimes shocked him with her improper stories.[4] Ricketts made her a set of four dolls, illustrating characters in her brother's drawings, mentioned by Yeats in one of the unpublished poems he wrote of her:

> Although she has turned away
> The pretty waxen faces
> And hid their silk and laces
> For mass was said to-day
> She has not begun denying
> Now that she is dying
> The pleasures she loved well. . . .[5]

He paid tribute to her gallantry in "Upon a Dying Lady" in *The Wild Swans at Coole:*

> With the old kindness, the old distinguished grace,
> She lies, her lovely piteous head amid dull red hair
> Propped upon pillows, rouge on the pallor of her face.*

Poor Mrs. Beardsley outlived her children by many years. A lonely old age was further embittered by poverty. A Thames flood destroyed many of Aubrey's pictures and she had no insurance. She died at Hurstpierpont, Sussex, where she was living in one room of a cottage, in January, 1931, at the age of eighty-five.

When Gertrude Atherton went to the mass for Beardsley she saw Ernest Dowson, whom she had tried to reform a few years before at Pont Avon. He drifted past her with unseeing eyes, very shabby, very poor, looking "more like a lost soul than ever,"[6] for Dowson too was caught in the scourge of this decade. Two years later he died at the home of Robert Sherard in

---

*Quoted from *The Wild Swans at Coole,* copyright 1919 by The Macmillan Company, by permission of the publisher.

Catford. He was only thirty-three. His relatives gave him "a good funeral—quite a good funeral," said Edgar Jepson.[7]

Lionel Johnson lived two years longer than his fellow Rhymer—years dimmed by drink and drugs. In spite of his increasing irresponsibility, Henry Nevinson gave him reviewing to do for the *Chronicle,* and he turned in good copy. But in late September, 1902, Nevinson was summoned to St. Bartholomew's Hospital. A man found dying on the corner of Whitefriars Street had a letter addressed to him. Johnson died without regaining consciousness.[8]

By the end of the nineties John Davidson was looking seriously toward the theatre, which Bernard Shaw and Stephen Phillips were finding so profitable. He had already translated Coppée's *Pour la Couronne* for a Lyceum production with Mrs. Pat Campbell, who found his "grave manner and inimitable Scotch accent" delightful.[9] She often recited his little poem "Butterflies." In 1904 she produced Davidson's translation of Victor Hugo's *Ruy Blas* in blank verse. Unfortunately it ran only a fortnight, for the critics pronounced it "tedious," a literary achievement but not a play.[10] This was a tragic outcome for Davidson, who had hoped desperately for a success. Now he turned to journalism, but after a long absence from newspaper offices, he could not write under such circumstances. Richard Whiteing saw him, "a miserable fellow creature with his hands in his hair, and a welter of torn beginnings on the floor," and shortly afterward he gave it up "with a handful of his failures in his pocket."[11] Some of his friends managed a small pension for him, and Mrs. Campbell commissioned him to translate *Phèdre,* but it was never produced. He had written himself out as a poet, telling Yeats, "The fires are out . . . and I must hammer the cold iron."[12] Still he had what he thought was a great poetic drama in his head, and the usually tight-fisted Shaw agreed to lend him £250 so that he might write it. But instead he wrote a cheap sensational melodrama which he thought would make money. The play was worthless and, realizing his failure and haunted by the morbid fear of cancer, he killed himself. "In short," said Shaw, "he died of poverty."[13]

Harland felt the end of the *Yellow Book* more keenly than anyone else. He wrote *The Cardinal's Snuff Box* during the "monstrous dark and dour and sour London winter" of 1897-98,[14] and money was scarce at Cromwell Road. Hamlin Garland, whom Howells called Harland's "rhyme," being invited to dinner during a stay in London was much entertained by his host's account of "the adroit methods by which he outwitted the various sheriffs who came to collect bills,"[15] but Mrs. Harland did not enjoy the stories. Upon the publication of the novel, however, Harland emerged into the third of his literary roles as an author of best-sellers, for the book, with a heroine modeled on Aline, sold enormously, and his old friends in Norwich heard he had made at least $70,000 on it. Illness again overtook him, but rest and a visit to the Italian Lakes helped him, though he was never to be free from its threat. He published *The Lady Paramount* in 1902, and *My Friend Prospero* ran in *McClure's* in 1903. All these romances were written by Henry Harland, convert to Rome, for he and his wife had been received into the Church after the end of the *Yellow Book,* and the characters in them, "good practical Catholics," turned the thoughts of many toward the Church.

He and Aline visited the States in 1902 and 1903, spending much time at Sentry Hill, Norwich, Connecticut, with his mother. Finding the estate run down, he tried to restore its former glory with such effect that after his death he was identified in the Norwich *Bulletin* as the "one who transformed land at corner of Washington Street and Taftville Road from an unsightly vacant lot to a beautiful parklike plot of ground." Though he loved Sentry Hill he was always homesick for London, even for its yellow fogs which were so bad for him. American doctors urged him to go to Colorado or to Switzerland if he must go abroad, but instead he returned to London.

Severe hemorrhages sent him to San Remo, Italy, where he began *The Royal End,* his last book, completed after his death by his wife. Even when he was too ill to "put his hand to his unfinished book" he still hoped for a turn in his disease that would allow him to "sit up and work, sit down and slog."[16] But the turn did not come, and his mother, who had been sent for, wrote from the villa at San Remo on November 20, 1905, to a Norwich friend: "You can understand that I have been greatly preoccupied and absorbed in my poor boy's condition. Alas, I still am, for he is no better—but I cannot speak of it. God alone knows the end. . . . Pray for me and mine, and love me all you can, for my heart is full of trouble."[17]

Here at San Remo, with his mother, his wife, his doctor, and a priest friend, Henry Harland died on December 20, 1905. His body was returned to Norwich for burial in the old Yantic Cemetery in specially consecrated ground.

After Henry's death Aline's restlessness increased; she flitted back and forth between New York and London, with visits to Paris and Italy, looking for the places where she and Henry had been together. In Italy in 1909, unnerved by the tragic death of her brother, she went into Retreat. More and more she turned to the Church for solace. Later that year she wrote from Russell Square: "And though when I sat me down among my Gallery of Dead Ladies, at the dinner hour, I asked myself 'Qu'est-ce-que tu fais dans cette Galère,' I knew very well that I was also a 'dead lady' and that this indeed was just the place for me. And when Harry and I went into the Chapel after dinner, and felt that sweet flowing love of the Blessed Sacrament, once more . . . I realized that it is better to be a Dead Lady with God and Harry, than a living one without either."[18]

She had already completed *The Royal End* ("Love is the Royal End"), and now she turned to a play which Harland and Crackanthorpe had written years before: "I am re-reading the most amusing play of Harry's which keeps me in a state of mirth and joy—and when it's finished I begin it over again. It sheds light upon my way, and lifts me into regions of high pranks and frolic which long ago I left be'ind me, as Tommy Atkins might say. No one has ever been so amusing as Harry. . . . I expect the Saints chuckle the whole day long, in whatever part of Heaven he finds himself. For, praise be to God, the Saints, at least, have a sense of humour."[19]

In 1917 she brought out this play, *The Light Sovereign*, a

farcical comedy in three acts, "published by Lady Henry Harland." She stayed in London during the war, which was "too horrible," hurrying back to Paris when it was over, distraught, unhappy, beset by memories and the need for money, antagonizing her friends by the Aline, Lady Harland manner.

Her death in 1939 followed a long period of incapacity during which she was confined in an asylum. Her body was placed beside Harry's in the elm-shaded cemetery under the Roman cross.

Though older than his *Yellow Book* editors, John Lane survived them both. He was happy in his marriage to Mrs. Annie Eichberg King, a well-to-do American and herself a writer. She was also an excellent cook and housekeeper, and Mrs. John Lane's cookbook brought culinary enlightenment to English housewives. Lane died in 1925 and his wife two years later. Their ashes were placed in the churchyard at Hartland, home soil for the man of Devon and not unfamiliar ground for the Bostonian. A Cornish cross with the inscription, "Nothing is here for tears," marks their graves.

A more impressive reminder of John Lane lives in the bequests he made of his art collections and in the publications of the Bodley Head. Though his spirit grew less adventurous in his later years, he still sought the work of new authors, Theodore Dreiser, Sherwood Anderson, and Julian Green among them. The American branch of the Bodley Head was closed in 1911, and the bow-fronted building on Vigo Street now houses an antiquarian book shop, but the firm carries on from a different address.

Sir Muirhead Bone, the artist, whose early etchings had been sent by D. Y. Cameron to Lane for Volume XIII, lived to record pictorially Britain's part in two World Wars, and died in 1949. Sir Max Beerbohm, though frail in health for several years, lived pleasantly at Rapallo, each successive birthday celebrated with appropriate observances by ardent admirers. Illness slowed his body but not his mind. A short time before his death in May, 1956, he was married to his devoted secretary, Elizabeth Jungmann. She survived him by less than three years, dying in January, 1959. Penrhyn Stanlaws, friend of Beardsley, who contributed drawings under the name of Sydney Adamson, had lived for years in the States. He was burned to death in a fire in his studio in Los Angeles in May, 1957, at the age of eighty.

In July, 1958, Mrs. Hicks Beach, the Susan Christian of Volume VII, replied to a query about her latest book, *Yesterdays behind the Door* (University of Liverpool Press, 1958), "I have your Air Letter, asking if I am still alive. I have contrived to be," but in February, 1959, she acknowledged mortality. Laurence Housman was the last to go, at the age of ninety-three, having lived twenty-six years longer than he expected. In 1932 he had written his obituary for the Manchester *Guardian*; it was printed on February 26, 1959, six days after his death.

So one by one the children of that "new Jerusalem," as Stedman called it, have slipped away until not one remains. "Each age believes—and should believe," said Ethel Colburn Mayne, "—that to it alone the secret of true art has been whispered."[20] Why should one live to learn otherwise?

NOTES

I

1. *New Statesman and Nation,* June 2, 1945, p. 352.
2. *The Works of Max Beerbohm* (London, 1896), p. 160.
3. Quoted by Holbrook Jackson, *The Eighteen Nineties* (New York, 1927), p. 139.
4. Quoted by Thomas Beer, *The Mauve Decade* (New York, 1926), title-page.
5. Jackson (see note 3), p. 46.
6. *The Letters of Henry James,* ed. E. F. Benson (London, 1930), p. 1.
7. "Editor's Study," *Harper's Magazine,* Feb., 1895, p. 481.
8. Richard Le Gallienne, *Prose Fancies* (London, 1896), II, 93.
9. Letter to the author of this book.

II

1. Walter Pater, *Studies in the History of the Renaissance* (London, 1873), pp. 249-50.
2. *Ibid.*
3. Quoted by Richard Le Gallienne, *The Romantic '90s* (Garden City, 1925), p. 30.
4. E. A. Robinson, *Untriangulated Stars* (Cambridge, Mass., 1947), p. 93.
5. *Bookbuyer,* XII, Aug., 1895, 389.
6. *Saturday Review,* June, 1895, p. 731.
7. *Letters of Sir Walter Raleigh,* ed. Lady Raleigh (New York, 1926), I, 227.
8. Edward Marsh, *A Number of People* (London, 1939), p. 103.
9. Arthur Machen, *Things Near and Far* (New York, 1923), p. 145.
10. Thomas Beer, *The Mauve Decade* (New York, 1926), p. 179.
11. *Blackwood's Magazine,* June, 1895, p. 839.

12. *The Letters of George Gissing*, ed. Algernon and Ellen Gissing (London, 1927), p. 182.

13. Max Beerbohm, *Around Theatres* (London, 1924), II, 265.

14. Hesketh Pearson, G.B.S., *A Full Length Portrait* (New York and London, 1942), p. 125.

15. Lawrence Pearsall Jacks, *Life and Letters of Stopford Brooke* (London, 1917), p. 554.

16. *Nineteenth Century*, April, 1894, p. 624.

17. Mark Longaker, *Ernest Dowson* (Philadelphia, 1945), p. 135.

III

1. William Gaunt, *The Aesthetic Adventure* (New York, 1945), p. 71.
2. *Harper's*, Nov., 1893, pp. 858-67.
3. Richard Le Gallienne, *Retrospective Reviews* (London, 1896), I, 25.
4. *Blackwood's*, June, 1895, pp. 833-45.
5. Max Nordau, *Degeneration* (New York, 1895), p. 8.
6. C. Lewis Hind, *The Diary of a Looker-on* (New York, 1908), p. 251.
7. *Bookman* (New York), April, 1895, p. 180.
8. Bernard Shaw, *The Sanity of Art* (London, 1908), p. 65.
9. E. A. Robinson, *Untriangulated Stars* (Cambridge, 1947), p. 249.
10. Quoted in *Nation*, LVIII, 432.
11. *Tomorrow*, I, June, 1896, 219.
12. Henri Murger, *Scènes de la Vie de Bohème* (Paris, 1888), p. vi.
13. *Critic*, XXVII, N. S. (1897), 9.
14. Conversation with the author of this book.
15. W. B. Yeats, *The Trembling of the Veil* (London, 1922), p. 179.
16. H. D. Traill, *The New Fiction* (London, 1897), p. 1.
17. Max Beerbohm, *Around Theatres* (London, 1924), II, 265.
18. *Fortnightly Review*, March, 1894, pp. 377-92.
19. Quoted by Ernest Rhys, *Everyman Remembers* (New York, 1931), p. 84.
20. Jerome K. Jerome, *My Life and Times* (New York and London, 1926), p. 88.
21. Laurence Housman, *My Brother, A. E. Housman* (London, 1938), p. 174.
22. "Ouida," *Views and Opinions* (London, 1895).
23. *Bookbuyer*, XI, Aug., 1894, 337.
24. *Bookbuyer*, XI, Sept., 1894, 380.
25. Doris Langley Moore, *E. Nesbit* (London, 1933), pp. 182, 227.
26. Elizabeth Robins Pennell, *Nights* (Philadelphia and London, 1916), p. 158.
27. Quoted by Grant Richards in *A. E. Housman (1897-1936)* (Oxford, 1941), p. 9.
28. C. Lewis Hind, *Naphtali* (New York, 1926), p. 55.
29. Jerome Hamilton Buckley, *William Ernest Henley* (Princeton, 1945), p. 156.
30. C. Lewis Hind, *More Authors and I* (London, 1922), p. 257.
31. George Bernard Shaw, *The Quintessence of Ibsenism* (London, 1930), p. 76.
32. *The Letters of George Gissing*, ed. Algernon and Ellen Gissing (London, 1927), p. 196.
33. Sir Henry Lucy, *The Diary of a Journalist: Later Entries* (London, 1922), p. 71.

IV

1. Richard Le Gallienne, *Retrospective Reviews* (London, 1896), I, xix.
2. Ford Madox Ford, *Return to Yesterday* (London, 1931), p. 39.
3. A. S. Hartrick, *A Painter's Pilgrimage* (Cambridge, 1939), p. 106.
4. *Bookbuyer*, XVII, Jan., 1899, 600.
5. *The Journal of Arnold Bennett* (New York, 1933), p. 73.
6. Ernest Rhys, *Everyman Remembers* (New York, 1931), p. 24.
7. Walter Besant, *Autobiography* (London, 1902), pp. 265-66.
8. *Bookbuyer*, XXV, 608.
9. *Munsey's*, XIII, 202.
10. E. A. Robinson, *Untriangulated Stars* (Cambridge, Mass., 1947), p. 181.
11. James Milne, *The Memoirs of a Bookman* (London, 1934), p. 110.
12. J. H. Harper, *The House of Harper* (New York, 1912), p. 531.
13. Douglas Sladen, *My Long Life* (London, 1939), p. 81.
14. *Robert Ross, Friend of Friends*, ed. Margery Ross (London, 1952), p. 29.

288

15. *Elkin Mathews, Books of the "Nineties"* (London, n.d.), p. 30.
16. Marie Belloc Lowndes, *Where Love and Friendship Dwelt* (New York, 1943), p. 157.
17. Katharine Tynan [Hinkson], *The Middle Years* (London, 1916), p. 105.
18. Ella Hepworth Dixon, *As I Knew Them* (London [1930]), p. 61.
19. Edith Wharton, *A Backward Glance* (New York, 1934), p. 305.
20. *The Letters of Henry James*, ed. E. F. Benson (London, 1930), p. 11.
21. Gertrude Atherton, *Adventures of a Novelist* (New York, 1932), p. 258.
22. *Bibelot*, XVIII, 290.
23. Elizabeth Robins Pennell, *Nights* (Philadelphia and London, 1916), p. 234.
24. "An Apostle of the Grotesque," *Sketch*, IX, April 10, 1895, 561.
25. John Berryman, *Stephen Crane* (New York, 1950), p. 188.
26. *Westminster Gazette*, Jan. 21, 1895, p. 2.
27. C. Lewis Hind, *Authors and I* (London, 1921), p. 320.
28. Arthur Symons, *The Café Royal* (London, 1923), p. 2.
29. *Journals of Thomas James Cobden-Sanderson, 1879-1922*, ed. R. Cobden-Sanderson (London, 1926), I, 329.
30. *Evening Transcript* (Boston), Feb. 16, 1895, p. 16.
31. W. B. Yeats, *Autobiographies* (New York, 1927), p. 370.
32. Virginia Woolf, *Roger Fry: A Biography* (London, 1940), p. 92.
33. Unpublished and undated letter of Max Beerbohm to Ada Leverson in the possession of the author.
34. Jerome K. Jerome, *My Life and Times* (London, 1926), p. 101.
35. Grant Richards, *Memories of a Misspent Youth* (New York and London, 1933), p. 300.
36. *Ibid.*, p. 295.
37. C. Lewis Hind, *Naphtali* (New York, 1926), p. 118.
38. Dixon (see note 18), p. 41.
39. Elizabeth Robins Pennell, *The Life and Letters of Joseph Pennell* (Boston, 1929), I, 248.
40. Hind (see note 37), p. 89.
41. Manchester *Guardian*, Jan. 19, 1924, p. 7.
42. Patrick Chalmers, *Kenneth Grahame, Life, Letters and Unpublished Work* (London, 1933), p. 65.
43. Manchester *Guardian* (see note 41).
44. Florence Emily Hardy, *The Later Years of Thomas Hardy* (New York, 1930), p. 46.
45. Netta Syrett, *The Sheltering Tree* (London, 1939), p. 93.
46. Arthur Waugh, *One Man's Road* (London, 1931), p. 291.
47. Clement K. Shorter, *C.K.S.: An Autobiography* (London, 1927), p. 131.
48. Roger Lancelyn Green, *Andrew Lang* (Leicester, 1946), p. 175.
49. New York *Times*, Feb. 26, 1895, p. 4.
50. John Dickson Carr, *The Life of Sir Arthur Conan Doyle* (New York, 1949), p. 112.
51. Joseph Hone, *W. B. Yeats, 1865-1939* (New York, 1943), p. 78.
52. *Bookman* (London), Dec., 1894, p. 73.
53. *The Letters of Henry James*, ed. Percy Lubbock (New York, 1920), I, 203.
54. *The Letters of Maurice Hewlett*, ed Laurence Binyon (London, 1926), p. 107.
55. Richard Le Gallienne, *Attitudes and Avowals* (London, 1910), pp. 38 ff.

V

1. *The Life of Sir Thomas Bodley Written by Himself*, with an Introduction by John Lane (London, 1894), p. v.
2. J. Lewis May, *The Path through the Wood* (London, 1930), p. 167.
3. Arthur Waugh, *One Man's Road* (London, 1931), p. 251.
4. Evelyn Sharp, *Unfinished Adventure* (London, 1933), pp. 55-56.
5. Gertrude Atherton, *Adventures of a Novelist* (New York, 1932), p. 235.
6. *Critic*, Nov. 11, 1893, p. 310.
7. J. Lewis May, *John Lane and the Nineties* (London, 1936), p. 213.
8. *The Book of Bodley Head Verse*, ed. J. B. Priestley, Preface by J. C. Squire (London, New York, 1926), p. xi.
9. Sharp (see note 4), p. 57.
10. May (see note 7), p. 35.

11. Stephen Gwynn, *Experiences of a Literary Man* (London, 1926), p. 143.
12. Sir William Rothenstein, *Men and Memories* (London, 1931), I, 165.
13. Laurence Housman, *The Unexpected Years* (Indianapolis, 1936), pp. 103-4.
14. Atherton (see note 5), p. 312.
15. James Milne, *Memoirs of a Bookman* (London, 1936), p. 91.
16. Anthony Hope [Hawkins], *Memories and Notes* (London, 1927), p. 162.
17. E. F. Benson, *As We Were* (London, 1930), p. 271.
18. Waugh (see note 3), pp. 252-53.
19. W. Pett Ridge, *I Like to Remember* (New York, 1925), p. 198.
20. *Sketch*, Dec. 4, 1895, Supplement, p. 6.
21. Grant Richards, *Memories of a Misspent Youth* (New York and London, 1933), p. 211.
22. Statement of Miss Ella D'Arcy.

VI

1. *The Library of Edmund Gosse*, comp. E. H. M. Cox (London, 1924), p. 37.
2. E. T. Raymond, *Portraits of the Nineties* (London, 1922), p. 198.
3. C. Lewis Hind, *The Uncollected Work of Aubrey Beardsley* (London, 1925), p. 68.
4. Ernest Rhys, *Everyman Remembers* (New York, 1931), p. 148.
5. *Robert Ross, Friend of Friends*, ed. Margery Ross (London, 1952), p. 27.
6. Elizabeth Robins Pennell, *The Life and Letters of Joseph Pennell* (Boston, 1929), I, 250.
7. J. Lewis May, *John Lane and the Nineties* (London, 1936), pp. 46-48. For permission to use this and other quotations from this book I am grateful to the Bodley Head.
8. A. W. King, *An Aubrey Beardsley Lecture* (London, 1924), p. 62.
9. Richard Le Gallienne, *The Romantic '90s* (Garden City, 1925), p. 232.
10. King (see note 8), p. 75.
11. Ross (see note 5), p. 28.
12. Thomas Beer, *The Mauve Decade* (New York, 1926), p. 179.
13. Sir William Rothenstein, *Men and Memories* (London, 1931), I, 182.
14. Boris Brasol, *Oscar Wilde* (New York, 1938), p. 225.
15. Frances Winwar, *Oscar Wilde and the Yellow 'Nineties* (New York and London, 1940), p. 214.
16. Mrs. Patrick Campbell, *My Life and Some Letters* (London, 1922), p. 74.
17. E. R. and J. Pennell, *Life of James McNeil Whistler* (London, 1909), p. 140.
18. Rothenstein (see note 13), 1, 135.
19. *Bookbuyer*, XVII, Oct., 1898, 212.
20. *Ibid.*
21. *Sketch*, IX, April 10, 1895, 561.
22. Le Gallienne (see note 9), p. 233.
23. May (see note 7), p. 53.
24. Henry Harland in *Academy*, LV, 437.
25. C. J. Holmes, *Self and Partners* (London, 1936), p. 229.
26. Doris Langley Moore, *E. Nesbit* (London, 1933), p. 130.
27. *Evening Transcript* (Boston), Feb. 16, 1895, p. 16.
28. *Idler*, XI, March, 1897, 198.
29. See note 27, above.
30. Hind (see note 3), p. x.
31. *Critic*, XXXIV, 442.
32. *Academy* (see note 24).
33. Aubrey Beardsley, *Letters to Smithers* (London, 1937), Letter CXLV.
34. Aymer Vallance in *The Magazine of Art*, XXII, May, 1898, 368.
35. John Rothenstein, *The Artists of the 1890's* (London [1928]), p. 173.
36. Beardsley (see note 33), Letter XVII.
37. Ford Madox Ford, *Return to Yesterday* (London, 1931), p. 45.
38. *Studio*, May, 1898, p. 252.
39. *Idler*, XIII, May, 1898, 539.

VII

1. Francis L. Bickley in *Dictionary of National Biography*, Second Supplement, ed. Sir Sidney Lee (London, 1912), II, 213-14.

2. "G. Glastonbury" (Aline Harland), *Irish Monthly*, April, 1911, p. 210.
3. Unpublished MS by Miss Louise Howe, Norwich, Connecticut.
4. Evelyn Sharp, *Unfinished Adventure* (London, 1933), pp. 62-63.
5. Richard Le Gallienne, *The Romantic '90s* (Garden City, 1925), p. 233.
6. Sharp (see note 4), p. 63.
7. Statement of Miss Ella D'Arcy.
8. Conversation with Miss Howe.
9. Laura Stedman and George M. Gould, *Life and Letters of Edmund Clarence Stedman* (New York, 1910), II, 320.
10. MS by Miss Howe.
11. *Ibid.*
12. Stedman and Gould (see note 9), II, 251.
13. *Ibid.*, p. 97.
14. MS by Miss Howe.
15. *The Letters of Henry James,* ed. Percy Lubbock (New York, 1920), I, 208.
16. *Irish Monthly*, April, 1911, p. 218.
17. *Ibid.*, p. 212.
18. Le Gallienne (see note 5), p. 234.
19. Statement of Miss Margaret Fuller, Norwich, Conn.
20. Stedman and Gould (see note 9), II, 358-59.
21. *Nation,* Oct. 20, 1898, p. 299.
22. Arthur Waugh, *One Man's Road* (London, 1931), p. 214.
23. Mrs. Mabel Kitcat, *Bookman* (New York), XXIX, 610.
24. Max Beerbohm, *Seven Men* (London, 1919), p. 19.
25. Letter to the author.
26. Elizabeth Robins Pennell, *Nights* (Philadelphia and London, 1916), p. 172.
27. Beerbohm (see note 24), p. 19.
28. Le Gallienne (see note 5), p. 233.
29. Richard Le Gallienne, *R.L.S. and Other Poems* (London, 1895), p. 30.
30. *Irish Monthly*, April, 1911, p. 218.
31. C. Lewis Hind, *Naphtali* (New York, 1926), p. 90.
32. Statement of Miss Ella D'Arcy.
33. Patrick Chalmers, *Kenneth Grahame, Life, Letters and Unpublished Work* (London, 1933), p. 66.
34. Pennell (see note 26), p. 228.
35. Richard Le Gallienne, *The Romantic '90s* (Garden City, 1925), p. 237.
36. D. S. MacColl, *London Mercury*, XXXIX, 290.
37. MS by D. S. MacColl, presented to the author.

VIII

1. *London Mercury*, XXXIX, 292.
2. *Ibid.*
3. Letter to the author.
4. MS by Miss Howe.
5. *Irish Monthly*, April, 1911, p. 214.
6. Netta Syrett, *The Sheltering Tree* (London, 1939), p. 80.
7. MS by Miss Howe.
8. *Evening Transcript* (Boston), Feb. 16, 1895, p. 16.
9. Patrick Chalmers, *Kenneth Grahame, Life, Letters and Unpublished Work* (London, 1933), p. 66.
10. *Critic*, XXI, Jan. 20, 1894, 42-43.
11. Aubrey Beardsley, *Under the Hill* (London, 1921), p. v.
12. J. M. Richards, *The Life of John Oliver Hobbes* (London, 1911), p. 79.
13. *Sketch*, V, April 11, 1894, 557.

IX

1. *The Selected Letters of Henry James,* ed. Leon Edel (New York, 1955), p. 98.
2. *The Novels and Tales of Henry James* (New York, 1909), XV, v-vii.
3. The Hon. Evan Charteris, *Life and Letters of Sir Edmund Gosse* (London, 1931), p. 348.
4. Arthur Waugh, *One Man's Road* (London, 1931), pp. 253-58.

5. John Rothenstein, *The Life and Death of Conder* (London, 1938), p. 100.
6. Laurence Housman, *The Unexpected Years* (Indianapolis, 1936), p. 103.
7. Walter Crane, *An Artist's Reminiscences* (New York, 1907), p. 416.
8. A. S. Hartrick, *A Painter's Pilgrimage* (Cambridge, 1939), p. 157.
9. J. Lewis May, *John Lane and the Nineties* (London, 1936), p. 49.
10. *Ibid.*, pp. 48-49.
11. *Robert Ross, Friend of Friends*, ed. Margery Ross (London, 1952), p. 30.
12. *Ibid.*, p. 31.
13. Prospectus ("Announcement"), *Yellow Book.*
14. *Granta*, VII, April 21, 1894, 271.
15. *Critic*, May 5, 1894, p. 300.
16. Ross (see note 11), p. 30.
17. *Critic*, XXI, 290.
18. *Ibid.*, p. 360.
19. May (see note 9), p. 74.
20. Elizabeth Robins Pennell, *Nights* (Philadelphia and London, 1916), p. 186.
21. *Critic*, XXI, 311.
22. Letter to the author.
23. *Critic* (see note 21).
24. Victor Plarr, *Ernest Dowson* (London, 1914), p. 98.
25. Alfred Thornton, "Diary of an Art Student of the Nineties," *Artist*, May, 1935 p. 86.
26. *Critic*, XXI, 312.
27. Arthur Waugh, *One Man's Road* (London, 1931), p. 255.

X

1. Statement of Miss Ella D'Arcy.
2. William Archer, *Poets of the Younger Generation* (London, 1902), p. 251.
3. Owen Seaman, *The Battle of the Bays* (London, 1896), p. 38.
4. E. A. Robinson, *Untriangulated Stars* (Cambridge, Mass., 1947), p. 180.
5. H. C. Beeching, *Pages from a Private Diary* (London, 1899), p. 115.
6. John Churton Collins, *Ephemera Critica* (Westminster, 1901), p. 109.
7. Arthur Waugh, *One Man's Road* (London, 1931), p. 254.
8. *Yellow Book*, I, 129.
9. *Evening Transcript* (Boston), Feb. 16, 1895, p. 16.
10. *National Observer*, X, April 21, 1894, 588-89.
11. *Times* (London), April 20, 1894, p. 3.
12. *Westminster Gazette*, April 18, 1894, p. 3.
13. *Daily Chronicle*, April 16, 1894, p. 3.
14. *Ibid.*, April 17, 1894, p. 3.
15. *Punch*, May 5, 1894, p. 208.
16. *Granta*, VII, April 28, 1894, 278.
17. *Evening Transcript* (Boston), Feb. 16, 1895, p. 16.
18. *Critic*, May 19, 1894, p. 344.
19. *Academy*, April 28, 1894, p. 339.
20. *The Journal of Arnold Bennett* (New York, 1933), p. 33.
21. *Oxford Magazine*, May 17, 1894, Special extra number, p. 2.
22. *The Letters of Henry James*, ed. Percy Lubbock (New York, 1920), I, 222.
23. "Jean Paul Raymond" and Charles Ricketts, *Oscar Wilde* (Bloomsbury, 1932), p. 52.
24. Frances Winwar, *Oscar Wilde and the Yellow 'Nineties* (New York and London, 1940), p. 240.
25. *Ibid.*
26. *Spectator*, May 19, 1894, p. 695.
27. *Sketch*, May 2, 1894, p. 16.
28. *Saturday Review*, April 28, 1894, p. 455.
29. *Speaker*, April 28, 1894, p. 468-69.
30. *Punch*, April 28, 1894, p. 198.
31. *Ibid.*, p. 203.
32. *Granta*, VII, April 28, 1894, 285.
33. *Isis* (Oxford), May 5, 1894, p. 261.
34. *Harper's*, Aug., 1894, p. 476.
35. *Nation*, May 24, 1894, p. 390.

36. *Bookbuyer*, XI, June, 1894, 261, 262.
37. *Critic*, May 19, 1894, p. 360.
38. *Dial* (Chicago), June 1, 1894, pp. 335-36.
39. Robinson (see note 4), p. 168.
40. Prospectus, Volume II.

XI

1. J. M. Richards, *Life of John Oliver Hobbes* (London, 1911), p. 86.
2. *Ibid.*, p. 43.
3. G. B. Burgin, *Memoirs of a Clubman* (London, 1921), p. 133.
4. Gertrude Atherton, *Adventures of a Novelist* (New York, 1932), pp. 248-49.
5. *Bookman* (New York), I, 221.
6. *Munsey's*, X, 640.
7. *Bookman* (New York), II, 461.
8. *Bookbuyer*, XI, April, 1894, 127.
9. *Ibid.*, X, Nov., 1893, 409.
10. C. Lewis Hind, *Naphtali* (New York, 1926), p. 109.
11. Florence Emily Hardy, *Later Years of Thomas Hardy* (New York, 1930),
pp. 26, 120.
12. George Moore, *Vale* (Carra Edition, New York, 1935), p. 79.
13. *Ibid.*, p. 87.
14. W. B. Yeats, *Dramatis Personae* (New York, 1936), p. 71.
15. Joseph M. Hone, *The Life of George Moore* (London, 1936), p. 373.
16. Malcolm Elwin, *Old Gods Falling* (New York, 1939), p. 99.
17. Richards (see note 1), p. 91.
18. *Munsey's*, XIII, 553.
19. *Bookman* (New York), March, 1897, p. 10.
20. Hind (see note 10), p. 74.
21. James Milne, *Memoirs of a Bookman* (London, 1936), p. 240.
22. Eileen Bigland, *Ouida* (New York, 1951), p. 227.
23. *Letters of George Meredith* (London, 1912), II, 529.
24. *Ibid.*, p. 551.
25. Yeats (see note 14), p. 50.
26. Hone (see note 15), p. 190.
27. Burgin (see note 3), p. 133.
28. Hardy (see note 11), p. 120.
29. Quoted in *Current Literature*, XLI, 405.
30. *North American Review*, CLXXXIII, Dec., 1906, 1261.
31. Ella Hepworth Dixon, *As I Knew Them* (London, 1930), p. 56.
32. Yeats (see note 14), p. 55.
33. Atherton (see note 4), p. 161.
34. Richard Le Gallienne, *The Romantic '90s* (Garden City, 1925), p. 11.
35. Charles Morgan, *Epitaph on George Moore* (New York, 1935), p. 8.
36. Susan Mitchell, *George Moore* (New York, 1916), p. 13.
37. James Whitall, *English Years* (New York, 1935), p. 74.
38. George Moore, *Ave* (New York, 1911), p. 26.
39. *Ibid.*, p. 35.
40. *The Journal of Arnold Bennett* (New York, 1933), p. 616.
41. Vincent O'Sullivan, *Aspects of Wilde* (New York, 1936), p. 87.
42. Yeats (see note 14), p. 21.
43. *Ibid.*
44. Sir William Rothenstein, *Men and Memories* (London, 1931), I, 231.
45. Clement K. Shorter, *C.K.S.: An Autobiography* (London, 1927), p. xvi.
46. Somerset Maugham, *The Summing Up* (New York, 1938), p. 21.
47. Morgan (see note 35), p. 2.

XII

1. D. S. MacColl, *Life, Work and Setting of Philip Wilson Steer* (London [1945]),
pp. 2, 3, 7.
2. *The Cambridge History of English Literature*, ed. Sir A. W. Ward and A. R.
Waller, XIV (Cambridge, 1932), 208.

3. Edward Marsh, *A Number of People* (New York and London, 1939), p. 52.
4. *Punch,* March 9, 1895, p. 118.
5. *Times* (London), July 20, 1894, p. 4.
6. *Westminster Gazette,* July 20, 1894, p. 2.
7. *Punch,* Aug. 11, 1894, p. 66.
8. Elizabeth Robins Pennell and Joseph Pennell, *The Art of Whistler* (New York, 1928), p. 25.
9. *Bookman* (London), Dec., 1896, p. 94.
10. *Yellow Book,* II, 179-90.
11. *Ibid.,* pp. 281-84.
12. *Ibid.,* p. 269.
13. *Times* (London), July 20, 1894, p. 4.
14. *The Best of Friends: Further Letters to Sydney Carlyle Cockerell,* ed. Viola Meynell (London, 1956), pp. 32-34.
15. Charlotte Mew, *Collected Poems* (London, 1953), p. 44.
16. Virginia Moore, *Distinguished Women Writers* (New York, 1934), p. 191.
17. R. L. Stevenson, *Strange Case of Dr. Jekyll and Mr. Hyde* in *Works* (New York, 1906), XIV, 313.
18. *Letters of Robert Louis Stevenson,* ed. Sidney Colvin (New York, 1902), II, 6.
19. *Stevenson's Letters to Charles Baxter,* ed. Ferguson and Waingrow (New Haven, 1956), pp. 175-217.
20. Charles Archer, *William Archer* (London, 1931), p. 215.
21. Norman Gale, *Orchard Songs* (New York, 1893), p. 112.
22. E. A. Robinson, *Untriangulated Stars* (Cambridge, Mass., 1947), p. 180.
23. *National Observer,* XII, Aug. 18, 1894, 359.
24. Quoted by Douglas Ainslie, *Adventures Social and Literary* (London and New York, 1922), p. 196.
25. The Hon Evan Charteris, *John Sargent* (New York, 1927), p. 142.
26. *Nation,* Aug. 23, 1894, p. 143.
27. *Critic,* Aug. 18, 1894, p. 108.
28. Thomas Beer, *The Mauve Decade* (New York, 1926), p. 247.
29. Richard Le Gallienne, *The Romantic '90s* (Garden City, 1925), p. 238.
30. *Savoy,* No. 2, p. 124.
31. *Chap-Book,* I, Sept. 15, 1894, 240-41.

XIII

1. Review of *Lover's Lexicon, Bookbuyer,* April, 1894, p. 150.
2. Richard Le Gallienne, *The Romantic '90s* (Garden City, 1925), p. 231.
3. *Speaker,* Nov. 24, 1894, p. 572.
4. *Bookman* (New York), I, 329.
5. H. C. Beeching, *Pages from a Private Diary* (London, 1899), p. 39.
6. *Ibid.,* p. 3; see p. 7 for the phrase "My poet Davidson."
7. Owen Seaman, *The Battle of the Bays* (London, 1896), p. 26.
8. *The Critic,* XXIV, Aug. 3, 1895, 77.
9. Edgar Jepson, *Memories of a Victorian* (London, 1933), p. 239.
10. William Archer, *Poets of the Younger Generation* (London and New York, 1902), p. 119.
11. *Bookman* (London), April, 1896, p. 10.
12. W. B. Yeats, *Autobiographies* (New York, 1927), p. 389.
13. *Bookman* (London), Nov., 1894, p. 49.
14. *Letters of Charles Eliot Norton* (Boston and New York, 1913), II, 226-27.
15. Edmund Gosse, *Critical Kit-Kats* (New York, 1896), pp. 218-23.
16. Quoted in *New Statesman and Nation,* Feb. 17, 1945, p. 111.
17. Victor Plarr, *Ernest Dowson* (London, 1914), p. 9.
18. Arthur Symons, *Poems and Prose of Ernest Dowson* (New York, 1919), p. 12.
19. *Academy,* Nov. 2, 1907, p. 95.
20. *Yellow Book,* III, 109.
21. *Some Winchester Letters of Lionel Johnson* (London and New York, 1919), p. 69.
22. George Santayana, *Persons and Places* (New York, 1944), p. 14.
23. Douglas Ainslie, *Adventures Social and Literary* (London and New York, 1922), p. 98.
24. *Elkin Mathews. Books of the "Nineties"* (London, n.d.), p. 48.
25. *Letters of Louise Imogen Guiney* (New York and London, 1926), II, 210-11.

26. Ernest Rhys, *Everyman Remembers* (New York, 1931), p. 221.
27. Sir William Rothenstein, *Men and Memories* (London, 1931), I, 157.
28. *Letters of Louise Imogen Guiney* (see note 25), I, 74.
29. George Santayana, *The Middle Span* (New York, 1945), p. 60.
30. W. B. Yeats, *Autobiographies* (New York, 1927), p. 375.
31. Mathews (see note 24).
32. *Yellow Book*, III, 143-52.
33. Santayana (see note 29), p. 56.
34. Grant Richards, *Memories of a Misspent Youth* (New York and London, 1933), p. 338.
35. *Robert Ross, Friend of Friends*, ed. Margery Ross (London, 1952), p. 29.
36. *Bookman* (London), Jan., 1894, p. 129.
37. *Saturday Review*, Oct. 27, 1894, p. 469.
38. *National Observer*, XIII, Nov. 17, 1894, 23.
39. *Idler*, XIII (1898), 544.
40. *Bookbuyer*, XVII, Oct., 1898, 214.

XIV

1. Charles Newton-Robinson, biographical sketch in Preface of *Moods and Metres* (London, 1913).
2. Elizabeth Robins Pennell, *Nights* (Philadelphia and London, 1916), pp. 157-58.
3. Elizabeth Robins Pennell, *The Life and Letters of Joseph Pennell* (Boston, 1929), I, 282-83.
4. Laura Stedman and George M. Gould, *Life and Letters of Edmund Clarence Stedman* (New York, 1910), II, 185.
5. C. Lewis Hind, *More Authors and I* (London, 1922), p. 115.
6. *Ibid.*, p. 218.
7. Grant Richards, *Memories of a Misspent Youth* (New York and London, 1933), p. 158.
8. Edgar Jepson, *Memories of an Edwardian* (London, 1937), p. 20.
9. H. G. Wells, *Experiment in Autobiography* (New York, 1934), p. 516.
10. Hesketh Pearson, *G. B. S.* (New York and London, 1942), p. 96.
11. Doris Langley Moore, *E. Nesbit* (London, 1933), p. 154.
12. *Ibid.*
13. Noel Coward, *Present Indicative* (New York, 1937), p. 11.
14. Moore (see note 11), p. 288.
15. Richard Le Gallienne, *The Romantic '90s* (Garden City, 1925), p. 165.
16. Moore (see note 11), p. 259.
17. *Punch*, May 21, 1924, p. 562.
18. *Chap-Book*, III, 112.
19. *Munsey's*, XIV, 244.
20. *Bookman* (London), July, 1893, 120.
21. Marie Belloc Lowndes, *The Merry Wives of Westminster* (London, 1946), p. 23.
22. Obituary New York *Times*, March 27, 1945, p. 19.
23. *International Studio*, IV, 239.
24. William Rothenstein, *Men and Memories* (London, 1931), I, 341.
25. Jacques Émile Blanche, *Portraits of a Lifetime,* trans. and ed. Walter Clement (New York and London, 1938), p. 80.
26. Sir William Rothenstein, *Men and Memories* (London, 1931), I, 90.
27. Sir John Lavery, *The Life of a Painter* (Boston, 1940), p. 76.
28. Laurence Binyon, *English Water-Colours* (London, 1933), p. 190.
29. Rothenstein (see note 26), II, 178.
30. *Irish Monthly*, April, 1911, p. 214.
31. Desmond McCarthy, *Experience* (London, 1935), p. 89.
32. Edith Wharton, *A Backward Glance* (New York, 1934), p. 222.
33. Gertrude Atherton, *Adventures of a Novelist* (New York, 1932), p. 290.
34. *Tomorrow*, Aug., 1896, p. 165.
35. *The Letters of George Meredith to Alice Meynell* (London and San Francisco 1923), p. 52.
36. Derek Patmore, *Portrait of My Family* (New York, 1935), p. 232.
37. Quoted by Amy Cruse, *After the Victorians* (London, 1938), p. 52.
38. Patmore (see note 36), p. 255.
39. Cruse (see note 37), p. 52.

40. *Bookman* (New York), I, March, 1895, 82.
41. Atherton (see note 33), p. 245.
42. A. F. Tschiffely, *Don Roberto* (London, 1937), p. 264 note.
43. *Westminster Gazette,* Jan. 24, 1895, p. 3.
44. Stephen Gwynn, *Experiences of a Literary Man* (London, 1926), p. 142.
45. *Evening Transcript* (Boston), Feb. 16, 1895, p. 16.

XV

1. Aubrey Beardsley, *Under the Hill* (London and New York, 1928), p. viii.
2. Elizabeth Robins Pennell, *The Life and Letters of Joseph Pennell* (Boston, 1929), I, 294.
3. *Evening Transcript* (Boston), Feb. 16, 1895, p. 16.
4. *Bookbuyer,* XII, March, 1895, p. 79.
5. New York *Times,* April 4, 1895, p. 5.
6. J. Lewis May, *John Lane and the Nineties* (London, 1936), p. 80.
7. *Ibid.*
8. *Times* (London), April 8, 1895, p. 13.
9. C. Lewis Hind, *Authors and I* (London, 1921), p. 291.
10. Conversation with the author.
11. Violet Hunt, *I Have This To Say* (New York, 1926), p. 87.

XVI

1. *The Library of Edmund Gosse,* comp. E. H. M. Cox (London, 1924), pp. 299-300.
2. *Times* (London), May 10, 1895, p. 42.
3. *Westminster Gazette,* May 6, 1895, p. 3.
4. *Sketch,* May 22, 1895, p. 180.
5. *Bookman* (New York), July, 1895, p. 423.
6. *Evening Transcript* (Boston), March 30, 1895, p. 15.
7. Statement of Miss Margaret Fuller to the author.
8. Grant Richards, *Memories of a Misspent Youth* (New York and London, 1933), p. 150.
9. Alfred Austin, *English Lyrics,* ed. William Watson (London, New York, 1896), p. xxiv.
10. *Munsey's,* XXII, July, 1895, 343.
11. *Bookman* (London), April, 1893, p. 5.
12. *Ibid.,* Nov., 1894, p. 37.
13. Ella Hepsworth Dixon, *As I Knew Them* (London [1930]), p. 53.
14. *Friends of a Lifetime: Letters to Sydney Carlyle Cockerell,* ed. Viola Meynell (London, 1940), p. 201.
15. New York *Times,* Aug. 14, 1935, p. 19.
16. Obituary, Sir William Watson, *Observer* (London), Aug. 18, 1935, p. 12.
17. *Ibid.*
18. Douglas Ainslie, *Adventures Social and Literary* (London and New York, 1922), p. 225.
For the verses quoted from Watson, see "The Unknown God," *Poems* (London, 1899), p. 280, and *New Poems* (London, 1909), pp. 64-65.
19. Sir William Rothenstein, *Men and Memories* (London, 1931), I, 287.
20. Max Beerbohm, *More* (London, 1899), p. 106.
21. G. S. Street, *Some Notes of a Struggling Genius* (London, 1897), p. vi note.
22. *Bookbuyer,* XII, April, 1895, 174.
23. J. Lewis May, *John Lane and the Nineties* (London, 1936), p. 176.
24. Maurice Baring, *The Puppet Show of Memory* (Boston, 1923), pp. 156-57.
25. Archibald Marshall, *Out and About* (London, 1933), p. 27.
26. Edward Marsh, *A Number of People* (London, 1939), p. 73.
27. Maisie Ward, *Gilbert Keith Chesterton* (London, 1944), p. 387.
28. G. K. Chesterton, *Autobiography* (London, 1936), p. 228.
29. "Since Maurice Died," *Commonweal,* Feb. 15, 1946, p. 447.
30. Charles Baudelaire, *The Painter of Victorian Life,* trans. P. G. Konody (London, 1930), p. 172.
31. *Yellow Book,* V, 249.
32. Frances Winwar, *Oscar Wilde and the Yellow 'Nineties* (New York and London, 1940), p. 306.

33. *Ibid.*, p. 313.
34. Richards (see note 8), p. 300.
35. *Punch,* Nov. 28, 1896, p. 253.
36. Osbert Sitwell, *Noble Essences* (Boston, 1950), p. 160.
37. Ada Leverson, *The Limit* (London, 1950), pp. 231-32.
38. Sitwell (see note 36), p. 160.
39. Leverson (see note 37), p. 231.
40. Grant Richards, *A. E. Housman (1897-1936)* (Oxford, 1941), pp. 113-14.
41. Grant Richards, *Author Hunting* (New York, 1934), p. 191.
42. Richards (see note 40), *loc. cit.*
43. Sitwell (see note 36), p. 181.

XVII

1. Conversation with the author.
2. A. F. Tschiffely, *Don Roberto* (London, 1937), p. 350.
3. Richard Aldington, *Life for Life's Sake* (New York, 1941), p. 245.
4. Frances Winwar, *Oscar Wilde and the Yellow 'Nineties* (New York and London, 1940), p. 199.
5. *Nation,* June 6, 1895, p. 448.
6. *Punch,* April 13, 1895, p. 178.
7. Haldane Macfall, *Aubrey Beardsley* (London, 1928), pp. 67-68.
8. Aubrey Beardsley, *Letters to Smithers* (London, 1937), Letter IX.
9. W. B. Yeats, *Autobiographies* (New York, 1927), pp. 406-7.
10. Arthur Symons, *The Art of Aubrey Beardsley* (New York, 1918), p. 15.
11. Patrick Chalmers, *Kenneth Grahame, Life, Letters and Unpublished Work* (London, 1933), p. 83.
12. Conversation with the author.
13. Statement to the author by D. S. MacColl.
14. Walter Shaw Sparrow, "Some Drawings by Patten Wilson," *International Studio,* XIV, 189-92.

XVIII

1. *Munsey's,* XII, 311.
2. Henry James, *Theatre and Friendship,* ed. Elizabeth Robins (London, 1932), p. 166.
3. *Evening Transcript* (Boston), Jan. 30, 1895, p. 6.
4. James (see note 2), p. 167.
5. Walford Graham Robertson, *Time Was* (London, 1931), p. 269.
6. *Bookman* (New York), Aug., 1909, p. 611.
7. James (see note 2), p. 170.
8. *Bookman* (New York), Feb., 1895, p. 9.
9. *The Notebooks of Henry James,* ed. F. O. Matthiessen and Kenneth B. Murdock (New York, 1947), p. 180.
10. *Ibid.*, p. 28.
11. *Anne Douglas Sedgwick: A Portrait in Letters,* ed. Basil de Sélincourt (Boston and New York, 1936), p. 47.
12. James (see note 9), p. 143.
13. *The Letters of Henry James,* ed. E. F. Benson, p. 17.
14. Elizabeth Robins Pennell, *The Life and Letters of Joseph Pennell* (Boston, 1929), I, 286.
15. James (see note 9), pp. 151-52.
16. *Ibid.*, p. 160.
17. *The Novels and Tales of Henry James* (New York, 1909), XV, xvii.
18. *Ibid.*, p. viii.
19. James (see note 9), p. 236.
20. MS by Miss Howe.
21. Gertrude Atherton, *Memories of a Novelist* (New York, 1932), p. 234.
22. Edith Wharton, *A Backward Glance* (New York, 1934), pp. 243-44.
23. *The Diary of Arthur Christopher Benson,* ed. Percy Lubbock (New York, 1926), p. 47.
24. *Bookman* (New York), Aug., 1909, p. 611.
25. James Whitall, *English Years* (New York, 1935), p. 94.

26. *The Journal of Arnold Bennett* (New York, 1933), p. 8.
27. W. Pett Ridge, *I Like to Remember* (London, 1925), p. 180.
28. *Bookman* (New York), July, 1905, 464-66.
29. *Ibid.*, Feb., 1912, p. 590.
30. Wharton (see note 22), p. 178.
31. Max Beerbohm, *Around Theatres* (London, 1924), II, 428-29.
32. The Hon. Evan Charteris, *The Life and Letters of Sir Edmund Gosse* (London, 1931), p. 350.
33. Conversation wtih the author, 1954.
34. MS by Miss Howe.
35. *Bookbuyer*, XVIII, 184.
36. *Ibid.*, June, 1894, p. 244.
37. *Bookman* (New York), VI, Dec., 1897, 284.
38. *Westminster Gazette*, April 18, 1894, p. 3.
39. Cornelius Weygandt, *A Century of the English Novel* (New York, 1925), p. 348.
40. Malcolm Elwin, *Old Gods Falling* (New York, 1939), p. 314.
41. *The Letters of Henry James*, ed. Percy Lubbock (New York, 1920), I, 237.
42. *The Journal of Arnold Bennett* (New York, 1933), pp. 18-19.
43. *Ibid.*, p. 20.
44. *Ibid.*, p. 193.
45. Arnold Bennett, *The Truth about an Author* (Westminster, 1903), pp. 95-96.
46. Bennett (see note 42), p. 10.
47. *Ibid.*, p. 72.
48. *Sketch*, July 31, 1895, p. 7.
49. *Westminster Gazette*, July 30, 1895, p. 3.
50. Thomas Hake and Arthur Compton-Rickett, *The Life and Letters of Theodore Watts-Dunton* (London, 1916), II, 189.
51. Clara Watts-Dunton, *The Home Life of Swinburne* (London, 1922), p. 72.
52. Richard Whiteing, *My Harvest* (London and New York, 1915), p. 263.
53. Sir William Rothenstein, *Men and Memories* (London, 1931), I, 231.
54. Charles Archer, *William Archer* (London, 1931), p. 267.
55. Sedgwick (see note 11), p. 80.
56. E. V. Lucas, *Reading, Writing and Remembering* (New York and London, 1932), pp. 142-43.
57. Laura Stedman and George M. Gould, *Life and Letters of Edmund Clarence Stedman* (New York, 1910), II, 52.
58. Lucas (see note 56), p. 102.
59. Ernest Rhys, *Everyman Remembers* (New York, 1930), p. 219.

XIX

1. Richard Le Gallienne, *Young Lives* (London, 1898), p. 311.
2. Jerome K. Jerome, *My Life and Times* (London, 1926), p. 190.
3. *Chap-Book*, III, 178.
4. J. Lewis May, *John Lane and the Nineties* (London, 1936), p. 90.
5. *Yellow Book*, VIII, 165.
6. *Critic*, XXVII, April 10, 1897, 262.
7. *The Journal of Arnold Bennett* (New York, 1933), p. 139.
8. Richard Le Gallienne, *The Romantic '90s* (Garden City, 1925), p. 229.
9. Le Gallienne, *From a Paris Garret* (New York, 1936), p. 64.
10. Quoted in R. Thurston Hopkins, *Rudyard Kipling* (New York, 1916), p. 347.
11. *Ibid.*
12. Richard Le Gallienne, *The Beautiful Lie of Rome* (New York and London, n.d.), pp. 53-54.
13. Lionel Johnson in *Academy*, Nov. 20, 1897, p. 428.
14. Aubrey Beardsley, *Letters to Smithers* (London, 1937), Letter XC.
15. Sir William Rothenstein, *Men and Memories* (London, 1931), I, 208.
16. Reprinted in *Critic*, XXVII, Jan. 30, 1897, 84.
17. Grant Richards, *Memories of a Misspent Youth* (New York and London, 1933), pp. 342-45.
18. Lawrence Pearsall Jacks, *Life and Letters of Stopford Brooke* (London, 1917), II, 528.
19. *Academy*, Nov. 20, 1897, p. 428.
20. Conversation with the author.

21. Vincent Starrett, *Buried Caesars* (Chicago, 1923), p. 136.
22. Hubert Crackanthorpe, *Last Studies* (London, 1897), p. ix.
23. Le Gallienne (see note 8), p. 165.
24. Beardsley (see note 14), Letter CX.
25. *Ibid.*, Letter CXXII.
26. William Freeman, *The Life of Lord Alfred Douglas* (London, 1948), p. 159.
27. *Ibid.*, p. 250.
28. M. C. Stopes, *Lord Alfred Douglas* (London, 1949), pp. 21-22.
29. Olive Custance, *The Inn of Dreams* (London and New York, 1911), pp. 24-25.
30. *The Notebooks of Henry James*, ed. F. O. Matthiessen and Kenneth B. Murdock (New York, 1947), p. 132.
31. Evelyn Sharp, *Unfinished Adventure* (London, 1933), p. 120.
32. Letter to the author.
33. *Bookman* (London), June, 1897, p. 74.

XX

1. Conversation with the author.
2. Stephen Gwynn, *Experiences of a Literary Mqn* (London, 1926), p. 140.
3. H. G. Wells, *Experiment in Autobiography* (New York, 1934), p. 330.
4. *Ibid.*, p. 159.
5. New York *Times*, Aug. 17, 1946, p. 13.
6. *Letters of George Gissing to Members of His Family* (London, 1931), p. 192.
7. Richard F. Niebling, "The Early Career of George Gissing," Ph.D. dissertation, Yale, 1943, p. 22.
8. Wells (see note 3), pp. 482-83.
9. Edward Clodd, *Memories* (London, 1916), p. 178.
10. *The Letters of Henry James*, ed. Percy Lubbock (New York, 1920) I, 398.
11. Wells (see note 3), pp. 491-93.
12. Henry James, *Notes on Novelists* (New York, 1914), pp. 438-39.
13. *Letters of George Gissing*, ed. Algernon and Ellen Gissing (London, 1927), p. 213.
14. *Ibid.*, p. 182.
15. *Ibid.*, p. 183.
16. *Ibid.*, p. 138.
17. *Yellow Book*, VIII, 38.
18. *Selections Autobiographical and Imaginative from the Works of George Gissing* (New York, 1929), pp. 218-19.
19. Niebling (see note 7), p. 98.
20. Wells (see note 3), p. 493.
21. Gwynn (see note 2), p. 116.
22. Frank Swinnerton, *Autobiography* (London and New York, 1936), p. 119.
23. *Bookman* (London), Nov., 1895, p. 46.
24. *The Journal of Arnold Bennett* (New York, 1933), p. 13.
25. Quoted in *Academy*, Dec. 11, 1897, p. 525.
26. Letter to the author.

XXI

1. Edgar Jepson, *Memories of a Victorian* (London, 1933), p. 245.
2. Conversation with the author.
3. Arthur Symons, *Studies in Prose and Verse* (London, 1904), p. 285.
4. Arthur Symons, *Poems* (London, 1916), I, 31.
5. Arthur Symons, *Images of Good and Evil* (London, 1899), p. 178.
6. *Bookman* (London), April, 1897, p. 16.
7. *Chap-Book*, IV, 98.
8. George Moore, *Ave* (Carra Edition, New York, 1935), p. 19.
9. Sir William Rothenstein, *Men and Memories* (London, 1931), I, 250.
10. *Ibid.*
11. *Savoy*, No. 1, p. 5.
12. *Ibid.*, p. 66.
13. Aubrey Beardsley, *Letters to Smithers* (London, 1937), Letter IX.
14. *Ibid.*, Letter XXIII.
15. *Ibid.*, Letter XVI.
16. Mark Longaker, *Ernest Dowson* (Philadelphia, 1945), p. 280.
17. Quoted in advertisement, *Savoy*, No. 2, p. 203.

18. Beardsley (see note 13), Letter XXVI.
19. *Ibid.,* Letter XLIII.
20. *Ibid.,* Letter XLII.
21. *Ibid.,* Letter XLIV.
22. W. B. Yeats, *Autobiographies* (New York, 1927), p. 399.
23. *Savoy,* No. 3, p. 103.
24. Beardsley (see note 13), Letter XLV.
25. Quoted in advertisement, *Savoy,* No. 5, p. 88.
26. Beardsley (see note 13), Letter XLVI.
27. *Ibid.,* Letter LVIII.
28. *Letters from Joseph Conrad 1895-1924,* ed. Edward Garnett (Indianapolis, 1928), p. 62.
29. *Savoy,* No. 7, p. 6.
30. Katharine Tynan [Hinkson], *The Middle Years* (London, 1916), p. 131.
31. *The Letters of George Meredith to Alice Meynell* (London and San Francisco, 1923), p. 47.
32. *Ibid.,* p. 79.
33. Cornelius Weygandt, *A Century of the English Novel* (New York, 1925), p. 356.
34. *Savoy,* No. 8, pp. 91-92.
35. *Critic,* XXVII, Jan. 2, 1897, 12.
36. *Yellow Book,* XI, 58.
37. *Letters of George Meredith Collected and Edited by His Son* (New York, 1913), II, 462.
38. Henry S. Salt, *Company I Have Kept* (London, 1930), p. 138.

XXII

1. *Letters of Sir Walter Raleigh,* ed. Lady Raleigh (New York, 1926), I, 184.
2. *Ibid.,* II, 350.
3. Arnold Bennett, *Books and Persons* (London, 1917), p. 45.
4. Raleigh (see note 1), II, 357.
5. *Ibid.,* p. 521.
6. Robert P. Eckert, *Edward Thomas* (New York, 1937), p. 19.
7. Helen Thomas, *As It Was* (London, 1926), p. 72.
8. *Critic,* April 25, 1896, p. 297.
9. H. D. Traill, *Saturday Songs* (London, 1890), pp. 108, 110.
10. H. D. Traill, *The New Fiction* (London, 1897), p. 2.
11. *Ibid.,* p. 5.
12. Charles Archer, *William Archer* (London, 1931), p. 213.
13. Hind, *Authors and I* (New York and London, 1921), pp. 330-31.
14. *The Journal of Arnold Bennett* (New York, 1933), p. 184.
15. Hind (see note 13), p. 334.
16. G. B. Burgin, *Many Memories* (New York, 1923), p. 124.
17. *Bookman* (London), March, 1898, p. 175.
18. *Ibid.,* April, 1895, p. 140.
19. The Hon. Evan Charteris, *John Sargent* (New York, 1927), p. 78.
20. *The Library of Edmund Gosse,* comp. E. H. M. Cox (London, 1924), p. 179.
21. Walter Crane, *An Artist's Reminiscences* (New York, 1907), p. 229.
22. Obituary, Theo. Marzials, *Times* (London), Feb. 12, 1920, p. 17.
23. The Hon. Evan Charteris, *The Life and Letters of Sir Edmund Gosse* (New York, 1931), p. 76.
24. *Ibid.,* p. 31.
25. Arthur Waugh in *Bookman* (London), Sept., 1896, p. 166.
26. Charteris (see note 23), p. 201.
27. *Ibid.,* p. 197.
28. Grant Richards, *Memories of a Misspent Youth* (New York and London, 1933), p. 223.
29. *The Letters of Robert Louis Stevenson,* ed. Sidney Colvin (London, 1923), III, 182.
30. Archer (see note 12), p. 297.
31. Marie Belloc Lowndes, *Merry Wives of Westminster* (London, 1946), p. 180.
32. Siegfried Sassoon, *The Old Century and Seven More Years* (London, 1938), pp. 102-3.
33. *National Observer,* XI, April 21, 1894, 588.

34. *Letters of Louise Imogen Guiney* (New York and London, 1926), I, 54.
35. *Letters of Robert Browning,* ed. Thurman L. Hood (New Haven, 1933), p. 187.
36. G. B. Burgin, *Memories of a Clubman* (New York, 1922), p. 219.
37. Somerset Maugham, *The Summing Up* (New York, 1938), p. 4.
38. Osbert Sitwell, *Noble Essences* (Boston, 1950), p. 40.
39. Sassoon (see note 32), p. 102.
40. *Century,* Feb., 1894, p. 488.
41. *Bookbuyer,* XI, Aug., 1894, 348.
42. *Bookman* (London), Oct., 1894, p. 27.
43. *Academy,* Dec. 11, 1897, p. 518.
44. Archibald Marshall, *Out and About* (London, 1933), p. 26.
45. *Bookman* (London), March, 1896, p. 187.
46. New York *Times,* Aug. 24, 1952, VI, 18.
47. *The Diary of Arthur Christopher Benson,* ed. Percy Lubbock (New York, 1926), p. 39.
48. *Ibid.,* p. 39.
49. Charteris (see note 23), p. 375.
50. Rupert Hart-Davis, *Hugh Walpole* (London, 1952), pp. 286-87.

XXIII

1. Frederic Whyte, *William Heinemann* (New York, 1929), p. 69.
2. C. Lewis Hind, *More Authors and I* (London, 1922), p. 114.
3. *Bookbuyer,* XVII, Jan., 1899, 601.
4. *The Letters and Journal of Brand Whitlock* (New York, 1936), I, 6.
5. *Bookbuyer,* XVII, Jan., 1899, 602.
6. Rupert Hart-Davis, *Hugh Walpole* (London, 1952), p. 179.
7. *Observer* (Utica), Oct. 22, 1898, p. 9.
8. John Berryman, *Stephen Crane* (New York, 1950), pp. 237-46.
9. Vincent Starrett, *Buried Caesars* (Chicago, 1923), p. 85.
10. *Bookbuyer,* XX, July, 1900, 433.
11. Starrett (see note 9), pp. 128-29.
12. "The Phoenix Nest," *Saturday Review of Literature,* March 16, 1946, p. 59.
13. Richard Le Gallienne, *George Meredith* (New York and London, 1890), p. xc.
14. *Letters of George Meredith Collected and Edited by His Son* (New York, 1913), II, 387, 388.
15. *Ibid.,* II, 478.
16. *The Letters of Henry James,* ed. Percy Lubbock (New York, 1920), II, 163.
17. *Sketch,* Jan. 23, 1895, p. 637.
18. *Bookman* (New York), I, 54.
19. Charles Archer, *William Archer* (London, 1931), pp. 244-45.
20. Norman Hapgood, *The Changing Years* (New York, 1930), p. 95.
21. Marie Belloc Lowndes, *The Merry Wives of Westminster* (London, 1946), p. 66-67.
22. Walter Crane, *An Artist's Reminiscences* (New York, 1907), p. 352.
23. *Vanity Fair,* LIV, July 18, 1895, 55.
24. *Bookman* (London), April, 1894, p. 25.
25. *Critic,* XXIV, Nov. 30, 1895, 374.
26. *Fortnightly Review,* April 1, 1898, pp. 653-54.
27. *Academy,* May 3, 1902, p. 459.
28. *Saturday Review,* June 1, 1895, p. 730.
29. Van Wyck Brooks, *The Confident Years* (New York, 1952), p. 266.
30. *Yellow Book,* IX, 21.

XXIV

1. A. J. A. Symons, *The Quest for Corvo* (New York, 1955), p. 29 note.
2. Somerset Maugham, *The Summing Up* (New York, 1938), p. 171.
3. Quoted in Frederick Baron Corvo, *Letters to Grant Richards* (London, n.d.), p. 44.
4. Symons (see note 1), p. 249.
5. Osbert Burdett, *The Beardsley Period* (New York, 1925), p. 235.
6. William C. Frierson, *The English Novel in Transition* (Norman, 1942), p. 58.
7. Neta Syrett, *The Sheltering Tree* (London, 1939), p. 100.

301

8. Letter to the author.
9. *Ibid.*
10. *Ibid.*
11. *Critic,* XXVII (Jan. 2, 1897), 11.
12. Max Beerbohm, *Around Theatres* (London, 1924), I, 501.
13. Laurence Housman, *The Unexpected Years* (Indianapolis, 1936), p. 192.
14. Letter to the author.
15. Syrett (see note 7), p. 256.
16. Harold Williams, *Modern English Writers* (London, 1925), p. 467.
17. *Academy,* March 1, 1902, p. 220.
18. Evelyn Sharp, *Unfinished Adventure* (London, 1933), p. 53.
19. *Ibid.,* p. 59.
20. *Ibid.,* p. 72.
21. *Bookbuyer,* XII, Oct., 1895, 519.
22. Stephen Gwynn, *Experiences of a Literary Man* (London, 1926), p. 137.
23. H. V. Nevinson, *Fire of Life* (London, 1935), p. 85.
24. *Ibid.,* p. 121.
25. H. V. Nevinson, *Changes and Chances* (London, 1923), p. 117.
26. Nevinson (see note 23), pp. 265-66.
27. Gwynn (see note 22), p. 138.
28. Sharp (see note 18), p. 64.
29. Anthony Hope [Hawkins], *Memories and Notes* (New York, 1928), p. 123.
30. *National Observer,* XII, Aug. 18, 1894, 359.
31. Patrick Chalmers, *Kenneth Grahame, Life, Letters and Unpublished Work* (London, 1933), p. 55.
32. E. A. Robinson, *Untriangulated Stars* (Cambridge, Mass., 1947), p. 197.
33. Syrett (see note 7), p. 97.
34. *Bookman* (London), Sept., 1896, p. 161.
35. *Academy,* Jan. 1, 1898, p. 4.
36. Amy Cruse, *After the Victorians* (London, 1938), p. 81.
37. Charles Archer, *William Archer* (London, 1931), p. 246.
38. Gwynn (see note 22), p. 184.
39. Cruse (see note 36), p. 82.
40. Coulson Kernahan, *In Good Company* (London and New York, 1917), p. 148.
41. Lena Ashwell, *Myself a Player* (London, 1936), p. 90.
42. Gwynn (see note 22), pp. 179-80.
43. Constance Benson, *Mainly Players* (London, 1926), p. 67.
44. Ernest Rhys, *Everyman Remembers* (New York, 1931), p. 69.
45. *The Book of Bodley Head Verse,* ed. J. B. Priestley (London and New York, 1926), p. 147.
46. William Archer, *Real Conversations* (London, 1904), p. 73.
47. Ella Hepworth Dixon, *As I Knew Them* (London [1930]), p. 250.
48. *The Works of Max Beerbohm* (London, 1896), pp. 8-9.
49. Walford Graham Robertson, *Time Was* (London, 1931), p. 310.
50. St. John Ervine, *Bernard Shaw* (New York, 1956), p. 339.
51. Max Beerbohm, *Around Theatres* (London, 1924), I, 4.
52. *Ibid.,* I, 3.
53. Doris Arthur Jones, *Life and Letters of Henry Arthur Jones* (London, 1930), p. 254.
54. *Academy,* June 10, 1899, p. 631.
55. *The Journal of Arnold Bennett* (New York, 1933), p. 171.
56. Max Beerbohm, *Mainly on the Air* (London, 1946), p. 99.
57. Constance Collier, *Harlequinade* (London, 1929), p. 155.
58. *Saturday Review of Literature,* July 3, 1948, p. 4.
59. *Tomorrow,* III, Jan., 1897, 28.
60. Beerbohm (see note 51), I, 5.
61. *Ibid.,* II, 355-56.
62. *Bookman* (New York), Nov., 1900, p. 268.
63. Beerbohm (see note 51), II, 488-89.
64. Conversation with the author.
65. Frank Harris, *Contemporary Portraits,* Fourth Series (New York, 1923), p. 132.
66. *Times Literary Supplement* (London), Feb. 23, 1924, p. 138.
67. Clippings from *Daily Mail* (Nov.-Dec., 1906) in British Museum.
68. Beerbohm (see note 48), p. 160.

69. Max Beerbohm, *More* (London, 1899), p. 137.
70. Osbert Sitwell, *Noble Essences* (Boston, 1950), p. 171.
71. Sir William Rothenstein, *Men and Memories* (London, 1931), I, 240.
72. Richard Aldington, *Life for Life's Sake* (New York, 1941), p. 376.
73. Frederic Whyte, *A Bachelor's London* (London, 1931), p. 229.
74. *Ibid.*, p. 228.
75. Ethel Colburn Mayne, *Browning's Heroines* (London, 1913), pp. vii-ix.
76. *Academy*, July 31, 1897, p. 94.
77. *Bookman* (New York), Aug., 1909, p. 611.

XXV

1. The Hon. Evan Charteris, *John Sargent* (New York, 1927), pp. 245-48.
2. *Bookman* (New York), XXXII, Nov., 1910, 231-32.
3. *Forum*, April, 1911, p. 449.
4. A. C. Benson, *Memories and Friends* (London, 1924), p. 60.
5. Marie Belloc Lowndes, *Where Love and Friendship Dwelt* (New York, 1943), p. 176.
6. Elizabeth Robins Pennell, *The Life and Letters of Joseph Pennell* (Boston, 1929), I, 118.
7. Anne Douglas Sedgwick: *A Portrait in Letters*, ed. Basil de Sélincourt (Boston and New York, 1936), p. 9.
8. *Bookman* (London), Oct., 1931, p. 21.
9. *Forum*, April, 1911, p. 456.
10. Katharine Tynan [Hinkson], *Twenty-five Years* (New York, 1913), p. 330.
11. E. C. Stedman, *A Victorian Anthology* (New York, 1895), p. 579.
12. *Yellow Book*, X, 214.
13. Séan O'Faoláin, *Constance Markievicz* (London, 1934), p. 20.
14. W. B. Yeats, *The Winding Stair and Other Poems* (New York, 1933), p. 1. Copyright 1933 by The Macmillan Company; used with the publisher's kind permission.
15. A. Norman Jeffares, *W. B. Yeats* (London, 1949), p. 188.
16. H. W. Nevinson, *Changes and Chances* (London, 1923), p. 210.
17. *Yellow Book*, XIII, 12.
18. "The Grey Rock," in *Poetry*, II, 17. Reprinted in *Collected Poems* by Yeats, copyright 1903-56 by The Macmillan Company; used with the publisher's kind permission.
19. Katharine Tynan [Hinkson], *The Middle Years* (London, 1916), p. 39.
20. Arthur Compton-Rickett, *I Look Back* (London, 1933), p. 142.
21. Frederic Whyte, *The Life of W. T. Stead* (New York and London, n.d.), I, 252.
22. Walter Crane, *An Artist's Reminiscences* (New York, 1907), p. 268.
23. Hesketh Pearson, *G.B.S., A Full Length Portrait* (New York and London, 1942), p. 66.
24. J. Lewis May, *John Lane and the Nineties* (London, 1936), p. 210.
25. A. F. Tschiffely, *Don Roberto* (London, 1937), p. 344.
26. *The Journal of Arnold Bennett* (New York, 1933), p. 781.
27. Marie Belloc Lowndes, *Merry Wives of Westminster* (London, 1946), p. 173.
28. The Ranee Margaret of Sarawak, *Good Morning and Good Night* (London, 1934), p. 237.
29. Lowndes (see note 27), p. 177.
30. Gertrude Atherton, *Adventures of a Novelist* (New York, 1932), p. 464.
31. The Ranee Margaret of Sarawak (see note 28), p. 129.
32. H. G. Wells, *Experiment in Autobiography* (New York, 1934), p. 591.

XXVI

1. *Chap-Book*, V, 30.
2. Quoted in advertisement, *Savoy*, No. 3, p. 106.
3. *Bookman* (London), June, 1896, p. 90.
4. Letter to the author.
5. Douglas Ainslie, *Adventures Social and Literary* (London and New York, 1922), pp. 74 ff.
6. *Ibid.*, p. 259.
7. *Ibid.*, p. 252.
8. Letter to the author.

9. Florence Emily Hardy, *The Later Years of Thomas Hardy* (New York, 1930), p. 107.

10. William Archer, *Poets of the Younger Generation* (London, 1902), p.117.

11. C. Lewis Hind, *Naphtali* (London, 1926), p. 103.

12. Letter to the author.

13. Ernest Rhys, *Everyman Remembers* (New York, 1931), p. 54.

14. Richard Le Gallienne, *Retrospective Reviews* (London, 1896), II, 9.

15. W. B. Yeats, *Letters to Katharine Tynan* (Dublin, 1953), p. 124.

16. *Bookman* (London), Aug., 1895, p. 146.

17. Douglas Goldring, *South Lodge* (London, 1943), p. 71.

18. David Garnett, *The Golden Echo* (London, 1954), pp. 124-26.

19. Rhys (see note 13), p. 246.

20. *Times* (London), Feb. 15, 1938, p. 10.

21. *Ibid.*, March 30, 1938, p. 16.

22. *Ibid.*, Dec. 16, 1942, p. 7.

23. *Academy*, April 30, 1910, pp. 416-18.

24. *Observer*, Dec. 9, 1930.

25. Oscar Wilde, *Complete Works*, ed. Robert Ross (London, 1909), IX, 293.

26. H. W. Nevinson, *Changes and Chances* (London, 1923), p. 287.

27. *Bookman* (London), Dec., 1894, p. 86.

28. Samuel C. Chew, *Thomas Hardy* (New York, 1921), p. 90.

29. Laurence Housman, *The Unexpected Years* (Indianapolis, 1936), p. 137.

30. J. Lewis May, *John Lane and the Nineties* (London, 1936), p. 69.

31. W. B. Yeats, *The Trembling of the Veil* (London, 1922), p. 58.

XXVII

1. Sir William Rothenstein, *Men and Memories* (London, 1931), I, 232.

2. *Bookbuyer*, June, 1894, p. 262.

3. *Munsey's*, XI, 430.

4. Elizabeth Robins Pennell, *Nights* (Philadelphia and London, 1916), p. 189.

5. *Evening Transcript* (Boston), Feb. 16, 1895, p. 16.

6. *Times* (London), Jan. 29, 1897, p. 14.

7. *Ibid.*, May 28, 1897, p. 15.

8. *Critic*, XXVIII, July 17, 1897, 38.

9. *The Journal of Arnold Bennett* (New York, 1933), p. 50.

10. *Letters from Joseph Conrad, 1895-1924*, ed. Edward Garnett (Indianapolis, 1928), p. 106.

11. Ford Madox Ford, *Return to Yesterday* (London, 1931), p. 45.

12. Haldane Macfall, *Aubrey Beardsley* (London, 1928), p. 72.

13. Conversation with the author.

14. *Academy*, May 3, 1902, p. 459.

15. Conversation with the author.

16. *Irish Monthly*, April, 1911, p. 215.

17. MS by Miss Howe.

18. Conversation with B. W. Willett, Director, Bodley Head, in 1930.

19. James Milne, *The Memoirs of a Bookman* (London, 1934), p. 230.

20. *Critic*, Jan. 2, 1897, p. 12.

21. M. H. Spielmann and G. S. Layard, *Kate Greenaway* (New York, 1905), p. 187.

22. Grant Richards, *Memories of a Misspent Youth* (New York and London, 1933), p. 277.

23. *New Review*, X, March, 1894, 309.

24. *Savoy*, No. 8, p. 92.

25. Arnold Bennett, *Books and Persons* (London, 1917), p. 243.

26. Lawrence Pearsall Jacks, *Life and Letters of Stopford Brooke* (London, 1917), II, 518.

27. Aubrey Beardsley, *Letters to Smithers* (London, 1937), Letter XXXI.

28. *Munsey's*, XII, 104.

29. Letter to the author.

30. *Chap-Book*, II, May 1, 1895, 386.

31. *Yellow Book*, II, 261.

32. Max Beerbohm, *Seven Men* (London, 1919), p. 6.

33. *New Review*, May, 1894, p. 681.

34. Patrick R. Chalmers, *Kenneth Grahame* (London, 1933), p. 66.

35. A. J. A. Symons, *An Anthology of 'Nineties' Verse* (London, 1928), p. xvii.
36. *Yellow Book*, II, 262, 267.
37. MS by Miss Howe.

XXVIII

1. Aubrey Beardsley, *Letters to Smithers* (London, 1937), Letter CLXXXV.
2. Gertrude Atherton, *Adventures of a Novelist* (New York, 1932), p. 262.
3. Violet Hunt, *I Have This To Say* (New York, 1926), p. 80.
4. *The Letters of W. B. Yeats,* ed. Allan Wade (London, 1954), pp. 574-75.
5. A. Norman Jeffares, *W. B. Yeats* (London, 1949), pp. 166-67. Quoted by permission of Routledge and Kegan Paul and the Yale University Press.
6. Atherton (see note 2), p. 262.
7. Edgar Jepson, *Memories of a Victorian* (London, 1933), p. 263.
8. H. W. Nevinson, *Changes and Chances* (London, 1923), p. 192.
9. Mrs. Patrick Campbell, *My Life and Some Letters* (London, 1922), p. 110.
10. *Ibid.,* p. 184.
11. Richard Whiteing, *My Harvest* (London and New York, 1915), pp. 278-79.
12. W. B. Yeats, *Autobiographies* (New York, 1927), p. 392.
13. Grant Richards, *Author Hunting* (New York, 1934), p. 224.
14. *Irish Monthly,* April, 1911, p. 215.
15. Hamlin Garland, *Roadside Meetings* (New York, 1930), p. 441.
16. *Irish Monthly,* April, 1911, p. 219.
17. Unpublished letter to Miss Howe.
18. *Ibid.*
19. *Ibid.*
20. Ethel Colburn Mayne, *Browning's Heroines* (London, 1913), p. x.

Index

Academy: and Arnold Bennett, 174, 175; awards by, 213, 244; bought by John Richards, 99-100; edited by Lewis Hind, 100, 213; on Katherine Douglas King, 253; review of Realms of the Unknown Kings, 220; on Ronald Campbell Macfie, 268; George Saintsbury a critic for, 85; on Yellow Book, 274; mentioned, 53, 90, 174, 201, 210, 238, 244

Achurch, Janet, 9

Adams, Francis, 15, 270

Adamson, Sydney. See Stanlaws, Penrhyn

Adcock, St. John, 278

A. E. See Russell, George William

Aestheticism, 11-13

Ainger, Alfred; and Austin Dobson, 7; quoted, 38; mentioned, 115, 177, 239

Ainslie, Douglas: and Harland, 263-64, 278; and Sarah Bernhardt, 264; and Benedetto Croce, 264; and Henry James, 264; and Lionel Johnson, 123; name change of, 264; and Oriental philosophy, 264-65; and Yellow Book, 263-64; death of, 265

Albermarle, edited by Hubert Crackanthorpe, 183

Albermarle Club, 139

Aldington, Richard: and the Radfords, 267; on Reginald Turner, 251; quoted, 161

Alexander, George, 166, 245

All the Year Round, 210

Allen, Grant: and Churton Collins, 217; and Edmund Gosse, 217; and Gladstone, 41; and the new hedonism, 16; and Vivian Cory, 253; on Whitman, 9; uncle of Netta Syrett, 253; mentioned, 12, 133, 149; The Woman Who Did, 211, 253, publication of, 40

Alma-Tadema, Sir Lawrence, 19, 219

Alma-Tadema, Lady, sister of Nellie Gosse, 219

Alma-Tadema, Laurence (daughter of Sir Lawrence Alma-Tadema), 219; literary contributions of, 220; Realms of the Unknown Kings, 220

Anderson, Sherwood, 286

Anti-Jacobin, 114, 124

Archer, William: and Watts-Dunton, 177; on Beardsley, 113; on F. B. Money-Coutts, 265; on Francis Watt, 212; on Norman Hapgood, 227; on Rosamund Marriott Watson, 129; on Stephen Phillips, 244; on Symons, 200; translates Ibsen, 9; quoted, 84; mentioned, 110, 246

Aristophanes, Lysistrata, Beardsley's drawings for, 53

Arliss, George, 251

Arnold, Edwin, 150

Arnold, Matthew: critical of contemporary mores, 4; on religious uncertainties, 5; mentioned, 6, 145, 151, 217, 218

Art for Art's Sake, excesses of devotees, 13-15

Ashwell, Lena, 245

Asquith, Margot, and William Watson, 151

Astor, William Waldorf, and Pall Mall Budget, 213

Athenaeum, and Watts-Dunton, 177; on Harold Frederic, 224; on the Savoy, 204; mentioned, 118, 132, 201, 247

Atherton, Gertrude: and Ernest Dowson, 26, 282; and George Moore, 102; and Henry Harland, 138; on Frank Swettenham, 262; on Mrs. Craigie, 95-96; on John Lane, 40; quoted, 137, 170, 281; Patience Sparhawk, publication of, 38; "The Striding Place," refused by Yellow Book, 138

Atkinson, Elizabeth, 225

Austin, Alfred, 150

Austin, Jane, 159

"B., J. M." (J. M. Bulloch), quoted, 41

Backhouse, E. Trelawny, 78

Bacon, Sir Francis, essays edited by John Buchan, 197

Balfour, Arthur, 99

Balfour, Marie Clothilde, as writer, 269; mentioned, 263

Ball, Wilfred, 175

Balzac, Honoré de, Beardsley on, 44-45; mentioned, 159; La Fille aux Yeux d'Or, 205

Baring, Edward Charles, Lord Revelstocke, 154

Baring, Maurice: career of, 154-56; on Anatole France, 153; and Aubrey Beardsley, 154; and Edmund Gosse, 155; and G. K. Chesterton, 155; and Hilaire Belloc, 155; as novelist, 155-56; Catholicism of, 155; linguistic ability of, 155; on Russian writers, 9; mentioned, 29, 256

Barr: Robert: and Harold Frederic, 223; in London, 22; on death of Stephen Crane, 225

Barrie, Sir James M., early work of, 7; and H. B. Marriott Watson, 130; mentioned, 27, 197

Barlas, John, see Douglas, Evelyn

Battersby, H. F. P.: and H. W. Nevinson, 269; and Oscar Wilde, 268-69; career of, 268-69; mentioned, 263

Baudelaire, Charles, mentioned, 85, 153, 156; Les Fleurs du Mal, 8

Baxter, Charles, 109, 110

Beach, Mrs. Hicks. See Christian, Susan

Beardsley, Aubrey: and Lord Alfred Douglas, 139-40; and Arthur Symons, 198, 199, 201; and Charles Conder, 136; and critics of, 51; and Edward Burne-Jones, 44; and Frederic Brown's Art School, 44; and Frederick Evans, 44; grotesque element in, 49, 52-53; and Haldane Macfall, 162-63; and Henry Harland, 164; and John Lane, 76; and

Maurice Baring, 154; and Max Beerbohm, 74; and Olive Custance, 186; and Oscar Wilde, 47-49, 73, 139-140, 143-47, 160, 162; and Philip G. Hamerton, 107; and Robert Ross, 76-77; and the *Savoy*, 164, 198, 202, 203, 205-06, 207; and the *Yellow Book*, 3, 35, 55, 67, 68, 69, 72, 75, 76, 112-13, 126-27, 128, 139-47, 227, 273, 274-75; and *Sunday Times*, 203-04; and *Daily Chronicle*, 88-89; childhood of, 43-44, 54; compares Balzac to Shakespeare, 44-45; difficulties of, 163-64; dress of, 43, 50; elected to New English Art Club, 49; entertains at home, 50; encouraged by A. W. King, 44, 47; first exhibit of, 44; introduces Netta Syrett to the Harlands, 236; method of work, 49-51, 52-53; buys home, 49; proposes a *Comedy of Masques*, 67; obscenity in work of, 53-54; proposes to go to America with Lane, 51; shares studio with Will Rothenstein, 50; successful career of, 50; death of, 15, 281; Netta Syrett visits grave, 238; drawings for Aristophanes' *Lysistrata*, 53; drawings for Malory's *Morte d'Arthur*, 45, 46-47; drawings for Oscar Wilde's *Salomé*, 47-49, 50; translates *Salomé*, 48; on black as a color, 87; on Verlaine, 24; on William Watson, 152; on Wratislaw, 126; on W. B. Yeats, 204; on the *Yellow Book*, 271; *Westminster Gazette* on, 88; quoted, 26, 29, 82, 183, 264, 275; mentioned, 7, 25, 26, 30, 33, 35, 60, 63, 70, 78, 80, 81, 83, 94, 112, 114, 129, 148, 157, 158, 166, 175, 190, 191, 203, 230, 241, 247; *Under the Hill*, 53, 71, 140, 203, 205; "Comedy-Ballet of Marionettes," 113; "Night Piece," 87; "Portrait of Madame Réjane," 113; "Portrait of Mrs. Patrick Campbell," 87, 88-89; "L'Education Sentimentale," 87; "The Three Musicians," 203; "The Toilet of Helen," 203

Beardsley, Mabel: and Aubrey Beardsley, 43; and Netta Syrett, 236; death of, 281-82; mentioned, 31, 33, 44, 49, 77, 157, 237, 238, 264, 281

Beardsley, Mrs. (mother of Aubrey and Mabel Beardsley): entertains writers, 31; death of, 282; mentioned, 43, 45, 50, 164, 238, 281

Beeching, H. C.: and Davidson, 115-16; on George Saintsbury, 85

Beer, Thomas: and Madame Réjane, 113; on Oscar Wilde, 48; quoted, 8

Beerbohm, Max: career of, 152, 246-51; as theatre-goer and critic, 247-48, 249-50; attractiveness of, 246-47; replaces Shaw as drama critic of the *Saturday Review*, 247; and A. C. Benson, 221; and Constance Collier, 248-49; and critics, 107-08; and Ada Leverson, 159; and Florence Kahn, 249, 250; and the Harlands, 246; and Henry Harland, 62; and Henry James, 171; and John Davidson, 128; and Kipling, 34; and Mabel Beardsley, 282; and Philip G. Hamerton, 107; and Richard Le Gallienne, 181; and Stephen Phillips' *Herod*, 246; and Will

Rothstein, 128; and *Yellow Book*, 74, 95, 246, 247; in America, 23, 148; in Italy, 250; on Alice Meynell, 137; on Aubrey Beardsley, 55; on John Lane, 39; on Henry Harland, 276; on W. E. Henley, 18; on Ibsen, 9; on G. S. Street and "Ouida," 152-53; on Netta Syrett's *The Finding of Nancy*, 237; on G. B. Shaw, 247; on the *Yellow Book*, 3, 67, 148; on knighthood, 250; on his satiric temperament, 249; on social behavior, 248; *Westminster Gazette* on, 88; death of, 286; quoted, 1, 16, 30, 277; mentioned, 7, 15, 47, 68, 78, 82, 83, 93, 114, 140, 158, 172, 175, 203, 209, 232, 237, 241, 264, 276; *Caricatures of Twenty-five Gentlemen*, 247; *The Happy Hypocrite* (play), 248, 251-52; *The Works of Max Beerbohm*, publication of, 246; *Zuleika Dobson*, 249; "A Letter to the Editor," 95, 107; "A Peep into the Past," 84; "Defence of Cosmetics," 84, 107; "The Happy Hypocrite" (short story), 247, 251; "The Incomparable Beauty of Modern Dress," 84; "The Mote in the Middle Distance," 171; "Note on George the Fourth," 126; "No. 2 The Pines," 177

Beerbohm, Mrs. (mother of Max Beerbohm), 252

Beerbohm-Tree, Sir Herbert. *See* Tree, Sir Herbert Beerbohm

Bell, R. Anning: mentioned, 78; "A Book Plate," 87

Belloc, Hilaire: and Maurice Baring, 155; mentioned, 237

Belloc, Marie. *See* Lowndes, Marie Belloc

Benét, William Rose, quoted, 226

Bennett, (Enoch) Arnold: career of, 174-75; and Gissing, 195; and John Buchan, 174-75; and John Lane, 273; and Julie Norregard, 180; and *Yellow Book*, 174; on George Moore, 103; on Henry James, 170; on John Buchan's popularity, 197; on Lewis Hind, 214; on Robert Barr, 22; on R. B. Cunninghame Graham, 261; on Walter W. Raleigh, 210; quoted, 248, 275; mentioned, 90, 213, 236, 273; *Journal*, 175; *Journalism for Women: A Practical Guide*, 175; *A Man from the North*, 273; "A Letter Home," 174

Benson, A. C.: career of, 220-22; prose style criticized, 221; and poetry, 221; essays, 221; biographies, 221; and Edmund Gosse, 221-22; on Henry James, 170; on Violet Paget, 256; Hugh Walpole on, 222; mentioned, 25, 42, 74, 78, 85, 155, 168; *Le Cahier Jaune*, 3

Benson, Constance: on Stephen Phillips, 245

Benson, E. F.: on John Lane, 41

Benson, Eugene: marriage of, 228; in Italy, 228; essay on d'Annunzio, 228; *Gaspara Stampa*, 228; *From the Asolan Hills*, 228

Benson, Sir Frank, 243

Benson, Hugh: and Baron Corvo, 233

Bentzon, Th.: and Henry Harland, 59

Bernhardt, Sarah: and Douglas Ainslie, 264; and *Salomé*, 48; mentioned, 155

Besant, Walter: on book clubs, 20; on New York, 23; on Ibsen's *A Doll's House*, 9-10; mentioned, 149

Besant, Mrs.; and the Cunninghame Grahams, 260

Beyle, Henri, 227

Binyon, Laurence, 7, 15, 67, 243, 270; *London Visions*, 27

Birmingham School, in *Yellow Book*, 191

Björnson, Björnstjerne, 9, 173

Black and White, 66, 158, 268

Blackwood's, 9, 12, 234, 235

Blätter für die Kunst, founded by Stefan George, 21

Blaikie, John Arthur, and Edmund Gosse, 216

Blake, William, 85, 204

Blanc, Madame. *See* Bentzon, Th.

Blanche, Jacques Émile: and Charles Conder, 135; mentioned, 202, 203

Bland, Hubert: and E. Nesbit, 131-32; mentioned, 5, 133, 233

Bland, Mrs. Hubert. *See* Nesbit, Edith

Blast, 280

Blavatsky, Mme. Elena Petrovna, 260

Blind, Mathilde, 203

Blunt, Wilfrid, 187

Bodley Head: as symbol of Elkin Mathews and John Lane, 35-36; and Aubrey Beardsley, 140; and John Lane, 262-63; and *Yellow Book*, 190, 274; in the twentieth century, 286; mentioned, 33, 141, 143, 149, 150, 161, 172, 175, 178, 179, 181, 188, 191, 197, 232, 272, 274, 275. *See also* Elkin Mathews and John Lane, Lane, John, Vigo Street

Bone, Sir Muirhead, 286

Book clubs, in nineties, 20

Bookbuyer, the: on Mrs. Craigie, 96; on Evelyn Sharp, 238; on "George Egerton," 172; review of *Yellow Book*, 93; on *Yellow Book*, 271; "The Rambler," column in, 141; mentioned, 153

Bookman (English periodical): on A. Bernard Miall, 263; on William Watson, 150; on Wratislaw's *Caprices*, 126; mentioned, 34, 133, 172, 189, 196

Bookman (U.S. periodical): Annie Macdonell London representative of, 114; on Mrs. Craigie, 96; on Meredith and the *Yellow Book*, 138; review of *Yellow Book*, 148; mentioned, 34, 56

Borrow, George, 176

"Bosie," Alfred Douglas, 48, 187

Bourget, Paul, 25, 261

Braithwaite, Lillian, 237

Brandes, Georg: and Julie Norregard, 179-80

Bridges, Robert, 27, 42, 130, 270

Brieux, Eugène, 263

British Museum, 7, 214, 215, 216, 225

Brooke, Honor (daughter of Stopford Brooke), 10

Brooke, Margaret, Ranee of Sarawak: career of, 261; and Oscar Wilde, 261; and Frank Swettenham, 262; and W. H. Hudson, 262; in Paris, 261; and Vernon Lee, 262

Brooke, Stopford: on death of Crackanthorpe, 186; on Henry James, 185; on Ibsen's *A Doll's House*, 10; quoted, 275; mentioned, 33, 244, 261

Brooks, Van Wyck: on Henry Harland, 231; on Violet Paget, 255, 256-57; mentioned, 255

"Broughton, Philip" (Aubrey Beardsley), 127

Broughton, Rhoda: on Margaret Brooke, Ranee of Sarawak, 261

Brown, Ford Madox, 205

Brown, Frederic: and Beardsley, 44; mentioned, 65, 66

Browning, Elizabeth Barrett, 127

Browning, Robert: on Dobson, 112; on Nellie Gosse's paintings, 219; and Violet Paget, 255; Ethel Colburn Mayne on, 252-53; mentioned, 6, 139, 167, 212, 217, 218, 268; *Asolando*, 255; *Pippa Passes*, 4

Buchan, John: career of, 196-97; and Arnold Bennett, 174; edits Bacon's essays, 197; as reader for Elkin Mathews and John Lane, 37; and *Yellow Book*, 196, 197; mentioned, 265; *Scholar Gypsies*, 197; *Sir Quixote of the Moors*, 197

Buchanan, Robert, and Dante Gabriel Rossetti, 4

Bucke, Dr. R. M., quoted, 22

Bumpus', 80

Burdett, Osbert: on Ella D'Arcy, 234

Burgess, Gelett: and the *Lark*, 21

Burgin, G. B.: on Richard Garnett, 214; mentioned, 101

Burne-Jones, Edward: and Beardsley, 44, 47; mentioned, 2, 45, 191

Burne-Jones, Philip, 29, 33

Burns, John: and R. B. Cunninghame Graham, 260

Burr, Mrs. Godfrey. *See* Katherine Douglas King

Burrow, Charles K., 270

Burton, Sir Richard, and yellow breakfasts, 2; mentioned, 202

Butcher, Eleanor, fiancée of Charles Furse, 87

Butler, Ellis Parker, 273

Butterfly, the, 20

Byron, George Gordon, Lord, 253

Café Royal, 28, 29, 124

Caine, Hall, 6, 243, 250, 273

Caird, Mona: and yellow, 2; mentioned, 10, 18

Cambridge Observer, founded by Oswald Sickert and Stanley V. Makower, 106

Cameron, D. Y.: and John Buchan, 197; mentioned, 191, 286

Campbell, Mrs. Patrick: and John Davidson, 283; mentioned, 35, 49, 113, 248, 251

Capuana, Luigi, 9

Carlyle, Thomas, 4, 117, 212

Carman, Bliss, 208, 229

Carpenter, Edward: and H. S. Salt, 208; brochure on "Sex Love," 208; riots of Bloody Sunday, 208; quoted, 260; mentioned, 208

Cassell and Company, 58, 180

of *Maggie*, 24; death of, 225; quoted, 26; mentioned, 14, 22, 52, 153, 222; *Maggie*, 24; *The Red Badge of Courage*, 24

Crane, Walter: and Aubrey Beardsley, 75; and Eugene Benson, 228; and Theo Marzials, 216; illustrates Marzials' *Pan-pipes*, 216

Crawhall, Joseph, quoted, 136

Critic, the: and Arthur Waugh, 70-71; on Aubrey Beardsley, 90; on the *Savoy*, 208; review of *Yellow Book*, 93; on Le Gallienne, 180; quoted, 274; mentioned, 16, 80

Croce, Benedetto, 264

Crockett, S. R., 197

Crosland, T. W. H., and Frank Harris, 33

Cross, Victoria. *See* Cory, Vivian

Crowley, Aleister: poetry of, 270; and W. B. Yeats, 270

Cunninghame-Graham, Gabriele. *See* Graham, Gabriele Cunninghame

Cunninghame-Graham, Robert Bontine. *See* Graham, Robert Bontine Cunninghame

Curzon, George Nathaniel, Lord: and Mrs. Craigie, 99, 100; mentioned, 101

Curzon, Mary Lester, Lady, 99, 100

Cust, Harry, and John Davidson, 116

Custance, Colonel Frederick Hambledon, 186

Custance, Olive: career of, 186-88; and Aubrey Beardsley, 186; and Lord Alfred Douglas, 186-87; mentioned, 41, 114, 127; *The Inn of Dreams*, 187; *Opals*, 186-87

Dalmon, Charles W.: career of, 267-68; and Tennyson, 267; mentioned, 128, 263; "Parson Herrick's Muse," 126

Daly's Theatre, 95

"Dane, Hal." *See* Macfall, Haldane

d'Annunzio, Gabriele: London writers interested in, 228; mentioned, 9, 21

D'Arcy, Ella: career of, 234-36; procrastination of, 235; interest in P. B. Shelley, 235; and Beardsley, 145; and Frederick Chapman, 37; and Rimbaud, 235-36; and Leila Macdonald, 183; and Netta Syrett, 235; and the Williamsons, 235; and the Wilde affair, 144; and Henry Harland, 56, 190, 233; and *Yellow Book*, 77, 190; in Paris, 236; on Baron Corvo, 232; on authorship of "Women—Wives or Mothers," 114; on death of *Yellow Book*, 274; quoted, 185; mentioned, 17, 32, 41, 78, 87, 114, 126, 165, 180, 232, 237, 272; "Irremediable," 84, 234, 235

Darwin, Charles: Victorian attitude toward, 5

Daudet, Alphonse: and Henry James, 25; and Henry Harland, 60

Davidson, Annie Smith, 117

Davidson, John: career of, 7, 116-18, 283; as reader for Elkin Mathews and John Lane, 37; in London, 117; in the theatre, 283; marries, 117; writes plays, 117; controversy over "Ballad of a Nun," 115-16; parodies of "Ballad of a Nun," 116; translates Coppée's *Pour la Couronne*, 283; translates Victor Hugo's *Ruy Blas*, 283; contributions to *Yellow Book*, 117-18; death of, 14; quoted, 179;

mentioned, 27, 28, 29, 42, 70, 74, 78, 85, 114, 128, 133, 181, 238, 268; "Ballad of a Nun," 115-16, 278

Davis, Richard Harding, 22

Day, Fred Holland, 72

Dearmer, Mabel: and Henry Harland, 191; mentioned, 31, 232

Dearmer, Percy, 191

Decadence, defined by Symons and others, 11-12

Degas, Hilaire Germain Edgar, 34, 104

Degeneration, by Max Nordau, 12, 13

De la Mare, Walter, 108

De Morgan, William, 17

Denny, Norman, 280

Dent, J. M., 45-46

Dial, 19, review of *Yellow Book*, 93-94

Dickens, Charles, 234

Dictionary of National Biography, 55, 56

Dircks, Rudolf, 202

Dix, Gertrude, 41

Dixon, Ella Hepworth: and George Moore, 102; on Max Beerbohm, 247; on William Watson, 150; mentioned, 18

Dixon, Hepworth, 247

Dixon, Marion Hepworth, 128

Dobson, Austin: career of, 112; and gossip, 34; in nineties, 7; mentioned, 78; *Sat est Scripsisse*, 111

Dome, 20, 199

Dostoievsky, Feodor Mikhailovich: mentioned, 9, 175; *Poor Folk*, Lena Milman translates, 188

Douglas, Lord Alfred: and Olive Custance, 186-87; and Lionel Johnson, 123; introduces Lionel Johnson to Oscar Wilde, 161; and Wilde, 139; and Wilde's *Salomé*, 48; editor of *Spirit Lamp*, 84; mentioned, 91

Douglas, Evelyn, 208

Douglas, Lady Olive. *See* Custance, Olive

Dowie, Ménie Muriel: career of, 133-34; reception of *Gallia*, 134; mentioned, 78, 81, 127; *Gallia*, 134; *Women Adventurers*, 134

Dowson, Ernest: career of, 119-22; and Adelaide Foltinowicz (Missie), 121, 122; and Brittany, 121-22; and Lionel Johnson, 28, 124; and the *Savoy*, 205; biographers of, 119; collaboration with Arthur Moore, 121; in France, 26; marriage of "Missie," 122; skill at languages, 120; prose of, 120; death of, 15, 282-83; on Ibsen's *A Doll's House*, 10; on John Lane, 204; on John Lane and the *Savoy*, 204; quoted, 24, 82; mentioned, 7, 29, 39, 42, 78, 114, 202, 203, 209, 259; "*Non Sum Qualis Eram Bonae sub Regno Cynarae*," 120; "*Amor Umbratilis*," 120; "Apple-Blossom in Brittany," 122

Doyle, Sir Arthur Conan, 23, 34

Dreiser, Theodore: quoted, 159; mentioned, 286

Dürer, Albrecht, 165

Duff, Sir Mountstuart Grant, 264

Dujardin, Édouard, 135

Dumas, Alexandre, père, 243

311

Dumas, Alexandre, fils: *La Dame aux Camélias,* 127
Du Maurier, George, 11
Dunham, O. M., 58
Dunne, Finley Peter: on Henry James, 171; quoted, 172
Dunne, J. J., 172
Dunne, Mary Chavelita. *See* "Egerton, George"

Eden, Sir William, controversy with Whistler, 175, 177; "The Screen," 175; Watts-Dunton on, 177
"Egerton, George": career of, 171-73; Scandinavian influence on, 9, 173; and Henry James, 171, 172, 173; and *Yellow Book,* 173; mentioned, 12, 41, 77, 78, 81, 85; *Discords,* 171, 173; *Keynotes,* 171, 172, 173; "Lost Masterpiece," 94
Eglantine, Mlle., 200
"Eliot, George," 4, 167
Elkin Mathews and John Lane: first publication of, 36; choice of authors, 37; readers for, 37; notoriety of, 38; Arthur Waugh on, 37; Evelyn Sharp on, 37; dissolution of, 38-39, 114; mentioned, 71, 91, 92
Ellis, Havelock: and Fabian Society, 5; and study of sex, 16; mentioned, 24, 38, 131, 200, 203, 206, 208
Elwin, Malcolm: on "George Egerton," 173
Emery, Winifred, 128
English Men of Letters series, 221
Eustace, Jennie, 231
Evans, Frederick: and Beardsley, 44, 45; mentioned, 205
Evergreen, 20, 199, 269

Fabian Society, the: and the Blands, 131; mentioned, 5, 17, 259, 266
Fabre, Lucien, 263
Falconer, Lanoe, 78
Field, Eugene, 23
"Field, Michael": quoted, 17; mentioned, 39, 78
Fields, Annie, 21
Finch, Constance, 263
Fisher Unwin, 37, 197
Fisher, Harrison, 273
Fitzgerald, Major E. A., 134
FitzGerald, Edward, 264
Flaubert, Gustave, 8
"Fleming, George." *See* Fletcher, Constance
Fleming, John, 273
Fletcher, Constance, 228
Fletcher, Henrietta, 228
Fleury, Gabrielle: and George Gissing, 193, 194
Flower, Desmond, 119
Foltinowicz, Adelaide ("Missie"), 121, 122
Forbes-Robertson, Sir Johnston, 95
Ford, Ford Madox: career of, 205; interest in Whitman, 9; and *Savoy,* 205; and *Transatlantic Review,* 205; on *Yellow Book,* 273; mentioned, 208, 253
Forster, E. M., 133

Fortnightly Review: review of *Yellow Book,* 115; mentioned, 149, 192, 256
"Foschter, Albert" (Aubrey Beardsley), 127
Fourier, François Marie Charles, 57
France: and Nineties, dominant literary influence on, 8, 9
France, Anatole: and *Yellow Book,* 153-54; on Hérédia, 118; mentioned, 255
Frederic, Harold: career of, 222-24; London correspondent for New York *Times,* 22; and John Lane, 40; mentioned, 29
Frierson, William C.: on Ella D'Arcy, 234-35
Fry, Roger: and Hubert Crackanthorpe, 30; on Aubrey Beardsley, 52; mentioned, 183
Fuller, Margaret, 149
Fullerton, William M.: career of, 226-27; and George Meredith, 226
Furse, Charles: mentioned, 26, 29, 78; "Portrait of a Lady," 86-87

Gale, Norman: career of, 111; and *Yellow Book,* 111; mentioned, 27, 28, 42, 78; *A Fellowship of Song,* 111; *Close of Play, Poems on Cricket,* 111; *Cricket Songs and Other Trifling Verse,* 111; *Orchard Songs,* 111
Gallatin, A. E., 43
Gandhi, Mohandas K.: on "Plea for Vegetarianism," 209
Gardner, Mrs. Jack, 135
Garland, Hamlin: on Henry Harland, 284
Garnett, Constance, 214, 267
Garnett, David, 214, 267
Garnett, Edward: and Joseph Conrad, 206, 273; mentioned, 214, 261, 267
Garnett, Richard: and Nora Hopper, 215; and T. E. Lawrence, 214; in nineties, 7; interest in Italian literature, 214; keeper of printed books at the British Museum, 214; contributions to *Yellow Book,* 214; quoted, 54; mentioned, 78, 81, 87, 93, 128, 210; "The Love-Story of Luigi Tansillo," 85
Gaskell, Mrs.: *Wives and Daughters,* finished by Frederick Greenwood, 114
Gaunt, William: quoted, 11
Gautier, Théophile: on Hérédia, 118; quoted, 8
"Gawsworth, John" (Terence Ian Fytton Armstrong), 119, 121
George, Stefan: founded *Blätter für die Kunst,* 21
Gentleman's Magazine, 197
Germ, the, 4, 20
Ghouls, 29
Gilbert, H., 270
Gilbert, W. S.: *Patience,* 11
Gilchrist, R. Murray: as writer, 207; leader of Symbolist school, 207; and William Sharp, 207; and Hugh Walpole, 207
Gilder, Jeannette: and Grant Allen, 16; on death of Hubert Crackanthorpe, 14; quoted, 185; mentioned, 273
Gissing, George: career of, 192-96; acceptance by Meredith of *The Unclassed,* 6; as realist, 193; independence of, 192-93; marriages of,

Hardy, Thomas: and Charlotte Mew, 108; and Mrs. Craigie, 97; and Edmund Gosse, 219; critics of, 269; published in America, 23; on death of Mrs. Craigie, 101; on sex education, 278; quoted, 33; mentioned, 99, 114, 265, 270; *Jude the Obscure*, 23, 24; *Tess of the D'Urbervilles*, 6, 23, 219

Harland, Aline Merriam: history of, 58-59; and Aubrey Beardsley, 45; and Henry Harland, 59, 63; Mistress of the Grob, 64; completes Henry Harland's work, 285-86; contributions to *Yellow Book*, 229-30; and Catholicism, 284, 285; painted by Whistler, 33; Saturday evenings at, 32; and inception of *Yellow Book*, 68; death of, 286; on *Yellow Book*, 136; on death of *Yellow Book*, 274; mentioned, 32, 55, 56, 67, 82, 83, 90, 105, 113, 164, 183, 186, 236, 243, 284

Harland, Henry: origin of, 55-56, 57; literary career of, 55-56; literary influence of, 61, 62; short stories of, 60; Jewish novels of, 56-58, 59; university study, 57; at Harvard, 57-58; and *Yellow Book*: 69, 71, 72, 127, 138, 166, 168-69, 190-91; inception of, 68; first issue of, 85; art in, 191; as editor of the *Yellow Book*: 3, 35, 190-91, 232, 272, 276-77, 278-79; Douglas Ainslie on Harland as editor of, 263-64; Americans in *Yellow Book*, 222-32; as "Yellow Dwarf," 139, 230; as editor: recognizes Ella D'Arcy, 77; solicits Alice Meynell for a contribution to *Yellow Book*, 137-38; and death of *Yellow Book*, 284; and competition from *Savoy*, 198, 209; and Aubrey Beardsley, 45, 51-52, 53, 145, 164, 209; and Max Beerbohm, 62; and Alma Strettell, 215; and Baron Corvo, 232, 233; and Catholicism, 284; and Charles Conder, 66, 75; and Mrs. Craigie, 95; and Coventry Patmore, 138; and Douglas Ainslie, 263; and Dauphin Meunier, 113; and Ella D'Arcy, 77, 190, 235; and Henry James, 59-60, 167-68, 169, 170, 171; and James's *Guy Domville*, 167; and Stanley Makower, 252; and Stephen Phillips, 243, 246; and Paris, 63; and young writers, 190; and women writers, 233; influence of Daudet on, 60; influence of Maupassant on, 60; influence of Mérimée on, 60; absent from London during the Wilde affair, 146; dislike for Oscar Wilde, 61; feud with Frank Harris, 33; Saturday evenings at, 32; translates Matilde Serao's *Fantasia*, with Aline Harland, 9; precarious health of, 15, 60; stories reflect enchantment with Continent, 230-31; in America, 284; in Brittany, 64-66; on his exile from America, 59-60; death of, 284-85; on *Yellow Book*, 280; on death of *Yellow Book*, 274; on W. E. Henley, 18; quoted, 59; mentioned, 7, 24, 26, 70, 74, 78, 81, 83, 86, 91, 95, 105, 114, 115, 129, 135, 147, 152, 154, 174, 175, 176, 183, 186, 189, 192, 202, 227, 230, 236, 237, 238, 247, 272; *The Cardinal's Snuff Box*, 113, 284; *From Generation to Generation* (retitled *As It Was Written*), 58; *Grandison Mather* or

An Account of the Fortune of Mr. and Mrs. Thomas Gardner, 58; *The Light Sovereign*, with Hubert Crackanthorpe, edited by Aline Harland, 285-86; *Mademoiselle Miss and Other Stories*, 60, 67; *Mea Culpa*, 60, 62; *Mrs. Peixada*, 58; *The Royal End*, 57, completed by Aline Harland, 284, 285; *The Yoke of the Thorah*, 58, 59

Harland, Mrs. Irene Jones (mother of Henry Harland): and death of Henry Harland, 285; quoted, 56

Harland, Thomas (father of Henry Harland), 57

Harper, J. H.: and Thomas Hardy, 23

Harris, Frank: and Max Beerbohm, 247, 250; and Harold Frederic, 224; and T. W. H. Crosland, 33; and Joseph Pennell, 33; feud with Harland, 33; and *Yellow Book*, 139; and the "Yellow Dwarf," 230; on Harland, 231; mentioned, 70, 78, 91, 214, 224, 276

Harrison, Alma Strettell. *See* Strettell, Alma

Harrison, Frederic: and Gissing, 193; mentioned, 196

Harrison, Lawrence: and Alma Strettell, 215; and Will Rothenstein, 215; and John Singer Sargent, 215

Harte, Bret, 22, 222

Hartrick, A. S.: and *Yellow Book*, 75; quoted, 22; mentioned, 175

Hayes, Alfred: mentioned, 28; *A Fellowship of Song*, 111; "My Study," 108, 110

Haymarket Theatre, 166

Heinemann, William, 223, 276. *See also* William Heinemann

Henley, William Ernest: and Henry Harland, 33; and Robert Louis Stevenson, 110; and Stephen Phillips, 244; and Francis Watt, 212; as journalist and editor, 18; entertains *Observer* men, 31; interest in Whitman, 9; on Housman's *A Shropshire Lad*, 132; quoted, 83; mentioned, 15, 85, 109, 130, 139, 152, 218, 241, 270, 276; *London Voluntaries*, 26

Hérédia, José Maria de: and *Yellow Book*, 118-19; co-founder of *Parnasse Contemporain*, 118; *Les Trophées*, 118; "Fleurs de Feu," 119

Hewlett, Maurice: quoted, 35; mentioned, 213

Hichens, Robert, *The Green Carnation*, 11

"Hickson, Mrs. Murray." *See* Mrs. Mabel Kitcat

Higginbotham, Elsie, 263

Hind, C. Lewis: career of, 213; and Aubrey Beardsley, 46, 53, 213; contribution to *Yellow Book*, 213; editor of *Academy*, 100, 213; lauded new literary works in *Academy*, 213; left Academy, 213; with *Pall Mall Budget*, 213; with *Studio*, 48, 213; as music and art critic, 213; in America, 213; on own works, 213, 214; on *Daily Telegraph*, 19; on Arnold Bennett, 214; on F. B. Money-Coutts, 265; on H. B. Marriott Watson, 130; on Harold Frederic, 223; on Mrs. Humphry Ward, 145; on Stephen Phillips' *Christ in Hades*, 244;

quoted, 13, 63, 130; mentioned, 28, 31, 32, 43, 179, 210, 212, 232, 248

Hinkson, Katharine Tynan. See Tynan, Katharine

Hobby Horse: founded by Herbert Horne and Selwyn Image, 20; mentioned, 120, 124

Hofmannsthal, Hugo von, 21

Hogarth Club, 72

Hope, Anthony: and Kenneth Grahame, 241; on A. P. Watt, 37; on *Yellow Book,* 241

Hopper, Nora: career of, 214; and Richard Garnett, 215; studied Icelandic sagas, 215; and Celtic revival, 215; listed among Archer's younger generation poets, 215; mentioned, 41

Horne, Herbert: and *Hobby Horse,* 20; Reginald Turner and, 251; mentioned, 39, 42, 120, 200

Housman, A. E.: and Laurence Housman, 270; and E. Nesbit, 132; on Ada Leverson's *The Limit,* 159; and *Yellow Book,* 270; on suffrage, 17; quotation attributed to, 42; mentioned, 27; *A Shropshire Lad,* 40, 132, 181

Housman, Laurence: and E. Nesbit, 133; and Francis Thompson, 36, 270; and John Lane, 40, 270-71; and A. E. Housman, 270; and suffrage, 17; death of, 287; mentioned, 7, 75, 78, 159, 239; *Prunella,* 237; "The Reflected Faun," 87

Howard Ainslie Company: publisher of the *Yellow Kid,* 273

Howard, Francis, 152

Howarth, Mary, 270

Howe, Julia Ward, 26

Howells, William Dean: and Henry James, 34; London, yearly visits to, 22; quoted, 61, 284; mentioned, 57, 149, 173, 222, 224; *A Hazard of New Fortunes,* 94

Hudson, W. H.: and Margaret Brooke, 262; mentioned, 27, 261

Hueffer, Ford Madox. See Ford, Ford Madox

Hugo, Victor, 123, 283

Hunt, Violet: on Mabel Beardsley, 281; mentioned, 205, 253, 260

Hunt, William Holman, 135

Huntley, Francis. See Ethel Colburn Mayne

Hutton, Richard Holt: on Stephen Phillips' *Christ in Hades,* 244; mentioned, 149

Huysmans, Joris Karl: influence on George Moore, 8

Hyde, William, 78

Ibsen, Henrik: and Beerbohm Tree, 35; plays translated, 9; reception in London of plays, 9, 19; mentioned, 237, 248; *A Doll's House,* 9; *Ghosts,* 19, 246; *Pillars of Society,* 35

Image, Selwyn: and *Hobby Horse,* 20; mentioned, 39, 78, 120, 203, 208

Impressionism, defined by Symons, 11-12

"Iola" (Mrs. Mannington Caffyn), 2

Isis (Oxford periodical): and *Yellow Book,* 92-93

Italian writers: and influence on English writers, 9

J. M. Dent and Sons, 37

James, Henry: career of, 167-71; and Americans in London, 21-22; and American humorists, 170-71; and Daudet, 25; and Douglas Ainslie, 263; and Evelyn Sharp, 238; and "George Egerton," 172, 173; and Hubert Crackanthorpe, 184-85; and Lena Milman, 188-89; and Max Beerbohm, 171; and Violet Paget, 255, 256; and William Dean Howells, 34; and Henry Harland, 59-60, 169, 170, 171; *Yellow Book:* promises to contribute to, 69; *What Maisie Knew* originally intended for, 169; and *Yellow Book,* 136, 166, 167, 168-69; attitude toward Frederic scandal, 224; Douglas Ainslie and, 264; entertains, 33; in the theatre, 166-67; interest in Ibsen, 10; life in London, 169; mature style, 6; on London, 167; on Henry Harland, 60, 230; on *Yellow Book,* 90-91; on George Gissing, 194; on William M. Fullerton, 69; quoted, 3; 32, 73; mentioned, 33, 61, 78, 81, 87, 93, 105, 122, 158, 221, 222, 232, 233, 247, 261, 276; *Guy Domville,* 166-67; *What Maisie Knew,* 169; "The Coxon Fund," 108, 168-69; "The Death of the Lion," 83, 90-91, 94, 167, 171; "The Next Time," 167, 169; "She and He," 169

James, Humphrey, 202

James, William: and Violet Paget, 256; mentioned, 90

"Jean de France" (John Lane), 42, 78

Jefferies, Richard, 209

Jepson, Edgar: on Arthur Symons, 199; on Dowson, 121; on Dowson's funeral, 283; on Hubert Bland, 131; on William Watson, 150; mentioned, 119, 264

Jerome, Jerome, K.: quoted, 16; mentioned, 31

Jewett, Sarah Orne, 21, 59

John, Augustus, 200

Johnson, Lionel: career of, 123-26; and Arthur Symons, 124; and Catholicism, 125-26; and Ernest Dowson, 28, 124; and Douglas Ainslie, 123; and the Meynell circle, 125; and George Santayana, 123; and H. W. Nevinson, 283; and Pater, 124; and Will Rothenstein, 124; and Oscar Wilde, 161; and Lord Douglas, 123; and the *Savoy,* 205; death of, 15, 283; on Annie Macdonell's *Thomas Hardy,* 269; on Hubert Crackanthorpe, 182-83; on Crackanthorpe's *Last Studies,* 185; on his library, 125; mentioned, 7, 29, 39, 78, 82, 114, 209, 244, 259; *The Art of Thomas Hardy,* 6, 124; *Some Winchester Letters of...,* 123; "By the Statue of King Charles at Charing Cross," 27

Jones, Henry Arthur, 248

Jungmann, Elizabeth, 250, 286

Kahn, Florence: as actress, 249; Max Beerbohm and, 249-250

Kailyard School, 197

Karageorgevitch, Prince Bojdar, 175

Kegan Paul, 40, 265, 268

Kelly, Gerald, 237, 238

317

New Reform Club, 266
New Review, 15, 219, 275, 276, 278
New Vagabonds, 29
New Writing, 280
New York *Tribune*: review of Henry Harland's *As It Was Written*, 58
New York *Times*, 144
Newlyn School: in *Yellow Book*, 191
Newman, J. H., Cardinal, 123, 125
Newton-Robinson, Charles: in *Yellow Book*, 128; *Viol of Love*, 128
Nicholson, Frances, 263
Nicoll, William Robertson: literary influence of, 34; quoted, 178
Niebling, Richard: on Gissing, 193, 195
Nietzsche, Friedrich, 117
Nineteenth Century, 16, 33
Nineties, the: London, literary life in, 21-35, Chelsea, 28, restaurants in, 28-29; as literary center, 26-28, Bloomsbury, 28, Fleet Street, 28; clubs in, 29-30; interior decoration in, 30; entertainment in, 31-33; gossip, 34-35; Americans in, 21-23; English writers during, publication in America of, 23-24; writers in France, 24, 26; French writers in England, 24-25; divergent ideas about, 1-2; journalism in, 18-19; masculine pen names of women writers, 17; "new" as catchword of, 15-16; and the new woman, 16-17; periodicals of, 199; preoccupation with yellow, 2
Noble, Helen. *See* Thomas, Helen Noble
Noble, James Ashcraft: career of, 210-11; and *Yellow Book*, 211; death of, 211; on A. C. Benson, 220; mentioned, 149, 209; *The Sonnet in England*, 211
Nordau, Max: *Degeneration*, quoted, 12-13
Norman, Henry: and Ménie Muriel Dowie, 134; mentioned, 22, 81, 88, 144
Norman, Mrs. Henry. *See* Dowie, Ménie Muriel
Norman, Nigel, 134
Norregard, Julie: career of, 180-81; in Paris, 180; and Richard Le Gallienne, 179-81; and Georg Brandes, 179; mentioned, 237
Norton, Charles Eliot: on *Yellow Book*, 118; mentioned, 22
Nott, J. S. Pyke, 270
Novello, Ivor, 251
Nye, Edgar Wilson, "Bill Nye": in England, 23; mentioned, 69

Observer, the: 133, 268
Odd Volumes, 29
O'Faoláin, Séan: on Eva Gore-Booth, 258
Omar Khayyám Club, 29, 116, 192
Order of the Golden Dawn, 270
O'Sullivan, Vincent, 101; "The Twilight People," 258
"Ouida" (Marie Louise de la Ramée): on d'Annunzio, 228; on the new woman, 17; quoted, 100; mentioned, 150, 152, 209, 255
Oxford Magazine: on *Yellow Book*, 90

Pageant, 20, 246
Paget, Lady, 262

Paget, Violet: career of, 254-57; and Browning and Anatole France, 255; and Pater, 255; and Amy Levy, 257; and Henry James, 255, 256; and William James, 256; and John Singer Sargent, 255; and Maurice Baring, 156; and *Yellow Book*, 262; in Italy, 255; in London, 256; on her lack of recognition, 256; *Studies of the Eighteenth Century in Italy*, 255; quoted, 216
Palgrave, Francis Turner, 264
Pall Mall Budget: Aubrey Beardsley in, 89-90; mentioned, 48, 75, 213
Pall Mall Gazette, 18, 19, 114, 116, 129, 130, 138, 153, 264, 266, 268; and H. G. Wells, 192
Pan, 20, 21
Parade, 199, 246
Paris, attitude of English writers toward, 26
Parker, the Reverend John, 97
Parry, Albert, and Henry Harland, 56
Partridge, J. Bernard, 78
Pater, Walter: and Violet Paget, 255; influences George Moore, 8; influences Oscar Wilde, 5; disciple of Ruskin, 5; mentioned, 78, 84, 85, 124, 161, 212, 279; *The Renaissance*, quoted, 5; *Marius the Epicurean*, 5
Patmore, Coventry: and the Meynells, 31, 137-38; and *Yellow Book*, 138; on the *Observer*, 19; mentioned, 18, 150, 182
Paul, Mrs. Sidney Austin. *See* Kitcat, Mrs. Mabel
Pauling, Sydney, quoted, 33
Payn, James, 196
Payne-Townshend, Charlotte, marries G. B. Shaw, 208; mentioned, 263
Pennell, Mrs. Elizabeth Robins: and the Harlands, 63; and Whistler, 22; evenings at home, 32; on Henry Harland, 62; on Harold Frederic, 223; on Rosamund Marriott Watson, 129; on Violet Paget, 256; on *Yellow Book*, 271; quoted, 26; mentioned, 26, 50, 74, 78, 81, 82, 83
Pennell, Joseph: and Beardsley, 46; and Whistler, 22; and Frank Harris, 33; on Beardsley, 141; quoted, 129-30, 168; mentioned, 74, 75, 78, 86, 87, 203, 204, 227
Periodicals, in nineties, 20-21
Peters, William Theodore, death of, 15
Petit, Roland, 156
Phillips, Claude, 135
Phillips, Stephen: career of, 243-46; and Max Beerbohm, 246; and W. E. Henley, 244; and *Yellow Book*, 246; in the theatre, 245; decline of, 245; mentioned, 213, 232, 237, 248, 265, 268, 283; *Christ in Hades*, 244; *Herod*, 246; *Paola and Francesca*, 244-45
Piggott, Mostyn: on *Yellow Book*, 93
Pinero, Sir Arthur Wing, mentioned, 248; *Letty*, 237
Pissarro, Camille: and Bernhard Sickert, 105
Plarr, Marian, and Dowson, 119
Plarr, Victor: on Dowson, 119; quoted, 213; known by D. Ainslie, 264; mentioned, 10, 24, 29, 82, 119
Ponsonby, Lady, 274

320

322

reviews of, 148, Gosse's unique copy of, 147-48, Beardsley plates removed from, 147; Vol. VI of, 166-67, 175, 176, 178; Vol. VII of, 178, 186, 191; Vol. VIII of, 191, 196, 197-98; Vol. IX of, 191, 220; Vol. X of, 229, 253, 269; Vol. XI of, 230, 265, 267, 270; Vol. XII of, 105, 229, 246, 263, 269, 271; Vol. XIII of, 271-80; advertising in, 275; art editorship of, 164-66; critical reception of, 83, 87-90, 91-95, 106-07, 111, 112-13, 148, 176, 271-72; and editors, 94, of American edition, 93-94; financial success of, 274; hostility toward, 136-37, 138; limited circulation of, 275; minor writers in, 269-70; poets in, 270-71; omissions, 270-71; poetry in, 278-79; popularity of, 90-91; stature of, 276, 279; compared with *Savoy*, 199; Sotheran reprints of, 275, 280; selections from, 280; and John Lane, 39; and Beardsley, 55; and Max Beerbohm, 67; mentioned, 20, 33, 35, 53, 62, 66

"Yellow Dwarf." *See* Harland, Henry

Young, Filson, 74

Zangwill, Israel, 78, 139

Zola, Émile: and French Academy, 118; in England, 25; mentioned, 82, 98, 121, 255